The Mennonite Church
in the
Second World War

By

GUY FRANKLIN HERSHBERGER

Professor of History and Sociology
Goshen College

Reproduced by permission of
Herald Press

Wipf and Stock Publishers
150 West Broadway • Eugene OR 97401
2000

The Mennonite Church in the 2nd World War

By Hershberger, Guy F.
Copyright© by Herald Press

ISBN 978-1-5326-6710-7

Reprinted by *Wipf and Stock Publishers*
150 West Broadway • Eugene OR 97401

Previously published by Herald Press, .

TO CLARA
CO-WORKER IN ALL MY LABORS
THIS BOOK IS AFFECTIONATELY DEDICATED

Foreword

The great war of 1939-45, commonly called the second World War, was the most extensive, costly, and destructive war in which the United States and Canada have ever engaged. For the almost 300,000 Mennonites (including children), resident in these two countries, it was also the most thorough and far-reaching test of their Christian nonresistance which they have ever experienced. A first claim on our historians is a complete report and evaluation of this experience for the total Mennonite brotherhood in both countries and of all branches. This report should include not only the record of the alternative service programs, part of which has been fully and competently given in the exhaustive work by Melvin Gingerich, *Service for Peace* (Akron, Pennsylvania, 1949), but also all aspects of the life, work, and witness of the church as it was affected by the war. We need such an account both for the inspiration and challenge of a test well met, as well as for the lessons we can learn from it for the future.

Guy F. Hershberger, the author of *War, Peace, and Nonresistance*, has made a major contribution toward this full history in the volume which is here presented. It is not merely an account of the direct relation of the church to the war, although there is a complete coverage of all phases of our "war relations." There are also chapters on missions, education, relief, voluntary service, and inter-group relations both within and without the Mennonite family. Here one can find fairly and honestly told the complete story of one branch of that family during one of the most important periods in recent history.

We are perhaps too close to the events of 1939-45 for a final understanding and evaluation of this period of our history, but this book gives us both the necessary basic record and helpful signposts on the road toward this evaluation, particularly in its concluding chapter. As we enter into another period of international tension, and a possible third world war, we will need every available help which we can secure toward a better achievement of full Christian discipleship both as individuals and as a church. Those who were in the midst of the leadership in the work and the problems of the recent past will be doubly grateful for the reviewing of their stewardship which this book calls forth. Thousands of others will also want to read this clear and challenging account and check the record of the Mennonite Church in the second World War. It is a good book and deserves the widest distribution. The Peace Problems Committee, which has sponsored the manuscript, is happy to recommend it.

HAROLD S. BENDER.
Chairman of the Peace Problems
Committee of the Mennonite Church

Author's Preface

This is a history of the Mennonite Church, sometimes referred to as the (Old) Mennonite Church, during the period of the second World War. Although it frequently speaks of Civilian Public Service, this book is not a history of Mennonite Civilian Public Service. That task has been done by Melvin Gingerich in his *Service for Peace*, published by the Mennonite Central Committee in 1949. Neither is it a history of Mennonite relief and voluntary service, although two chapters are devoted to these subjects, and much is said about the work of the Mennonite Central Committee, as well as the work carried on by the Relief Committee of the Mennonite Board of Missions and Charities. Frequent mention, by way of reference and comparison, is also made of other Mennonite groups and conferences, such as the General Conference Mennonite Church, the Mennonite Brethren Church of North America, the Old Order Amish Mennonite Church, the Conservative Amish Mennonite Church, and others. This is not a history of Mennonitism, however, nor even of American Mennonitism, in the second World War. It is merely a wartime history of one Mennonite group, that officially known as the Mennonite Church, which in 1950 had approximately 66,000 baptized members, about 57,000 of whom resided in the United States, 46,000 of them east of the Mississippi River.

In the period following the first World War it was frequently said that the Mennonite Church had not been adequately prepared for that crisis. Numerous church leaders, as well as young men who were conscripted in 1917-18, said that in the event of another war greater preparation would need to be made if the church was to meet the crisis successfully. This conviction led the Mennonite General Conference,[1] which is the representative general organization of the (Old) Mennonite Church, to appoint a Peace Problems Committee, which since 1925 has been officially responsible for this task. Its labors during the following fifteen years did much to prepare the church for the events of the 1940's. These events and the world situation of that time were much more serious than those of 1917, however, and thus the question can still be asked whether, relatively, the church was better prepared for the crisis of the second World War than for that of the first.

It is the author's hope, however, that the present study will contribute something to an understanding of the war's effect upon the life

---

[1] Not to be confused with the above-mentioned General Conference Mennonite Church (formerly known as the General Conference of the Mennonite Church of North America). The General Conference Mennonite Church is the official name of the second largest Mennonite group in North America, with about 44,000 baptized members, most of whom reside in western Canada and in the United States west of the Mississippi River.

and work of the Mennonite Church, and that this in turn may be able to provide some guidance for the future. It is also his hope that similar studies will be made of other Mennonite groups, both in America and in Europe, and that these will be followed by a general synthesis of the history of Mennonitism in the second World War.

The author desires to acknowledge his obligation to all who assisted in any way in the preparation of this work. The members of the Peace Problems Committee, at whose request the task was undertaken, have read the manuscript, as have representatives of the Publishing Committee of the Mennonite Publication Board. Carl Kreider read Chapter XIV. Nelson P. Springer, then in the service of the Mennonite Research Foundation, gave research assistance. Melvin Gingerich gave counsel at various stages of the work and also read the entire manuscript. Beulah Loucks prepared the index. My wife, Clara Hooley Hershberger, assisted in the task of proofreading. These friends have saved the author from numerous errors; those which remain must be charged to his account alone.

Goshen, Indiana
September 15, 1950

GUY F. HERSHBERGER

Contents

CONTENTS

CONTENTS

Chapter I

The Peace Problems Committee

As explained in the author's preface, the representative general organization of the (Old) Mennonite Church, hereinafter referred to by its official name, the Mennonite Church, is the Mennonite General Conference. Much of the work of the Mennonite General Conference is carried on through its General Council and a group of ten boards and standing committees. One of these ten is the Peace Problems Committee. This committee was first appointed in 1917 as a special committee to deal with the emergency problems of the first World War, and was sometimes referred to as the Military Committee. In 1919, however, it was made a standing committee of General Conference and officially named the Peace Problems Committee. In 1925 the Peace Problems Committee was reorganized so as to consist of six members, three from the United States and three from Canada. The committee remained this size until 1941. In that year, because of increased responsibilities arising from the second World War, the membership was increased to ten, with six from the United States and four from Canada. In 1943 it was increased again so that now there were twelve American representatives and four Canadian, making a total membership of sixteen. In 1947 the membership was reduced to ten, with the distribution of members the same as in 1941. In 1949, however, three younger men with C.P.S. experience were added to the committee, making a total membership of thirteen, four from Canada and nine from the United States.

Since 1925 the Peace Problems Committee has provided an aggressive leadership for the promotion of peace thought and action in the Mennonite Church. In 1925 Orie O. Miller became the secretary of the committee, a position he was still holding in 1951. E. L. Frey was chairman of the committee from 1925 to 1936. His successor was Harold S. Bender who also was still serving in this capacity in 1951. In its report to General Conference in 1927,[1] the committee outlined its threefold task as follows: (1) The strengthening of the nonresistant faith of the Mennonite people themselves by various means, especially through the publication of peace literature, and aggressive peace teaching. (2) Representing the church in making her peace position known to government officials; in obtaining information concerning legislation and trends affecting that position; and in taking the lead in planning proper courses of action in response to such trends. (3) Interpreting the nonresistant faith

1

to other people, particularly Christians seeking information on the subject.

From 1925 on, much of the committee's efforts were devoted to carrying out the first of the three tasks outlined above. An important phase of this task was the publication of peace literature. The response to this challenge began almost immediately, and since 1927 there has been a continuous flow of peace literature within the Mennonite Church, due largely to the influence of the Peace Problems Committee. This significant feature of the committee's work is treated separately in Chapter XVII. Other methods of strengthening the nonresistant faith of the church, however, were also used. The committee urged the inclusion of topics on peace and nonresistance in the curriculum of the Sunday school and the young people's meeting. The schools and colleges of the church were encouraged to further the teaching of peace both through curricular and extracurricular activities. District conferences and other agencies of the church were urged to be active in the work as well. These efforts bore fruit. In its report to General Conference in 1929, the committee reported a growing interest in peace in the church colleges. Both Goshen and Hesston had active peace committees, which were co-operating with the Peace Problems Committee. In 1933 the committee reported that these activities were continuing and that Sunday-school conferences, young people's institutes, and similar meetings were continuing to give attention to the teaching of peace. In 1937 the committee reported the organization of the Goshen College Peace Society, which took the place of the earlier peace committee. During each year of that biennium the Peace Problems Committee had given financial assistance to the Goshen College Peace Society for the purchase of permanent material. The financial records of the committee show that this practice has continued regularly since 1937.

One of the most significant things which the Peace Problems Committee did was to hold two peace conferences at Goshen College in February, 1935, and April, 1939. These were study conferences, primarily for church leaders. The first was a conference on war and peace. The introduction to the mimeographed proceedings says that the purpose of the conference was to enable those present "to arrive at conclusions and convictions on points that bear upon the application of the Scriptures to the conditions of the present day." The report also says that "the present status of international and world conditions lent a serious and earnest atmosphere to the . . . conference. Everyone felt the timeliness of the discussions. With war clouds . . . low over different parts of the world, it was a solemnizing thought to all that the young brethren now in high school and college might be called upon to face the realities of war in a very practical way, even sooner than many might suppose." The sessions were devoted to a variety of topics including the Scriptural teaching on peace and war; experiences in the first World War; an examination of modern peace movements; the meaning of nonresistance; and the non-resistant Christian in a possible future war. Perhaps the most significant thing which emerged from this conference, however, was a clarification of current thinking on the question of alternative civilian service as opposed to noncombatant military service. It cited the Russian Mennonite experience in forestry service as a worthy example, thus taking a definite step in the direction of the Mennonite C.P.S. program inaugurated in 1941.

The second of these conferences, held in April, 1939, was a conference on applied nonresistance dealing with such subjects as litigation, propaganda, industrial relations, and the Christian and the state. Perhaps the most significant thing which emerged from this conference leading to early action was a stimulation of the thinking of the church on the question of industrial relations, and on the importance of a strong Mennonite community life for the promotion of the doctrine of nonresistance. In the fall of 1939, following this meeting, the Mennonite General Conference appointed a new Committee on Industrial Relations to deal with these problems. Following the precedents of the conferences of 1935 and 1939, numerous local peace conferences of an educational type were held throughout the church, beginning as early as 1935 and continuing to the beginning of the second World War. During the war, as mentioned in Chapter XVIII, peace educational work was continued through special meetings of various kinds. Following the war, especially with the threat of universal military training and the revival of Selective Service in 1948, these efforts were renewed with considerable vigor.

Another significant achievement of the Peace Problems Committee was the preparation of the classic statement on *Peace, War, and Military Service* which was officially adopted by the Mennonite General Conference in 1937. In 1940 Paul Comly French, the executive secretary of the National Service Board for Religious Objectors, called this "the most concise and the most logical of the stated views of any church group."[2] When the Peace Problems Committee in its 1937 report presented the above statement to General Conference for approval, it also reported that the Conservative Amish Mennonite Conference "has expressed a desire to work with us in such matters," and recommended an invitation to this conference "to share in the work of the Peace Problems Committee, and authorize the Peace Problems Committee to receive the representative appointed by the Conservative A.M. Conference . . . as a member of the committee for such a length of time and such purposes as his conference may see fit to determine. We also recommend that General Conference authorize the Peace Problems Committee, in case a war emergency should arise, to extend its aid and help to other nonresistant Mennonite bodies who may desire such help and who are willing to cooperate with us on the basis of our established policies." These recommendations were approved by General Conference, and since 1937 Shem

Peachey has served as the Conservative A.M. Conference representative on the Peace Problems Committee.

In its report to the Mennonite General Conference in 1939, the Peace Problems Committee said that most of the American district conferences had endorsed the General Conference statement on *Peace, War, and Military Service.* Several had not yet found occasion to give it consideration. The Conservative A.M. Conference had also accepted the statement as its own. "Quite a number of Old Order Amish congregations have also adopted the statement and asked that we include them in our further representations to the government," the report said. During 1938, the Peace Problems Committee gave wide distribution to printed copies of the statement. Copies were sent to secretaries of district conferences of the Mennonite Church for distribution to all ministers within the conferences. Three copies of the statement, accompanied by a form letter, were sent directly to each of 1,889 ministers of other Mennonite branches. The Ontario Amish Mennonite Conference distributed 2,000 copies among its constituency, one copy for each church member.[3]

Numerous congregations in the Mennonite Church made similar distributions to all of their members. In the United States the statement on *Peace, War, and Military Service* was mailed to the President, to Cabinet members, to the Chief Justice of the Supreme Court, to the chairmen of the Foreign and Military Affairs Committees in both House and Senate, and to the governors and United States senators of all states where congregations of the church were located. In Canada, the comparable officials of the Dominion government received copies, and it was also reported that the Mennonite conferences in India, Argentina, and Tanganyika planned similar action with respect to their governments. It should also be observed that following 1939, and perhaps in some cases even before this, a number of district conferences of the Mennonite Church organized peace committees, either under that name or some other, which concerned themselves with local problems related to war and peace. Conferences which appointed such committees were Franconia, Lancaster, Virginia, Ontario, Southwestern Pennsylvania, and Illinois.

THE WITNESS BEYOND THE CHURCH

The second and third tasks of the Peace Problems Committee as outlined in its report of 1927 were to represent the church before governments and to witness to others, especially other Christians, concerning the nonresistant faith. These two points looked toward an aggressive outreach such as had not been envisioned by the earlier committee which had served largely to meet the emergency of the first World War. In an article announcing the program of the new committee, the secretary said:

Our experience during the recent war painfully showed us how little some of our own people knew as to the true and Biblical basis for the position, and

how little we had done in acquainting others with the true basis of our belief
. . . . There are today many individuals outside of our nonresistant denominations who are sincerely longing and searching for a way through which the
world may be saved from another sickening experience such as the last war
brought us . . . . Our committee is now studying the various peace movements
in other churches and groups. In various ways which shall be consistent with
the other vital tenets of our belief, the committee wants to let others know how
and why we have always stood as we have on the war question.[4]

This aggressive outlook on the part of the secretary, no doubt, was
largely responsible for the reorganization and continuation of the Peace
Problems Committee in 1925. The secretary has explained elsewhere
how earlier in 1925 he had attended a peace conference in Washington
sponsored by representative American religious leaders, and how he had
found there a deep concern to find the Scriptural answer to war. This
meeting, he says, gave him a new vision of what the Mennonite Church
could and should do by way of a peace witness. Later, when he attended
General Conference in the summer of 1925, he discovered in conversation
with a member of the old Peace Problems Committee that since the
committee had been inactive, and since there seemed little for it to do,
its plan was to recommend to General Conference that it be discontinued.
Miller then suggested that now was the time when the committee had a
unique opportunity for work and witness, and that instead of discon-
tinuing it, it should be enlarged and charged with new responsibilities.[5]
Fortunately this suggestion was accepted, with the result that General
Conference appointed the new and enlarged committee.

As early as 1927 there was evidence of aggressive work on the part
of the Peace Problems Committee. In that year the committee reported
to General Conference on having written letters "to government officials
in connection with the Welsh Bill before the last Congress which aimed
to take the compulsory feature out of military training in our public high
schools and colleges. Other letters were forwarded at the time when the
international situation as regards Nicaragua, Mexico, and China seemed
acute and to encourage our President in his program of naval reduction.
Much more should have been done. We owe it to the 'powers that be'
to let them know our position on this question." The 1929 report mentioned further activity along this line, and recommended that at this
session of General Conference a message of appreciation be sent to President Herbert Hoover for his effort in behalf of peace. This recommendation was approved, and messages were sent both to President Hoover
and to Prime Minister Mackenzie King of Canada. In 1931 the committee
reported a communication with government officials encouraging efforts
at disarmament at the London Naval Conference in 1930, and the disarmament conference planned for 1932. The 1939 report suggested the
advisability of making "personal contact with the President and other
leading government officials on the part of a carefully chosen delegation
during the early part of each new administration."

RELATIONS WITH OTHER PEACE GROUPS

The 1927 report to General Conference also shows that the new Peace Problems Committee was attempting to discover what its relation should be to the organized peace movement in general. The report says that "through attendance at meetings of various peace organizations and a study of their literature as well as a study of the pronouncements made by other denominations on war and peace, we know there is dire need for, and a present opportunity of, spreading among many now seeking the light, a fuller interpretation of the doctrine than they now have. We hope more can be done along this line in the future." In 1931 the committee reported the receipt of a manifesto published by a group of Dutch Mennonite leaders protesting against the position and activities of the new peace movement within the Mennonite Church of the Netherlands.[6] The Peace Problems Committee sponsored a reply to this manifesto setting forth the attitude of the American Mennonites toward military service, which was signed by twenty-two brethren in responsible positions in the general activities of the Mennonite Church, and forwarded in June, 1931.[7] The report of 1933 says that "calls from other denominational committees and from a variety of societies and groups interested in the peace question, for literature or for information regarding our viewpoint or work indicate a continuing need for witness in that direction and an especial need for sound literature to meet these calls."

The 1935 report again refers to the nonresistance movement among the Mennonites of Holland with which the Peace Problems Committee had continued to keep in touch. The committee also reported concerning inquiries from peace committees of other branches of Mennonites in America, as well as exchanges of correspondence with them concerning methods of work. The committee then suggested that perhaps the Mennonite Central Committee could serve as a co-ordinating agency for the various Mennonite peace committees, enabling them to work unitedly in their approaches to the government, especially to obtain concessions for suitable forms of alternative service in case of war. Early in 1936, a proposed *Mennonite Peace Manifesto* prepared by Jacob ter Meulen, the secretary of the Dutch Mennonite Committee against Military Service, was circulated by the Peace Problems Committee for signatures. This *Manifesto* was signed by about 140 leaders of eight different branches of Mennonites in America. About one half of the signers were from that branch of the church which is served directly by the Peace Problems Committee. A letter from the Peace Problems Committee explained that the *Manifesto* was intended to serve "as an encouragement for those who intend to stand for the Biblical principle in these troublous times, and as a witness to those others who are wavering on this principle or have lost it altogether . . . . We owe a witness, not only to the world, but also to our Mennonite brethren in various lands such as Holland, Germany,

Russia, Switzerland, France, and Poland, where the principle is well-nigh lost, as well as to our brethren in the refugee colonies in Paraguay and Brazil who are struggling to maintain it."[8] The *Manifesto* reads as follows:

MENNONITE PEACE MANIFESTO

We, the undersigned Mennonite groups, organizations, and individuals, scattered throughout the world,

Believing in the Gospel of Jesus Christ which calls men to the service of peace and to stand against the sin of war,

And being convinced that God condemns the atrocious means and measures of war which are now being prepared by all nations in a constantly increasing stream,

Call all Mennonites throughout the world to fulfill the task entrusted to us by the history of our Mennonite forefathers, in the propagation of the Gospel of peace.

We therefore appeal to all brethren and sisters to witness vigorously to our peace testimony in our congregations everywhere, and to work together to the end that we may give spiritual and material help to all who are convinced that God has called them to refuse military service, as well as to all others who may be called upon to suffer for their peace convictions.

INTERNATIONAL MENNONITE PEACE COMMITTEE

The Third Mennonite World Conference was held in the Netherlands, June 29 to July 3, 1936. On the following day, July 4, 1936, representatives of several Mennonite peace committees from North America, of the Dutch Mennonite Committee against Military Service, and of other interested persons, a total of about twenty-five, met in a peace conference and organized the International Mennonite Peace Committee. "It was encouraging to find a unanimous stand by those present on the principle of absolute Gospel nonresistance and peace."[9] Present at this meeting were Harold S. Bender and Orie O. Miller of the Peace Problems Committee, as well as C. Henry Smith, P. C. Hiebert, P. R. Schroeder, C. F. Klassen, and David Toews, representing the General Conference Mennonite Church and the Mennonite Brethren Church of North America. Harold S. Bender was chosen chairman of the new International Mennonite Peace Committee, and Jacob ter Meulen of the Netherlands was chosen secretary-treasurer. The new organization endorsed the *Mennonite Peace Manifesto* referred to above, as had been done earlier by the Dutch Mennonite Committee against Military Service and the various American Mennonite groups and peace committees, as well as by Mennonite leaders in Europe and South America. This document was now printed and widely circulated by the organization among the Mennonites of the world.

The International Mennonite Peace Committee was not thought of as an official body, but rather as a working organization for the promotion of the cause of peace among Mennonites throughout the world, with the various peace committees in Holland and America, including the

Peace Problems Committee, listed as supporting committees. The work envisioned by the committee was outlined as follows by its chairman:

> The function of the committee is primarily to provide for helpful contact between the various Mennonite groups throughout the world interested in promoting the historic Mennonite principle of Biblical nonresistance and peace. Specifically the following types of co-operation were suggested: (a) Exchange of information regarding the activities, programs, problems, and needs of the various peace committees in the various Mennonite lands. This exchange of information was to be accomplished chiefly through the agency of a mimeographed news sheet published occasionally, probably twice a year. (b) Issuance of joint statements such as the Peace Manifesto and similar statements, pamphlets or booklets, as may be desired by the group committees. (c) Joint aid to Mennonites compelled to suffer for their peace convictions. (d) Exchange of information regarding possible concrete and constructive expressions of our peace testimony through service such as relief work in needy areas.[10]

CO-OPERATION WITH HISTORIC PEACE CHURCHES

In 1937 the Peace Problems Committee reported to General Conference its supporting relationship to the new International Mennonite Peace Committee. It also reported that its secretary was serving on a continuation committee of three members representing the historic peace churches, the Brethren, the Friends, and the Mennonites, a committee whose task it was to discover means whereby the peace testimony of these groups "might be more effective if unitedly made." This co-operation with the historic peace churches goes back as far as 1922, or indeed to the first World War. The Mennonite relief program of that era received its start through co-operation with the Quakers when over fifty Mennonites served with the Friends Reconstruction Service in France.[11]

Although the Mennonite Relief Commission for War Sufferers had been organized by the Mennonite Church in 1917, this agency considered itself too young and inexperienced at the moment to attempt an independent work. In 1920, however, the Mennonite Central Committee was organized by several of the Mennonite branches for the purpose of carrying on relief work in Russia. In time it became the official Mennonite relief agency, operating in a large way in all parts of the world, and supported by all of the Mennonite groups. Following the second World War it had more relief workers on the field and was operating in a larger number of countries than was the American Friends Service Committee, although the total volume of its operations was smaller and its budget was about one half that of the A.F.S.C. The secretary of the Mennonite Central Committee was certainly correct some years earlier, however, when in referring to the Mennonite experience of 1918 and 1919 he said: "We leaned heavily on Quaker leadership to show us certain constructive opportunities. Certain irreparable losses to us through the loss of some of our young brethren in these connections may have been due to our unreadiness to lead at this strategic moment."[12]

It is not surprising, then, that following the war there should have been occasional meetings of what came to be known as the Conference of Pacifist Churches. The first of these, held at Bluffton, Ohio, in 1922, was promoted to a large extent by Wilbur K. Thomas, a prominent leader in the relief work of the American Friends. Subsequent conferences were held in 1923, 1926, 1927, 1929, and 1931. The chief participants in these conferences were Brethren, Friends, and Mennonites, although Moravians, Schwenckfelders, and other peace groups were invited, and on occasion attended the meetings. These conferences were unofficial and informal in character, for the purpose of comparing views and methods of work, and for an exchange of experiences. In 1935 a new series of meetings known as conferences of the historic peace churches was initiated on a new basis by H. P. Krehbiel, a prominent minister of the General Conference Mennonite Church.[13] The first of these meetings, held at Newton, Kansas, October 31 to November 2, 1935, was attended by fifty-seven delegates besides other interested persons. This was by far the most important meeting of this kind held so far, since all were aware of the current grave international situation and realized its significance for the peace churches. The work of the Newton conference has been summarized by Melvin Gingerich as follows:

A report for the conference was . . . adopted . . . . The first part was a statement of position, stressing that the church's peace principles are rooted in Christ and His Word, that war is sin, and that their supreme allegiance is to God. Section two presented "Our Concept of Patriotism." The next three sections called for a joint committee of the historic peace churches, exchanging of literature, and a program of united action. Section six was a "Plan of Unified Action in Case the United States Is Involved in War." This included seven points, among which was one encouraging the members of the peace churches to accept only "alternative service of nonmilitary nature and not under military control."[14]

The joint committee mentioned above was appointed, and came to be known as the Continuation Committee. It functioned from 1935 to 1940, when its work was largely taken over by more official organizations, particularly the National Service Board for Religious Objectors, operating to meet the exigencies of conscription and war. The Mennonite representative on the Continuation Committee was Orie O. Miller, who was secretary of the Mennonite Central Committee, which appointed him, as well as of the Peace Problems Committee. The other two members of the committee were R. W. Balderston and C. Ray Keim, representing the Friends and Brethren, respectively. In 1936 the Continuation Committee sponsored a conference on peace literature at which time a committee on literature was appointed. This committee never accomplished very much although it did meet once or twice, and initiated certain ideas which eventually resulted in the publication of the *Pacifist Handbook* in 1939. This book is primarily the work of the peace section of the American Friends Service Committee, however, and of certain persons connected with the Fellowship of Reconciliation. The latter organization holds the copyright. The peace section of the American Friends Service Committee also published mimeographed bibliographies of peace literature from time to time, and it is possible that the literature committee made some slight contribution to this work.

In 1936 the Continuation Committee arranged for a joint delegation of the historic peace churches to bring personal greetings and a testimony for the Christian way of peace to the general conference of the Methodist Episcopal Church. In the same year, a delegation was sent on a similar mission to the conference of the Reformed Presbyterian Church. In 1937 representatives of the Friends, the Brethren, and the Mennonites called on President Franklin D. Roosevelt at the White House. Each of the three groups presented a letter stating its views on war and peace, and giving reasons why those who adhere to this faith cannot conscientiously bear arms. A similar delegation visited President Roosevelt again on January 10, 1940, with concrete proposals for alternative service in case of conscription. The Continuation Committee also sponsored a peace institute at Manchester College in the spring of 1937, and another conference with special emphasis on peace work among college students at Winchester, Indiana, in October of that year. In 1938 a missions and peace conference was held, giving attention to the peace emphasis in the work of foreign missions.

THE MENNONITE CENTRAL PEACE COMMITTEE: A PLAN OF ACTION IN CASE OF WAR

On March 10 and 11, 1939, the historic peace churches met in Chicago, this time with special emphasis on possible procedure in case of war. Since the Continuation Committee was an unofficial organization, and since the Mennonite representative on this committee was appointed by the Mennonite Central Committee, a relief organization, there was in reality no person or committee who could speak authoritatively for all Mennonite groups concerning a procedure in case of war. Consequently the secretary of the M.C.C. called a meeting, also on March 10, 1939, of representatives of the various Mennonite groups, the representatives to be the official peace committees of these groups in case they had such. Representatives of seven Mennonite groups were present, and steps were taken toward the formation of a Mennonite Central Peace Committee.

A temporary organization was set up until such time as the various co-operating groups would appoint their official representatives to the committee. After these appointments were made, the permanent organization was completed on September 30, 1939, with P. C. Hiebert as chairman, E. L. Harshbarger, vice-chairman and treasurer, and Harold S. Bender, executive secretary. This was now an official body with authority to act, although its actions would need to be ratified from time to time by the supporting bodies, which in the case of the Mennonite Church was the Peace Problems Committee and the General Conference to which it was responsible. At the meeting of March 10, 1939, an effort was made to acquaint all Mennonite groups with each other's work, and serious attention was given to ways in which American Mennonites working co-operatively might be helpful to the Mennonites of Europe and South America in the maintenance of their peace testimony. The work of the International Mennonite Peace Committee was endorsed and encouraged, and greetings were sent to the Mennonites in South America as well as to officials of the Mennonite peace group in Holland.

With the beginning of the second World War, early in September, 1939, the Mennonite Central Peace Committee directed its energies to the formulation of a definite plan of action in case the United States should actually become involved in war. On September 16, 1939, officials of the committee met with representatives of the Church of the Brethren and of the Friends. At this meeting, the representatives drew up a general outline of a plan of action in case of war, which they believed would meet the approval of all three groups. On September 30, this outline was presented to the entire Mennonite Central Peace Committee and adopted as its own plan of action. All of the co-operating Mennonite groups later gave their official approval to this plan which proposed that the church follow a course which would separate its members as completely as possible from the military organization, and which would make possible a constructive program of alternative service. The plan proposed the following specific steps:

1. All persons subject to conscription "should register when called to do so, indicating at the time of registration their conscientious objection to military service and their willingness, if called, to render other useful service of a nonmilitary character."

2. When the individual is called for service, he should "state his inability as a Christian to accept induction into the army, and should at that time offer himself for nonmilitary service of such a nature as his conscience will permit."

3. The church should offer to the President of the United States "its co-operation in providing forms of service acceptable to our Christian conscience and conformable to the principles of the Gospel, and which can be approved by the church and placed as much as possible under some form of church direction and supervision. Among acceptable forms of service the following might be included: relief for war sufferers; relief for refugees or evacuated civil populations; reconstruction work in war-stricken areas; resettlement of refugees; reclamation or forestry service in the United States or elsewhere; farm service similar to that provided under the farm furlough system in operation in the last war; relief and reconstruction work in local communities in the United States; medical,

nursing, and health service in connection with any of the above projects or independently, both for men and women."

4. "The church should endeavor to secure an arrangement whereby the service provided for conscientious objectors would be placed by the President under a civilian board of control especially set up for this purpose as was the case in the last war."

5. "Inasmuch as the government plans for mobilization apparently empower the President to determine the status and service of conscientious objectors, and inasmuch as the plans are apparently prepared in detail and are designed to go into effect as soon as possible after the declaration of war and the passage of a conscription law, and inasmuch as it will be necessary for the President to provide procedure and machinery to deal with conscientious objectors coincidentally with those inducted into military service, we believe that the fundamental position of the Mennonite Church, together with concrete proposals such as those mentioned above, should be presented soon to the President for his consideration with the request that plans be made in advance to care for the conscientious objectors."

Since it appeared that the other historic peace churches were also ready to give official approval to this plan of action for their own groups, the Mennonite Central Peace Committee and its supporting organizations approved the idea of having representatives of the Mennonites present to the President, jointly with representatives of the Friends and Brethren, the proposals agreed upon. Accordingly, a delegation of Mennonites, Friends, and Brethren visited the President at the White House on January 10, 1940, presenting to him a letter setting forth their general purposes and desires. Accompanying the letter was a memorandum containing concrete and somewhat detailed proposals embodying the ideas outlined in the general plan of action above.

In all of these proceedings, the Peace Problems Committee played an important role, always moving cautiously so as to make sure that it was carrying out the wishes of the church which it represented. The October 5, 1939, issue of the *Gospel Herald* carried "A Message from the Peace Problems Committee" reporting on what the committee was doing. It was keeping in touch with the various branches of Mennonites and with the Friends and Brethren. The meeting of the M.C.P.C. on September 30 was referred to. The committee was working closely with the moderator and the Executive Committee of General Conference and "is giving careful consideration to various problems involved in our position on war and military service." Special mention was made of a possible delegation to the President and of possible plans for alternative service in case of war. The committee asked for the prayers and the counsel of the church to the end that it might have divine guidance in the performance of its tasks. Congregations and members were urged to give special attention to the nonresistant doctrine, to study the Scriptures, "and to become thoroughly familiar with the position of the church as expressed in the General Conference statement on *Peace, War, and Military Service,* as adopted at Turner, Oregon, in 1937."[15]

On October 20, 1939, the Peace Problems Committee met at Goshen, Indiana, with the moderator of General Conference, to review the recent happenings and to plan for the larger meeting of the following day. The chairman gave a full report of the circumstances which led to the organization of the Mennonite Central Peace Committee and of his service on this committee as its secretary. The service which the M.C.P.C. would be expected to render was discussed at length, and it was agreed that in meeting these needs the central committee could function more effectively than could the several groups working separately. It was also agreed that "subject to objectionable trends in the Mennonite Central Peace Committee's work," the chairman should continue his connection with it. The plan of action formulated by the M.C.P.C. on September 30, 1939, was carefully considered and found "consistent with the General Conference position as stated at Turner, Oregon, in 1937."[16]

On the following day, October 21, 1939, the Peace Problems Committee met with a larger group of about twenty-five men, consisting of representatives of the Executive Committee of General Conference, of the Executive and Relief committees of the Mennonite Board of Missions and Charities, and of the various district conferences, including Franconia, Lancaster, and the Conservative Amish Mennonite Conference, and a few other leaders. Representatives from the Old Order Amish group were also present. At this meeting, presided over by Harry A. Diener, moderator of General Conference, the Peace Problems Committee reviewed its work and that of the Mennonite Central Peace Committee, and presented the proposed "Plan of Action in Case of War" to the entire delegation. After considerable discussion it was moved and passed, "without a dissenting vote," that the plan of action be approved. The meeting also approved a recommendation of the Peace Problems Committee that it appoint a committee of six to co-operate with Harold S. Bender in representing the Mennonite Church to the government. It was understood that in case a joint delegation of the historic peace churches visited the President, Bender should be the member of that delegation representing the Peace Problems Committee constituency. In case of a Mennonite delegation making a separate representation to government officials, responsibility was also to be placed in Bender's hands. In either case, the committee of six were to be his official advisers. The committee members as finally appointed were: Amos S. Horst, Simon Gingerich, E. B. Frey, Orie O. Miller, Eli J. Bontreger, and Shem Peachey. The first four persons were appointed at the meeting on October 21. The last two were appointed later by the Old Order Amish and the Conservative Amish groups.[17]

The meeting of October 21, 1939, also heard reports from the Relief Committee of the Mennonite Board of Missions and Charities. The status of the committee's relief program in Spain was explained, as well as its decision to approve the organization of war relief through the Mennonite Central Committee, which had not taken part in the program in Spain. "It was then moved and passed without dissenting vote to approve of the thoughtful way in which the Relief Committee had gone about its work and its plans for the future, and that they be urged to continue along the lines suggested." It is clear that the church representatives assembled on October 21, 1939, were thinking in terms of a long-range program of relief, and also of alternative service in case the United States were actually drawn into the war. The minutes of this meeting were published in the *Gospel Herald* shortly afterward,[18] thus giving the church full information of what the Peace Problems Committee and its co-operating official bodies were doing. Following the mission of the representatives of the historic peace churches to see President Roosevelt on January 10, 1940, a full report of what was done at this time was also published in the *Gospel Herald*.

The report reviewed the meeting of October 21, 1939, authorizing the mission. It then explained that during the forenoon of January 10 the seven delegates of the historic peace churches met with the Mennonite committee of counselors appointed by the meeting of October 21, and with "several additional counselors from the other two churches," to prepare for the meeting with the President which took place at 12:30 P.M. The report then describes the visit with the President, followed by visits with Attorney General Murphy, with Robert H. Jackson who had been appointed as Murphy's successor, and with Secretary of War Woodring. The report is signed by Harold S. Bender and the members of the advisory committee. Following the report is a printed copy of the formal letter presented to President Roosevelt by the delegates representing the historic peace churches.[19] These reports illustrate the policy of the Peace Problems Committee in keeping the church fully informed of all that it was doing. Later in the year, after the Selective Training and Service Act had been passed and while steps were being taken to open the C.P.S. program, the chairman of the Peace Problems Committee wrote the editor of the *Gospel Herald* saying that the Mennonite people desired as much information as possible concerning Selective Service and C.P.S. and expressing the hope that the *Herald* would provide space for all necessary announcements and publicity.[20]

The meeting of the representatives of the peace churches with the President and other officials had come none too early. Prospects for a draft law were great, and continual vigilance on the part of all was required. For a time much of the planning for the proposed conscription program seemed to be centered in the office of Francis Biddle, the Solicitor General of the United States. On June 6, 1940, Orie O. Miller, with representatives of the Friends and the Brethren, had a conference with Biddle, who requested: information concerning British C.O.'s in the current war; a statement of what service the peace churches would be willing to perform in case of war; suggestions for C.O. provisions which might be written into a possible draft law; and a man-power report from the three churches. The peace churches were able to comply with the first three requests almost immediately. The man-power report, however, required time for making a statistical survey. In carrying out their part of this task, the Mennonite Central Peace Committee laid plans for a man-power survey by means of a questionnaire. The Peace Problems Committee then assumed responsibility for administering the survey in its section of the Mennonite constituency. The survey was completed during the summer and the report submitted to the Solicitor General.

THE DRAFT ACT: CIVILIAN PUBLIC SERVICE

In the summer of 1940, the Burke-Wadsworth Bill was introduced in Congress, and in September it became a law known as the Selective Training and Service Act of 1940. Despite the efforts of peace churches, however, including the mission to President Roosevelt on January 10, 1940, the later conference with the Solicitor General, and other activities before and after, the Burke-Wadsworth Bill in its original form had practically the same provision for conscientious objectors as had the draft law of 1917. Representatives of the Mennonite Central Peace Committee and of the Quakers, Brethren, and other interested bodies immediately got in touch with the sponsors of the bill, however, and pointed out that noncombatant military service would be altogether unacceptable to a large group of conscientious objectors. They also pointed out that many persons not of the traditional peace churches were conscientious objectors, and that these should be included in the provisions of the act. These representatives therefore urged the inclusion of a provision assigning to civilian service all persons who could not conscientiously serve in the army. They testified at hearings of the Military Affairs Committees of House and Senate. The sponsors of the bill consulted with military officials who also agreed that genuine conscientious objectors ought not to be inducted into the army.

As a result of these efforts, the law as passed provided that all persons "who by reason of religious training and belief" were conscientiously opposed to all forms of military service, should, if conscripted for service, "be assigned to work of national importance under civilian direction." An effort was also made to obtain the complete exemption of men with conscientious objection to all forms of service, including civilian service, under conscription. It was pointed out that the British conscription laws provided for such absolutists. This effort failed, however, with the result that the Selective Training and Service Act of 1940 made no provision for the absolutists.

During this period Orie O. Miller was more active in behalf of the M.C.P.C. and the Peace Problems Committee than any other person, making frequent trips to Washington, although E. L. Harshbarger and Harold S. Bender also were active. On one occasion, Amos S. Horst in the absence of Orie O. Miller spoke at the hearings of the House Military Affairs Committee. In this phase of the work, however, more work was done by the Friends, especially Paul Comly French and E. Raymond Wilson, than by either the Mennonites or the Brethren. Melvin Gingerich says that while the draft legislation was in process, French and Wilson conferred personally with more than seventy-five senators and 250 congressmen, and then adds: "It would appear . . . that the Brethren and Mennonites had taken the leadership in working out plans for action in case of conscription and war but that the Friends had taken the leadership in getting these concepts into the Selective Training and Service Act of 1940."[21]

Even though the conscientious objector clause was included in the bill, and the law passed, the peace churches realized that their greatest task was still before them. The law provided that conscientious objectors should be assigned to civilian service, but nothing was said of ways and means for administering such a civilian service program. What would be the procedure for assigning a conscientious objector to civilian service? What would be the nature of the service? How would it be financed? Would the peace churches be permitted to direct and supervise the social and religious life of the men assigned to service, as suggested in the memorandum given to the President in January, 1940? These and many other questions remained to be answered. In course of time the Selective Service System placed the classification of conscientious objectors into the hands of local draft boards, and not into the hands of a special board of control as the peace churches had proposed to the President. In case the draftee was dissatisfied with his classification, however, it was provided that he might appeal his case to an appeal board under a plan in which the Department of Justice investigated the sincerity of his claims and made final recommendation.

THE NATIONAL SERVICE BOARD FOR RELIGIOUS OBJECTORS

In order to co-ordinate their own organizations so as to have a unified approach to the problem, as well as to the government agencies, the historic peace churches, on October 5, 1940, took steps to set up a National Council for Religious Conscientious Objectors for the formulation of policies and the giving of advice relating to the problems of C.O.'s. In addition, it was agreed to organize a Civilian Service Board whose function it would be to deal with the problems of alternative service. On November 26, 1940, however, the two organizations were merged and the resulting new organization was named the National Service Board for Religious Objectors. The N.S.B.R.O. now became the agency through which the peace churches worked in dealing with Selective Service. The latter, likewise, dealt with the peace churches through the N.S.B.R.O. From this point onward, the Continuation Committee was relatively inactive until after the war, when it was revived again. The peace churches, following a conference with Clarence A. Dykstra, the first director of Selective Service, presented a plan for setting up Civilian Public Service camps in which the work projects would be under the direction of government technical men, and the social and religious life of the drafted men under the supervision of the church agencies. The plan was adopted by Selective Service and presented to President Roosevelt who approved it on December 19, 1940. Following the issuance of the executive order, the Mennonite Central Committee, the American Friends Service Committee, and the Brethren Service Committee, through the National Service Board for Religious Objectors, were authorized by Selective Service to operate the Civilian Public Service camp program.[22]

In the above account it was observed that during 1939 and 1940 the task of preparing the various Mennonite groups for the emergency of war was carried on by the Mennonite Central Peace Committee, which adopted its plan of action on September 30, 1939. When the M.C.P.C. was faced with the actual problem of operating C.P.S. camps, however, in the fall of 1940, it assigned the task to the Mennonite Central Committee, an organization which seemed better fitted for this task, in view of its twenty years of experience in foreign relief and colonization projects. Thus there were two organizations working on different aspects of the same problem. The M.C.P.C. served as a general policy making organization in matters relating to the fundamental Mennonite position on war, peace, and military service, while the M.C.C. was the operating organization for C.P.S. In practice, however, there was some overlapping of functions, resulting in a certain amount of confusion. It became clear, therefore, that it would be better to merge the two organizations, which was done in January, 1942. With this action the M.C.P.C. ceased to exist, being replaced by a Peace Section within the M.C.C.

The different Mennonite groups co-operating with the M.C.C., however, continued to have active peace committees for the promotion of peace teaching within the groups. These committees continued to publish literature, to do publicity work through their own church papers, and to lead in the peace thinking of their particular groups. The role of the Peace Problems Committee in this respect is dealt with in virtually every chapter of the present work.

NOTES AND CITATIONS

[1] For the reports of the committee see the biennial reports of the Mennonite General Conference, printed by the Mennonite Publishing House, Scottdale, Pa.

[2] P. C. French, *We Won't Murder* (New York, 1940), 128.

[3] Correspondence in files of the Peace Problems Committee.

[4] Orie O. Miller, "Aggressive Peace Work," *Gospel Herald* (Jan. 14, 1926), 18:858.

[5] Report of interview with Orie O. Miller, Oct. 10, 1947, in the files of Melvin Gingerich.

[6] This *Manifesto* was a four-page leaflet, with forty-one signers, members of the Dutch Mennonite Committee for Warning Against Propaganda for Refusal to Render Military Service and for One-sided Disarmament.

[7] This reply was a four-page leaflet, entitled, *The Position of the Mennonite Church in America on Peace and War*. It was signed by the members of the Peace Problems Committee, the Executive Committee of the Mennonite General Conference, the heads of the colleges and boards of the church, and a few other individuals.

[8] From the files of the Peace Problems Committee.

[9] Orie O. Miller and Harold S. Bender, "A Brief Account of the Third Mennonite World Conference," *Mennonite Quarterly Review* (January, 1937), 11:11.

[10] Harold S. Bender's letter to P. R. Schroeder and E. L. Harshbarger, Dec. 31, 1936, in Peace Problems Committee files.

[11] J. S. Hartzler, *Mennonites in the World War* (Scottdale, Pa., 1921), 194. See also Guy F. Hershberger, *War, Peace, and Nonresistance* (Scottdale, Pa., 1944), 140-42; and Melvin Gingerich, *Service for Peace: A History of Mennonite Civilian Public Service* (Akron, Pa., 1949).

[12] Orie O. Miller, "The Place, Purpose, and Program of the Peace Problems Committee," *Report of Mennonite General Conference* (1933), 69.

[13] For a fuller discussion of this movement, see Ch. XIX, p. 247 ff.

[14] Melvin Gingerich, *Service for Peace*, 27. Ch. III in this book, "Interchurch Co-operation," is an excellent treatment of the whole subject.

[15] *Gospel Herald* (Oct. 5, 1939), 32:570.

[16] Peace Problems Committee Minutes, Oct. 20, 1939.

[17] *Ibid.*, Oct. 21, 1939.

[18] "Minutes of Meeting of Church Representatives held at Goshen College, Goshen, Ind., Saturday, October 21, 1939," *Gospel Herald* (Nov. 2, 1939), 32:670.

[19] "A Visit with the President," *Gospel Herald* (Feb. 22, 1940), 32:1004-5.

[20] Letter in Peace Problems Committee files, Nov. 21, 1940.

[21] Melvin Gingerich, *Service for Peace*, 50. See Ch. IV, "The Coming of Conscription," for a detailed treatment of the subject.

[22] For a detailed account of the origins and the operations of the N.S.B.R.O., see Gingerich *op. cit.*, Chs. V and VI. Also see below, Chs. XIX and XX, for a discussion of certain issues raised concerning the relations of the Peace Problems Committee and its constituency with the M.C.C. and the N.S.B.R.O.

Chapter II

The Coming of Selective Service

The Selective Training and Service Act became law on September 16, 1940, one year to the day after representatives of the historic peace churches had drawn up their outline of "A plan of action in case of war." On October 16, 1940, all men aged twenty-one to thirty-five years, inclusive, were registered for the draft. By June 30, 1942, a total of five registrations had taken place, which now included all men aged eighteen to sixty-five in the United States. After January 1, 1943, all younger men registered upon reaching the age of eighteen.

KEEPING THE CHURCH INFORMED

As soon as the law was passed the M.C.P.C., with the co-operation of the N.S.B.R.O. and the peace committees of the various Mennonite groups, prepared literature for distribution to the membership in every Mennonite congregation. This literature gave counsel, not only to men subject to conscription, but also to ministers and to the entire brotherhood, concerning the best course to be followed by nonresistant Christians in time of conscription. Responsibility for the preparation of this literature was largely that of Henry A. Fast, who had earlier served the Peace Committee of the General Conference Mennonite Church as its executive secretary. Beginning in September, 1940, he gave full-time service to the M.C.P.C., representing its interests in Washington until he became the general director of Civilian Public Service under the M.C.C. in mid-November. Fast was in constant touch with Selective Service and the N.S.B.R.O. in Washington, and with the M.C.C. office in Akron, Pennsylvania. As important information was obtained and prepared by him, it was relayed to their various constituencies by the peace committees co-operating with the M.C.P.C.

On September 19, 1940, three days after the draft law was signed, the *Gospel Herald*[1] carried a copy of a mimeographed letter which had previously been mailed by the secretary of the Peace Problems Committee to all ministers of the Mennonite Church. This letter described the provisions of the draft law as they affected conscientious objectors. Even though the complete rules for registration, classification, and induction had not yet been announced by the Selective Service System, the general procedure was known, and this information was included in the letter. The letter said that upon registration the individual should indicate, "in the proper section of the registration blank," the fact that he is a conscientious objector. It was explained that following registration local

19

draft boards would classify registrants and pass upon the sincerity of conscientious objectors, assigning them to "work of national importance under civilian direction" if found sincere, or to service in the army if not found sincere. Anyone not satisfied with his classification might appeal to an appeal board which would refer the case to the Department of Justice for inquiry and hearing. After the Department of Justice had conducted its hearing, it would report its findings and recommendations to the appeal board. The latter would then give its decision, which would be considered final. The letter also explained that Selective Service had not yet clearly defined the term "work of national importance under civilian direction." This matter would be cleared up later on.

On October 3, 1940, the *Gospel Herald* published a "Further Word on Conscription Act Procedure."[2] This communication corrected a point made in that of September 19, saying: "It seems clear now that the registration set for October 16 is for identification and assignment of numbers only. It is not necessary and perhaps would not be advisable to indicate one's C.O. status at the time of registration.[3] Subsequent to registration, and after the order in which the numbers are to be called up is determined, questionnaires will be mailed to all holders of these numbers. At that time the conscientious objector's position needs to be clearly given." It was stated that contacts made with Selective Service officials "indicate intention on their part to be as lenient as possible with those adjudged sincere religious objectors."

Full details of appeal procedures, however, had not been announced. Neither was it known as yet how the civilian service program would operate, nor precisely what would constitute work of national importance. It was hoped, however, that the program would follow the general pattern outlined in the communication of January 10, 1940, to the President. Representatives of the peace churches had been in conversation with responsible government officials looking toward that end. Moreover, it now seemed that the Mennonite Central Committee would be the most appropriate agency for the administration of the church's part of this program, whatever that would be. The *Gospel Herald* statement of October 3 emphasized, however, that no commitments would be made by the Peace Problems Committee without first obtaining the approval of the officials of the Mennonite General Conference. As rapidly as new information was available, it would be announced to the constituency.

COUNSEL TO MENNONITE YOUNG MEN

The next mailing of important information directly to ministers of the church took place on October 8. This contained various items, including a copy of that section of the Selective Training and Service Act which referred to conscientious objectors. Another item was a four-page leaflet entitled, *Counsel to Mennonite Young Men Regarding the Selective*

Training and Service Act of 1940 As It Applies to Conscientious Objectors. This leaflet was reprinted in the *Gospel Herald* of October 10.[4] Its contents were divided into parts as follows: (1) Registration. (2) The questionnaire. (3) Inquiry and hearing before the local board. (4) The assignment to service. (5) Possibility of appeal. (6) Failure or refusal to register. (7) Words of counsel to young men facing military conscription. The last section urged the registrant: (a) To "make certain that you are able to give a simple and clear statement of the Scriptural basis of your convictions." (b) To "endeavor to manifest a truly Christian attitude always." (c) Not to "argue or try to convince authorities of the truth of your position," but rather to state that position quietly and confidently, knowing that it is within the law. (d) To "be prepared to be misunderstood." (e) To remember that "the government has the right to inquire into the sincerity of your convictions." (f) To "thank God for a government that tries to respect the rights of individual conscience." (g) To "remember that you will need daily fellowship with God and daily study of His Word if you would be faithful to your Christian profession and a true witness of the Better Way."

Section 3 of the above leaflet gave counsel concerning possible appearance before a local draft board for inquiry and hearing. The registrant was advised to:

... Have thought through beforehand clearly and carefully your religious and Scriptural reasons for objecting to participation in military training so that you are sure of your ground and can give a clear and intelligent statement of your Christian conviction. You ought to understand thoroughly and if possible know from memory certain great teachings of Jesus and the apostles that have become basic in determining your opposition to military training and war, probably passages like the following: Matthew 5:9, 38, 43, 44; 25:52; Romans 12:17-21; I Peter 2:21-23; and others.

You should also try to have an answer to give when asked to explain such sayings of Jesus as: "Render unto Caesar the things that are Caesar's"; "I came not to send peace but a sword"; "He that hath no sword, let him buy one"; or the problem of warfare in the Old Testament, or other similar difficult passages of Scripture, which are sometimes given as arguments against Christian nonresistance.

You should also have thought through such questions as the following, which in some form or other might be asked by a board of inquiry: What would you do if somebody would attack your mother or your wife and children? What would you do if your country were invaded? The charge that you lack patriotism because you will not take up arms or resort to methods of violence or defend your country. The charge that you are a coward and are merely seeking an easy escape from an unpleasant demand. Anticipate other possible questions.

In general the right position and the safest position for you to take in all such questions is that of the humble, faithful Christian believer, who desires to follow Christ and obey His teachings. You may not be able to answer satisfactorily all the questions which may be asked, but you can always say that you believe the Spirit and teachings of Jesus and the New Testament to be opposed to all taking of human life in any form and that therefore you cannot take part in war or preparation for it.

On October 11, 1940, the Peace Problems Committee made another mailing which included a four-page leaflet, *Additional Counsel to Mennonite Young Men Regarding the Selective Training and Service Act of 1940 As It Applies to Conscientious Objectors.* This leaflet re-emphasized the advice of the previous one with respect to policy and attitude, gave more detailed information, and also corrected a few minor points in the previous leaflet with regard to the administration of the act. It was emphasized that all persons aged twenty-one to thirty-five must register on October 16, and that each registrant must retain the registration card or certificate received at that time. The registration and classification procedures were described in considerable detail. It was made clear that following registration, an assignment of numbers as drawn by lot would determine the order in which the registrants would receive their questionnaires. It also was emphasized that in this questionnaire the section entitled "Series X, Conscientious Objection to War" would need to be filled out with care. The counsel of the Peace Problems Committee on this point was as follows:

The following is a copy of that section of the registration questionnaire dealing with the conscientious objector. Those preferring civilian service will need to place an "X" in both boxes in order to indicate their position.

SELECTIVE SERVICE QUESTIONNAIRE

SERIES X. CONSCIENTIOUS OBJECTION TO WAR

INSTRUCTIONS—Only registrants who are conscientiously opposed to combatant or noncombatant military service by reason of their religious training and belief shall fill in this series, and shall obtain from the Local Board a special form on which to give substantiating evidence of conscientious objection. The Local Board will determine whether the registrant shall be classed as a conscientious objector on the basis of information contained in the special form, and not merely on the basis of the statements in this questionnaire.

I am conscientiously opposed, by reason of my religious training and belief, to the types of service checked below:

(Put an "X" in the applicable box or boxes)

( ) Combatant military service

( ) Noncombatant military service

The above-mentioned mailing also included a supply of church membership cards to be used by such registrants as might find them helpful. This was a small card 2½ x 4 inches in size, which when signed by the minister certified the holder as a member in good standing in the Mennonite Church. The card was patterned after one used by the Church of the Brethren. The mimeographed letter which accompanied the material explained that since there was no official action requiring the use of this card, "you will, therefore, decide for yourself whether you wish to use it." The letter also announced the appointment by the Peace

Problems Committee of Amos S. Horst, D. A. Yoder, and Harry A. Diener as regional counselors, "in order to provide for proper help and counsel in cases of difficulty in connection with the operation of the Selective Service Act . . . . These brethren are prepared to give their service to ministers and registrants if called upon. All requests for aid in dealing with local problems should be sent directly to them." Horst was assigned to the region east of Ohio; Yoder, to Ohio, Indiana, Michigan, and Illinois; Diener, to all territory west of the Mississippi River. The Peace Problems Committee explained that the service of these counselors "will be available not only to our own congregations, but to our brethren in the Conservative Amish Mennonite Conference, the Old Order Amish, and the Old Order Mennonites, in so far as their service is requested."

The October 24, 1940, issue of the *Gospel Herald* announced that "another mailing of material helpful to conscientious objectors and their pastors" was being sent out that week. This mailing included a sample of DSS Form 47, the special questionnaire for conscientious objectors, which was to be used by the registrant who had completed Series X of the general questionnaire. Form 47 requested considerable information on various points, such as the name and address of the registrant; his general background, including a complete description of his education; a chronological list of all occupations, positions, jobs, or types of work; the addresses and dates of residences where the registrant formerly lived; and his participation in organizations, such as membership in military, religious, or other organizations.

If a member of a religious organization, the registrant was asked to give: its name and the name and location of its governing body; the name and location of the local congregation commonly attended; the name and address of the pastor; and a statement of the creed, or official statement of the church as it relates to participation in war. The registrant was also asked to give as reference the names of persons "who could supply information as to the sincerity of your professed convictions against participation in war." In the section of the questionnaire called Series I, the registrant was required to sign a claim of exemption from military service. If he objected to all military service, both combatant and non-combatant, he signed the following: "I claim the exemption provided by the Selective Training and Service Act of 1940 for conscientious objectors, because I am conscientiously opposed by reason of religious training and belief to participation in any service which is under the direction of military authorities."[5]

The heart of Form 47 was the section entitled "Series II: Religious Training and Beliefs." This section had six questions as follows:

1. Describe the nature of your belief which is the basis of your claim made in Series I above.
2. Explain how, when, and from whom or from what source you received the training and acquired the belief which is the basis of your claim made in Series I above.

3. Give the name and present address of the individual upon whom you rely most for religious guidance.

4. Under what circumstances, if any, do you believe in the use of force?

5. Describe the actions and behavior in your life which in your opinion most conspicuously demonstrate the consistency and depth of your religious convictions.

6. Have you ever given public expression, written or oral, to the views herein expressed as the basis for your claim made in Series I above? If so, specify when and where.

Accompanying sample Form 47, sent by the Peace Problems Committee to the ministers during the week of October 24, 1940, was a two-page leaflet, *Counsel for Mennonite Young Men in Answering the General Selective Service Questionnaire and the Supplementary Special Questionnaire for Conscientious Objectors.* This leaflet said that local draft boards would begin mailing out the general questionnaire, "probably soon after November 1." Men were urged to "use great care" in filling out their questionnaires, and they were reminded that if they were able to accept neither combatant nor noncombatant service in the army, they must mark an "X" in both boxes in Series X of the general questionnaire. They were urged to return the general questionnaire promptly and then to secure Form 47 and return it promptly also. Registrants were advised to fill out Form 47 "with unusual thoughtfulness and care. Make your answers brief but clear and honest and intelligent . . . . The counsel of your minister or an older trusted friend will be of great help to you here. Such an adviser must, however, also sign your questionnaire."[6] The leaflet then gave explanations designed to be helpful in answering the six questions of Series II in Form 47 listed above. Finally the leaflet explained again that "what is meant by 'work of national importance under civilian direction,' and how it is to be administered, has not yet been determined. Responsible leaders of the historic peace churches are actively working with government officials on the whole question and announcement of plans and projects will be made as soon as possible."

COUNSEL TO MENNONITE MINISTERS

About this time or soon afterward the Peace Problems Committee circulated a two-page mimeographed letter, "A Word to Mennonite Ministers in Regard to the Draft."[7] The letter stated:

As Christian people we should face such a time of testing as is now upon us not with a spirit either of fear or defiance, nor yet of martyrdom, but rather of quiet confidence, calm and courage, certain that God has called us to witness to the Better Way of Jesus . . . . The realization that God has a definite witness for us to bear should make us humble and grateful but also brave and sacrificing in our life and service so that we may not fail in our God-appointed task and opportunity. It should also make us sympathetic and understanding toward others who share our Christian position and concern.

As ministers we should help our people at home to face their daily tasks and their relations in the community in this spirit and also help our young men to undertake their service to the country in this spirit. We want our communities at home, as well as our young men in service, to give a convincing witness to the nature and the power of the Christian way of life, rather than merely to seek exemption from military service or seek to avoid burdens.

The letter then enumerated a number of services which ministers should render to the young men of their congregations. A point especially stressed was the minister's "legal right to advise his people and his young men about the issues of conscription." Quotations from the *Congressional Record* were cited as

. . . Evidence that a minister may frankly discuss and analyze the issues presented by the conscription law or the rules and regulations for its administration, provided he does not counsel evasion. Discussing various types of services open to conscientious objectors is merely trying to help the young man to understand his rights under the law. Advising young men to refuse noncombatant service and accept civilian service is legal. Helping a young man to understand and fill out his questionnaire is likewise permissible. And it should also be added that the law in no way abridges the right of our churches or of our ministers to testify to our nonresistant Christian faith. Our country is not at war; it is still at peace.

The *Gospel Herald* for November 21, 1940,[8] reported a mailing by the Peace Problems Committee that week of the following items: (1) "Instructions to All Mennonite Pastors": a one-page sheet giving instructions for the next month or two. (2) "Report of Mennonite Registrants": a two-page form on which each pastor was asked to report to the chairman of the Peace Problems Committee the names and addresses of all registrants of his congregation. The report indicated the type of service chosen by the registrant, and the classification given him by his draft board. This report was designed to be used by the committee for statistical purposes. (3) "Report of Class IV-E Conscientious Objector": a card to be filled out by each conscientious objector and mailed to the executive secretary of the Mennonite Central Committee. (4) "The Mennonite Civilian Service Program": a six-page folder describing the type of service being planned for IV-E men.

CLASSIFICATION AND INDUCTION PROCEDURES

Selective Service had by this time announced its classification scheme under which those in class I-A to I-E were declared available for military service; those in class II were declared necessary in their present civilian capacity; those in class III were deferred because of dependents; and those in class IV-A to IV-F were deferred for one reason or another. IV-E was the classification of a "conscientious objector available only for civilian work of national importance." The card provided by the Peace

Problems Committee was to be filled out by the registrant and sent to the Akron office of M.C.C. as soon as he received his IV-E classification from the local draft board. The purpose of this was to help the M.C.C. to anticipate as nearly as possible how many C.P.S. inductions to expect.

The folder describing the civilian service program explained that "only those conscientious objectors who would ordinarily have been placed in class I-A will be placed in IV-E and called for civilian service .... Men who are placed in any deferred class, on any ground whatsoever, will not be classed as conscientious objectors in IV-E but will be classed in a deferred classification in class II, class III, or class IV." The folder went on to say that while Selective Service regulations for the assignment and induction of conscientious objectors had not yet been published, "the expected substance of these rules and regulations is known," therefore the following unofficial information could be tentatively given:

1. Conscientious objectors in class IV-E will be called for service according to their draft numbers, in the same order as if they were in I-A.
2. When a C.O. is called, the local board will notify the Director of Civilian Service Administration in Washington. The local board will not assign the C.O. to service until the assignment order has been sent from Washington.
3. Upon assignment the C.O. will proceed direct from the local board to the post of service to which he has been assigned.
4. The assignment of service will be made by the Director of Civilian Service in consultation with the church organization handling the service project.

The folder then went on to explain other matters, such as the types of service which would be available; the relation of the M.C.C. and other agencies to the N.S.B.R.O. and to the Selective System; the financial aspects of the C.P.S. program; and the spirit of the Mennonite service program.

On December 19, 1940, the Civilian Public Service program, as it was later operated by the M.C.C. and other agencies, was finally approved by President Roosevelt.[9] On that day, following numerous conferences with representatives of the churches and of the N.S.B.R.O., Clarence A. Dykstra, the first director of Selective Service, presented a memorandum to the President presenting a plan whereby the church agencies through the N.S.B.R.O. would be responsible for the operation of C.P.S. camps. The War Department would furnish or loan cots, bedding, and other camp equipment "so far as feasible and necessary." The Department of Agriculture and other government agencies would provide technical supervision for soil conservation and similar projects. Selective Service would be responsible for general supervision and inspection, and would pay the transportation of the inducted men to the camps. The N.S.B.R.O. and its affiliated agencies would agree for a temporary period to finance and manage the camp program, including subsistence, buildings, hospital care, and generally all things necessary for the care and maintenance of the men."

When the director of Selective Service reported the President's approval of the plan, Paul Comly French, the Executive Secretary of the N.S.B.R.O., replied that the agencies which he represented were "prepared to organize and finance within the limits of their ability" this program for an experimental period subject to later review. The following day, December 21, 1940, the M.C.C. in its annual meeting authorized its Executive Committee to proceed with its part of this program and approved a budget necessary for this purpose.[10]

NOTES AND CITATIONS

[1] "A Description of the Selective Service Act of 1940," *Gospel Herald* (Sept. 19, 1940), 33:544.

[2] "Further Word on Conscription Act Procedure," *ibid.* (Oct. 3, 1940), 33:570.

[3] Actually the registration card when completed contained the following information: the name, address, and telephone number of the registrant; the date and place of birth; the country of citizenship; the name, address, and relationship of a person who will always know his address; the name of his employer and the place of his business. There was also a physical description of the registrant, giving his race, height, weight, complexion, color of eyes and hair. The card also had space for the order and serial numbers.

[4] *Gospel Herald* (Oct. 10, 1940), 33:603-4.

[5] In case the registrant was willing to accept noncombatant service he signed the following: "I claim the exemption provided by the Selective Training and Service Act of 1940 for conscientious objectors, because I am conscientiously opposed by reason of my religious training and belief to participation in combatant military service or training therefor; but I am willing to participate in noncombatant service or training therefor under the direction of military authorities."

[6] Form 47 provided space for the signature of such adviser.

[7] See files of Peace Problems Committee.

[8] *Gospel Herald* (Nov. 21, 1940), 33:730-31.

[9] This approval was not obtained, however, without some difficulty. For a more detailed account of this part of the story see Melvin Gingerich, *Service for Peace,* Ch. V.

[10] Minutes in files of Peace Problems Committee.

Chapter III

Local Draft Boards

Once the plans of the peace churches and the N.S.B.R.O. had been approved, the general outlines of conscription and the C.P.S. program under the Selective Training and Service Act of 1940 were fairly clear. Registration had taken place; general questionnaires, followed by Form 47, were being received; Mennonite and other C.O.'s were obtaining their IV-E classifications; the general pattern of the C.P.S. program had been established; the site of the first M.C.C. camp at Grottoes, Virginia, had been selected; and now there was widespread expectancy until this first camp actually opened in May, 1941. On the whole, the conscription machinery operated perhaps more smoothly than had been anticipated; and relations between registered C.O.'s and their draft boards were better than many had dared to hope. Nevertheless, throughout the entire period of conscription, and especially in its early stages, the problems which continually arose were numerous, some of them perplexing indeed, requiring the continuous attention of the M.C.C., the Peace Problems Committee, regional counselors, local pastors, and other responsible persons.

MINOR PROBLEMS

The November 28, 1940, issue of the *Gospel Herald* carried a note from the Peace Problems Committee warning all C.O.'s to insist on obtaining Form 47, and making it clear that unless they received a deferred classification they should be placed in IV-E. If they were given some other classification, they should appeal at once. A week later, ministers were asked to report to the M.C.C. office "*at once*, the name and address of every man in your congregation who is *denied* his claim for exemption as a conscientious objector. See that an appeal is made to the appeal board." It was explained that the M.C.C. office would follow each appeal case in Washington. In April and June, 1941, the Peace Problems Committee announced that IV-E men with slight physical disabilities, which would ordinarily place them in I-B, would be classified as "IV-E limited service," subject to call at such time as I-B men are called. On April 16, 1942, the committee announced a suggestion by the Consultative Council of the N.S.B.R.O. that C.O.'s aged forty-five to sixty-five who would register on April 27 might wish to write on the back of their registration cards a statement of inability to contribute to the war effort, with willingness to serve in a civilian capacity along constructive lines which would relieve human need and suffering.

The correspondence of the Peace Problems Committee bears evidence of desire on the part of the church to play square with Selective Service, and to seek no special favors. In October, 1942, the Franconia Conference passed a resolution advising its registrants "not to appeal the decision of the local draft board on any grounds except in case of not being recognized as a conscientious objector." In April, 1944, the Peace Problems Committee of the same conference sent invitations to 632 registered men, requesting their attendance at a special meeting in the Franconia meetinghouse. Here the men were informed of complaints by local draft boards that some young men with farm deferments were putting in too much time at other work. The church leaders urged the registrants not to violate the intent of their deferments.[1]

In January, 1945, a minister, evidently writing in behalf of someone who felt his call overdue, inquired whether IV-E men whose call had been delayed for a considerable period of time should "feel ethically bound to call the attention of the fact to the draft board." At times it seemed advisable for a member of the Peace Problems Committee, or someone representing it, to visit local communities or areas in need of counsel or help. Early in 1941, for example, D. D. Miller of Middlebury, Indiana, spent a week on the Pacific Coast helping the congregations in this area, which were rather far removed from the headquarters of the committee, or of the M.C.C.[2] About the same time Bishop Ira Nissley of the Old Order Amish congregations in Southeastern Iowa reported that he was working closely with the Mennonite and Conservative A.M. ministers of his area. He was also planning to visit certain Amish communities elsewhere in connection with conscription problems.

MORE SERIOUS DIFFICULTIES WITH CERTAIN BOARDS

While the relationship between local draft boards and C.O. registrants was on the whole satisfactory, and most boards made a genuine effort to treat the sincere C.O. fairly, there was nevertheless considerable difficulty in certain cases. In the early days of Selective Service, for example, the local board at Warsaw (Kosciusko County), Indiana, refused to give Form 47 when the registrant asked for it, claiming that it must first be determined whether or not he is to be given a deferred classification. A similar attitude was taken by one of the Allen County boards at Fort Wayne. However, after the chairman of the Peace Problems Committee called these irregularities to the attention of the State Director of Selective Service, they were corrected.[3] Interestingly enough, another local board in Indiana was co-operative to the extent that it almost insisted on C.O.'s securing Form 47 immediately upon the receipt of the general questionnaire, and then filing the two forms simultaneously.[4]

At the beginning of classification, the local board at Arthur, Illinois, insisted on placing in IV-E all men who had filed Form 47, whether or not they would otherwise be placed in class II or III.[5] At one time or another there were reports from Elida, Ohio; Atwater, California; Albany, Oregon; and numerous other places to the effect that local boards were refusing IV-E classifications. The Atwater board claimed to have orders not to give any more IV-E classifications.[6] In December, 1941, the Albany board declared that since the United States had entered the war, there would be no more IV-E classifications. It had tentatively classified a Mennonite C.O. farmer as I-A.[7] A considerable number of local boards, at one time or another, required all IV-E claimants to appeal their case. One report indicates that in January, 1945, this was the case of the local board at La Junta, Colorado.[8] In the early days of Selective Service, certain local boards in the area of Peoria, Illinois, also refused IV-E classifications. After a member of the Peace Problems Committee and local ministers called on the State Director of Selective Service, however, the matter was corrected.

One of the more outstanding difficult cases was the local board of Iowa City (Johnson County), Iowa. This board persistently gave I-A classification to men who had filed Form 47, but then delayed calling them up. When Mennonite ministers of the county objected, the board said the men should be satisfied with a I-A classification since they were not being inducted into service. The board seemed to consider the request for IV-E classification an attempt to evade the draft. The ministers replied that their young men were ready and willing to go to C.P.S. The board, however, seemed to regard a IV-E classification as a blot on its record, and preferred to keep the men on the farm as delayed I-A's. There also were charges that attendance at local Mennonite churches had risen markedly since the beginning of the war; that a Mennonite teacher had refused to raise the flag in his school; and that Mennonites were raising money to fight the draft. Mennonite leaders denied these charges, however, and even invited the board to inspect the church records.[9] A visit of a member of the Peace Problems Committee and local ministers with the State Director of Selective Service helped to correct the matter temporarily. Following instructions from state headquarters, the local board now began to give IV-E classifications.

Throughout most of the war, however, there was intermittent difficulty in the area of the Iowa City board. As late as November, 1944, Claude C. Shotts of the N.S.B.R.O. made a trip to Iowa where he had conferences with the local draft board, the county War Labor Board, the state Selective Service office, and with Mennonite leaders. Instead of placing IV-E men into I-A as it had formerly done, the Mennonites felt that now the board was giving IV-E classification, and inducting into service, men who should have been classified II-C. At least they felt that there was discrimination against registrants who had filed Form 47. The county War Labor Board said that there were prejudices against the Mennonites, originating from the time of the first World War when Mennonite men were allowed, under the farm furlough plan, to return to the farm while other citizens served in the army.

The War Labor Board also believed that this prejudice was accentuated in several ways: by the manner in which Mennonites were said to be taking advantage of their farm earnings to buy farms; by the opinion of the draft board that if ministers had not assisted their young men in completing their questionnaires, more of them would have accepted military service; by unwise statements made by Mennonites; and by the failure of the draft board to call on the War Labor Board for help in evaluating the men's agricultural activities. The draft board, on the other hand, claimed to be acting without prejudice. It objected to ministers filling out Form 47 for the registrants; it said the ministers had promised the board that their men would not ask for deferment if they received IV-E classification (which the ministers denied); it said Mennonites themselves were pointing out cases where their men had violated the intent of their classification; and it said appeals to higher boards showed a lack of appreciation for the efforts of the board, whose members were serving without pay.

The head of the state Selective Service said he had visited the Johnson County board and found no evidence of serious discrimination against the Mennonites. He felt that the removal of Mennonite farmers from the county was not as serious as in the case of non-Mennonites, since Mennonites shared work with each other to a greater extent than others did. He admitted, however, that he had not talked with the Mennonites themselves; that the Johnson County board had acted with independence and discrimination in some cases; and that the Washington County board to the immediate south of Johnson County, which also had many IV-E registrants, was one of the best in the state and had shown special skill in handling its problems. The same Mennonite ministers who experienced so much difficulty with the Johnson County board were having no difficulty in Washington County. Claude C. Shotts' conclusion in regard to the Johnson County situation was that the local board had shown discrimination against the Mennonites, and that some of this discrimination was encouraged by imprudence in word and action on the part of some Mennonites.[10]

The Johnson County, Iowa, board was one of the more unsympathetic boards with which the Peace Problems Committee and its constituency had to deal. It was not the most unsympathetic board in Mennonite territory, however. Perhaps that "honor" goes to the local board of Washita County, Oklahoma, the home of 1,600 members of the General Conference Mennonite Church and of the Mennonite Brethren Church. In this county there seems to have been a kind of conspiracy on the part of the draft board, the U.S.D.A. War Labor Board, and the ration board. Persons filing Form 47 were denied farm deferments regardless of the size of their farms or the number of children in their families. The ration board refused to grant these same persons gasoline, tires, and farming implements. In some cases Mennonite ministers were refused gasoline and tires to carry on their church work, while ministers of other denominations were receiving all they requested.

As in the case of Johnson County, Iowa, the opposition to the Mennonites in Washita County, Oklahoma, is traceable to the first World War, at which time a vigorous campaign was carried on to prohibit the speaking of German in the county. During the second World War the opposition was less widespread, perhaps limited to a small group of people in Cordell, the county seat, who expressed a desire "to drive the Dutchmen out." While they were unable to carry out this desire, their point of view nevertheless had enough representation on the draft and other wartime boards to cause a great amount of trouble.[11]

OTHER DIFFICULTIES: MENNONITES IN PRISON

In addition to the general problems described above, a few Mennonite C.O. registrants experienced individual difficulties of an unusual character, such as denial of IV-E classification, induction into the army, or even prison sentence. In some cases, these experiences were due to unsympathetic boards; in some, to the registrant's lack of information on procedures for registration and appeal; in others, to negligence on the part of the registrant; and in some cases, to embarrassing circumstances which draft boards interpreted as an invalidation of the registrant's claims as a conscientious objector. It was very unusual for a man to be released from the army in order that he might enter C.P.S. Nevertheless there was at least one Mennonite who had this experience. Apparently this was a case of misunderstanding the procedure for filing IV-E claims. After being inducted into the army, however, this man stated his C.O. convictions in an effective manner. As a result, the military authorities did not require him to take training. He did errands about the camp for a time and then was discharged from the army and reclassified; after this he was inducted into C.P.S., serving for three years and eight months.[12] There were other cases of army induction, however, in which attempts to secure release were unsuccessful.

From the various Mennonite groups, more than forty men were sentenced to prison for violation of the Selective Training and Service Act of 1940. At least twenty of these men were Old Order Mennonites of Eastern Pennsylvania who first received IV-E classification, and then refused to report for induction into C.P.S. Apparently not more than nine of the men receiving prison sentences were from the Mennonite Church. One of these was refused a IV-E classification on the ground that he had worked in a defense plant, although the man himself contended that he had not engaged in defense work. When he refused to accept induction into the army, he was sentenced to prison for three years. He was paroled, however, after serving about six months of his sentence. Another man had appealed a I-A classification, but failed to appear for his hearing. After serving nine months in prison, he was paroled to a hospital where he served as an X-ray technician.

One man of Amish background who served a prison sentence was refused IV-E classification because he had joined the Mennonite Church after registering for the draft. He was under instruction for baptism at the time his questionnaire was filed. Several of the men who served prison sentences were refused IV-E classification after their boards challenged their sincerity. In one or two of these cases, it was a matter of having joined the church only recently. In others there were alleged unfavorable records in the past conduct of the men. Men from other Mennonite groups who served time in prison were given their sentences for reasons similar to those listed above. No one from any of the Mennonite groups refused to register under the Selective Training and Service Act of 1940. After registering, however, one man from one of the groups repudiated his registration, and notified his board that it no longer had jurisdiction over him. Following a brief prison sentence, he was paroled to his father's farm.[13]

NOTES AND CITATIONS

[1] Minutes of Peace Problems Committee of the Franconia Conference, April 13, 1944.

[2] *Gospel Herald* (March 6, 1941), 33:1033.

[3] Correspondence in files of Peace Problems Committee.

[4] *Ibid.*, Nov. 18, 1940.

[5] *Ibid.*, Nov. 20, 1940.

[6] *Ibid.*, Feb. 5, 1941.

[7] *Ibid.*, Dec. 22, 1941.

[8] *Ibid.*, Jan. 11, 1945.

[9] *Ibid.*, June 12, 1941.

[10] Report of Claude C. Shotts, in *ibid.*, Nov. 14, 1944.

[11] Report of Claude C. Shotts, June 4, 1944, in files of Peace Problems Committee.

[12] Correspondence in files of Peace Problems Committee.

[13] For a fuller treatment of this subject see Gingerich, *Service for Peace*, 389-92.

Chapter IV

Response to the Draft

Early in the war the Peace Section of the M.C.C., in co-operation with the Peace Problems Committee and the peace committees of the other Mennonite groups, undertook a census to determine the draft record of the Mennonite churches. The first results were compiled as of November 1, 1942. Later the census was continued and the statistics compiled as of December 1, 1944.[1] The latter compilation was used by Howard H. Charles in preparing a comprehensive report on how the draft affected the membership of the Mennonite churches. The Charles report[2] contains fourteen pages of tables and twenty-one pages of interpretation, giving statistics on church membership; on the numbers and percentages of men registered and drafted; on numbers and percentages of men in II-C and other deferred classifications; on numbers and percentages of men in C.P.S. and in the army; and on correlations of draft status with other factors, such as church standing, education, occupation, and age.

After Selective Service was ended in 1947, the draft census was completed, making available the statistics for the entire conscription period, 1940-47. From this completed census the M.C.C. prepared tabulations showing the total number of Mennonites drafted from each congregation, conference, and group, with the numbers and percentages of drafted men in each of three classifications, I-A, I-A-O, and IV-E. The present chapter is based on the Charles report and the detailed materials on which it was based, plus the M.C.C. tabulations of numbers and percentages of the three classes of drafted men.[3]

According to the Charles report, the total membership of the various Mennonite groups in the United States in 1944 was 126,354. The Mennonite Church comprised 39.7 per cent of this membership (50,177 members); and the General Conference Mennonite Church comprised 23.3 per cent (29,477 members). The total number of men drafted from all of the Mennonite branches was 9,809. Of this number, 33.3 per cent (3,272 men) came from the Mennonite Church, while 31.7 per cent (3,113 men) came from the General Conference Mennonite Church. That is, from more than 50,000 members in the Mennonite Church (1944) there had been drafted by the end of conscription (1947) a total of 3,272 men; and from less than 30,000 members in the General Conference Mennonite Church (1944), a total of 3,113 men had been drafted by the end of conscription. Putting it another way, even after allowing for an increase, between 1944 and 1947, of 5 per cent in the total church membership, a little more than 6 per cent of the membership of the Mennonite Church was drafted, whereas in the General Conference Mennonite Church 10 per cent of the membership was drafted.

GENERAL FINDINGS: VARIATIONS AMONG CONFERENCES AND GROUPS

These figures illustrate the great variation which existed among the Mennonite groups as to the effect of the draft. Interestingly enough, in many cases there was as great a variation among the twelve United States district conferences of the Mennonite Church as there was among the different branches of Mennonites. For example, in the combined Mennonite branches the total number of men classified by December 1, 1944, was 18,735. This means that on the average, according to the report, 14.8 per cent of the church membership was classified for the draft. This figure is not quite reliable, however, since in some of the branches not all congregations responded to the census questionnaire, making the actual figure higher than is here shown. In the case of the Mennonite Church all congregations responded, hence these figures are complete. These show that in the Mennonite Church, 15.3 per cent of all members were classified. In most of the census statistics the figures for the Mennonite Church are, as a rule, about the same as the average for all groups, with the Old Order Amish representing the extreme in one direction and the Mennonite Brethren in Christ the opposite extreme. It would seem to be a good guess, therefore, that the actual percentage of all Mennonites classified was somewhere near 15.3 per cent, as in the case of the Mennonite Church.

Within the Mennonite Church, however, the variation was surprisingly great, ranging from 11.1 per cent in the Virginia Conference to 24.85 per cent in the North Central (Dakota-Montana) Conference. The percentage for the Indiana-Michigan Conference was 16.3. Here, as in most cases, the Indiana-Michigan Conference represents about the average between the extremes among the district conferences. The Franconia Conference has the second highest classification rate, with 19.3 per cent. The Southwestern Pennsylvania Conference has the second lowest classification rate, with 12.24 per cent; and the Lancaster Conference next with 13.5 per cent. These figures would seem to show that the Virginia, Southwestern Pennsylvania, and Lancaster conferences had a low percentage of their members in the eighteen to forty-five age group, whereas the Washington County, Maryland, and Franklin County, Pennsylvania, Conference, the Franconia Conference, and especially the North Central Conference, had a high percentage of their members in this group, with the other conferences having percentages nearing the medium. It should be remembered, however, that North Central is a very small conference with only 433 members, hence not of great weight in the total statistical picture.

The second interesting thing to note in this study is the percentage of registrants drafted, and the percentage deferred, in the various groups and conferences. The percentage of all classified Mennonites who were drafted was 37.7, leaving 62.3 per cent in the various deferred classes. In the Mennonite Church the percentage drafted was 33.8, slightly below the general average. In this category the extreme on the one hand is represented by the Krimmer Mennonite Brethren Church with 89.5 per cent of its classified men drafted, and the Mennonite Brethren in Christ Church with 72.5 per cent drafted. At the other extreme are the Old Order Mennonites with 5 per cent of their classified men drafted, and the Old Order Amish with 14.4 per cent drafted. The latter can be explained in part by the fact that the Amish and Old Order Mennonites are farmers for the most part, and that many of their men received farm deferments. In fact the statistics show that 69.2 per cent of the former were in class II-C, the classification of those engaged in, and considered necessary to, agriculture. Among the Old Order Mennonites, 66.6 per cent of the classified men were in II-C.

In the case of the Mennonite Church, even though the number drafted was 33.8 per cent of the total classifications within the entire branch, the percentage varied among the district conferences from 10.14 per cent in Franconia to 74 per cent in Southwestern Pennsylvania. In the Indiana-Michigan Conference the percentage drafted was 34, almost exactly the same as that for the entire branch. A striking point in this picture is the fact that the four eastern conferences, Franconia, Washington-Franklin, Lancaster, and Virginia, in the order named, had the lowest percentage of drafted registrants; Southwestern Pennsylvania had the highest percentage, with the conferences from Ohio westward in between. These figures certainly reflect differences in the policies of local draft boards.

Off hand one might expect conferences in the Middle West to have had the largest percentage of agricultural deferments (II-C). The conference with the highest percentage of II-C's, however, was Franconia, in eastern Pennsylvania, located midway between the industrial cities of Philadelphia, Allentown, and Bethlehem. A survey made in 1940 shows that at that time only 39 per cent of the employed male members of this conference were making their living on the farm, whereas 61 per cent made their living "in various types of commercial and industrial pursuits."[4] And yet 67 per cent of all the registered men in this industrial area were classified II-C. The explanation seems to be that local boards in this area were very lenient with C.O.'s engaged in agriculture; consequently a considerable number of men who formerly had been otherwise employed shifted to the farm during the war. In commenting on the survey referred to above, John E. Lapp says:

The picture did change somewhat during World War II because of local draft boards who were favorable to deferring all men, especially conscientious objectors, who were employed on farms. This encouragement persuaded a number of young men to change their employment from industry and commerce to agriculture. Since the war's end, a number have left the farm; however, there are more engaged in farm work today than there were at the beginning of the war. According to a survey made in the autumn of 1946 there are approximately 43 per cent of the men employed on farms today.[5]

Apparently a similar policy was followed by draft boards in the Washington-Franklin and Lancaster Conference areas which had 65.4 per cent and 58 per cent of II-C classifications, respectively. Virginia had only 40.1 per cent II-C's, but had 34.5 per cent of non-II-C deferments, which is higher than that of any other conference district. The only other conference with a II-C rate comparable with that of the three eastern conferences was North Central with a percentage of 60.1. It will be remembered, however, that this is the conference with one fourth of its membership classified. This conference had the distinction of having 31.4 per cent of its classified men drafted and 60.1 per cent in agricultural deferment. The conferences in what might be considered the agricultural section in the middle states had percentages of II-C's ranging from 43.9 per cent down to 36 per cent. In the Pacific Coast Conference 27.8 per cent of the classified men had a II-C classification, while 27.9 per cent had some other type of deferment. This places the Pacific Coast Conference next to Virginia in the nonagricultural deferment class. In these conferences apparently a large number of nonagricultural workers were engaged in occupations considered essential by their draft boards.

Third in the list of nonagricultural deferments is the Southwestern Pennsylvania Conference with 23.2 per cent of its classified men in this category. This conference, however, had only 2.8 per cent of its classified men in II-C. The average for all Mennonites of all branches was 43.3 per cent of the classified men in II-C. The rate for the Mennonite Church was 46.5 per cent, and that of the Indiana-Michigan Conference 43.9 per cent. Here again, the figure for the Indiana-Michigan Conference is near the average of the Mennonite Church. In the nonagricultural deferment class the average figure for the various Mennonite branches is 18.8 per cent, and the figure for the Mennonite Church is 19.7 per cent. In this case the percentage of the Lancaster Conference coincides exactly (19.7 per cent) with that of the average for the district conferences of the Mennonite Church. The Indiana-Michigan Conference had 22.1 per cent of its classified men in the nonagricultural deferment class. The Iowa-Nebraska Conference had the lowest rate of nonagricultural deferments, the percentage being twelve. In agricultural deferments this conference was about average, with 42.5 per cent of its classified men in II-C.

Early in this chapter it was stated that by the end of Selective Service approximately 10 per cent of the membership of the General Conference Mennonite Church had been called by the draft, and a little more

4

than 6 per cent of the membership of the Mennonite Church. This section of the chapter will now be concluded by observing the range of percentages among the district conferences of the Mennonite Church. The Southwestern Pennsylvania Conference had the highest rate, with 9.3 per cent of the membership, or one member out of every eleven, called by the draft. Washington-Franklin had the lowest rate with 3.3 per cent, or only one member out of thirty called by the draft. The Franconia and Lancaster conferences were next lowest in rank, with 3.7 per cent and 3.8 per cent, respectively. Next to Southwestern Pennsylvania the conferences with the highest percentages were Iowa-Nebraska with 8.6 per cent drafted, and Ohio and Eastern A.M. with 8.3 per cent. As usual, Indiana-Michigan is somewhat near the average of the church as a whole, with 7.1 per cent of its membership drafted, or one out of every fourteen members. The average for all Mennonite groups is 7.4 per cent, and for the Mennonite Church, 6.2 per cent.

PROPORTION OF MEN IN C.P.S.

The most significant revelation of the draft census is the number of men who chose civilian service, and the number who accepted induction into the armed forces. It had been rather commonly assumed that with generous provision for civilian service, relatively few Mennonites would enter the army. The Selective Service System was not in operation very long, however, until it became evident that this was not the case. This revelation, no doubt, hastened the taking of the first census late in 1942. When the results of this census were in, it was discovered that 31 per cent of the drafted men within the Mennonite Church had entered the army. When the Peace Problems Committee made its report to General Conference in August, 1943, it said: "We can rejoice at the large number of our young men who have taken a clear-cut loyal stand on the consistent position for complete nonparticipation in war in any form. A large majority of our men have victoriously met this test . . . . However, we regret to report that all too large a number of our men in the younger ages have failed to meet the test of conscience and have entered the army voluntarily, choosing rather to surrender the faith of their fathers, even under the most favorable circumstances, and become a part of the war machine."[6]

The report also cited evidence that the proportion of drafted men accepting military service since November, 1942, had increased. "This is a startling report," said the Peace Problems Committee, "and challenges our most serious concern." The committee felt that more information would be necessary, however, before final conclusions could be drawn from these statistics. It therefore proposed to continue the census and in doing so to obtain information about the men entering the army "which may help in working at the problem of recovering the lost ground."

The district conferences also expressed concern because of what the census revealed. The Southwestern Pennsylvania Conference, for example, reported as follows in August, 1943: "We can all see that the picture with regard to the stand taken by many of our brethren is not a flattering one and should give us as a conference body grave concern."[7] The report of the Iowa-Nebraska Conference contains the following statement: "Each bishop reported on his respective field of oversight. A note of alarm was expressed by each one of them because of the light consideration manifested in the attitude toward the nonresistant principles . . . ."[8]

With the tabulation of the final figures, we now know what the percentages were. The total number of drafted men in all Mennonite groups was 9,809. Of this number, 4,536[9] were in C.P.S., and 5,273 in the armed forces; or 46.2 per cent in C.P.S., and 53.8 per cent in the armed forces. As in the case of other items revealed in the census, the percentage of drafted men who chose C.P.S. varies considerably among the various branches of Mennonites. In this case again the extreme on one side is represented by the Old Order Mennonites and the Old Order Amish, with 100 per cent and 93.5 per cent, respectively, classified in IV-E; in this case the percentage of the Church of God in Christ Mennonite is exactly the same as that of the Old Order Amish. The opposite extreme is represented by the Defenseless Mennonite and the Mennonite Brethren in Christ churches, with 10.2 per cent and 4.8 per cent, respectively, in IV-E. The Mennonite Church had 59.5 per cent of its drafted men in IV-E. This percentage is 13.2 points higher than the average for all Mennonites. The group whose rate coincides most nearly with that of the Mennonite Church is the Evangelical Mennonite Brethren, with 58.8 per cent of its drafted men in C.P.S.

A summary of the final draft census of all Mennonites, broken down according to church groups, giving the number of men and the percentages in each classification, for the entire conscription period, 1940-47, follows:[10]

	I-A		I-A-O		IV-E		
Name of Group	No. of Men	Percentage	No. of Men	Percentage	No. of Men	Percentage	Total
(Old) Mennonite	980	29.9	349	10.6	1,943	59.5	3,272
General Conference Mennonite	1,799	57.7	486	15.6	828	26.6	3,113
Old Order Amish	23	2.9	27	3.5	722	93.5	772
Mennonite Brethren	225	31.5	228	31.9	260	36.4	713
Mennonite Brethren in Christ	527	78.5	112	16.7	32	4.8	671
Conservative Amish Mennonite	34	13.8	24	9.7	187	76.3	245
Brethren in Christ	63	25.9	56	22.2	126	51.8	245
Church of God in Christ Mennonite	10	5.0	3	1.5	187	93.5	200
Defenseless Mennonite	91	54.8	58	34.9	17	10.2	163
Krimmer Mennonite Brethren	65	48.1	21	15.5	49	36.3	135
Evangelical Mennonite Brethren	16	14.6	29	26.6	64	58.8	109
Old Order Mennonite	0	0.0	0	0.0	72	100.0	72
United Zion Children	41	74.6	3	5.5	11	20.0	55
Hutterian Brethren	2	6.2	1	3.1	29	90.6	32
Reformed Amish Christian	0	0.0	0	0.0	6	100.0	6
Church of God (Mennonite)	0	0.0	0	0.0	3	100.0	3
Summary	3,876	39.5	1,397	14.2	4,536	46.2	9,809

The above table shows a great variation among the different Mennonite groups as to the proportion of their drafted men who chose Civilian Public Service. Among the district conferences of the Mennonite Church there is a similar, although a much lesser, variation, ranging from the Washington-Franklin Conference, which reports 97.8 per cent of its men in IV-E, to the Southwestern Pennsylvania Conference with 41.8 per cent in IV-E. It is interesting to note that the conferences representing these extreme figures are both eastern conferences. In all of the conferences except one, the percentage of IV-E's is disappointingly low.

A summary of the final census, broken down according to district conferences of the Mennonite Church, for the entire conscription period, 1940-47, follows:[10]

Conference	I-A		I-A-O		IV-E		
	No. of Men	Percentage	No. of Men	Percentage	No. of Men	Percentage	Total
Washington County, Md., & Franklin County, Pa.	0	0.0	1	2.1	46	97.8	47
Independent Churches	1	4.1	4	16.6	19	79.1	24
North Central	4	14.8	3	11.1	20	74.0	27
Pacific Coast	24	16.5	22	15.1	99	68.2	145
South Central	57	23.8	22	9.1	161	67.9	240
Ohio and Eastern A.M.	187	25.5	62	8.4	483	65.9	732
Indiana-Michigan	115	26.0	49	11.1	277	62.8	441
Virginia	64	36.5	7	4.0	104	59.4	175
Lancaster	150	29.0	66	12.7	301	58.2	517
U.S.A. Canadian Conf. Churches	11	39.2	2	7.1	15	53.5	28
Franconia	49	35.3	20	14.3	70	50.4	139
Iowa-Nebraska	132	39.6	38	11.4	163	48.9	333
Illinois	90	38.6	38	16.3	105	45.0	233
Southwestern Pennsylvania	96	50.2	15	7.8	80	41.8	191
Totals for the Mennonite Church	980	29.9	349	10.6	1,943	59.5	3,272

The census was taken by asking some person, usually the minister, in each congregation to fill out a report sheet giving the number of men from his congregation in IV-E, in I-A-O, in I-A, in II-C, and in other deferred classes. For each man drafted the informant was asked to give: the man's age at the time of induction; his classification; the extent of his education; his church standing before being drafted, whether it was good, poor, or backsliding; and his occupation, whether it was farmer, factory laborer, teacher, or what. Finally, in the case of each man who entered the armed forces, the informant was asked to give his opinion as to why this man chose military service. As an aid in answering the last question, a number of possible reasons were suggested. In each case, the informant was asked to check those reasons which were applicable, and to add any others which he believed would help to explain the case. By making a series of correlations between the draft status of the individual and the other information and evaluations given by the ministers, it is possible to obtain some further light on the question why draftees chose the type of service which they did. Here again, however, in comparing the various Mennonite branches and conferences one finds considerable variation.

DRAFT STATUS AND CHURCH STANDING

In correlating the draft status of the individual with his church standing, we find that 88.5 per cent of the men in the Mennonite Church drafted up to December 1, 1944, and who were rated as in good standing by their ministers, accepted IV-E; while 11.5 per cent of those rated as in good standing joined the armed forces. On the other hand, 78.3 per cent of the men rated as in poor standing accepted military service. Over one fifth (21.7 per cent) of these poor members, however, were classified IV-E. Of the backsliders, 95 per cent were in military service and 5 per cent in C.P.S. Approaching the problem from another point of view, we find that 20.4 per cent of the men in I-A were rated as having been in good standing, 44.7 per cent in poor standing, and 34.9 per cent as backsliding. Of the men in I-A-O, 46 per cent were rated as in good standing, 40.7 per cent as in poor standing, and 13.3 per cent as backsliding.

It is obvious, of course, that these classifications represent merely the ministers' evaluations, and not until after the man had made his choice between C.P.S. and military service was the minister asked to rate him. It would be interesting to know how many men who joined the army, and later were rated as having been poor or backsliding members, would have been rated as in good standing if rated earlier. In some of the report sheets there seems to be a tendency to rate the men chiefly on the basis of whether or not they were classified IV-E. Whatever the truth may be on this point, the fact remains that, as of December 1, 1944, the ministers of the Mennonite Church rated one third of their drafted men as poor or backsliding members, and only two thirds as in good standing. The fact remains that two out of every five men drafted accepted military service, and only three out of five proved loyal to the nonresistant position of the church. If 12.1 per cent of the church members were backsliders, and another 21.8 per cent were members in poor standing, was there not entirely too much "dead wood" in the church? Does not this mean that the Mennonite Church today is in need of a great awakening which will rekindle the spiritual life of its members?

In comparing the reports of the various conference districts, one finds considerable variation in this matter of church standing, as well as on other points. As of December 1, 1944, the percentage of men in IV-E who were rated as in good standing was uniformly high, ranging from 86 per cent in the Washington-Franklin Conference to 98.5 per cent in Virginia. As to the percentage of men in good standing who chose IV-E there is more variation. In the Illinois Conference 65.7 per cent of the men in good standing chose IV-E, and in Virginia the percentage was 98.5. Southwestern Pennsylvania, which on December 1, 1944, had only 45.7 per cent of its drafted men in IV-E, nevertheless reported 82.9 per cent of its men who were in good standing to have taken IV-E. This means that exactly one half of the drafted men from this conference were rated by their ministers as not in good standing. The conference reporting the highest percentage of its drafted men as in good standing was Washington-Franklin with 86 per cent. Virginia comes second with 75 per cent, and Illinois third with 67 per cent. As mentioned before, in the church as a whole, 66.1 per cent of the drafted men were rated as in good standing, 21.8 per cent as in poor standing, and 12.1 as backsliding. In Virginia, however, 75 per cent were rated as in good standing, 1.2 per cent as in poor standing, and 23.3 per cent as backsliding.

An analysis of the statistics in other branches of the church would reveal even greater variation. The percentage of men rated as in good standing among all Mennonites was only two points higher (68 per cent) than the average for the Mennonite Church, and the percentage of backsliders was two points lower (10 per cent). The most striking difference, however, appears in the percentage of men in good standing who chose IV-E. Whereas for the Mennonite Church the percentage was 88.5, for Mennonites as a whole it was only 60 per cent. This means that among Mennonites as a whole, 40 per cent of the men who were considered in good standing, and who presumably participated actively in the work of the church, chose the armed forces in preference to C.P.S. In some of the Mennonite branches the ratio was far above 50 per cent.

DRAFT STATUS AND EDUCATION

The draft census also included information on the educational status of the individual. From this information we learn that, as of December 1, 1944, 39 per cent of the drafted men of the Mennonite Church had a grade-school education only; 49 per cent had one or more years of high school; 10.8 per cent had one or more years of college; and 0.34 per cent had advanced training beyond four years of college. This places the educational level of the drafted men of the Mennonite Church somewhat below that of the general average for all Mennonite branches. In the latter case the figures are as follows: grade school only, 29.2 per cent; one or more years of high school, 55.1 per cent; one or more years of college, 15.1 per cent; and advanced training beyond four years of college, 0.6 per cent. Apparently, however, the educational factor was not tabulated in the case of the Old Order Amish. If this omission were supplied, the figures would change somewhat and the level of the Mennonite Church would approach more nearly the general average for all Mennonites. Excluding the Old Order Amish, the educational extremes are represented by the Church of God in Christ Mennonite and the General Conference Mennonite Church. The former had 91.2 per cent in grade school only; 8.8 per cent with one or more years of high school; and none with college training. The General Conference group had 15.5 per cent in grade school only; 61.6 per cent with one or more years of high school;

21.7 per cent with one or more years of college; and 1.2 per cent with training beyond the four years of college.

There was also considerable educational variation among the district conferences of the Mennonite Church. On December 1, 1944, in the Washington-Franklin Conference, 76.7 per cent of the drafted men had a grade-school education only. The Ohio Conference had the lowest percentage of men in this category, with 25.3 per cent. This was still 10 points higher, however, than the average for the General Conference Mennonite Church. Within the Mennonite Church the Indiana-Michigan Conference, as usual, coincided with the church as a whole, with 39.4 per cent of its drafted men in the grade-school category. Those conferences with a higher than average percentage of men with a grade-school education only were Washington-Franklin, North Central, Franconia, Lancaster, Pacific Coast, and Iowa-Nebraska. Those with a lower than average percentage were Southwestern Pennsylvania, Missouri-Kansas (South Central), Virginia, Illinois, and Ohio.

Perhaps the most significant revelation of this part of the study is the fact that of the drafted men, the high-school group had a lower percentage of IV-E's than either the college group or the group with a grade-school education only. This holds for Mennonites as a whole, all of the branches taken together; it also holds for the Mennonite Church as a whole; and it holds for most of the district conferences within the Mennonite Church. The figures for the combined Mennonite branches are: of those with a grade-school education, 57.6 per cent were in IV-E; of those with a high-school education, 37.4 per cent; and of those with a college education, 50.2 per cent. For the Mennonite Church the comparable percentages are: grade school, 63.8 per cent; high school, 57.3 per cent; and college, 76.3 per cent.

In all of the district conferences of the Mennonite Church except three, the college-trained group had a higher percentage of IV-E's than either the high-school or grade-school groups. The three exceptions are Washington-Franklin, North Central, and Illinois. Of these, the first two are small conferences with a combined total of only seventy-seven drafted men. In the case of Washington-Franklin, both the high-school and college groups were 100 per cent IV-E. In nine of the twelve conferences the college group had 75 per cent or more of its men in IV-E. In the Ohio Conference the grade-school group had 61 per cent in IV-E, and the high-school group 63 per cent. The two conferences in which the high-school group made a notably better showing than the grade-school group were Lancaster and Franconia. In the former case, the grade-school group had 54.3 per cent in IV-E, and the high-school group 63.2 per cent. In Franconia the figures were 47 per cent and 68.7 per cent, respectively, a most striking variation. The lowest percentage of IV-E's found anywhere in the Mennonite Church was in the high-school group of Southwestern Pennsylvania, with 35.7 per cent in IV-E. In this same conference, however, the college group had 84.6 per cent in IV-E.

These are the facts as revealed by the census, as of December 1, 1944. How shall they be interpreted? While one needs to be cautious in drawing conclusions, it would seem a safe generalization that many of the men with only a grade-school education lived in a more or less sheltered rural environment, and were therefore not so subject to influences militating against the nonresistant faith; hence the high percentage of IV-E's. One might also assume that the high-school group had the lower percentage of IV-E's because of the many influences in the public high school militating against the nonresistant faith. This would perhaps be especially true of the younger men drafted while in high school or soon after graduation. In the case of the college group, it may be assumed that most of the men attended Mennonite colleges where the environment was favorable; hence the high percentage of IV-E's among them.

On the other hand, how shall we interpret the case of Lancaster and Franconia where the high-school group made a better showing than did the grade-school group? Is the low percentage of IV-E's in the grade-school group due to the formalism which is sometimes said to characterize these conferences? Or were the potential IV-E's given farm deferments, leaving the factory workers to be drafted? (The census results also show that factory workers had a lower percentage of IV-E's than farmers.) In these two conferences the percentage of high-school men among the draftees was also low. Obviously, therefore, a low percentage of the conference membership had a high-school education. Does this mean that the public high school is not widely patronized in the Lancaster and Franconia conferences, and that a high percentage of those who do go to high school attend Mennonite high schools where the environment is favorable to the nonresistant position? Perhaps this is the explanation.

DRAFT STATUS AND OCCUPATION

In analyzing the occupations of the drafted men, and correlating these with their draft status, some more interesting facts are discovered. Among all branches of Mennonites, 40.2 per cent of the men drafted were farmers; 35.6 per cent were day laborers or workers in factories and shops; 4.1 per cent were teachers; 2.9 per cent were office workers; and 17.2 per cent were engaged in miscellaneous occupations. In the Mennonite Church the figures are very much like those for Mennonites as a whole, with 39.7 per cent classified as farmers and 39 per cent as day laborers and workers in factories and shops. About an equal number from each of these occupational classes were drafted, even though the majority of the members of the Mennonite Church are engaged in agriculture. The explanation is, of course, that a large percentage of farmers were deferred in class II-C. In the Mennonite Church, as of December

1, 1944, the total number of men in II-C was 3,588. If 39.7 per cent of the drafted men were farmers, then 1,035 farmers were drafted. The sum of these figures is 4,623, or 60.1 per cent of the total number classified.

Some farmers were given other deferred classifications, although the number is unknown. Therefore it may safely be said that somewhat over 60 per cent of the classified men of the Mennonite Church were farmers, and somewhat less than 40 per cent were in all other occupations combined. Less than 40 per cent of the drafted men, however, were farmers. It is evident, therefore, that farmers were not represented among the drafted men in proportion to the other occupational groups. Even though a higher percentage of drafted farmers chose C.P.S. than was true of any other occupational group except teachers, farmers still constituted only 45.6 per cent of the C.P.S. population of the Mennonite Church. This is somewhat less than the average for all Mennonite branches which was 53.5 per cent.

As usual, there was considerable variation among the district conferences within the Mennonite Church. In Franconia, as of December 1, 1944, where 67 per cent of the classified men were in II-C, only 8.9 per cent of the drafted men were farmers, and 64.4 were classified as day laborers or workers in factories and shops. In Southwestern Pennsylvania where only 2.8 per cent of the classified men were in II-C, 22.3 per cent of the drafted men were farmers. In Ohio where 36 per cent of the classified men were in II-C, 33.2 per cent of the drafted men were farmers; and in Illinois where 37.7 per cent of the classified men were in II-C, 54.2 per cent of the drafted men were farmers. In the Lancaster Conference, even though 58 per cent (considerably more than the average) of the classified men were in II-C, nevertheless 37.1 per cent of the drafted men, or just a little below the average, were also farmers. As stated above, 45.6 per cent of the C.P.S. population of the Mennonite Church were farmers. On this point there was also considerable variation among the district conferences. Of the C.P.S. population of the Franconia Conference, only 7.1 per cent were farmers, whereas of the Iowa-Nebraska Conference the percentage was 72.8. In Southwestern Pennsylvania it was 28; in Virginia, 55; in Illinois, 61.2; and in the Indiana-Michigan Conference 39.2 per cent of C.P.S. men were farmers.

A most significant part of this study is to discover, if possible, what influence a man's occupation had on his choice, as between C.P.S. and military service. Putting the farmers of all the Mennonite branches together, we discover that 60.8 per cent of all drafted Mennonite farmers chose C.P.S.; the percentage of day laborers and workers in factory and shop who chose C.P.S. was 31.7; of teachers it was 56.3 per cent; of office workers, 47.1 per cent; and of all other occupations, 36.5 per cent. Within the Mennonite Church, C.P.S. was chosen by 70.8 per cent of the farmers; by 50 per cent of the day laborers and workers in factory and shop; by 73 per cent of the teachers; by 69 per cent of the office workers; and by 63 per cent of those engaged in the remaining occupations. In all of the district conferences except Franconia, the farmers had a higher percentage of IV-E's than did the day laborer and factory worker group. In the latter conference, however, only eight farmers had been drafted as of December 1, 1944; hence the number was hardly large enough to be significant. While the disappointingly low ratio of C.P.S. men among Mennonite draftees was due to a variety of factors, it seems quite clear that the occupational factor was one of them. Teachers and farmers had a considerably higher ratio of IV-E's than did day laborers and workers in factory and shop.

DRAFT STATUS AND AGE

Not only did education and occupation have a bearing on the draft status of the individuals; the age of the drafted man did likewise. Among Mennonites as a whole, on December 1, 1944, 32.1 per cent of the drafted men were in the 18 to 20 age group; in the Mennonite Church the percentage was 30.6. Among Mennonites as a whole, 34.2 per cent of the draftees were aged 21 to 23; in the Mennonite Church the percentage was 40.1. In the age group 24 to 26, the percentages were 17.1 and 17.6, respectively; for the age group 27 to 29, they were 7.8 per cent and 7.9 per cent; for the 30 to 32 age group, 4 per cent and 3.5 per cent; for the 33 to 35 age group, 2.2 per cent and 1.6 per cent; and for the 36 to 45 age group, 1.7 per cent and 1.5 per cent, respectively. Thus the age distribution within the Mennonite Church differs little from that among Mennonites as a whole. With 30.6 per cent of the drafted men in the 18 to 21 age group, and exactly two thirds of all drafted men aged 18 to 23, it is clear that these are the significant ages in case of wartime conscription.

The most significant revelation of this part of the study is the percentage of men in each age group who chose C.P.S. It is immediately apparent that the youngest age group (18 to 21) had the lowest percentage of men in IV-E. For the Mennonite Church this percentage was 45.4, or 15 points below the average for the church. Approaching it another way, the average percentage of IV-E's from the youngest age group, in the Mennonite Church as a whole, was the same as the average percentage of IV-E's from all age groups of that district conference which made the poorest showing. In the Illinois Conference the percentage of IV-E's in the 18 to 21 age group dropped as low as 18.4 per cent, as of December 1, 1944. In this conference, therefore, a little more than four out of five of the younger men accepted military service.

In Southwestern Pennsylvania the percentage of IV-E's in the 18 to 21 age group was 25.3, and in Franconia it was 27. The rate varied from this point upward, with a number of the conferences having considerably over 50 per cent of their younger men in IV-E. Yet the fact remains that on the average, as of December 1, 1944, 54.6 per cent of these younger men in the Mennonite Church entered military service. Taking the 18-year-old men alone, the figure is 55.6 per cent in the army and 44.4 per cent in C.P.S. It should also be noted that, in addition to this, 22 men under age 18 from the Mennonite Church enlisted in the army without being drafted. Among Mennonites as a whole, 54 men under age 18 enlisted. From these figures it is obvious that the crucial age group is the younger one, and that it is here where the church needs to concentrate its teaching efforts for the maintenance of its nonresistant testimony.

REASONS FOR ACCEPTING MILITARY SERVICE

In the case of those who accepted military service, the minister who gave the information was asked to state his opinion as to the reasons for the man's choice. It is obvious that this subjective opinion may not always have been correct. In some cases, for example, the minister himself may not have been thoroughly committed to the principle of non-resistance. He may have believed in the principle in a passive way, but if he was not thoroughly convinced, he may have lacked that quality of conviction which would have been necessary to bring a wavering young man to register IV-E in the face of opposition from friends or associates. In such a case the minister's attitude may well have been a real reason why some young men went into the army. And yet, in only one case do the census returns say that the minister's attitude was responsible for a man going into the army. Likewise, lack of peace teaching was rated low (in fourth place) by the ministers as a cause for men accepting military service. Nevertheless, there seems to be plenty of evidence that in many cases the task of peace teaching was not well done.

The one reason given more often than any other for men entering the army was the influence of associates. According to these ratings, 30.8 per cent of the backsliders who accepted military service were influenced by associates; 27.8 per cent of the men in poor standing, and 17.5 per cent of those in good standing who accepted military service were likewise influenced. The ministers also believed that 55.2 per cent of the high-school men who went into the army were influenced by associates. Only one half of this proportion of the grade-school men in the army were believed to have been so influenced, and still fewer in the case of the college men. The various age categories seem to have been influenced about equally (from 21 to 27.3 per cent of each group) by associates, there being no significant difference among the groups. The only exception to this statement is the case of the 30- to 32-year group, and this would appear to have been a matter of accident. Among the occupational groups there was great similarity also. From 23.4 to 32.8 per cent of each group who went into the army were said to have been influenced by associates.

It is not difficult to see why the registrant's associates may frequently have influenced him away from the nonresistant position of the church. It is rather distressing, however, to find that the reason given most frequently, next to associates, was the influence of the registrant's family. It is true that in the high-school group the associates are reported to have had far more influence than the family, but when the registrants are grouped as to church standing, education, and occupation, the influence of the family is relatively high. The third most frequently mentioned reason was finances; the fourth was lack of peace teaching; and the fifth, school influences. Lack of information about procedure in registration and answering of questionnaires rated low as a factor. Hostility of draft boards did likewise.

NOTES AND CITATIONS

[1] Draft Census Study. An M.C.C. study in mimeographed form.

[2] The Charles report as here described appeared in mimeographed form. It was later printed, in a somewhat condensed form, as "A Presentation and Evaluation of the M.C.C. Draft Status Census," in *Proceedings of the Fourth Annual Conference on Mennonite Cultural Problems* (North Newton, Kansas, 1945).

[3] The figures in the completed M.C.C. census are not entirely accurate. A careful review by John E. Lapp of the report from the Franconia Conference shows that the number of drafted men from that conference was 34 less than the number shown in the M.C.C. census. This alters the figures and the percentages in the report at a number of points. It is possible that the census reports contain other errors, although it is not likely that their correction would alter the percentages and general conclusions greatly.

[4] John E. Lapp, "The Other Days," *The Mennonite Community* (Scottdale, Pa., July, 1947), 1:4:6.

[5] *Ibid.*, 1:4:6.

[6] *Twenty-third Mennonite General Conference* (1943), 38.

[7] *Southwestern Pennsylvania Conference Report* (1943), 12-14.

[8] *Report of the Iowa-Nebraska Conference* (1943), 18.

[9] These figures are not entirely accurate. The *Directory of Civilian Public Service* reports a total of 4,665 Mennonites in C.P.S. The census reports, however, show a total of only 4,536 men in C.P.S. Evidently the discrepancy is due to incomplete census reports from the congregations. The completed reports, however, would not alter the percentages greatly.

[10] The tables on pages 39 and 40 show some variations from those of the Peace Problems Committee's report to the *Twenty-sixth Mennonite General Conference* (1949), 62-64. The chief variation is due to corrected statistics for the Franconia Conference, submitted to the author by John E. Lapp.

Chapter V

Civilian Public Service

When the Selective Training and Service Act was passed on September 16, 1940, and it was certain that some type of Civilian Public Service would be established, the peace churches as well as the responsible government agencies began to concern themselves with the form which this service should take. On October 24, 1940, the peace churches through the National Council for Religious Conscientious Objectors proposed a plan for two types of service projects.

The first proposal was for a program to be managed jointly by the government and the church agencies. This provided that in soil conservation and similar projects the government would control the work program, feed and house the men, and pay them wages more or less comparable to what was received by men in the army. The church agencies, on the other hand, would have charge of the men when off the work project, and the cost of this part of the program would be met by them. This would include the cost of camp directors, religious and educational leadership, dietitian and nursing service, literature, and other services essential for a wholesome camp life. The second type of program proposed was one in which the work project as well as the religious and social life of the men would be entirely under the supervision of the church agencies. It was assumed that this type of program would include humanitarian and service projects at home and abroad, such as the relief projects sponsored by the Mennonite Central Committee. It was also assumed that the entire cost of this program, including the maintenance of the men, would be met by the churches. Because of the nature of this service, however, it was hardly expected that the men engaged in it would receive wages, although it may have been assumed that they would receive a small allowance for incidentals, perhaps similar to that received by relief workers.

Selective Service and other governmental agencies accepted these proposals and added a third, providing for work projects "directly under governmental agencies, fully financed by the government agency involved, and mainly for technically trained persons." Then on November 29, 1940, Clarence Dykstra, the Director of Selective Service, submitted this threefold program to President Roosevelt. The President rejected the program, however, apparently believing that work in C.C.C. camps[1]

was too easy for conscientious objectors. Indeed, he is even said to have
threatened to have the C.O.'s drilled by army officers. The Director of
Selective Service then withdrew the proposal and gave it further study
before bringing it up again. Investigation convinced him, however, that
the program in the form as proposed by the churches could not receive
official approval. Funds available for the operation of Selective Service
could legally be used neither to finance the maintenance of the men nor
to pay wages for their services. The only way to legalize such expenditures would be to ask Congress for an appropriation specifically for this
purpose. He believed that, if requested, such an appropriation would be
granted; but he also believed that the price of such an appropriation
would be complete government administration of the entire camp program.

Selective Service officials therefore concluded that if the government would consent to finance the camp program, it would also insist on
administering it; that if the churches desired to administer the program,
they must finance it themselves. Moreover, because of the President's
attitude, they did not believe that government funds could be obtained
under any circumstances for the payment of wages to the men. The
Director of Selective Service, therefore, asked the church agencies whether they would be willing to undertake the administration of the entire
camp program, including the maintenance of the men, and to finance it
themselves. On December 10, 1940, the National Service Board for
Religious Objectors, with representatives of the peace churches and the
Fellowship of Reconciliation, agreed to accept this undertaking "on an
experimental basis within the limits of financial ability." It was understood, of course, that the administration and cost of the work projects,
the provision of tools, and the transportation of the men to the camps
would be the responsibility of the government. This revised program as
accepted by the church agencies was approved by President Roosevelt
on December 19, 1940. On the following day Selective Service and the
National Service Board for Religious Objectors acknowledged their mutual agreement through an exchange of letters.[2]

C.P.S. ADMINISTRATION[3]

In the administration of C.P.S. which was thus established, ultimate
responsibility was vested in the Director of Selective Service. Under
the Director of Selective Service, in immediate charge of the C.P.S. program, was Camp Operations, an office headed by Colonel Lewis F.
Kosch. It was the duty of Camp Operations to locate, equip, maintain,
and supervise the C.P.S. camps and special projects. Camp Operations
assigned, transferred, and discharged men from C.P.S., and reviewed their
classifications. It initiated and recommended policies and administrative
action having to do with the entire C.P.S. system. The administration

of C.P.S. was a co-operative arrangement in which government agencies and technical men were responsible to Camp Operations for the work projects; and the church agencies and camp directors were responsible for camp life and discipline, and the nonworking time of the men.

Since three church agencies were responsible for the administration of camps, the National Service Board for Religious Objectors served as liaison between Selective Service and these agencies. For the most part, Selective Service dealt directly with the various technical agencies and project superintendents having to do with C.P.S. Normally, however, Selective Service dealt with the M.C.C., the Brethren Service Committee, and the American Friends Service Committee indirectly through the N.S.B.R.O., although frequently there were direct relations and negotiations between these agencies and Selective Service.

Since the administration of C.P.S. was a co-operative arrangement in which the church agencies were responsible for the camp life and the nonworking time of the men, and since they were also vitally concerned with the nature of the work projects to be selected, the N.S.B.R.O. and the church agencies were consulted by Camp Operations in the formulation of its policies, and in the beginning at least, they had a genuine share in developing the program. In matters of camp regulations, leaves, transfers, and discipline they had a considerable degree of freedom.

At the head of the M.C.C.-C.P.S. administration was the general director. When the program was at its peak there were four regional directors serving under the general director, besides assistant directors in charge of specialized services, as hospital units and farm and dairy testing assignments. These directors with their secretaries, assistants, and other helpers, clerical and otherwise, made up an administrative staff of approximately sixty persons at the Akron headquarters of the M.C.C. The first general director of M.C.C.-C.P.S. was Henry A. Fast. He was succeeded in 1943 by Albert Gaeddert, and later by Elmer Ediger. An important function of the Akron office was information service and publicity. There were continuous releases to the various Mennonite periodicals and to M.C.C. members. Beginning in 1941 there was an M.C.C. *Headquarters Letter* issued every few weeks to a small selected mailing list, giving the latest relief and C.P.S. news. Beginning in 1942 there was also a *C.P.S. News Letter* which was published under various names until the close of C.P.S. in 1947. As an additional means of keeping local camp staffs and campers informed concerning M.C.C. policies, and the operation of the C.P.S. system, the M.C.C. conducted numerous training schools and conferences for actual and potential camp directors and unit leaders, educational directors, business managers, dietitians, and other C.P.S. leaders, as well as prospective relief workers.

In the operation of the draft machinery, when the number of a IV-E registrant came up his name was forwarded to the state Selective Service office, and from thence to the national office in Washington. Camp

Operations, through the N.S.B.R.O., then assigned the man to a camp. If he was a Mennonite he was assigned to an M.C.C. camp, except in certain special cases. Once his assignment to camp had been made the man's relations with Selective Service were carried on through the M.C.C. almost entirely. The general director of M.C.C.-C.P.S. issued instructions to the man and informed the local camp director of the impending arrival of the new assignee. From the time of his arrival in a given camp, until his transfer or discharge, the assignee was responsible to this local director. The camp director kept a record of the time given by the man to the work project; he granted leaves and furloughs; and made reports to the M.C.C. headquarters at Akron, Pennsylvania, which in turn forwarded them to Selective Service at Washington. Requests for transfer, or any other requests other than routine ones, were made for the camper by the director to M.C.C., who in turn passed the request on to Camp Operations.

CAMP GROTTOES: THE WORK PROJECT

The first C.P.S. camp to be put into operation under the M.C.C. was Camp No. 4, a soil conservation project, located near Grottoes, in Rockingham County, Virginia, about twenty miles from Eastern Mennonite College. The camp was selected as early as November, 1940, following an inspection by representatives of Selective Service, the Department of Agriculture, the N.S.B.R.O., the M.C.C. and others, and was formally opened on May 22, 1951. Grottoes was a former C.C.C. camp considerably in need of repairs. By the time the camp was opened the M.C.C. had spent $1,400 on repairs and $1,100 on camp equipment, with more expenditures to follow. This involved a question of camp administrative policy in which Selective Service agreed to furnish camps in good condition in the future, and to maintain them in repair. Selective Service provided the camp with 175 cots and mattresses, besides stoves, kitchen and dining room equipment, obtained from the C.C.C., and over 500 blankets obtained from the army.

The work project under the Soil Conservation Service covered most of Rockingham and Augusta counties. Technicians from the S.C.S. arranged with farmers for the inauguration of soil conservation methods, S.C.S. furnishing the C.P.S. labor and the farmers agreeing to keep up the methods and practices inaugurated. "The C.P.S. men cleared pasture lands, stabilized gullied banks, planted thousands of seedlings, removed and constructed miles of fence, and laid much drainage tiling. Others built diversion ditches and farm ponds. Not all of the work was in the area of soil conservation. One man was stationed in a fire-lookout tower and many man days were spent in fighting forest fires. One crew worked on blister rust control, while another one kept the fire trail clear in the Shenandoah National Park." The records show that in four years' time the Grottoes C.P.S. men built 53,394 rods of fence, sodded 1,000 acres of pasture, sloped 464,399 square rods of bank and completed 37,515 linear feet of ditch diversion. They also gave 17,150 man days of labor to farm work, and 1,792 man days to fighting forest fires. Among other specific types of work listed were "minor road building, constructing terrace outlet structures, preparing land for strip cropping, clearing and cleaning channels and levees . . . food and cover planting and seeding, making surveys, technical service buildings maintenance, constructing telephone lines, building of foot trails, tree and plant disease control, emergency work, laying tile lines, and building small reservoirs."[4] One man who spent more than four years at Grottoes, calculating at the rate of fifty cents per hour, estimated that he had donated $4,296 worth of labor to the government. The fire fighting service was also of great importance. In the month of April, 1942, alone, "Grottoes men traveled a total of 4,083 miles in forest fire fighting, using 690 man days of labor." In this connection the project superintendent said: "I can honestly say that I know of no case where a boy of this camp has failed when the call came. The whole operation of fire fighting is based on team work and co-operation. This I have found in abundance and cannot compliment the personnel here too highly."[5] This description of the work project may be considered as typical of all Soil Conservation and Forestry Service camps.

CAMP LIFE AT GROTTOES

Much of the planning for the opening of the Grottoes Camp was in preparation for the life of the campers during their nonworking hours. In the very beginning a building was reserved for use as a chapel. Class rooms were provided for Bible classes, and it was announced that the faculty of Eastern Mennonite College was planning to co-operate in offering extension courses which could be taken for academic credit. Another building contained a shop where the men could occupy their spare time in woodworking or other hobbies. Before arriving at camp each man received a letter of welcome, with an attached list of provisions which he should bring with him. Upon his arrival he received a physical examination and vaccinations for smallpox and typhoid. The daily camp schedule began with a rising bell at 5:45, followed with breakfast at 6:15, morning worship at 6:45, and reporting for work at 7:30. The work day ended at 5:00 p.m., and supper was served at 5:30. Classes and recreation came after supper.

The camp organization included a camp council, made up of dormitory leaders from each unit and their assistants. This council gave leadership in the maintenance of camp morale. There were six committees: Religious activities, social and recreational, buildings and grounds maintenance, subsistence, safety, and the *Olive Branch* committee. The latter was responsible for the camp paper, the *Olive Branch*. The following quotation from Gingerich's *Service for Peace* packs into a few sentences numerous details in the daily life of the Grottoes campers.

5

Camp life was a novel experience to nearly all of the men reporting for C.P.S. Sleeping in barracks, eating in a large dining hall, living with a large group constantly, meeting with men from differing backgrounds, taking orders from government officials, and enjoying little privacy were all part of this new way of living to which the thousands of men who went through C.P.S. had to become accustomed. An effort was therefore made to provide interests and recreation which would help make the adjustment easier and provide a wholesome experience throughout the period of service.

The *Camper's Manual* described to the incoming men the facilities and opportunities of this new way of living. There was a barber shop, a bulletin board, and a canteen. In the latter, toilet supplies, stationery, and other items could be purchased. The hospital was equipped to care for minor injuries and sicknesses. A laundry was operated for the convenience of the men. A library and reading room with several hundred volumes and current periodicals was used by all the men. A prayer room with several booths for privacy encouraged spiritual growth. For indoor games there was the recreation room. A social room afforded a place for the entertainment of guests. The workshop appealed to those who liked to work with wood. Later considerable attention was given to leatherwork. A photography darkroom interested many of the campers. There was also adequate provision for outdoor recreation. A clay court was used for basketball, volleyball, and tennis. Softball, croquet, horseshoes, and archery also received their share of attention.[6]

During the four years of its life a number of special conferences were held at the Grottoes Camp. In January, 1943, there was a two-day Bible conference under the leadership of Arthur Ruth, J. C. Clemens, and John E. Lapp. On a week end in March, Paul Mininger of Goshen College gave a series of inspirational talks on "Youth Faces Life." April, 1943, saw the beginning of a six-week cooking school with twenty men from different camps enrolled. In 1944 there was a ten-day art institute directed by John P. Klassen of Bluffton College. Later in the same year there was a three-day business managers' and dietitians' conference.

THE RELIGIOUS AND EDUCATIONAL PROGRAM OF C.P.S.

The above description of religious and educational activities at Grottoes provides a good sample of the religious and educational program throughout C.P.S. The M.C.C. considered it of utmost importance that a strong religious program be maintained in all of the camps. Indeed, a major reason for desiring church administered camps was the opportunity which they would provide for maintaining such a program. For this reason, as said in Chapter VIII, the first men selected as camp directors were ministers who were expected to provide spiritual leadership for the camp as well as assuming administrative responsibilities. Later, however, the camp directors came to be chosen from the ranks of the drafted men. Many of these men did excellent work as administrators, but since they were not ministers additional means were sought to provide spiritual leadership, through the appointment of camp pastors and pastoral visitation committees, as also discussed and evaluated in Chapter

VIII. Most camps had a committee whose responsibility it was to plan the weekly religious services. Base camps had Sunday school each Sunday morning, followed by a preaching service. If there was no minister present, the camp director or sometimes a camper took the service. In some camps services were held early to give the men an opportunity to attend services in near-by churches. Sunday evening services varied, some having no regular service, and other camps having preaching or discussion meetings, regularly. Most camps had a weekly prayer meeting. Base camps had morning devotions at the breakfast table. Working hours in the hospital units were not uniform, making it difficult for these units to maintain a regular worship schedule. Most of them managed to have at least one religious service a week. The religious program of C.P.S. is discussed in considerable detail in Gingerich's *Service for Peace*, Chapter XVIII.

C.P.S. had not developed very far until the M.C.C. adopted the policy of appointing an educational director for each base camp. In October, 1941, a meeting of educational directors from the various camps adopted the following objectives for the C.P.S. educational program: 1. Appreciation of our Mennonite heritage and mission in the world. 2. Understanding the Christian's relation to the state and the community. 3. Deepening Christian experience. 4. Promoting personal growth. In line with these objectives an effort was then made to enroll all Mennonite campers in a *core course* consisting of six units of study covering the first three of the above four objectives. For the teaching of these units the M.C.C. then published a series of six booklets under the general title, *Mennonites and Their Heritage*, to be used as texts, as follows: 1. *Mennonite Origins in Europe*, by Harold S. Bender. 2. *Mennonites in America*, by C. Henry Smith. 3. *Our Mennonite Heritage*, by Edward Yoder. 4. *Our Mission as a Church of Christ*, by Ed. G. Kaufman. 5. *Christian Relationships to State and Community*, by Guy F. Hershberger. 6. *Life and Service in the Kingdom of God*, by P. C. Hiebert. Mennonite assignees were urged to take the course during the first quarter in camp. In order to make this possible the course was repeated at regular intervals in each camp. A number of camps offered a course in the Biblical basis of nonresistance, using Edward Yoder's, *Must Christians Fight?* as a basis for discussion.

Bible study was an important feature of the C.P.S. educational program, and Gingerich says, "Judging from the wide offerings of courses and the average attendance in these classes, it appears that Bible courses were more generally supported than any other kind of studies."[7] These courses included Bible doctrine, Old and New Testament Survey, Biblical Introduction, Teachings of Jesus, and the study of various books. Courses in first aid were also given, the standard course being required of all campers, and the advanced course offered for those who desired it. Besides these there was among the various camps a variety of courses taught in such subjects as music, German, Spanish, public speaking, current affairs, woodworking, photography, typewriting, and foods and nutrition.

Beginning in October, 1942, an educational secretary in the Akron office was made responsible for the direction of the educational program throughout C.P.S. He received reports from all educational directors. This office was first filled by Robert Kreider, then by Elmer Ediger and others. "The development of special schools [such as farm and community schools, cooking schools, Christian workers' schools, and others], the beginnings of voluntary service, the establishment of the orientation program, and many other aspects of C.P.S. education had their origin or vitalization in the educational secretary's office. The office was also responsible for the educational records of the assignees. This included keeping a detailed course description of each credit course offered as well as a record of all grades received and amount of college or high school credits earned. Early in the program, an activities and educational record was kept for each camper; later in the program records were kept by courses and activities of the camp or unit."[8] Many campers took courses for high school or college credit. A committee appointed by the Council of Mennonite and Affiliated Colleges approved courses worthy of such credit, and recommended the amount of credit which a given course should merit. By October, 1944, the task of processing courses desiring recognition for academic credit, and keeping the records of the men enrolled in these courses, was large enough to warrant the creation of a special office known as that of the educational liaison. This office was filled by Roy Umble. The M.C.C. educational office also made use of General Educational Development and other tests to measure the academic value of correspondence courses or other forms of educational experience presented for credit. The academic features of the C.P.S. educational program, as well as the foreign relief training program, are described more fully in Chapter XIV.[9]

In addition to the formal education here described there was also a large amount of informal education in C.P.S. The project itself, whether it was soil conservation, forestry, or mental health, involved a considerable amount of "on-the-job training." As time went on, many of the camps adopted orientation programs in which the new camper was given a week or more of preliminary training before taking up the duties of the job assigned to him. All of the camps had libraries, many of them well arranged, with a good assortment of books and periodicals. Most of the camps published a camp paper which had an educational value. Music in the form of quartettes and choruses played an important part in the life of many camps. Much use was made of visual education in the form of illustrated lectures. All of the camps made use of special lectures on a variety of topics, and in most of them there was a wholesome development in the field of crafts and hobbies, such as leathercraft, photography, and woodworking.

THE BASE CAMPS

The M.C.C. operated a total of 23 base camps, 10 of which were under the Soil Conservation Service. In the early days of C.P.S., from one half to two thirds of the Mennonite campers were in soil conservation work. In August, 1942, the M.C.C. was operating fourteen camps, nine of which were soil conservation camps with 1,147 of the 1,725 men then in M.C.C.-C.P.S. When it was pointed out that millions of acres of American agricultural land had lost their topsoil, it was not difficult for a rural people like the Mennonites to recognize soil conservation as work of national importance. During their C.P.S. experience numerous Mennonite farm youths gained a valuable education in conservation methods, from which their home communities will profit for years to come. The soil conservation camps ranged from Grottoes, Virginia, and Powellsville, Maryland, in the East, to Colorado Springs and Ft. Collins, Colorado, and Downey, Idaho, in the West. Soil conservation camps between these areas were Sideling Hill and Howard in Pennsylvania; Henry, Illinois; Denison, Iowa; and Weeping Water, Nebraska.

In December, 1942, about 14 per cent of the men in M.C.C. camps were in forestry service, and even in 1945, after large numbers had entered mental health and special service projects, 12 per cent were in this service. The forestry service camps were at Marietta, Ohio; Bluffton and Medaryville, Indiana; Missoula, Montana; and Camino and North Fork, California. The United States Forestry Service has general administration over 160 national forests. The C.P.S. men in this service were engaged in such work as the planting and cultivating of young trees, disease control, and fire prevention and control. The forest service camp receiving the most public attention in C.P.S. days was the camp at Missoula, Montana, where the Smoke Jumpers Unit was located. This was a unit of fire fighters, trained in parachute jumping from airplanes as a means of speedy arrival at the location of the fire. The Smoke Jumpers Unit did an important piece of work, which was highly appreciated by the Forestry Service. The Camino, California, camp had a higher than average percentage of non-Mennonite campers, some of whom did not understand, or were unsympathetic with, the M.C.C. policies. As a result, this camp had perhaps more than its share of administrative problems. The Camino camp also had some public relations problems, because of sections in the neighboring population who did not appreciate the presence of a conscientious objector camp, although there were a few other camps which had a similar experience.

Four of the Mennonite camps were under the National Park Service. These were at Galax and Luray, Virginia; Belton, Montana; and Three Rivers, California. Usually about ten per cent of the Mennonite campers were in the National Park Service. Two camps, Hill City, South Dakota, and Lapine, Oregon, were under the Bureau of Reclamation. At each

of these camps the project was the construction of a large dam for purposes of irrigation and water supply. The Terry, Montana, camp also had
some of its men assigned to the Bureau of Reclamation, but about two
thirds of them were under the Federal Security Administration. At Terry
these two agencies co-operated in the development of a large irrigation
project. The Terry camp was noted for its high morale and for its splendid
public relations with the neighboring community.

SMALLER AGRICULTURAL UNITS

In addition to the base camps devoted to soil conservation or related
agricultural work, there were a number of smaller agricultural units.
Camp No. 24 at Hagerstown, Maryland, consisted of five units, three of
which were operated by the M.C.C., and two by the Brethren Service
Committee. The three M.C.C. units each having about 35 men, were
located on farms owned by Mennonite Church agencies. In addition to
the soil conservation work done, Soil Conservation Service thought of the
Hagerstown units as experimental units in farm management and rural
self-subsistence. The M.C.C. also saw in this set-up an opportunity to
experiment in the production of a share of the camp's food supply, as
well as to study the overhead expenses in small units as compared with
the larger base camps. A similar arrangement was had at Lincoln, Nebraska, in the two farm units of Camp No. 138. Unit No. 2 of this camp,
located near Malcolm, was operated by the Peace Problems Committee.
Closely associated with these units was Camp No. 106, a small unit under
the Agricultural Experiment Station of the University of Nebraska. Both
the Hagerstown and the Nebraska units emphasized agriculture in their
educational programs, both of them conducting special farm and community schools.

The year 1942 saw the beginning of a program in which C.P.S. men
were given assignments in dairying, especially on dairy farms where a
labor shortage was handicapping milk production. By the autumn of
1945 over 590 men were engaged in this type of work. Most of them were
on dairy farms. Some were doing dairy herd testing. Over 30 worked
with dairy herds owned by agricultural colleges, and about a dozen were
engaged in artificial insemination work. These dairy farm and dairy testing units were located in the dairy sections of Wisconsin, California,
Colorado, Michigan, Ohio, Pennsylvania, Iowa, and Maine. One unit was
located at the United States Dairy Experiment Station, which is part of
the Agricultural Research Center at Beltsville, Maryland. This unit
helped to relieve the labor shortage at the Dairy Station where an experimental herd of 500 cattle was kept. One of the relief training units
described in Chapter XIV was located with the Beltsville unit.

MENTAL HOSPITALS AND TRAINING SCHOOLS

No type of C.P.S. service was held in higher esteem, either by the men themselves or by the general public, than were mental hospital and related services. With more than three fourths of a million patients in some type of mental institution, and with a great shortage of labor in these institutions, there was no doubt that this was work of national importance. The first hospital units for C.P.S. men were organized in 1942, and by October, 1943, one out of every six men in C.P.S. was working in a mental hospital. In September, 1945, there were over 1,000 men in 26 M.C.C. mental hospital and training school units. By the end of 1945 over 1,500 men had given service in such units. Altogether, the M.C.C. operated 25 mental hospital and 5 training school units. Mental hospitals are not noted, as a rule, for their good management, satisfactory working conditions, or high standards of treatment of their patients. In numerous cases the C.P.S. units coming into hospitals were able to make an excellent contribution to the work of the institution and to raise the standards materially. The most ideal situation among mental hospitals was that in the Ypsilanti, Michigan, State Hospital. It was of modern construction, with the best of equipment and high standards of service, under the direction of Dr. O. R. Yoder, a most sympathetic superintendent who co-operated in a splendid way with the C.P.S. unit. The Ypsilanti unit consisted of about 75 C.P.S. men. Usually 35 wives and other friends of the men worked there also, making a total of over 100. In 1944 and 1945, summer service units of women worked at the hospital. Ypsilanti was also the location of one of the relief training units described in Chapter XIV. Two other such relief training units were located with the Hudson River State Hospital unit at Poughkeepsie, New York, and the State Hospital at Howard, Rhode Island.

PUBLIC HEALTH SERVICE

Another useful form of service rendered by C.P.S. was in the field of public health. The first C.P.S. project of this type was organized in 1942 at Crestview, Florida, under the Brethren Service Committee, with some Mennonite assignees in the unit. In 1943 an M.C.C. unit was established at Mulberry, Florida, and then in 1946 it moved to a more desirable location at Bartow. The unit was engaged in a hookworm control project which required the construction of a large number of sanitary toilets. By September, 1945, over 1,800 toilets had been installed in Polk County, Florida. One of the C.P.S. relief training units was located at Mulberry. In February, 1945, a similar project was opened at Gulfport, Mississippi. In addition to the hookworm control work, members of the C.P.S. unit worked in the laboratory of the Harrison County Health Department making tests in hookworm control, venereal disease control, and milk sanitation. The camp nurse gave much of her time to the County Health Department, visiting schools where vaccinations and immunizations were given. Both the Mulberry and Gulfport units served as a means of introducing the Mennonite campers to a variety of new social and economic problems, making them conscious of the social implications of Christianity as they had not been before.

One of the most significant services of C.P.S. was that given by the Puerto Rican Reconstruction Administration unit in the La Plata community project near Aibonito, Puerto Rico. A medical clinic was opened in December, 1943, and the new hospital, which had been built and to some extent furnished and equipped with C.P.S. labor, was dedicated in August, 1944. The community building program emphasized agricultural education, recreation, and community relief. Since there was no house of worship in the community, it was clear that the La Plata community offered real possibilities for missionary work. In 1945 work was begun on the construction of a chapel, which was dedicated in March, 1946. In the meantime the Mennonite Board of Missions and Charities had begun a mission project in the neighboring community of Pulguillas. Eventually, in 1950, as explained in Chapter XIII,[10] the La Plata project was also transferred to the Mission Board which then carried on the program in both communities. The La Plata C.P.S. project did a significant piece of work. The hospital report for the year 1945 reports 9,335 outpatient clinical visits, and 1,134 patients hospitalized. There were 240 major and 594 minor operations. The number of dental patients seen was 5,701. In five subsidiary clinics a total of 15,780 outpatient visits was recorded. The total attendance at the community centers for the year was 226,022. Two milk stations were in operation, a boys' summer camp was operated, and a school health program and a variety of other projects were included in the total program.

Another significant type of Public Health project was what was known as the "guinea pig" projects, under C.P.S. Unit No. 115, directed jointly by the Brethren, Friends, and Mennonites under the Office of Scientific Research. In this unit the number of Mennonite assignees was never large, although a number participated in such projects as the starvation experiment at the University of Minnesota; the New England experiment in working while infected with body lice, as a means of studying methods for the extermination of lice and combating typhus; the experiment in nutrition in tropical climates carried on at the University of Illinois; and the experiment with atypical pneumonia at Pinehurst, North Carolina.

The M.C.C. also had two health units in veterans' hospitals, one in California and the other in Oregon. A number of Mennonite campers was included in the hospital unit administered by the Association of Catholic Conscientious Objectors (later by the Brethren Service Committee), at Alexian Brothers Hospital in Chicago; and several in the Duke

University Hospital unit administered by the Methodist Commission on World Peace.

DEMOBILIZATION

When the C.P.S. program began in 1941, it was assumed that the men were enrolled for one year of service. With the entrance of the United States into the war in December of that year, however, everyone knew that C.P.S. service would now continue for the duration of the war. Even with the end of the war in September, 1945, it was discovered that demobilization would require time. As early as 1943, C.P.S. men over 38 years of age could be placed into the C.O. reserve, provided they found employment on farms. In April, 1945, men 42 years old and over were discharged. There were only 10 such men in C.P.S., however. In June, 1945, it was announced that men 40 years of age and over would be released. Not until November, 1945, however, did the demobilization of C.P.S. men really get under way. By November 14 a total of 118 men had been released on the basis of age and length of service. Soon afterwards it was announced that men with four years of service as of December 31, those 35 to 37 years old with two years of service, and men 38 years old, could take their physical examination for release, beginning November 26, 1945. Beginning in January, 1946, a plan was inaugurated for the release of all men with three years of service, and by February 1, 1946, a total of 1,350 men had actually been released from M.C.C.-C.P.S. From now on qualifications for release were reduced from time to time, resulting in a steady stream of releases until demobilization was completed and C.P.S. finally closed in March, 1947.

SOME PROBLEMS OF ADMINISTRATION

Earlier in this chapter it was said that in the early period of C.P.S. the church agencies had a genuine share in developing the camp program, and a considerable degree of freedom in the matter of camp regulations. After the United States entered the war, however, and the number of men in C.P.S. camps reached into the thousands, there was a tendency on the part of Camp Operations and Selective Service to assume more direct control of discipline and camp regulations, and to formulate policies without consulting the church agencies. This may have been due in part to the increased problems of wartime which gave the Director of Selective Service less time for consultation. It was also due in part, no doubt, to an increase in the number of disciplinary problems, particularly in Quaker camps, which caused Camp Operations to conclude that the church agencies were unable to exercise the amount and quality of discipline necessary for efficient camp administration. It must be remembered that Selective Service and Camp Operations were in the hands of military men whose ideas of discipline would not always coincide with those of a Mennonite or a Quaker. Furthermore, in some camps there were men who lacked the spirit of co-operation to such an extent as to create a difficult situation. This was especially true of certain types of political objectors and of members of certain religious groups, such as the Russian Molokans and the Jehovah's Witnesses. Often these men objected to conscription as such, as much as to the performance of military service. There were a few who had no conscience against disregarding camp rules, being absent without leave, or loafing on the project to which the camp program was committed.

Enforcement of Selective Service regulations upon such unwilling men would seem to require methods which a nonresistant camp director could not employ. One result of this was the establishment of three government camps, operated directly by Selective Service, to which the more unco-operative campers were transferred. Even so, directors of Quaker camps, and the American Friends Service Committee which appointed them, found it increasingly difficult to work with Selective Service in the later period. This was one factor contributing to the withdrawal of the A.F.S.C. from the operation of C.P.S. in March, 1946, a year before the end of C.P.S.

Fortunately Mennonite camps had relatively few unco-operative campers of the type described above. The M.C.C. felt itself obliged, however, to admit to its camps a share of those IV-E men who were not members of the Mennonite, Quaker, or Brethren churches. Among those admitted were a few of the unco-operative type. This experience caused enough difficulty to induce the M.C.C. in September, 1943, to draw up a statement of policy regarding Mennonite Civilian Public Service, and to announce that it was inviting to its camps only such men as could freely and conscientiously subscribe to this policy. Among the points stressed in this statement of policy were the following: 1. The M.C.C. "considers that the men who choose its C.P.S. camps, do declare by that act their intention to live in the spirit of Christian brotherhood during their C.P.S. service." "The M.C.C. holds further that once a work assignment has been accepted it should be performed with the highest efficiency and dispatch and with a whole heart." With this policy it can be said that, at least until the last year of C.P.S., the Mennonite experience in camp administration was reasonably satisfactory. During the last year, however, problems in M.C.C. camps increased. The war was over, demobilization was in progress, and the men in camp were looking forward to their discharges. As members of the camp staffs received their own discharges, younger inexperienced men were appointed as directors and to other responsible positions, the turnover being very rapid at times. All of this contributed to a lowering of morale, so that M.C.C.-C.P.S. in the end period was not what it had formerly been. Mennonite campers were never of the unco-operative variety described earlier, as found in some camps. Not all Mennonites, however, were motivated by the desire for

Christian service to the extent that they should have been, especially in the last year of C.P.S.; and thus they contributed to the problems of the camp director. There were a few who shared the view of numerous men in Quaker and Brethren camps, that in undertaking to operate C.P.S. camps the church had made an alliance with the state which it should not have made. In spite of the difficulties, however, an opinion poll, as stated in Chapter XX, revealed the fact that the great majority of Mennonite C.P.S. men themselves believed the church had done the right thing in accepting the administration of the camps. Furthermore, in reviewing the experience, three years after the end of C.P.S., the M.C.C. was also of the opinion that in the event of future conscription involving C.P.S. camps, the church should have a share in their administration, although with certain improvements in the administrative set-up. A further evaluation of C.P.S., and some suggestions for a possible future program, are given in Chapter XX.

NOTES AND CITATIONS

[1] This refers to the Civilian Conservation Corps program operated during the 1930's. This program served the twofold purpose of providing employment for young men in the days of depression, and also doing important forestry and soil conservation work for the nation.

[2] For documentary materials on this question, see *The Origins of Civilian Public Service* (National Service Board for Religious Objectors, Washington, D.C.). For a detailed account of the origins of Civilian Public Service, see Melvin Gingerich, *Service for Peace*, Ch. V.

[3] The remainder of this chapter is based on Gingerich, *Service for Peace*.

[4] See below, p. 4. Gingerich, *Service for Peace*, 101-2.

[5] *Ibid.*, 104.

[6] *Ibid.*, 99.

[7] *Ibid.*, 299-300.

[8] *Ibid.*, 301.

[9] See below, p. 174 ff.

[10] See below, p. 167.

Chapter VI

Financing the C.P.S. Program

The moment the draft act was passed in September, 1940, with its provision for civilian work of national importance, the peace churches were aware that the Civilian Public Service program, whatever form it took, would cost them some money. It was generally assumed, however, that since the men would be engaged in government service, the government would also assume a substantial part of the financial responsibility. This assumption underlay the proposed plans for the types of service presented by the peace churches on October 24, 1940, as described in the previous chapter.[1]

THE CHURCH ACCEPTS FINANCIAL RESPONSIBILITY

When it became clear, however, that church-administered camps would need to be financed by the churches, the National Service Board for Religious Objectors and the peace churches accepted the undertaking "on an experimental basis within the limits of financial ability." The revised program as accepted by the church agencies was approved by President Roosevelt on December 19, 1940."[2]

While this revised program meant a financial load heavier than the churches had originally anticipated, the burden was actually lightened to a considerable extent by the fact that most of the base camps were located in abandoned C.C.C. camps. This made it unnecessary for the churches to build barracks for the housing of the men. The C.C.C. camp facilities were loaned to the church agencies free of rent. In addition to this, the War Department also loaned cots, bedding, stoves, and other items of camp equipment. If the church agencies would have had to provide all of these facilities, their expenditures would have been considerably greater than they were. In these negotiations of the peace churches, and of the National Service Board, with Selective Service, the Mennonite Central Committee and its constituent groups had an active part. The meeting of December 10, 1940, at which the peace churches accepted the responsibility for administering and financing the camp program on an experimental basis, was attended by Harold S. Bender and Orie O. Miller of the Peace Problems Committee and by Amos S. Horst of the Lancaster Mennonite Conference, as well as by Henry A. Fast and E. L. Harshbarger of the General Conference Mennonite Church, and by P. C. Hiebert of the Mennonite Brethren Church.

In the development of conscription and of C.P.S., the Peace Problems Committee had kept in touch with the leadership of the Mennonite

Church at every step of the program. At times, however, events moved so rapidly that important decisions had to be made before there was time to confer with representative groups of leaders. This was especially true during the weeks following November 29, 1940. By December 10, however, members of the committee had conferred with such individual leaders as they were able to get in touch with. This sampling of opinion, inadequate though it was, satisfied the Peace Problems Committee that, if the original program as proposed to President Roosevelt was not workable, the church would not hesitate to undertake the administration and financing of the entire camp program. Further sampling of opinion between December 10 and 21 strengthened this conviction.

Officials of the other Mennonite groups had the same experience, so that when the Mennonite Central Committee met for its annual meeting on December 21, 1940, it was ready officially to enter into the plan. This was done through the adoption of a resolution which said: (1) That the co-operating Mennonite groups had indicated a desire to undertake the C.P.S. program on the terms approved by the President. (2) That the M.C.C. and the M.C.P.C. had proposed an operating budget sufficient to cover all costs of C.P.S. to July 1, 1941. (3) That this budget could be met by an allocation of fifty cents per church member for the period ending July 1, 1941. (4) That the executive secretary was authorized to proceed with the C.P.S. program on this basis. (5) That each co-operating group was expected to assume official responsibility for its share of the budget; to report its action to the executive secretary of the M.C.C.; and promptly to pay its share monthly.[3]

This action having been taken by the Mennonite Central Committee, it was now the task of the co-operating groups to raise the needed funds. Before it was known that the church agencies would need to provide maintenance for the men, it had been estimated that the cost of operating the camp program would be fifty dollars per C.P.S. man annually. With this in mind, the Peace Problems Committee on November 7, 1940, had taken action asking the various congregations of the Mennonite Church to raise the money to meet this cost.[4] An announcement in the *Gospel Herald* two weeks later had asked that each congregation be responsible to provide fifty dollars for each of its members called to C.P.S. Payments were to be made through the treasury of the Mennonite Board of Missions and Charities at Elkhart, Indiana, and of the Eastern Board at Lancaster, Pennsylvania.[5] Correspondence in the files of the Peace Problems Committee, however, indicates that the committee believed this plan might work a hardship on some small congregations if they should happen to have an unusually large number of drafted men. In order to remedy this situation, the committee requested the district conferences to make this a conference problem, and to provide a way of relieving those congregations who might be carrying an unusually heavy burden.[6] At least one conference went farther than this, taking official action to make the conference, rather than individual congregations, responsible for the entire financial support of C.P.S.[7]

When the Mennonite Central Committee, on December 21, 1940, approved the new plan for financing the entire camp program, it also adopted a C.P.S. operating budget of $57,000.00 for a six-month period ending July 1, 1941. This amounted to an average of fifty cents per individual member of all the constituent groups. The Peace Problems Committee now changed its approach accordingly, and asked all congregations of the Mennonite Church to receive offerings of fifty cents per member for the first six months of 1941. Again the congregations were asked to send their contributions to the treasurers of the two mission boards who in turn would forward the money to the M.C.C. This seemed to be the best administrative procedure, since the mission boards appointed the persons who represented the Mennonite Church on the M.C.C.

On January 6, 1941, the Executive and Relief committees of the Elkhart Board took official action to co-ordinate the Board's work with the C.P.S. program. A Civilian Service Committee was appointed, consisting of S. C. Yoder, chairman; John L. Horst, secretary; and E. C. Bender, treasurer. It was the task of this committee to give information and to make financial appeals through the *Gospel Herald*. The monthly quota due the M.C.C. from the Elkhart treasury, for the first six months of 1941, was $2,800.00.[8] In the early stages of the program, however, the Peace Problems Committee took the initiative in bringing the new problem before the church. Between December 21, 1940, and January 13, 1941, the committee held meetings with the ministerial bodies of the Franconia, the Lancaster, the Southwestern Pennsylvania, the Ohio and Eastern A.M., the Indiana-Michigan, and the Iowa-Nebraska conferences, for the purpose of interpreting the new program and answering such questions as might arise. About the same time D. D. Miller of Indiana was sent as a special representative of the Peace Problems Committee, to meet with ministers of the Dakota-Montana (North Central) and the Pacific Coast conferences for the same purpose.[9]

C.P.S. REVIEWED AND CONTINUED

When the peace churches agreed to undertake the financing of the C.P.S. program "on an experimental basis within the limits of financial ability," the end of the experimental period was set for July 1, 1941. Later it was extended to September 15, due to some delay in the opening of the camps. In September, 1941, the entire C.P.S. program was given a thorough review, both by Selective Service and by the church agencies. The result was an agreement to extend the experimental period to January 1, 1943.[10] Shortly after the M.C.C. agreed to this extension of the C.P.S. program, the Peace Problems Committee called a meeting of representative leaders of the church to review with them the status of C.P.S., and to give careful consideration to the financial aspects of the program.[11]

The meeting was held in Chicago on October 24, 1941, with the moderator of General Conference serving as chairman, and with other conference officials present. The total attendance included fifty-three bishops, nineteen ministers, five deacons, and nine laymen of the Mennonite, the Conservative Amish, the Old Order Amish, and the Old Order Mennonite groups. Members of the Peace Problems Committee traced the history of C.P.S. They explained the relation of the M.C.C. and of the N.S.B.R.O. to C.P.S. The cost of the camp program was carefully analyzed, and the inability to secure a government subsidy for the church-operated camps was explained. The meeting discussed the method of raising funds for C.P.S., and the need for safeguarding the other giving of the church. The responsibility of M.C.C. for uncollectable charges against non-peace church C.O.'s was considered. Attention was called to the possibility of establishing C.P.S. farm units near Hagerstown, Maryland, on farms owned or leased by the M.C.C., and operated as soil conservation farm demonstration projects. The hope of using Mennonite C.P.S. men in foreign relief service in England, China, Paraguay, and elsewhere was also discussed.

Before the meeting closed, the following resolutions were adopted as expressing the views of the group:

1. *Resolved,* That inasmuch as the present selective service legislation and regulations permit the operation of church-directed Civilian Public Service camps, whereby we may maintain our nonresistant witness and safeguard and promote the moral and spiritual welfare of our young men who are called to service, we believe that, unless and until other provisions are made, the church should continue indefinitely to assume the responsibility to finance this service to the extent that may be required to make a church-directed program possible.

2. *Resolved further,* That we approve the general program and policies of Civilian Public Service as outlined by the Peace Problems Committee and as carried out by the Mennonite Central Committee, and that we encourage our Peace Problems Committee and the Mennonite Central Committee to continue their concern and efforts to maintain a clear and distinctive witness for the church through C.P.S. and to make the period of service of our young men a means of strengthening their own life and experience and upbuilding the church and the cause of Christ.

3. *Resolved further,* That we favor using civilian service men in foreign service, provided that the principles and policies expressed in the first two resolutions can be maintained, and provided that due care be taken to conduct an economical program. We favor co-operation between our civilian service and relief agencies in providing for such service through the Mennonite Central Committee or other Mennonite agencies, and would agree to a judicious use of relief funds to support such work.[12]

The spirit of the meeting was described in a graphic manner by Milo Kauffman, the moderator of the Mennonite General Conference, as follows:

Everyone present seemed to realize that the church was facing a momentous decision. A spirit of prayer and reverence prevailed . . . . The great problem before the Mennonite Church was: Shall she continue to finance the C.P.S. camps or shall they be financed by the government, which would mean also government control? . . . Resolutions were presented and adopted without a dissenting vote. While all realized that the decision was one of vital importance, all realized also that it was the only consistent position that could be taken. A discussion followed, which every member of the churches represented should have heard. A strong conviction was voiced by a number that the Mennonite Church can and will raise the necessary funds to carry on the work, also that the money raised for our camps should be above that normally given for the work of the church. Our relief work, charities, missions, and colleges should not have to suffer because of this program.

Could the entire church have been present at this meeting, the decision likely would have been the same. The decisions reached by the group, I believe, represent the mind of the great majority of the members of the Mennonite Church. Just as the Mennonite Church has faced other crises, so she will face this one. Not only are the C.P.S. camps a means of our young men following their convictions on the question of military training, but they are also a definite opportunity to express our peace testimony, and this work should accordingly have the united support of the entire church in prayer, concern, and money.[18]

RAISING THE FUNDS

Because the camp program developed more slowly during 1941 than had been anticipated, the period for the payment of the first quota of fifty cents per member was extended from July 1 to September 1. For the next six months, September 1, 1941, to March 1, 1942, the quota was set at one dollar per member. This represented a monthly contribution of about $9,000.00 per month for the Mennonite Church. The number of inductions increased steadily from now on so that for the six-month period, March 1, 1942, to September 1, 1942, the quota was set at $1.25 per member. When this was found to be insufficient, however, the period was shortened to five months, ending August 1. Following this, a quota of two dollars per member was set for the six-month period, August 1, 1942, to February 1, 1943. It was necessary, however, to shorten this period to four months, ending December 1, 1942, thus making a quota of fifty cents per member per month.

Even though the C.P.S. population continued to rise, an increasing number of men were now being assigned to detached service projects, such as mental hospitals. Since the M.C.C. did not need to provide for the maintenance of men on detached service, it was possible to continue the quota of fifty cents per member per month from August 1, 1942, to April 1, 1946, except that during the June- August quarter of 1945, an extra levy of fifty cents was made. For April, May, and June, 1946, the quota was forty cents per month. For July, August, and September, it was twenty-five cents per month. During the last quarter of 1946, the quota was twenty-five cents per member for the entire period. Thus the total quota per member of the Mennonite churches, for the duration of C.P.S., was $27.45.

The total contributions received by the M.C.C. for the operation of C.P.S., from its beginning in 1941 to its end on March 29, 1947, were $3,032,268.75. Of this amount, $2,886,280.64 was in the form of regular quota contributions from the churches. The remainder consisted of miscellaneous cash donations, including $1,426.07 from offerings given by C.P.S. men themselves, and gifts-in-kind, chiefly food supplies for the camps, valued at $134,129.37. Besides the contributions here listed, the M.C.C. also received, during the C.P.S. program, about $290,000.00 for the support of non-Mennonite men in camp, and for the support of Mennonites whose churches were not on the quota basis. This included contributions from non-Mennonite churches, from non-Mennonite campers, and other individuals. Of the quota contributions listed above, the share of the Mennonite Church, as paid through the treasuries at Elkhart and Lancaster, was $1,349,827.49, or about 47 per cent of the total. The church's share of the miscellaneous donations and gifts-in-kind would be difficult to determine.[14]

In the beginning of the C.P.S. program, especially after it was learned that the government would not provide maintenance for the men, some fears were expressed lest the church should be unable to provide the necessary finances. The results show, however, that these fears were unfounded. The spirit of the Chicago meeting of October 24, 1941, described earlier in this chapter, was evidently a reflection of the spirit of the entire church. There was a deep feeling that a cause was at stake; that the degree of support given to the C.P.S. program was a measure of the sincerity of the church's nonresistant faith; and that this support must be given in addition to the church's regular support of her mission and other necessary programs. Some congregations set aside a certain Sunday for the lifting of a large offering, sufficient to cover the congregation's quota for that entire quota period. Some took regular monthly offerings for C.P.S. Others raised their quotas by other means. From 1943 on, when the quota remained at fifty cents per member, it was taken for granted in many congregations that each month an offering would be lifted yielding at least one half as many dollars as there were members in the congregation.

Instead of injuring the church's giving to missions and other causes, contributions to C.P.S. seem to have stimulated greater giving in these areas as well. When an increase in the quota was announced in October, 1942, the chairman of the Peace Problems Committee said: "We are happy to know that the higher cost is due to the large number of our young men who stand faithful to the principles of the church."[15] At the same time an announcement in the *Gospel Herald* encouraged the brotherhood to respond to the program, saying: "The whole program is to be reviewed by the government soon. May we not let it be said that we failed to support what they have provided for us so that we might live true to our consciences and the teaching of the Word as we understand it."[16]

In its report to General Conference in 1943, the Peace Problems Committee, referring to the financial aspect of C.P.S., said: "Here there is cause for rejoicing, for our people have responded splendidly to the call for the support of C.P.S. without pressure . . . . Our relief funds have also been generously supported. Those who feared that C.P.S. would become too much of a burden and either fail financially or handicap our other giving have fortunately been disappointed. Never has the Mennonite Church given so generously to all causes, and we believe this will continue as long as there is need, and as long as our faith and convictions for our principles remain strong."[17] The chairman of the Peace Problems Committee, in reviewing the C.P.S. program for the year 1945, said: "The splendid record of the church in meeting its C.P.S. obligations has been a source of encouragement as well as a demonstration of what can be done financially when deep conviction motivates the work."[18]

GIFTS-IN-KIND

It was stated earlier in this chapter that the churches contributed to C.P.S., gifts-in-kind valued at more than $134,000.00, and that it would be difficult to estimate what proportion of this came from congregations of the Mennonite Church. We know, however, that publicity material concerning this work appeared regularly in the columns of the *Gospel Herald,* and that the congregations responded in a generous way. In May, 1943, the first year that the gifts-in-kind program was actively promoted, the Relief Committee reported to the annual meeting of the Mennonite Board of Missions and Charities, as follows: "We are glad to endorse the appeal for help in furnishing canned and dried food, both fruit and vegetables . . . . This is a service which our sisters in particular can render, and which will be a great help in the C.P.S. work. A letter regarding this will shortly go out to all our congregations."[19] Among the collection centers for canned goods, reported by William T. Snyder in the *Gospel Herald* in January, 1944, were: Kalona, Iowa; Fisher, Sterling, Eureka, and Arthur, Illinois; Goshen, Indiana; Milford, Nebraska; Orrville, Louisville, Elida, and Archbold, Ohio; Souderton and Lancaster County, Pennsylvania; and Broadway, Harrisonburg, and Fentress, Virginia. The article described the distribution of the canned food, the scope of the project, and the method of canning and packing. It also included testimonies from the camps, as well as from the local groups who did the work.[20]

Certain district conferences also gave official encouragement to the food preparation program. At the annual conference in 1943, the secretary of the Ohio and Eastern A.M. Conference "explained the fruit and vegetable canning and drying program for C.P.S. camps."[21] The following year the sisters' sewing circle of the Missouri-Kansas (South Central) Conference reported: "Canning for C.P.S. is an important part of the circles' work at the present time, although at the beginning of the year our district was poorly organized to take care of this work. Steps have been taken to co-operate more fully with the M.C.C."[22] At the 1943 meeting of the sewing circles of the Pacific Coast Conference "the home canning project for the C.P.S. work was discussed at length. It was tacitly agreed that every effort be put forth to increase production, canning, drying, and producing fresh food for the camps."[23] The conference at the same time took action asking S. E. Eicher, "in addition to his previously assigned duties" in connection with C.P.S., to "be our representative, to co-operate with the Mennonite Central Committee, sisters' sewing circle, and others in the district in supplying our C.P.S. camps with food and such other needs as may arise."[24] In 1944 the same conference appointed two additional brethren, Joe E. Slatter of Idaho and E. B. Harder of California, "to be responsible to co-operate with the M.C.C. in the canning of fruit and in other food preparation for C.P.S. camps."[25] In 1943 the congregation at Sweet Home, Oregon, furnished dressed turkey for Thanksgiving dinner at the Lapine and North Fork camps.[26]

News items, appearing in the *Gospel Herald* from time to time, reported that local congregations in all parts of the church were busy at work on these food preparation projects. A report from Nampa, Idaho, said: "The sisters' sewing circle has put in a busy season preparing food for the C.P.S. camps . . . . We have 1,176 quarts of vegetables and fruit canned and about 125 pounds of dried food for the camps."[27] A report from Fairview, Michigan, said: "This congregation canned 1,629 quarts of fruits and vegetables for the C.P.S. camps."[28] A note from Springs, Pennsylvania, reported: "Besides canning and drying foodstuffs for ourselves we were able to fill approximately 1,590 quarts of fruits and vegetables for the C.P.S. camps."[29] From Landis Valley, Pennsylvania, this report was published: "Our sisters met every Tuesday during the growing season after starting in July. They used the basement as a canning center, where bushel after bushel was donated and canned. At the close of the season three thousand quarts were sent to C.P.S."[30] These cases illustrate the manner in which the work was being done everywhere throughout the church.

It has been the purpose of this chapter to describe the part played by the Mennonite Church in the financing of the M.C.C. camp program. For the general picture of C.P.S. finances, including quota contributions, gifts-in-kind, maintenance projects on detached service, and other phases, as well as a table showing the quota contributions of each constituent group, the reader will wish to consult Melvin Gingerich, *Service for Peace*, Chapter XXI and Appendix 21.

NOTES AND CITATIONS

[1] See above, p. 49.

[2] See Gingerich, *Service for Peace*, Ch. V.

[3] Mennonite Central Committee Annual Meeting, Dec. 21, 1940, Minute No. 8.

[4] Minutes of Peace Problems Committee, Nov. 7, 1940.

[5] *Gospel Herald* (Nov. 21, 1940), 33:731.

[6] E.g., see letter of Harold S. Bender to A. J. Steiner, Nov. 12, 1940, in files of Peace Problems Committee.

[7] Minutes of the Peace Problems Committee of the Franconia Mennonite Conference, Dec. 3, 1940. On Jan. 30, 1941, following the adoption of the new quota plan by the M.C.C., the Franconia Conference in special session decided to support this program and raise fifty cents per member during the next six months. Incidentally, the minutes of this special session say that to date no IV-E classifications had been reported in that conference district.

[8] Report of the Civilian Service Committee, in "Report of the Thirty-fifth Annual Meeting of the Mennonite Board of Missions and Charities," *Gospel Herald* (June 5, 1941), 34:226.

[9] Harold S. Bender to N. M. Birky, Jan. 13, 1941, in Peace Problems Committee files.

[10] After this date the C.P.S. program was renewed a year at a time.

[11] Peace Problems Committee files, Oct. 14, 1941.

[12] Minutes of special meetings on C.P.S. and related problems, Oct. 24, 1941. In Peace Problems Committee files.

[13] Milo Kauffman, "The Chicago Meeting and Its Decisions," *Gospel Herald* (Nov. 21, 1941), 34:722.

[14] For a complete picture of the financial aspects of C.P.S., see Melvin Gingerich, *Service for Peace*, Ch. XXI.

[15] Harold S. Bender, printed letter to ministers in charge of Mennonite congregations, Oct. 30, 1942.

[16] "Concerning the Financial End of Civilian Service," *Gospel Herald* (Oct. 22, 1942), 35:645.

[17] "Report of Peace Problems Committee," *Twenty-third Mennonite General Conference*, Aug. 18-24, 1943.

[18] "Mennonite Civilian Public Service in 1945 and the Work of the Peace Problems Committee," *Mennonite Yearbook* (1946), 12.

[19] *Gospel Herald* (June 10, 1943), 36:224.

[20] *Ibid.* (Jan. 27, 1944), 36:916.

[21] *Report of the Ohio Mennonite and Eastern A.M. Joint Conference* (1943), 24.

[22] *Report of the Missouri-Kansas Conference* (1944), 13, 14.

[23] *Report of the Twenty-second Annual Mennonite Church Conference of the Pacific Coast District* (1943), 9, 10.

[24] *Ibid.*, 4.

[25] *Ibid.* (1944), 6.

[26] N. A. Lind to Mennonite Research Foundation.

[27] *Gospel Herald* (Dec. 16, 1943), 36:793.

[28] *Ibid.* (Nov. 25, 1943), 36:729.

[29] *Ibid.* (Dec. 2, 1943), 36:745.

[30] *Ibid.* (Oct. 28, 1943), 36:652.

Chapter VII

Financial Support of C.P.S. Men
and Their Families

While the M.C.C. provided maintenance and limited medical care for the men in C.P.S., the government paid them no wages for the work which they performed. From one to four years of service without pay, however, was bound to result in considerable need, and in some cases serious need. Besides maintenance, therefore, the M.C.C. also provided small additional allowances which were of some help.[1] In the beginning of the camp program, the amount was $1.50 per month, but this was discontinued in November, 1941. In the meantime local congregations and conferences began to provide small gifts to supplement such savings, personal income, earnings from work after hours, or help from immediate families, as the men in camp may have relied upon for spending money and for the purchase of clothing. Then, beginning January 1, 1944, the M.C.C. provided a monthly credit of $5.00 for each man who was not on a maintenance project which paid a nominal wage, as in the case of mental hospitals. The men were permitted to draw on this fund as they needed it, and those who did not need it were encouraged to contribute it to C.P.S., relief, or to C.P.S. rehabilitation. Men who received a regular monthly allowance of as much as $5.00 from their congregations were not eligible to use the M.C.C. credit. If a man received a monthly allowance of less than $5.00, he received an M.C.C. credit sufficient to bring it up to this amount. The purpose of the credit was to equalize the allowances of the men as much as possible.

As early as March, 1941, two months before the first camp opened, the *Gospel Herald* reported inquiries coming to the M.C.C. from sewing circles, asking what they could do to help equip the boys who would be called into service. In response, the M.C.C. recommended camp kits consisting of a laundry bag containing such items as towels, toilet articles, paper, postage, diary, sewing kit, etc., amounting to a total value of not over $5.00. It was suggested that these kits be given to the men at the "time of departure to camp or in connection with any special service which might be arranged by the congregation," for the men about to leave. These gifts, it was believed, would serve as practical symbols of the congregation's interest in the men, as well as an assurance that they were being remembered in prayer.[2] The M.C.C. also distributed an attractive folder among the women's organizations describing the camp kits. The response to this appeal was very generous.

How early certain congregations first provided regular cash allowances for their men in camp the writer does not know. In January, 1943, however, the chairman of the Peace Problems Committee received a letter from Sam N. Beachy reporting that the Old Order Amish congregations of his community in Illinois were planning to raise funds to help their C.P.S. men with the purchase of clothing, and also to provide something in the way of cash allowances. Beachy inquired whether this procedure would cause any difficulty within the camps, in case other men did not receive similar aid.[3] In April, 1943, the *Gospel Herald* reported the appointment of a Campee Aid Committee, representing the Lancaster Mennonite Conference and the Millwood, Morgantown, and Horning congregations. This committee had visited all of the eastern camps to determine the needs of the men. Two members of the committee traveled to Philadelphia, at their own expense, to purchase clothing, which was then distributed to the camps.[4] On April 7, 1943, the chairman of this committee reported to the Peace Problems Committee: "To date we have bought, paid for, and sent to camps in the East, in which many western brethren are placed, more than $5,000.00 worth . . . goods," including clothing, shoes, gloves, and smaller articles.[5]

On September 9, 1943, the Campee Aid Committee reported that it was contributing to the needs of men in the eastern camps, "irrespective of church or creed so long as they can establish their sincerity and wholehearted co-operation." Offerings were being lifted in the congregations of the Lancaster area. Voluntary donations were coming from other districts. To date $7,500.00 had come into the treasury, of which $7,100.00 had been expended.[6] In response to these efforts, the director of Camp No. 4 at Grottoes, Virginia, wrote that the services of the committee were greatly appreciated by the campers, "both because of the value of the articles given and also because of the manner in which they were given. I have especially appreciated the fact that these gifts have been made to all men regardless of their financial standing or church connection. This has helped a great deal to make the men feel that the C.P.S. program is the concern of the church as a whole, in which both the men in the camp and the church at home have equal concern, and in which we all work co-operatively."[7]

In addition to the aid described above, a number of congregations in the Lancaster Conference sent token gifts to their own members in camp. In some cases these were Christmas gifts, ranging from a few dollars to $15.00 or more each. A few congregations sent their men $5.00 or more per month regularly. Late in 1945 the Lancaster Conference took official action establishing a "Released Campers Aid Fund," which was built up by contributions from individuals, congregations, and Sunday schools. From this fund each C.P.S. man of the Lancaster Conference, following his discharge, was given $10.00 per month for his term of service. Thus a man who spent four years in camp received $480.00 following his release. The total amount of the discharge allowances paid by the Lancaster Conference was $89,926.21. The largest amount paid to any one man was $553.00. Actually these figures represent more than $10.00 per month per man. After all of the men had been paid at this rate, a total of $87,154.21 had been expended, leaving a balance of $2,772.00 in the treasury. This amount was then disposed of by allowing each man a bonus of $11.00, regardless of the length of his service. Thus the man with the highest payment received $542.00 as his $10.00 monthly allowance, plus $11.00 bonus, making a total of $553.00.[8]

The Illinois Conference had a C.P.S. Committee which sent a monthly letter and sermon to all men in service. This committee also received contributions from the churches for a fund from which each C.P.S. man received one gift of $10.00 while in service, and at the time of his discharge $2.00 for each month of service. Thus a man who had been in camp four years received a total of $106.00. These payments represent a conference expenditure of $7,627.00. After these payments were made, a balance of $1,175.83 remained in the treasury which was then distributed among the discharged men, on a pro rata basis, according to their term of service.[9] In addition to this, various congregations of the Illinois Conference reported payments, ranging from annual gifts of an unnamed amount to regular gifts of $5.00 per month. In the minutes of the Pacific Coast Conference we read that its district Mission Board canceled the note of a young man who had been loaned a sum of "students' aid money."[10] Some congregations of this conference reported payments, ranging from token gifts annually to regular payments of $5.00 per month.

In the spring of 1943 the Franconia Conference took official action giving all Franconia men in base camps allowances of $7.50 monthly, and those working in mental hospitals $5.00 per month. It was also decided to pay the traveling expenses, from camp to the home community and return, of men attending communion services in their home churches. Besides this, the conference paid certain medical expenses of its men in camp. In midsummer, 1945, the Franconia Conference took action providing for further C.P.S. allowances, on a graduated scale, at the time of discharge. The complete plan provided for a total gift of $90.00 to each man for his first year in camp. This was the $7.50 per month received currently, and referred to above. For the second year he was to receive $90.00 ($7.50 per month currently), plus 25 cents for each working day, counting 283 days per year. The latter amount was paid at the time of discharge. For the third year the Franconia men received $90.00, plus 50 cents per working day; for the fourth year, $90.00, plus $1.00 for each working day. In making the final settlement with each man, the sum of the monthly allowances mailed to him while in camp was deducted from the total amount due. Amounts paid for communion fares and medical expenses were not deducted.[11] Thus a man from the Franconia Conference who spent four full years in camp received a total of $784.50 from the conference, with possible additional amounts for communion fares and medical expenses. Reports from congregations indicate that in some cases there were additional gifts from Sunday-school classes, once a year or even oftener.

As early as 1943 the Virginia Conference appointed a C.P.S. Support Committee, which in 1944 was reorganized on a conference-wide basis. In January, 1944, the committee began paying monthly allowances to Virginia men in camp, the money being contributed by the congregations on a quota basis. In November, 1945, it took steps to make retroactive payments to men who had been in camp before 1944. By the close of C.P.S. the Virginia men had received from their conference $60.00 for their first year in a base camp, and $7.50 per month for the remainder of the time spent in a base camp. Men in detached service had received $15.00 per year. In addition to this, the committee established a discharge benefit fund, raising this money also by congregational offerings on a quota basis. From this fund, discharge allowances were paid on the following plan: For the first year in camp, no allowance; for the second year, $7.40 per month; for the third year, $10.00 per month; and for the entire time after the third year, $12.50 per month. By this plan a Virginia C.P.S. man who served four full years in a base camp received a total of $688.80 from his conference. The report of the C.P.S. Support Committee, June 1, 1947, shows that the committee had received in offerings from the congregations a total of $35,790.92. Of this amount, $12,379.77 was disbursed in the form of monthly allowances; $16,479.53 in discharge allowances; and $5,490.00 in dependency allowances. A small amount, $453.00 was used for student aid.[12]

Reports from those congregations in Iowa and Nebraska which responded to the questionnaire of the Mennonite Research Foundation indicate that in most cases there were at least token gifts, either by the congregation officially, or by members of the congregation individually. The conference itself, however, took no action in this matter. One congregation reports gifts of $10.00 per year; another $5.00 per month. One report says the congregation as such presented no gifts, but that members of the congregation did. The Wellman congregation gave its men $10.00 each year while in camp; then $100.00 at the time of discharge. The Wayland congregation gave its men $25.00 a year currently, to assist in the purchase of work clothing, plus a discharge allowance amounting to $200.00 for each year of service after the first. This allowance was comparable to that received by men from the Lancaster, Franconia, and Virginia conferences.[13]

Reports from the Indiana-Michigan Conference tell a similar story. Some congregations apparently did nothing. Some gave token gifts of $5.00 per year. The Forks and Kouts congregations report an allowance of $120.00 per year to each man. The Yellow Creek congregation reports a yearly gift by the literary and Sunday school; then at the time of discharge a sum which equaled $5.00 per month of service. The Nappanee congregation reports $5.00 per month. The most generous allowance reported is that of the Salem congregation which paid $180.00 per year currently to men in base camps, beginning about 1943, and a discharge allowance amounting to $6.00 per month per man for the entire period spent in C.P.S., plus transportation to and from home during times of furlough. A note in the *Gospel Herald* reports the Young People's Fellowship of the North Goshen congregation as sponsoring a potato-raising project in 1942. The proceeds of this project were sent to C.P.S. men, apparently to men of that congregation.[14]

In the Ohio and Eastern A.M. Conference some congregations do not report any gifts to their men. Some report $5.00 per year; one congregation reports $40.00 per year; several $5.00 per month. The Pike congregation of Elida, Ohio, reports gifts of $180.00 per year. The Central congregation, Archbold, reports discharge allowances totaling $16,519.34, with $511.65 as the highest amount going to any one man. The Oak Grove-Pleasant Hill congregation, Smithville, reports total gifts of $5,570.00 to its men in camp, besides $252.25 for medical service. Since this congregation had seventeen men in C.P.S., the average amount received per man for personal support was over $327.00, plus medical allowances. The method of distribution is not stated in the report. This congregation also reports contributions of $4,325.25 for the support of dependents of C.P.S. men, and $17,901.30 for the general support of the C.P.S. program. Thus the total contribution by this congregation for the support of the C.P.S. program, the men and their dependents, during the second World War, was $28,048.80.[15]

The congregations of the South Central Conference range from those who report no gifts to those who report regular monthly gifts to C.P.S. men. The Pleasant Valley congregation, near Harper, Kansas, reports gifts of $90.00 per year; La Junta, Colorado, $10.00 per month; Mt. Zion of Versailles, Missouri, and West Liberty, near Windom, Kansas, report $150.00 per year each.[16] Reports from the Southwestern Pennsylvania Conference are much the same. Some congregations report nothing. Some report unspecified amounts several times a year. Others report $5.00 per month, either currently, or at the time of discharge. The Pinto congregation reports $5.00 per month currently, plus $100.00 per year of service at the time of discharge.[17] The Conservative Amish Mennonite churches represent a similar range, from no report to $10.00 per year, and $180.00 per year. One congregation at Harrisburg, Oregon, reports a graduated discharge allowance, providing $10.00 per month for the first year in camp, $12.00 per month for the second year, $14.00 for the third, and $16.00 per month for the fourth year in C.P.S.[18]

The Canadian congregations responding to the questionnaire report only token current gifts to their men. One minister says, "The sending of gifts was mostly by the families directly concerned. Since our boys all received food and lodging and fifty cents per day from the government, the sending of gifts was not nearly so necessary."[19] Both the Ontario and Alberta-Saskatchewan conferences, however, received offerings for a fund from which their men were given allowances on the basis of the number of months spent in Alternative Service Camps. In both cases apparently the payments were made following discharge. In the Ontario Conference this applied only to men who served in camp more than five months. The conference report of 1945 shows a total of $3,025.93 thus distributed to the men.[20]

Under the Canadian Alternative Service Work system, conscientious objectors could be assigned either to government camps or to work for private individuals on farms or in factories. Men working on farms received board and room and $25.00 per month for themselves. Earnings beyond this point were withheld and given to the Canadian Red Cross. Men assigned to industrial work paid their own board and room, and then made payments to the Red Cross on a graduated scale, depending on the amount of their monthly earnings. Under this plan a man who earned more than $75.00 and not over $90.00 per month, paid $3.00 monthly to the Red Cross; while a man earning $131.00 to $140.00 paid $25.00 monthly; and a man earning more than $180.00 paid $50.00 monthly to the Red Cross. The total allocation to the Red Cross, from the wages of men in the Ontario Conference assigned to Alternative Service Work, was over $90,000.00, possibly as much as $100,000.00.[21] The Alberta-Saskatchewan Conference reports the establishment of a fund which it used to remunerate its men for one half of the amount which they paid to the Red Cross under the above plan.[22]

SUPPORT OF DEPENDENTS

When the United States entered the war, and Selective Service began to induct large numbers of married men who would remain in service for a long time, the church was confronted with the problem of caring for the dependents of these married men. This was a new problem, and the entire M.C.C. constituency was a bit slow in taking hold of it in an effective way. On May 30, 1942, the M.C.C. passed a resolution declaring it to be "the responsibility of the church to provide aid for needy dependents of men in C.P.S. camps who cannot be cared for by their families, and that assurance should be given to men facing the draft that the church will provide for this need to the utmost of its ability."[23] The M.C.C. believed, however, that the inducted man himself should provide for the maintenance of his wife and children as much as possible. After that his immediate family and circle of relatives should be considered responsible. Then, if need still remained, the local congregation should be considered responsible; after that the conference, and finally the M.C.C. itself.

Apparently the M.C.C. assumed its own task to be chiefly that of a clearing agency, seeing that cases of need would be brought to the attention of proper church officials. If there had never been more than a small number of dependency cases, this assumption would perhaps have been warranted. In most cases wives without children were able to work and provide for themselves. As soon as there were large numbers of wives with children, however, the situation was different, and it became apparent that the church could not perform its part effectively with the responsibility thrown entirely upon the local congregation. In December, 1943, the Peace Problems Committee of the Mennonite Church mailed a printed letter to all ordained men of the church. This letter was entitled, "A Message Concerning the Support of Dependents of Mennonite Men in C.P.S. Camps." It stated the facts of the dependency situation, and urged

that the local ministry be awake to the problem of dependency and *find out in advance* what the needs may be. We urge that an investigation be made at once of possible cases of need, and that brethren subject to draft be assured that their dependents would be provided for in case assistance is needed . . . . We urge that definite plans be made to provide for needy cases . . . that the congregation be made aware of its obligations . . . that the entire matter of dependency be treated as a matter of Christian duty . . . . We recommend that in case the burden becomes too great for the local congregations, the conference be asked for assistance. The Relief Committee of the Mission Board stands ready to help and will act in any cases submitted to it by the proper local or conference church authorities.

The appeal was stated urgently enough, but it did not bring the desired results. Dependency was a church-wide problem almost as much as was C.P.S. itself, and needed to be managed as such. Some congregations had many cases of dependency; others had few or none. Congregations also varied greatly in the extent to which they sensed the need and responded to it. This is illustrated by the varied manner in which they provided personal allowances for their men. It was only those conferences which took official action as conferences, and which had a workable plan with an organization to carry it out, that had effective programs of support universally applied.

Placing the responsibility for dependency support upon the congregation was also bound to result in inequities. By December, 1940, five months before any man had been called to C.P.S., the M.C.C. had changed its original plan of having each congregation finance the cost of keeping its own men in camp. To avoid inequities the quota system was adopted and each congregation was asked to raise its share of the quota. If this had not been done, the financial aspect of C.P.S. would likely have run into serious difficulty in its early stages. The dependency problem was similar in character, with this difference, however: A man's leaving for camp was something which everyone could see and be sure of, whereas the status of a bank account, or of other means for the support of a family, were less certain. In some cases this uncertainty brought a temptation to accept military service in order to obtain government support for the drafted man's family. When church leaders saw this happening, they began earnestly to seek a more satisfactory solution for the dependency problem.

In September, 1943, the M.C.C. appointed a committee to study the question. In February, 1944, the general director of M.C.C.-C.P.S. reported that "out of a group of 44 assignments for March whose questionnaires we have, there are 38 children and 19 wives listed as dependents. Of this total of 57 dependents, 41 dependents are Mennonites." Melvin Gingerich estimates that as early as September, 1943, "there were at least 690 wives, 198 children, and 140 other dependents of men in Mennonite C.P.S."[24] Finally on March 17, 18, 1944, the M.C.C. took action setting up a dependency support program with sufficient organization to make it effective. A basic principle approved at this time was stated as follows: "We consider all those dependents entitled to aid who cannot or ought not undertake to support themselves, excluding only those who have sufficient regular income for self-support. Those who can work are to be encouraged to support themselves."

Under this program each constituent group was still expected to provide the funds to care for its own dependents. A uniform schedule of dependency allowances was adopted, however, which the various groups were expected to follow. By this schedule a wife or dependent adult not in a position to support herself was to receive a regular current allowance of $25.00 per month, and each dependent child $10.00 per month. In cases of special need, special allowances might be granted. Under this plan the M.C.C. provided the entire administration of the program. It distributed dependency status forms to directors of C.P.S. camps and to ministers in local congregations, who were responsible to see that all C.P.S. men and prospective C.P.S. men received copies. These forms were then to be filed with the M.C.C., stating whether or not there were needs, and whether they were being met. Each case was then processed by the M.C.C. office, or by the man's own group, as previously agreed upon.

The Peace Problems Committee asked the Relief Committee of the Mennonite Board of Missions and Charities to raise the necessary funds and to administer the dependency program for its constituency, in coordination with the work of other groups, through the M.C.C. The Relief Committee accepted this assignment on March 18, 1944, and agreed:

(1) that provision be made on a church-wide basis; (2) that the work be undertaken at once; (3) that all congregations be asked to make a contribution for this purpose equal to a fifty cents per member allotment at this time; (4)

that dependency allowances be paid by E. C. Bender, treasurer, on the following basis: for a needy wife or adult dependent who cannot support herself, $25.00 per month; for each dependent child, $10.00 per month; (5) that each case be decided on the basis of a dependency report to be filled out by each man now in C.P.S. or about to be drafted; (6) that special provision be made for abnormal or emergency needs; (7) that local supplementary allowances by congregations be permissible where needed.[25]

By this action the Mennonite Church assumed the responsibility for supporting the dependents of its own C.P.S. men, raising the money by the quota plan. The Relief Committee asked the congregations for an initial offering of 50 cents per member to provide the funds, and began paying allowances as of April 1, 1944. By March 31, the committee had received 260 dependency status reports. Seventy of these had been approved for allowances, while 190 did not require any assistance.[26] By March 31, 1945, the committee had received more than $45,000.00 in contributions for C.P.S. dependency, and disbursed a total of $42,649.35. This represented a quota of about 50 cents per member per quarter for 1944, and 25 cents per member per month for 1945. On the above date approximately 130 cases were receiving dependency allowances through the Relief Committee.[27] From April 1, 1945, to March 31, 1946, the monthly quota continued at 25 cents per member. During the year the total amount of dependency allowances paid was $74,406.56, with a high mark of about $7,500.00 in the month of February, 1946. The maximum number of cases receiving the allowance in any one month was about 250.

In making its annual report, as of March 31, 1946, the Relief Committee said: "We have had many expressions of appreciation from the C.P.S. men and their families for this dependency aid, and feel that this was one of the most rewarding forms of relief carried on by the church during the past year."[28] By March 31, 1946, the discharge of C.P.S. men with dependents had already begun, and during the next six months it was practically completed. During the fiscal year April 1, 1946, to March 31, 1947, the receipts of the Relief Committee for dependency aid were only $28,612.83, and the disbursements were $13,285.10. At the end of the fiscal year an unused balance of $15,200.14 remained in the dependency fund. This was then used for C.P.S. students' aid through the Mennonite Board of Education.[29] Thus during the three years that the program was in operation, the Relief Committee paid allowances to dependents of C.P.S. men totaling $130,341.01.

It should be noted here, however, that the dependency funds administered by the Elkhart office of the Mission Board did not cover all of the C.P.S. dependency cases of the Mennonite Church. Four district conferences, Lancaster, Franconia, Virginia, and Washington-Franklin, raised their own funds and made payments out of their own treasuries. In addition, the congregations of Fulton County, Ohio, in the Ohio and Eastern A.M. Conference, operated their own dependency fund, and did not participate in the program under the Relief Committee. The Central congregation, Archbold, reported a total of $2,061.55 in dependency payments. On March 6, 1944, the Franconia Conference decided to grant dependent wives and children $25.00 and $10.00 per month, following the pattern of the M.C.C. and the Mennonite Relief Committee. These allowances were to be paid out of the conference treasury. In case the standard allowance was insufficient in specific cases, the local congregation was expected to provide additional funds.[30] The total amount of dependency payments by the Franconia Conference was $3,440.00.

In the Virginia Conference dependency allowances were administered through the C.P.S. Support Committee, which also administered personal allowances to C.P.S. men, both currently and at the time of discharge. When the Support Committee received the completed dependency status reports which had been distributed by the M.C.C., the families involved were "usually contacted to determine their wishes with reference to assuming some part of such support." General willingness was found on the part of families to assume such responsibility, "to the extent that they are reasonably able." The final report of the Support Committee shows total dependency allowance payments of $5,490.00.[31] The total amount of dependency allowances paid in the Lancaster Conference is difficult to determine, since the work was administered on a congregational basis, payments being made by the deacons. The conference does not seem to have collected the figures and totaled them. The Ontario Conference also had a dependency fund from which $468.80 was disbursed up to June 1, 1943. For the year 1944-45 the conference reported an unused balance of $344.37 in the dependency fund, which was then transferred to the equalization fund from which allowances were paid to men discharged from Alternative Service camps.[32]

MEDICAL CARE

A special phase of the C.P.S. support program was that of medical care for the men and their dependents. It was stated at the beginning of this chapter that the M.C.C. provided limited care for the men in camp. Actually, however, once the M.C.C. policy was fully developed, this came to include practically all medical and surgical needs of men who had been in camp one year or longer. This subject is treated more fully in Gingerich, *Service for Peace*, Chapter XXI. Expenses not covered by this plan, as well as medical and surgical expenses of dependents, had to be provided by other means. Unusual expenses, which the C.P.S. man or his family should not reasonably have been expected to pay, were generally met by the local congregation, and in some cases by the Mennonite Relief Committee, or even the M.C.C.

C.P.S. REHABILITATION

After C.P.S. had continued for several years, it was also realized that some of the men would need assistance in making the adjustment to civilian life following their discharge. In order to approach this problem in an intelligent manner, J. Winfield Fretz, then a member of the M.C.C. staff, was asked to make a study of C.P.S. rehabilitation needs. This study was begun June 1, 1943. On March 7, 1944, the M.C.C. established a Mennonite Aid Section, and on October 13, 1944, Fretz reported his findings to the new organization. He reported that 43 per cent of the men would need financial assistance from some source in order to get started in their lifework. He suggested that the Aid Section establish a counseling service, prepare a list of available employment situations in Mennonite communities, give guidance to local congregations in the development of mutual aid plans, and provide a plan of financial aid for those C.P.S. men whose own groups did not make such provision.

As early as February 9, 1944, however, the M.C.C. had agreed on the principle that primary responsibility for rehabilitation assistance should rest with the constituent groups, and not with the M.C.C. itself. The latter would gather the necessary information, and serve as a clearing agency for all of the groups, but would undertake actual assistance only in cases where this was not being done by a constituent group. At the 1945 annual meeting of the M.C.C. it was reported that at least eight of its constituent groups had made plans to help their own men. A year later it was reported "that by far the largest number of men would be able to establish themselves or be established by their own congregations or conference groups." As a result, the actual amount of direct financial aid by the M.C.C. for rehabilitation purposes was slight.[33]

In the Mennonite Church there was official discussion of the rehabilitation problem as early as April 10, 1943. On that date the Committee on Industrial Relations sponsored a meeting of thirty-five church leaders to consider the effect of current economic and social trends on the life of the church. One of the questions considered at this meeting was: "What can we do for our young men upon returning from the C.P.S. camps to help establish them in the life and work of our Mennonite communities?" At the close of the day the "sense of the meeting" was summarized by one of the members of the Committee on Industrial Relations as follows: "(1) Our old and century-long Mennonite ways of living are breaking up. New patterns are being set. (2) The present war is hastening this change and adding new elements, through C.P.S., and perhaps in other ways. (3) In this changing situation the church means to go along with its members to help where in conscience it needs to and can do so." The following three questions were then presented for consideration:

(1) Can we assume that the Committee on Industrial Relations is a study and policy recommending committee, and not an administrative organization? (2) Should we recommend to General Conference the formulation of plans, and the setting up of an organization, or the designation of an organization now in existence, to qualify to serve capital, credit, and financial counseling needs? (3) Should we recommend special attention to the rehabilitation of C.P.S. men?

The presentation of these questions was then followed by a general discussion and a resolution: "That it is the sense of this meeting that we encourage the Committee on Industrial Relations to continue its work on this problem and bring recommendations to General Conference."[34] At the 1943 General Conference the Committee on Industrial Relations then recommended the organization of a capital, credit, and financial counseling service, under the auspices of the Mission Board, to serve the needs of discharged C.P.S. men and others who might need help. General Conference approved the general idea, but believed a better plan of organization could be found. The committee was then asked to study the matter further and, if possible, to find this better plan.

Following this instruction from General Conference, the Stewardship Committee, the Committee on Industrial Relations, and the Peace Problems Committee gave much thought to the problem at hand. On December 4, 1943, they presented to the Interboard Committee and to the Executive Committee of General Conference a plan for the organization of a new church board to be known as Mennonite Mutual Aid. This plan was then approved in principle, after which the Executive Committee appointed a committee to draw up plans for the organization and incorporation of Mennonite Mutual Aid, and to present these plans to the district conferences and to General Conference for approval. The plans were drawn up and published in the *Gospel Herald* on April 14, 1944. In August, 1944, General Conference approved them; in course of time various district conferences did likewise.

General Conference then appointed a Board of Directors who completed the incorporation proceedings for the new organization on July 19, 1945. The purposes of Mennonite Mutual Aid and its methods of operation were explained in an article in the *Gospel Herald* of September 28, 1945. The article outlined a series of services which it ultimately hoped to provide. The immediate objective, however, was "assisting C.P.S. men who need help in establishing a home and/or a livelihood on discharge." A chief feature of this assistance was to be a counseling service. Capital for the making of loans to individuals was to be obtained through gifts and loans to Mennonite Mutual Aid. These loans might be made through the purchase of participation certificates, preferred certificates, or debenture notes.

The first loans by Mennonite Mutual Aid were approved on December 14, 1945, and the first loan check was issued on January 7, 1946. By

December 31, 1948, a total of $124,564.00 had been loaned to eighty-one C.P.S. men, the average loan being a little less than $1,538.00.[35] These loans were granted for a variety of purposes, such as the purchase of homes, business, livestock, farm equipment, trucks, autos, and for the payment of educational expenses. The average time spent in C.P.S. by these eighty-one men was thirty-six months. In certain cases where application was made to Mennonite Mutual Aid, the actual loan was granted by the Mennonite Board of Education, using its endowment funds. This was true especially of larger real estate loans. In some cases, where the application was for a project which seemed financially unsound or spiritually unwise, Mennonite Mutual Aid advised against the undertaking. Nevertheless, even though the times were "prosperous" and employment was easy to find, Mennonite Mutual Aid, as stated above, made loans to eighty-one men, totaling $124,564.00. It should be remembered, however, that this figure represents only a small portion of the total C.P.S. rehabilitation picture. The majority of men were able to obtain such financial assistance as they needed, either from members of their own families, from friends, or from local banks. In some instances aid was obtained from local congregations, and even from district conferences. The total amount of rehabilitation loans from these various sources would be very difficult to ascertain.

EDUCATIONAL GRANTS-IN-AID

An important special phase of C.P.S. rehabilitation was the assistance given to men continuing their education after discharge from camp. In December, 1945, the Mennonite Aid Section of the M.C.C. reported that "a rehabilitation program for C.P.S. men wanting to continue their education on the academy or college level has been worked out by a sub-committee of the Aid Section and the Council of Mennonite and Affiliated Colleges."[36] The plan provided that liberal scholarships or grants-in-aid be granted to ex-C.P.S. men in Mennonite colleges, the cost of the same to be shared by the colleges and the M.C.C., or its constituent bodies. Within the Mennonite Church it was then agreed that funds to be used for this purpose should be raised through the Relief Committee of the Mennonite Board of Missions and Charities, which had also been responsible for raising C.P.S. and C.P.S. dependency funds. In April, 1947, when C.P.S. had come to a close, the Mission Board treasury had a balance of $7,697.11 in the C.P.S. fund, and $15,374.39 in the C.P.S. dependency fund.[37] The Peace Problems Committee then took action to hold these amounts as the beginning of a fund, to be transferred to the Mennonite Board of Education for the use of Goshen, Hesston, and Eastern Mennonite colleges, as needed, for the payment of grants-in-aid to ex-C.P.S. men for as many college months as they had spent months in C.P.S., with twenty-seven months as a maximum.

7

To be eligible for this grant, a man was required to enter college within eighteen months of his discharge, and to complete his training within five years of his discharge. In special cases, such as men serving in relief work following discharge from C.P.S., the time limit described above was to become effective following the end of the relief assignment instead of following the discharge from C.P.S. The college announcements also stated that the issuance of the grants-in-aid was not automatic, but conditioned upon the availability of funds to provide for the grants. At the beginning of the program the grant-in-aid allowed by Goshen College was $100.00 per semester per man. Later it was raised to $110.00 per semester, which amount was still being granted in the academic year 1948-49. The 1949 catalog of Eastern Mennonite College announced exactly the same discount, or $220.00 per year. At Hesston, in the beginning, the C.P.S. grant-in-aid was $95.00 per semester. The amount was increased from time to time, however, the catalog for 1949-50 announcing the discount at $120.00 per semester.

This program meant that ex-C.P.S. men who were students in the three colleges of the Mennonite Church received about the equivalent of free tuition for a maximum of twenty-seven months each. Furthermore, this money was provided by the church through the Mennonite Relief Committee. The original amount received from the surplus of C.P.S. and C.P.S. dependency funds in the Elkhart treasury was increased as needed, from time to time, through contributions from the general relief fund of the Mission Board. For several years the Board had maintained a goal of fifty cents per member per month for the various C.P.S. and relief needs. With the close of C.P.S. this same goal was maintained for a time, and in this way both the relief and ex-C.P.S. educational needs of the church were met without any contributions from the church specifically designated for the latter purpose. The total number of ex-C.P.S. men receiving grants-in-aid from the three schools, Goshen, Hesston, and E.M.C., for the entire period 1946-50, was 240. The total amount of these grants-in-aid was $79,732.06, of which amount $66,616.39 was paid to the colleges by the Mission Board treasury at Elkhart.[38]

Ex-C.P.S. students who were not members of the Mennonite Church also received the regular C.P.S. grant-in-aid, although in this case the colleges, and not the church, provided the funds. It will also be recalled, as mentioned earlier in this chapter, that the Lancaster, Franconia, and Virginia conferences provided rather generous allowances to their C.P.S. men, both currently and at the time of discharge. These allowances, together with additional help frequently given their men, in themselves constituted a rehabilitation program. For this reason these eastern conferences did not share officially in the provision of funds for educational grants-in-aid, through the Relief Committee of the Mission Board at Elkhart. Generally speaking, it was also true that the Mennonite Board of Education did not award funds for grants-in-aid for men from these conferences. It is obvious that the ex-C.P.S. grants-in-aid, from whatever source received, covered only a portion of the student's total expenses. The student was required to provide the remainder himself, although the colleges were generous in providing opportunities for them to earn as much of this as possible. Colleges of the other Mennonite groups followed a similar plan for aiding their students who were ex-C.P.S. men.

NOTES AND CITATIONS

1 For a complete account of the M.C.C. allowance, medical, and dependency policy, see Melvin Gingerich, *Service for Peace*, Ch. XXI.

2 "Relief Notes" in *Gospel Herald* (March 13, 1941), 33:1069.

3 Sam N. Beachy to Harold S. Bender (Jan. 24, 1943), in P.P.C. correspondence.

4 M. R. Kraybill, "The Campee Aid Committee," *Gospel Herald* (April 1, 1943), 36:11.

5 Aaron H. Weaver to Harold S. Bender (April 7, 1943), in P.P.C. correspondence.

6 Aaron H. Weaver, "Campee Aid Committee," *Gospel Herald* (Sept. 9, 1943), 36:506ff. According to Harry E. Sauder, the treasurer, the total amount of contributions to the Campee Aid Fund by the various churches in the Lancaster area at the end of C.P.S. was $32,673.76.

7 "Appreciation for Aid to Campers," *Gospel Herald* (March 2, 1944), 36:1037.

8 Amos S. Horst, personal interview; reports of ministers to Mennonite Research Foundation; letter from Landis H. Brubaker, treasurer of the Camp Committee of the Lancaster Conference.

9 *Report of the Illinois Mennonite Church Conference and Associated Meetings* (1945-47), 18, 19.

10 *Report of the Twenty-fourth Annual Mennonite Church Conference of the Pacific Coast District* (June 5-7, 1946), 13.

11 Jacob M. Moyer, excerpts from minutes of the Peace Problems Committee of the Franconia Conference.

12 Typewritten report of the C.P.S. Support Committee, in files of the Peace Problems Committee.

13 Reports of congregations in the files of the Mennonite Research Foundation.

14 *Ibid; Gospel Herald* (Jan. 28, 1943), 35:937.

15 Reports of congregations in files of Mennonite Research Foundation.

16 *Ibid.*

17 *Ibid.*

18 *Ibid.*

19 Oscar Burkholder, *ibid.*

20 *Calendar of Appointments, Mennonite Church of Ontario* (1945-46), 31.

21 Report of Jesse B. Martin to the author.

22 Report of the Alberta-Saskatchewan Conference (1944). Also letter of Abram Reist in response to questionnaire of Mennonite Research Foundation.

23 See "Policy Regarding Cases of Dependency of Men in C.P.S.," *Gospel Herald* (Nov. 4, 1943), 36:667.

24 Melvin Gingerich, *Service for Peace*, 351.

25 "C.P.S. Dependency Needs," *Gospel Herald* (March 30, 1944), 36:1114.

26 *Report of the Annual Meeting of the Mennonite Board of Missions and Charities* (1944), 13.

27 *Ibid.* (1945), 15, 61.

28 *Ibid.* (1946), 23, 66.

[29] *Ibid.* (1947), 18, 77.

[30] Excerpts from records of the Franconia Peace Problems Committee, March 6, 1944.

[31] Report of Virginia C.P.S. Support Committee to Mennonite Research Foundation.

[32] *Calendar of Appointments of the Mennonite Church of Ontario* (1943-44), 22; (1945-46), 31.

[33] For a fuller discussion of this phase of the subject see Melvin Gingerich, *Service for Peace,* 352-55.

[34] Minutes of the Committee on Industrial Relations, April 10, 1943.

[35] Report of the secretary-treasurer of Mennonite Mutual Aid.

[36] M.C.C. Annual Report (1945).

[37] Report of H. Ernest Bennett, assistant treasurer, to the author.

[38] Statistics provided by the colleges and the treasurer of the Mennonite Board of Education.

Chapter VIII

Spiritual Ministry to C.P.S. Men

The church's major concern in the C.P.S. program was that there should be adequate opportunity for the cultivation of the social, intellectual, and spiritual life of the men engaged in government service. During working hours the campers were under the direction of the government technical staff. During the remainder of the time, however, they were responsible to the camp director and his assistants, who received their appointment from the M.C.C. Under the leadership of this staff, a religious and educational program was developed in all of the camps. This program, with its strengths and its weaknesses, is described in Gingerich, *Service for Peace*, Chapters XVIII to XX. The present chapter merely attempts to show what contribution the Mennonite Church made to that program.

RELIGIOUS LEADERSHIP IN THE CAMPS

Soon after the first M.C.C. camp was opened at Grottoes, Virginia, the church papers reported that "the Advisory Committee of six, representing the various groups of our Mennonite constituency, met with the staff . . . in order that they might see the camp and be informed of plans for its administration and in order to enlist their counsel on various problems of camp administration which concern both the boys and the church."[1] Each of the base camps had such an Advisory Committee which met with the staff from time to time to give counsel on spiritual and other matters. In the eastern part of the United States, the services of the Grottoes Advisory Committee were later extended to include all base camps in Virginia, Pennsylvania, and Maryland. In the early history of C.P.S. it was also the policy to appoint ministers as camp directors. These men were expected to serve not only as camp administrators, but also as spiritual leaders of the men. The first seven directors appointed by the M.C.C. were ministers.

After the United States entered the war, however, and the number of inductions increased, directors were chosen chiefly from the ranks of the campers. In course of time very few, if any, camp directors were ministers. It was evident therefore that further provision for the pastoral leadership of the camps was needed. Beginning July 1, 1943, Titus Books of the Brethren in Christ Church gave full-time pastoral service to four eastern camps, Sideling Hill, Hagerstown, Luray, and Grottoes. Beginning March 11, 1945, Newton Weber shared the pastoral work of the eastern camps and units with Books, being chiefly responsible for the hospital units. B. Charles Hostetter later shared this responsibility with

Weber, although both of these ministers discontinued their services in the summer of 1946. In some of the western camps a number of ministers from other Mennonite groups, including A. Warkentin, J. M. Regier, William Unruh, T. A. van der Smissen, and perhaps others, gave brief terms of pastoral service. Similar short terms of service were given in eastern camps by E. W. Kulp, P. L. Frey, and Harry Shetler of the Mennonite Church. These were only brief terms of service, however, and were not sufficient to meet the need.

PASTORAL MINISTRY

The M.C.C. took the attitude that each Mennonite group should, as much as possible, assume the pastoral oversight of its own men. In the Mennonite Church this responsibility was assumed by the Peace Problems Committee which, in October, 1942, appointed Harry A. Diener, D. A. Yoder, Amos S. Horst, and John E. Lapp as a special C.P.S. Pastoral Committee to be responsible for a systematic plan of keeping in personal touch with all members of the Mennonite Church in the camps. To this group were added two Amish bishops, Eli J. Bontreger and Ira Nissley. At a meeting of the Peace Problems Committee in Lancaster, Pennsylvania, on October 30, 1942, the details of the program were arranged. Camps and units assigned to Amos S. Horst were: Sideling Hill, Luray, Howard, Hagerstown, and Staunton. Assigned to John E. Lapp were: Grottoes, Galax, Beltsville, Wilmington, Marlboro, Norristown, and Crestview. D. A. Yoder's assignments were: Marietta, Medaryville, Denison, Weeping Water, Hill City, Belton, and the Dodge County, Wisconsin, farm unit. Harry A. Diener's assignments were: Colorado Springs, Fort Collins, Camino, North Fork, Downey, and Lapine. Eli Bontreger and Ira Nissley were to visit all Old Order Amish boys in M.C.C. camps. Horst, Lapp, Yoder, and Diener were also to include the Old Order Mennonite boys in their ministry. The minutes of the Peace Problems Committee state the purpose of the Pastoral Committee to be the bringing of "a spiritual ministry to the individual campees, to strengthen the bond with the home congregation and the church in general, and to assist campees in dealing with their personal problems." The work was to begin at once, and all camps and units were to be visited by March 1, 1943.[2]

These pastoral visits were carried out as planned. Harry A. Diener submitted periodic reports during the course of his itinerary, and a summary report at the close. He preached in the various camps in the western territory and had personal interviews with those men who were members of the Mennonite Church, and to some extent with others also. At some places he had private quarters for conducting his interviews; at others he found it necessary to interview the men wherever he could find them, which was not very satisfactory. Diener's reports manifested special concern for the smaller units, like the side camps, and the mental hospital unit at Provo, Utah, which found it difficult to maintain organized religious services. At one of the smaller units there seemed to be no special effort to meet the spiritual needs of the men. Some of the larger camps which did have an organized religious program, nevertheless seemed lacking in spiritual tone, attendance at meetings, and the general interest of the men not being what one would expect. At Downey, Idaho, for example, "many of the men freely expressed themselves that they felt their spiritual life had been strengthened while in camp; others frankly said that they were failing in their Christian life."[3]

It is evident from Diener's reports that the absence of a resident pastoral ministry was to a great extent responsible for what was lacking in the spiritual life of the camps. He gave a favorable report on the camp at Lapine, Oregon, where Sunday school was well attended, and the morning worship service still better, "with good interest and a fine response." Other spiritual services seemed to be much appreciated, and "the whole camp carries a good spiritual tone which one very soon senses." A partial explanation of this favorable situation is found in Diener's statement that the Mennonite congregations near Albany, Oregon, were making a real contribution to the life of the camp by sending a minister to the camp at least once a month.[4] In reporting on the California camps, Diener said: "As in the case of Downey, Idaho, the distance of these camps from any Mennonite churches was a spiritual handicap."[5] Both in his periodic reports, and in his summary report, Diener stressed the need for continued pastoral visitation in the western camps. "One director says we cannot have visitors too often. Others would like to have them once a month if possible."[6]

John E. Lapp also submitted rather detailed reports of his pastoral visits in the eastern camps. With the help of other ministers he held week-end Bible conferences at Grottoes and Galax. Lapp spent a week at each of these camps, and apparently interviewed each man in camp personally, regardless of denominational affiliation. While he reported the religious situation at these two camps as very encouraging, Lapp's reports, like those of Diener, emphasized the lack of pastoral oversight in C.P.S. camps, especially in the hospital and other smaller units. At the Bowie, Maryland, unit, which was administered co-operatively by the Friends, the Brethren, and the Mennonites, there was no provision for a Mennonite type of meeting. At the request of some of the men, Lapp attempted to remedy this matter somewhat by arranging for a weekly Bible class to be conducted by Ray Shenk of Cottage City.

At the Norristown, Pennsylvania, hospital unit, Lapp found a lack of group life, with a divided interest, very few meetings, and some of the men attending questionable amusements in the city. This situation, he felt, was due in part to the lack of a suitable meeting place for the unit members. He proposed to the unit a plan for regular weekly or biweekly meetings, with a minister present each time. The unit leadership was slow in acting, however, so that Lapp felt the Peace Problems

Committee or the M.C.C. should exercise some initiative in the matter. Lapp also mentioned a degree of dissatisfaction on the part of some of the men. In some cases this was due to financial problems, especially in the case of men having dependents. All in all, however, this report revealed a situation which could have been greatly helped by the presence of a resident pastor.[7]

At the Marlboro, New Jersey, hospital unit, Lapp found an interested group of men who were asking for spiritual help. They felt that they were not adequately supplied with literature, especially church periodicals, even expressing the feeling that the church was not doing as well as the Fellowship of Reconciliation in this respect. "This group wants more services. They are deserving and should have a minister to conduct services for them weekly. Someone should be with them for spiritual counsel and guidance." At Farnhurst, Delaware, Lapp found a hospital unit which had had only four preaching services in five months' time. "They tried to conduct services amongst themselves, but found they had nothing to talk about because they are together every day and talk about everything they know then." The report mentioned a number of other undesirable conditions at Farnhurst, and then said: "This group should not be blamed for this condition. The church is responsible for not supplying the spiritual guidance they stand in need of . . . ." In the summary report of his pastoral visitation experience, Lapp asked whether arrangements should not be made whereby each hospital unit would have a minister assigned to it as its regular pastor. He also raised the question of how best to provide pastoral care for those who were going into detached farm service.[8]

The pastoral reports of Harry A. Diener and John E. Lapp to the Peace Problems Committee were complete and detailed. Apparently Amos S. Horst and D. A. Yoder did not report very fully. Eli J. Bontreger and Ira Nissley who visited the Old Order Amish boys in the various camps, however, made a lengthy report, as did Elmer G. Swartzendruber of Wellman, Iowa, who made similar visits to members of the Conservative A.M. Church. In his tour of western camps, Swartzendruber was accompanied part of the time by M. S. Zehr of Pigeon, Michigan, a fellow bishop of the Conservative A.M. Church, and part of the time by D. J. Fisher of Kalona, Iowa, a bishop of the Mennonite Church. In his visits, Fisher gave particular attention to Mennonite campers from Iowa. At most of the camps the visitors had preaching appointments, followed by personal visits with the men, particularly with men from Iowa, or with those who were members of the Conservative A.M. Church.

Swartzendruber gave a very favorable report of his visits. "In all camps visited," he "found the members of the staff without exception eager to do all within their power to carry out the wishes of the churches from which the men came, desiring that everyone shall remain true to their convictions and someday return home better fitted to carry on the work the Lord may have for them." On the other hand, Swartzendruber emphasized "a definite need of a closer contact and greater concern for the welfare of the men in camp by those at home," a matter which he proposed to stress at the coming session of conference. He also believed that in all camps where a considerable number of men of any particular group were located, systematic efforts should be made for frequent preaching services by ministers from that group, thus again emphasizing the need for a more effective pastoral ministry.[9]

Eli J. Bontreger also gave a full report of his pastoral visitation tour with Ira Nissley. Accompanied by their wives, they visited all western camps where Old Order Amish men were located; and accompanied by Sister Nissley they visited the eastern camps and units. While the bishops visited the campers, their wives kept busy mending the campers' clothing. The boys "responded with enough mending at each place to keep the women busy mending during their stay in camp." They found no financial needs among the Amish boys. The Amish boys were advised to attend any "religious activities where they could gain any spiritual food, and if they felt they could, to also take part in such activities. We were pleased to learn that at some camps, our Amish boys have their German Sunday school."

Bontreger and Nissley held preaching services in the German language in the camps, and also had communion services for the Amish boys at Hill City, Belton, Lapine, North Fork, and Downey. While they found most of the boys living consistently with their faith, and ready to participate in the communion service, yet this was not true of all. Bontreger was concerned about conditions at Downey where certain campers, apparently humanitarian or political objectors, who were unsympathetic with camp regulations, "were doing harm to the morale of the camp by their antagonism to camp rules and their ridiculing of those who were living as Christians." Because of this situation, Bontreger and Nissley remained an extra day at Downey for another meeting with the Amish boys, at which time they spoke plainly about observance of camp rules and regulations, as well as concerning Christian conduct in general. The final report of Bontreger and Nissley emphasized the need for Amish ministers to write to their men in camp, as well as to visit the camps personally and conduct services in the German language.[10]

In August, 1943, the Peace Problems Committee reported the work of the Pastoral Committee to the regular session of General Conference, and recommended that this work be enlarged and extended. General Conference now increased the membership of the Peace Problems Committee from six members to twelve (in addition to the four Canadian members).[11] The enlarged Peace Problems Committee immediately appointed a Subcommittee on C.P.S. Pastoral Ministry, consisting of Amos S. Horst, John E. Lapp, O. N. Johns, D. A. Yoder, and H. A. Diener. On

February 16, 1944, the subcommittee held a meeting at which each member gave an oral report of his camp visitation experiences and observations. Apparently most of the camps had been visited by some member of the subcommittee since its appointment five or six months earlier. At this meeting it was decided:

(1) That we follow out our former plan of contacting our young brethren in camps and detached service units about twice a year if possible. (2) That we also provide a spiritual ministry for our sisters who are associated with said camps and units. (3) That we again divide our territory into districts which will enable us to work more economically and efficiently. (4) That the brother in charge of a district be instructed and authorized to provide preaching services and pastoral visitation throughout the year, the same to be done in cooperation with the local conferences as much as possible. (5) That in our camp and unit visits, we arrange for a number of Gospel messages when possible or advisable.[12]

The work as outlined above was continued through 1944 and 1945. In addition to this, Harold S. Bender, the chairman of the Peace Problems Committee, was asked to visit the far western camps, stopping en route at the Lincoln, Nebraska, farm units.[13] When the Subcommittee on Pastoral Ministry met on November 8, 1945, it gave lengthy consideration to the need of "securing a few brethren to devote full time to our pastoral work for three or six months." Beyond the services of Titus Books, Newton Weber, and B. Charles Hostetter, mentioned earlier in this chapter, however, no such full-time pastoral appointments were made. Since the war was now over, and the discharge of C.P.S. men would likely begin soon, the subcommittee also concerned itself with the returning C.P.S. men. Each member of the subcommittee was made responsible to write a personal letter to each C.P.S. man in his region who was about to be released; and also a letter to his pastor, expressing the committee's concern for the man, and giving helpful suggestions.[14]

COMMUNION SERVICES

An important phase of spiritual ministry in the life of the Mennonite Church is the semiannual communion service. Men located in C.P.S. camps which were within easy reach of some Mennonite congregation were able at times to participate in a service with that congregation. Some congregations and conferences made special efforts to have their C.P.S. men arrange their furloughs so as to be at home at the time of the regular communion service. Some congregations paid the travel expenses of men coming home for communion. Many men were located in distant camps, however, where it was not possible to be present at a communion service of any congregation of their church. In one of his pastoral visitation reports, Harry A. Diener stated that some of the men in western camps had not taken part in a communion service "for about two years."

From one point of view, it would seem to have been a simple matter for the pastoral visitor to conduct communion services in connection with his regular camp visits. It is the common practice of the Mennonite Church, however, to confine its communion service to members of its own group; and it did not seem too easy to conduct such a service in a camp made up of men from various Mennonite groups, as well as non-Mennonites, although this was done on several occasions. As mentioned earlier in this chapter, Eli J. Bontreger and Ira Nissley conducted communion services for members of the Old Order Amish Church in a number of the camps. In Harry A. Diener's report mentioned above, he spoke of a desire, on the part of many men, for a communion service in which members of all groups would participate. "In camps where the church differences can scarcely be seen they say if we separate communion service it would mar their now peaceful working together; and in camps where church differences can be noticed they would like to have communion service as a token of good will toward each other. To me this presents a problem and as yet I have no solution for it, but feel that someone should give it some careful study and helpful advice."[15]

How to make satisfactory provision for communion services, especially in view of the varying practices of the different groups represented in C.P.S., was a problem never entirely solved. In March, 1943, John E. Lapp reported that many of the men at the Norristown hospital unit had not attended a communion service since their induction into C.P.S. Since most of these men were members of the Indiana-Michigan Conference, he had asked D. A. Yoder to conduct a communion service for this group. Lapp also reported that some of the men in the Grottoes Camp found it embarrassing to join the Virginia congregations in a communion service, because of the ruling of that conference on the use of the radio.[16] As late as March 3, 1945, at a meeting of the Peace Problems Committee devoted to C.P.S. pastoral problems, "The communion practice in camps and units as related to accepted group practice loomed as a growing problem to all concerned. The pastoral ministry committee was instructed to make a special study of these problems and bring recommendations to the next meeting of the committee."[17]

These reports bring out rather clearly the difficulty found in applying a strict interpretation of the practice of close communion in situations where various Mennonite groups were working together as closely as they did in C.P.S. In actual practice, therefore, a more liberal interpretation was applied by ministers of the Mennonite Church in a number of instances where they conducted communion services, both in C.P.S. and on the foreign relief field. In these instances members of all groups present took part in the service. Apparently, however, neither the Peace Problems Committee, nor any official group, succeeded in developing a policy which came to be recommended for general application.

Included in the ministry of the church to C.P.S. men, was the publication and distribution of literature. Chapter XVII is a survey of the special peace literature published and made available during this period. To aid in this matter the Mennonite Publishing House, beginning in 1941, extended an annual credit of fifty cents per man to each C.P.S. camp and unit under the M.C.C., for the purchase of books and literature.[18] In addition to this, the regular budget of each camp included a specified amount for the purchase of literature. On August 17, 1944, the Peace Problems Committee approved a plan for the preparation and distribution among C.P.S. men of "a series of brief informative pamphlets on the major aspects of the work of the church, such as missions, education, publication, etc., these pamphlets to be illustrated and made attractive. This would express the deep interest of the church in enlisting the C.P.S. men for active and loyal participation in the future work of the church, and would help direct the minds of the men toward the church as they return."[19] This program was carried out and the following five pamphlets were published in 1946: *The Church and Returning C.P.S. Men,* a pamphlet of a general character; *Who Will Go for Us and Whom Shall We Send?,* describing the mission program of the church; *The Church Teaching the Word,* describing the work of the Mennonite Commission for Christian Education and Young People's Work; *Thou Shalt Write,* describing the work of the Mennonite Publishing House; and *Youth in Preparation for Service in Our Church Schools,* describing the work and objectives of the Mennonite Board of Education. A set of these pamphlets was mailed to each C.P.S. man at the time of his discharge, or soon thereafter.[20]

The Subcommittee on Pastoral Ministry continued its work through 1946 and into 1947, although after large numbers of men had been discharged the volume of the subcommittee's work was reduced, and finally came to an end with the close of C.P.S. in March, 1947. The subcommittee made its final report to the Peace Problems Committee on April 17, 1947, and was then discharged.[21]

MINISTRY OF DISTRICT CONFERENCES

In addition to the labors of the Peace Problems Committee for the spiritual welfare of the men in C.P.S., the various district conferences were also concerned in this task, and labored toward the same end. As early as June, 1941, the Pacific Coast Conference resolved that "inasmuch as our young men in Civilian Public Service camps will be deprived of their regular place of worship . . . an ordained brother be appointed by this body to have spiritual oversight of the said young men."[22] N. A. Lind was then appointed to have charge of this work, and was continuously reappointed to the end of C.P.S. In 1944, when Amos S. Horst of Pennsylvania spent some time visiting western camps, particularly in the interests of men from the eastern conferences who were stationed there, Lind was asked by his conference to accompany Horst in visiting the California camps. At the 1944 session of conference it was reported that about seventy men from the Pacific Coast Conference were in C.P.S. The conference passed a resolution expressing "sincere appreciation for their loyalty to God and the church," and the secretary was asked to write an appropriate letter expressing this appreciation "and encouraging them to continue in the faith and to rejoice in the Lord." The resolution was passed by the delegate body, and "the audience gave expression by uplifted hands." The letter was then sent to each C.P.S. man of the conference district personally.[23]

The Missouri-Kansas (South Central) Conference likewise expressed a warm interest in the C.P.S. program from the beginning. In 1941, and again in 1942, reports to the conference from the Manitou Springs congregation expressed appreciation for the presence of the men of the C.P.S. camp at near-by Colorado Springs: "The young men from the Civilian Public Service camp near here are a very welcome addition to our congregation and we admire their testimony against war."[24] At the 1942 conference one entire session was devoted to the C.P.S. program, with an address by Harry A. Diener, testimonies by C.P.S. men, and a discussion period by Gideon G. Yoder, director of the camp at Denison, Iowa.[25]

In January, 1943, the Missouri-Kansas Conference appointed Harry A. Diener the official C.P.S. camp pastor for that conference. He was to visit or direct visitation of camps in which men from the conference were located. In August, 1943, he reported that seventy-three men from the district were in C.P.S.: fifty in base camps, seventeen in hospital units, and six on farms.[26] E. M. Yost and Richard Showalter were then appointed assistants to Diener in this work.[27] These three men now constituted a committee known as the Spiritual Welfare Committee for Missouri-Kansas Conference Men in Government Service. A year later Showalter was replaced by Marcus Bishop.[28] As early as April, 1942, before these appointments were officially made, Diener began sending a monthly letter, accompanied by a sermonette, to all men from his home congregation at Yoder, Kansas, who were in government service, and also to a number of others in whom he had a special interest.

The circulation of Diener's letter was soon enlarged, and by the time of his official appointment as C.P.S. pastor it was being sent to all men from the conference district, who were in C.P.S. or in the army. Following the organization of the committee, an occasional letter was written by the other members, but most of the writing was done by Diener. Some of his letters were written at home, but many of them away from home. One is dated January 26, 1943, at Downey, Idaho, where Diener was visiting the C.P.S. camp located at that place.[29] A month later the the letter was sent from Goshen, Indiana, where Diener attended sessions of the Peace Problems Committee, the Mennonite Board of Education, and the Executive and Missions committees of the Mennonite Board of Missions and Charities. Besides speaking a word of encouragement to the men, Diener's letter included information concerning the work of these official church organizations.

The March, 1943, letter was written from Lapine, Oregon, and that of May, 1943, from Harrisonburg, Virginia, where Diener was attending the annual meeting of the Mennonite Board of Missions and Charities. The letters spoke of the crops, local draft boards, experiences in camp visitation, the material and spiritual needs of the world, the relief and missions program of the church, communion services, and other interesting matters, both material and spiritual. In August, 1944, the letter was sent from Hesston, Kansas, as "Greetings from the Missouri-Kansas Conference" which was then in session. The letter was six pages in length, containing a summary report of the conference, including a title page with a sketch of the conference tent, and a list of the conference officials. A year later a similar report was sent from the conference, including a report of contributions from the conference district to missions, relief, and C.P.S. One outstanding feature of this conference was an address by the chairman of the Peace Problems Committee on "Discharging Our Spiritual Responsibilities Toward Our Young Men Returning from Government Service." Another was a special service of thanksgiving for the end of the war with Japan, which came on the first day of the conference. The conference also adopted a suitable resolution of thanksgiving for the cessation of hostilities. Diener's letters continually related the man in C.P.S. to the work of the church. The August, 1945, letter, sent from the conference, spoke of the shortage of workers within the church, and expressed the hope that upon their release from camp some of the men in C.P.S. would be able to go into some of the needy places.

The Missouri-Kansas Conference and its Spiritual Welfare Committee were also concerned for the welfare of the men in the armed forces. At the 1943 conference L. C. Miller gave an address on "Our Responsibility to the Man in Uniform." Harry A. Diener's letters and sermonettes were sent to the men in uniform as well as to the C.P.S. men. In December, 1943, Richard Showalter, a member of the committee, visited members of the conference in military camps in Oklahoma and Texas.[30] In August, 1944, the committee reported that under its plan of work, Showalter was to visit as many as possible of the Mennonite boys in the armed forces, while the other two members of the committee concentrated on C.P.S. camps and units.[31] The attitude of the conference toward the men in uniform seems to have been expressed by Harold S. Bender in his address of August, 1945, when he reminded the conference: that some of these men were weak in the faith; that some had a lack of necessary information and guidance; that many of this group would be penitent; that the great spiritual responsibility of the church was restoration; that some men might be unwilling to be restored; and that these would then need to be released from church membership.[32]

Other district conferences followed a course similar to that of the Missouri-Kansas Conference in camp visitation and pastoral oversight, although the program was not always as elaborate or as well organized as in this conference. In September, 1943, the Iowa-Nebraska Conference appointed D. J. Fisher to represent the conference in providing pastoral oversight for C.P.S. men, "under auspices of the General Conference Peace Problems Committee."[33] This session of conference also adopted a special resolution of greeting and encouragement, which was sent to all men in camp. The following year the conference appointed "a committee of three to co-operate with sister conferences in providing the spiritual welfare of our drafted men." The committee consisted of D. J. Fisher, Amos Gingerich, and W. R. Eicher.[34] In 1946 the men from the C.P.S. unit at Malcolm, Nebraska, attended the Iowa-Nebraska Conference in session at Beaver Crossing, with the conference treasurer paying the transportation costs.[35]

The Illinois Conference also had a C.P.S. Committee. In August, 1945, this committee reported to conference that it had been sending out "monthly letters and sermons in an attempt to encourage our brethren and to help them know that the church has an interest in them. Many of them have written to express their appreciation for the interest and concern of those at home."[36] The length of time during which the letter had been mailed is not stated. The report of the following year said that since early in 1946 the letter has been "largely discontinued because of the discharge of the men."[37] The Indiana-Michigan Conference had no special C.P.S. committee, nor did it appoint any official pastor for C.P.S. men. In 1944 the conference adopted a resolution of appreciation for the faithfulness of the men in C.P.S., and sent a copy to all camps and units where members were serving.[38] The minutes of the 1946 conference refer to a report of C.P.S. camp visitation. This was probably a report by D. A. Yoder of the Indiana-Michigan Conference, who was a member of the Subcommittee on Pastoral Ministry appointed by the Peace Problems Committee. The report was accepted and the conference passed a motion "that arrangements be made to visit our C.P.S. men who may be in C.P.S. camps this coming year."[39]

In May, 1943, the Ohio and Eastern A.M. Conference adopted a resolution commending the men in C.P.S. for their faithful witness, and assuring them "of our continued support and prayers that the Lord's choicest blessings rest upon them, and that our secretary send a copy of this to each one."[40] The Executive Committee of the conference also reported having made "a little tour through the East, contacting the ministry in a number of our churches, visiting camps and hospitals, contacting our Ohio boys."[41] In 1944 the secretary of conference was instructed "to send monthly sermons to the brethren from our conference who have been inducted into C.P.S. or the armed forces."[42] The sermons were to be short and written by different brethren. In 1943 the Peace Committee of the Southwestern Pennsylvania Conference recommended a "more systematic visitation of brethren from our district in C.P.S. camps."[43] At the same session reports were heard "of communion services conducted in C.P.S. camps by Bros. John E. Lapp, T. E. Schrock, and Aaron Mast, who had been engaged in this service through arrangements by the Peace Problems Committee of General Conference."[44]

In 1944 the Peace Committee recommended that ministers "give faithful attention to keeping up contacts by correspondence and visitation of our brethren in C.P.S. camps." The committee itself was then instructed to work out a plan for camp visitation.[45] In 1945 the committee reported that it had published in the *Conference News* a list of C.P.S. men from the conference district, and suggested that ministers, when visiting camps, should see all men from the district. Roy Otto, a member of the committee, had visited a number of eastern camps in co-operation with Newton Weber, eastern camp pastor under the M.C.C. He was planning to continue these visitations. The committee then said: "We have had reports of considerable visiting by other brethren, but so far we have not succeeded in working out a systematic conference-sponsored visitation program."[46] Apparently the program finally got under way the following year. At any rate the committee reported in 1946 that its members had been active in visiting C.P.S. camps, hospitals, and other units. It also expressed appreciation for "the work of this kind that many of our ordained brethren have done."[47]

In June, 1943, the Peace and Industrial Relations Committee of the Virginia Conference reported that during the first quarter of the year it had been in touch with nearly all of the men in C.P.S. from that conference. "We adopted the general policy to have such a visit made each quarter of the year."[48] In 1944 the committee reported that although it had been unable to see each man each quarter, it nevertheless felt that the program of visitation was pretty well established, and that it should be continued for another year. At the suggestion of the bishops the committee mailed each of the men a schedule of communion dates, and urged them by personal letter to return to their home congregation for communion. While it was not possible for all of the men to follow this plan, "a large number of them appreciated the invitation and arranged accordingly."[49] In 1945 the committee reported that it was difficult to maintain a consistent visitation program, and asked whether it might not be advisable to appoint one or two conference pastors to serve the Virginia C.P.S. men.

The committee recognized, however, the advantages which went with a distribution of responsibility among a large group of ministers.

At any rate it was urged that in addition to whatever pastoral work is sponsored by the conference, all ministers should maintain a regular correspondence with C.P.S. men from their own congregations, and also visit them as they have opportunity.[50] Following this suggestion, the Virginia Conference authorized its Executive Committee and the Peace and Industrial Relations Committee jointly to work out a more satisfactory plan of pastoral visitation. The result was the appointment of John H. Shenk as full-time pastoral visitor for Virginia men in C.P.S. Shenk began his services in this capacity during the summer or autumn of 1945, and continued into the autumn of 1946, at which time the camp program was drawing to a close, and the need for pastoral visitation greatly reduced.[51] Following the close of C.P.S., the chairman of the Peace and Industrial Relations Committee reported that, before the appointment of the full-time pastor, those men in camps within close reach of the Virginia Conference were visited on an average of three times a year, and those at more distant points at least once a year. The committee aimed to visit all camps in which there were members of the conference.[52]

The Franconia Conference also had a special committee known as the Peace Problems Committee which assumed responsibility for the pastoral visitation of its men in C.P.S. In April, 1943, a schedule of visitation was prepared and carried out, which included ministerial visits every three months to the camps at Grottoes, Luray, and Galax, and monthly visits to the hospital unit at Howard, Rhode Island.[53] All C.P.S. camps, however, were visited by ministers of the Franconia Conference, as delegated by the conference Peace Problems Committee. The committee also sent monthly mimeographed letters to all men in C.P.S. from the Franconia district.[54] The Lancaster Conference had a special Conference Camp Committee, with Amos S. Horst as chairman, which sent monthly mimeographed letters to the men in camp, and carried out a systematic program of camp visitation. Camps west of the Mississippi River were visited once a year, and those east of the Mississippi more often. A considerable number of the Lancaster ministers shared in this visitation program.[55]

The Canadian system of Alternative Service camps was much less extensive than that of the United States. Due to the Canadian plan of assigning conscientious objectors to work in private life, a smaller percentage of the men were in camps than was the case in the United States. Their terms of service were also much shorter. All of this had a corresponding effect on the pastoral visitation program for the Canadian camps. The two Canadian conferences of the Mennonite Church, however, made an effort to keep in touch with the men in camp. In 1942, and again in 1943, the Ontario Conference sent official greetings to the men. In the latter year this included the sending of a letter to the wives of married men in camp.[56] In 1945 the Alberta-Saskatchewan Conference adopted a resolution commending "all those who had maintained a con-

8

sistent position on nonresistance."[57] This conference is small, and a total
of only 37 men was involved. The Ontario Conference, however, had
295 men in Alternative Service Work; and of these, 93 served in A.S.W.
camps at one time or another.

The Canadian camps were operated by the government, the church
having only a religious adviser or chaplain located in the camp. When
the first camp was opened in 1941, J. Harold Sherk of the Mennonite
Brethren in Christ Church served as spiritual adviser for a time. Other
ministers who served in a similar capacity, in this and other camps for a
time, were Edward Gilmore, Merle Shantz, H. W. Stevanus, and Harold
D. Groh. As chairman of the Military Problems Committee of the Ontario
Conference of Historic Peace Churches, Jesse B. Martin was a frequent
visitor in the camps.[58] The Peace Problems Committee of the Ontario
Mennonite Conference also had a planned program of camp visitation,[59]
although in the opinion of one minister the work done was "very hap-
hazard and spasmodic."[60] This program was co-ordinated with that of
the Alberta-Saskatchewan Conference, and with the camp visitation work
of the ministers of the various Russian Mennonite groups in Canada.

The Conservative Amish Mennonite Conference worked closely with
the Mennonite Church in all of its work relating to nonresistance and
the C.P.S. program. As early as June, 1941, the conference voted to create a fund with which to supply its official paper, and other religious
literature, to the men in camp. Fifty dollars was appropriated from the
general fund for this purpose, and the Old Order Amish brethren were
invited "to aid in this support as they see fit." This fund was to be in
charge of Shem Peachey, the Conservative A.M. Conference member on
the Peace Problems Committee. The conference also directed that "each
assignee from this conference to Civilian Public Service camps be reported to Shem Peachey by the church where his membership is held."[61]
In 1943, the Conservative A.M. Conference for the first time appointed a
Peace Problems Committee of its own, consisting of Shem Peachey,
chairman, Elmer G. Swartzendruber, and Nevin Bender. Shem Peachey
was also continued as representative on the Peace Problems Committee
of the Mennonite General Conference. The conference now gave to its
newly appointed Peace Problems Committee the responsibility for pastoral visitation of the men in C.P.S.[62] This work was then largely given
to Swartzendruber and Bender,[63] although others may have assisted in
the work also. At the 1943 conference, M. S. Zehr gave a report of his
C.P.S. camp visitation during the previous summer.[64]

MINISTRY OF LOCAL CONGREGATIONS

Another aspect of the ministry to C.P.S. men was that which operated through the local congregation. In the July 2, 1942, issue of the
Gospel Herald, the chairman of the Peace Problems Committee had an

article urging local congregations to keep in touch with their C.P.S. men, through correspondence and by other means. He emphasized the fact that unofficial contacts were more important than official ones. "If home ministers have been accustomed to fellowship with their young men at home it will be natural to continue that fellowship in C.P.S. camps . . . . It is not so important that congregations or conferences delegate officials to make official visits as that the stream of spiritual life should flow from the home church to the camps through channels of loving concern and sincere fellowship." He suggested that not only the minister, but other individuals of the congregation and also groups, such as Sunday-school classes, literary societies, Bible classes, and family groups, are natural groups for maintaining this fellowship.[65] A month later the *Gospel Herald* published a similar appeal from Amos S. Horst.[66]

In order to get a picture of what local congregations had done to keep in touch with their drafted men, the Mennonite Research Foundation sent a questionnaire to the ministry of each congregation, inquiring what was done by the congregation, officially or unofficially, through correspondence, visitation, or otherwise. Returns were received on only one third of the questionnaires, and many of these were answered in a general way only, so that it is difficult to obtain a detailed picture of what actually was done. Most of the replies, however, reported the writing of occasional letters. In the Missouri-Kansas (South Central) Conference, ministers from most of the congregations who had men in camp reported writing letters several times a year. Several mentioned occasional mimeographed letters. One congregation reported letters sent systematically from the congregation monthly. Some of the ministers visited a C.P.S. camp occasionally, but it is clear that the organized work of the Peace Problems Committee and of the conference was largely depended upon to do this task.

One minister writes: "We trusted the organized program of camp visitation by M.C.C. organization and our conference committee."[67] Another says: "All men were visited by camp pastor under conference."[68] One minister says: "This Missouri-Kansas Conference district had a plan of C.P.S. camp visitation that was effective. Also a mimeographed letter was sent out by Bro. Harry A. Diener to the boys regularly. I do not think there was any great lack or neglect of the camp boys."[69] Another minister of the same conference, however, says: "Our contact with our C.P.S. boys left much to be desired. As a ministry our letters were not so many and at no stated time; however, we tried to keep up with them through some correspondence and especially to contact them on their furlough. Most of the boys had parents and friends who did write regularly. Then, too, as a conference we had a Spiritual Welfare Committee who very definitely did try to keep up with the boys . . . . I do not feel that, as a ministry, we did all we could for our brethren in the camps by way of correspondence and visitation."[70] One minister included several samples of mimeographed letters giving congregational news, including a report of the annual business meeting, and a complete membership list of the congregation, with addresses. Another letter contained comments on the printed report of the recent session of conference which had been enclosed.

Most of the ministers from the Pacific Coast Conference reported correspondence with their men in C.P.S., one of them writing monthly letters. Several referred to the official conference camp visitation program. N. A. Lind, the official camp pastor, says that the reports from his conference would not be complete without reference to the work of S. E. Eicher, a layman of Albany, Oregon, who was appointed by the conference as a member of the C.P.S. Advisory Committee for the Pacific Coast camps. "While his work with the various C.P.S. camps was primarily in connection with the M.C.C., Bro. Eicher's natural gifts so well qualified him for the helpful touches and contacts he made among C.P.S. camps. Unhesitatingly I say no one man in our district rendered better service toward our brethren than did our Brother Eicher. This he did in a multitude of ways."[71]

All ministers of the Iowa-Nebraska Conference who replied, reported a certain amount of correspondence with C.P.S. men. One of them wrote about once a month, others less frequently. One minister reported writing at least once a year, and several times a year to those who replied. In one congregation a circle letter was maintained: "Each time it came around an old letter was taken out and a new one put in."[72] The same minister also referred to the official camp Pastoral Committee, and said that ministers outside the committee visited camps only when requested by the committee to do so, or when they happened to be near a camp where such visitation would be convenient.

All ministers of the Illinois Conference who replied, reported correspondence with their men. Several reported systematic correspondence from the congregation. A committee appointed by the conference was responsible to get in touch with the men once a month, and to send them $5.00 from a fund collected for this purpose. The financial part of the plan was changed later, and the money disbursed following the discharge of the men at the close of the war. Beginning in 1943, J. D. Hartzler, minister of the Waldo congregation near Flanagan, circulated a mimeographed monthly newsletter among his men in government service. The letter usually closed with a brief Scriptural meditation. The East Bend congregation near Fisher printed a monthly newssheet, beginning in 1945. This sheet occasionally featured a C.P.S. man, giving his picture and an account of his activity. H. J. King, minister in the congregation at Arthur, had a circle letter which circulated among the men in camp, with himself included. In this way he kept in touch with the men and they with each other. The Illinois Conference had no systematic plan of camp visitation. Most of the visiting which was done was in near-by camps. A. C. Good of Sterling reported visiting nine camps.

Most of the ministers of the Indiana-Michigan Conference reported writing to their men personally at least several times a year, a number of them monthly. A number of congregations sent the church bulletin regularly. The sewing circle of the Salem congregation near New Paris, Indiana, sent letters to the men once a month. In the case of the Prairie Street congregation in Elkhart, the minister sent monthly mimeographed letters to the men; in addition to this, church bulletins and mimeographed letters from the congregation were sent monthly. During 1945 the C.P.S. men from the Yellow Creek congregation near Goshen, Indiana, issued a monthly mimeographed letter to which each of the men was asked to contribute. It was known as the *Yellow Creek C.P.S. Letter*, and was edited and distributed by Ernest Lehman, an assignee at the Harrisburg State Hospital in Pennsylvania. The letter was mailed not only to the C.P.S. men, but also to a large number of subscribers in the Yellow Creek and Salem congregations. Men in the army, as well as C.P.S. men, contributed to the letter. In this way members of the home congregations were informed concerning the activities of the men in camp.

Some of the Indiana-Michigan ministers visited C.P.S. camps occasionally; but to a large extent they depended on D. A. Yoder, of the visitation committee appointed by the Peace Problems Committee, to perform this task systematically. Yoder, however, obtained the help of certain others in this work, especially toward the close of C.P.S. In the bulletin of the Prairie Street Church for November 25, 1945, John E. Gingrich, the minister, said: "Representatives of the Indiana-Michigan Conference have recently been appointed to visit all the C.P.S. boys from this conference district. Your pastor has been asked to visit the boys in Pennsylvania, New York, and the New England states. Since I will be quite close to the boys from this congregation who are in New Jersey, it seems advisable to stop off with them, too. Will you pray that this visit may be of real help to the boys?" Earlier in the year Gingrich had also spent several days with the camp at Denison, Iowa. Ira S. Johns of the Clinton Frame congregation reported that all of the men from that congregation were visited, but not all by local ministers. He personally did some of the visiting, however. He also said: "I endeavored to keep in touch with all our boys, writing to some in the army who responded. With some it was difficult; with others it was easy . . . . Many letters were written by the laity, but not systematically to my knowledge."[78]

A considerable number of ministers of the Ohio and Eastern A.M. Conference reported the writing of occasional letters, but in some cases apparently there was none. Few of them reported a systematic program. The Conestoga congregation at Morgantown, Pennsylvania, posted the names and addresses of its C.P.S. men, thus reminding members of the congregation to write personal letters. In this way "many were remembered and private gifts were sent. Also gifts were sent by Sunday-school classes, etc." The minister of one congregation wrote: "As far as I can determine there was nothing done in the way of contacts either in writing or visiting. This is certainly not the way it should have been, but it was." One minister reported personal letters sent to each man at least once a year, "as need required." Another minister, however, from whose congregation eighty-four men were drafted, said that during the first year of the draft personal letters were written monthly to all of the men, both in C.P.S. and in the army. After that, as the number of men increased, mimeographed letters were sent monthly for a time, and later several times a year.[75] The Oak Grove-Pleasant Hill congregation near Smithville, Ohio, had a systematic program of visitation to camps where its members were located. J. S. Gerig, the bishop, requested William G. Detweiler, the assistant pastor, to do the visiting, and Detweiler reported at least twenty-six visits to C.P.S. camps and units in the East.[76]

One minister said: "I have to confess that I did very little writing to the boys except to my own. I feel that I did not do my duty toward them." Another minister who wrote occasionally said: "It should be noted that individual members of the congregation kept the boys in touch with the home church."[77] One minister reported that there was a very active correspondence on the part of parents and young people of his congregation with the men in camp, although this was not a systematically organized program.[78] A. J. Steiner reported that the Midway-North Lima-Leetonia congregations systematically sent mimeographed letters about once a month to men in C.P.S. and in the army. This was in addition to frequent personal letters.[79] The Kidron congregation reported personal and mimeographed letters from the minister several times a year, besides systematic letters from the congregation at least once a year. The church bulletin was also sent to the men.[80] The Canton congregation also sent the church bulletin to its men.[81] Most of the remaining ministers who responded reported occasional letters.

From the Southwestern Pennsylvania Conference, a few ministers reported monthly or bimonthly personal letters to the men, and a number reported less frequent correspondence. None reported the sending of mimeographed letters or church bulletins from the congregation. It would seem that in this respect the ministry of this conference was less active than that of some other conferences. Only one minister of the Washington-Franklin Conference responded; he reported personal letters to the men in camp several times a year.[82] Less than one fourth of the ministers of the Lancaster Conference responded to the questionnaire. Of these, about one half reported personal letters to the men, some several times a year, some occasionally, some once a year. Two ministers reported that no letters were written, but one explained that all of the men from his congregation were located in near-by camps and came home frequently. One minister who himself was in C.P.S. for two years reported that his congregation had made it possible for all of its C.P.S. men to attend communion services at home. Another minister reported the systematic writing of personal letters by members of the congregation. Two ministers reported the sending of mimeographed letters. A number of ministers referred to the official camp committee of the Lancaster Conference, and its program of correspondence and visitation. Apparently the ministers of this conference depended largely on the leadership of the official committee, although, as noted before, a considerable number of them shared in the visitation program.

A number of ministers of the Franconia Conference reported that none of their men were drafted. This was to be expected, since the percentage of drafted men from this conference was unusually low. Several reported personal letters from minister to C.P.S. men, monthly or several times a year. A similar number wrote once a year. One minister reported monthly mimeographed letters from the congregation, and a number referred to the monthly letter sent by the official conference committee. As in the case of the Lancaster Conference, the ministers of the Franconia Conference seem to have depended largely on their official committee to carry on the ministry to C.P.S. men. Ministers of the Virginia Conference responded to the questionnaire through the conference Peace and Industrial Relations Committee. The chairman of this committee said that "approximately 20 per cent" of the Virginia ministers "wrote personal letters to C.P.S. men several times a year," although "this can hardly be interpreted to say it was done to each man. It was difficult to ascertain the percentage of ministers who wrote to men in the army, but there is evidence that quite a few of them did."[83] None of the Virginia congregations reported a systematic sending of letters by the congregation, although "at least two bishop districts sent their regular pastoral letters (about once a month) to C.P.S. men." In a few cases individual ministers also sent occasional mimeographed letters.[84]

The Ontario churches and their ministers apparently kept in touch with their men through correspondence in about the same manner and to the same extent as in the case of the congregations in the States. One minister reported the systematic sending of mimeographed sermons and letters; others reported the writing of personal letters, ranging from those written monthly to those sent only occasionally, or once a year. Reports of respondents from the Alberta-Saskatchewan Conference were similar. So likewise were reports from the respondents of the Conservative Amish Mennonite Conference in the United States. One of these ministers reported personal letters, with news, sermon outlines, and comments, sent out by the minister and congregation monthly.[85]

EVALUATION

The above account of the activities of the Peace Problems Committee, of its Subcommittee on Pastoral Ministry, of district conferences, and of local congregations, is evidence that the Mennonite Church had a genuine concern for the spiritual welfare of its men in C.P.S. The "Mennonite Preaching Mission" program of the General Conference Mennonite Church is evidence of a similar interest within that group. That much effort was put forth in this cause, there can be no doubt. The continuing generous sprinkling of items in the weekly news column of the *Gospel Herald,* reporting ministerial visits to C.P.S. camps, was impressive; that much good was accomplished, there is no question.

It is easily possible, however, for the superficial reader to overestimate the value of these many efforts. After all, the important question is not whether committees were busy, or even whether much good was accomplished. The important question is whether these efforts were sufficiently well planned and organized so as to bring a continuous daily and weekly spiritual ministry to all of the C.P.S. men during their stay in camp.

In all fairness it must be said that this result was not achieved. In 1943 John E. Lapp reported that a number of men at the Grottoes Camp had received no letters or visits from their home ministers, and that only a few received letters regularly. From Norristown he reported that "some of these brethren are dissatisfied with the interest shown in them by their home ministers." Earlier in this chapter mention was made of the Farnhurst, Delaware, unit which had had only four preaching services in a period of five months. The number of ministers visiting C.P.S. units on a given Sunday was always much smaller than the number of units, and many units were without the service of a minister for weeks at a time. The pastoral visitation program was a great help, but as Melvin Gingerich says:

> The value of the visitation program was diminished somewhat by a lack of co-ordination. The directors made an attempt to schedule these speakers in advance and to distribute them through the month, but sometimes preachers would arrive unannounced only to find that another preacher was already there and scheduled to preach. Sometimes ministers who came unannounced could not understand why the educational and recreational program of the camp could not be quickly rearranged in order to schedule church services. Obviously it was difficult to adapt the program under these conditions.[86]

Among the more alert C.P.S. men, especially among those who served in official capacities, there was a general feeling that, in the event of a future program similar to C.P.S., the only satisfactory way of maintaining a spiritual ministry would be by providing a resident pastor in each camp. One man wrote:

I also feel our church failed in the spiritual lives of the fellows. In many of our camps the program was left to the campers entirely which was far too often unsatisfactory . . . . How many of our conferences would let a church of 125 members go for several years without any good spiritual supervision? . . . I feel that there should have been a camp pastor . . . who would have been in charge of the religious life of the camp.[87]

Another man said:

Among the weaknesses that I would like to mention, perhaps of first importance, is the lack of a proper spiritual program in the camps during C.P.S. I had to think . . . that at no other time in the history of our churches . . . have groups of anywhere from 20 to 150 individuals been placed in isolated circumstances without proper spiritual leadership. In our branch of the church, at least, we found very few, if any places, where there are a dozen or more members without spiritual leadership . . . . A recommendation that certainly should be considered in case of a future program would be to have a spiritual life director in each camp or unit.[88]

Many testimonies of this type could be cited, not only from members of the (Old) Mennonite Church, but from the other Mennonite groups as well.

NOTES AND CITATIONS

[1] "Civilian Public Service News," *Gospel Herald* (May 29, 1941), 34:188.

[2] Peace Problems Committee Minutes, Oct. 30, 1942.

[3] Report in ∙Peace Problems Committee files, January, 1943.

[4] *Ibid.*, March 22, 1943.

[5] *Ibid.*, March 22, 1943.

[6] *Ibid.*, March 22, 1943.

[7] *Ibid.*, March 31, 1943.

[8] *Ibid.*, March 31, 1943.

[9] *Ibid.*, May 20, 1943

[10] *Ibid., December-March,* 1943.

[11] Prior to 1941 the committee consisted of three members from the United States and three from Canada. In 1941 it was enlarged to six from the United States and four from Canada. Now, in 1943, there were twelve from the United States and four from Canada. The United States section now consisted of the three members who had long served on the committee, Harold S. Bender, Orie O. Miller, and C. L. Graber, with the addition of nine bishops from eight district conferences as follows: H. A. Diener and Milo Kauffman, Missouri-Kansas; Simon Gingerich, Iowa-Nebraska; J. A. Heiser, Illinois; D. A. Yoder, Indiana-Michigan; O. N. Johns, Ohio and Eastern A.M.; Amos Horst. Lancaster; John E. Lapp, Franconia; and John L. Stauffer, Virginia.

[12] Peace Problems Committee Minutes, Feb. 16, 1944.

[13] *Ibid.*, Oct. 19, 1944.

[14] *Ibid.*, Minutes of the Subcommittee on Pastoral Ministry, Nov. 8, 1945.

[15] H. A. Diener Report, March 22, 1943.

[16] John E. Lapp Report, March 31, 1943.

[17] Peace ∙Problems Committee Minutes, March 3, 1945.

[18] Harold S. Bender letter to A. J. Metzler, P.P.C. file, July 20, 1942. The annual

report of the General Manager of the Publishing House for 1942-43 shows free literature, valued at $600.00 distributed to C.P.S. camps in that year.

[19] Peace Problems Committee Minutes, Aug. 17, 1944.

[20] Harold S. Bender to A. J. Metzler, P.P.C. file, July 25, 1946.

[21] Amos S. Horst, "The Peace Problems Committee in 1947," *Mennonite Yearbook* ('1948), 39:11

[22] *Report of the Twentieth Annual Mennonite Church Conference of the Pacific Coast District* (1941), 5

[23] *Ibid.* (Twenty-third Conference, 1944), 7.

[24] *Report of the Missouri-Kansas Church Conference* (1942), 12.

[25] *Ibid.*, 44.

[26] *Ibid.* (1943), 10.

[27] *Ibid.*, 4, 5.

[28] *Ibid.* (1944).

[29] See copies of letters in files of Harry A. Diener.

[30] *Gospel Herald* (Dec. 9, 1943), 36:760.

[31] *Report of the Missouri-Kansas Conference* (1944), 21.

[32] *Ibid.* (1945), 8.

[33] *Report of the Iowa-Nebraska Church Conference* (1943), 6.

[34] *Ibid.* (1944), 3.

[35] *Ibid.* (1946), 4.

[36] *Report of the Illinois Mennonite Church Conference* (1945), 18.

[37] *Ibid.* (1946), 18.

[38] *Report of the Indiana-Michigan Church Conference* (1944), 6.

[39] *Ibid.* (1946), 5.

[40] *Report of the Ohio and Eastern A.M. Joint Conference* (1943), 26.

[41] *Ibid.*, 24.

[42] *Ibid.* (1944), 10.

[43] *Southwestern Pennsylvania Mennonite Church Conference Report* (1943), 13.

[44] *Ibid.*, 4.

[45] *Ibid.* (1944), 14, 19.

[46] *Ibid.* (1945), 12.

[47] *Ibid.* (1946), 14.

[48] Report of the Peace and Industrial Relations Committee (1943).

[49] *Ibid.* (1944).

[50] *Ibid.* (1945).

[51] *Ibid.* (1945 and 1946).

[52] *Ibid.*, summary report to Mennonite Research Foundation, June 7, 1948.

[53] Report of Jacob M. Moyer to Mennonite Research Foundation, June 15, 1948.

[54] Report of J. C. Clemens, *ibid.*

[55] Report of Landis H. Brubaker and Amos W. Myer, *ibid.* The members of the Lancaster Conference Camp Committee were: Amos S. Horst, John R. Kraybill, Landis H. Brubaker, Jacob B. Mellinger, and Noah G. Good. Amos W. Myer of the Mummasburg congregation reports: "The Mummasburg congregation had only one member in C.P.S. As a pastor I visited that camp four times. I was also appointed pastoral visitor for a number of camps." In this capacity he visited Leitersburg four times, Powellsville and Luray twice each, and Grottoes, Sideling Hill, and Howard each once. "As I was one of many others appointed to visit these camps each one of us did not visit so often."

[56] *Calendar of Appointments of the Mennonite Church of Ontario* (1942-43), 10; (1943-44), 12, 23.

[57] *Report of the Alberta-Saskatchewan Conference* (1945).

58 Report of J. B. Martin to Mennonite Research Foundation.
59 Report of Roy Koch, *ibid.*
60 Report of Oscar Burkholder, *ibid.*
61 *Report of the Conservative A.M. Conference* (1941), 9.
62 *Ibid.* (1943), 6.
63 Letter from E. G. Swartzendruber in Harold S. Bender's P.P.C. file, Aug. 31, 1943.
64 *Report of the Conservative A.M. Conference* (1943), 3.
65 *Gospel Herald* (July 2, 1942), 35:299.
66 *Ibid.* (Aug. 6, 1942), 35:397.
67 Allen H. Erb to Mennonite Research Foundation.
68 W. R. Hershberger, *ibid.*
69 Leroy Gingerich, *ibid.*
70 Alva Swartzendruber, *ibid.*
71 N. A. Lind, *ibid.*, Jan. 9, 1948.
72 Simon Gingerich, *ibid.* It is not stated who was included in the circle letter.
73 Ira S. Johns, *ibid.*
74 Ira A. Kurtz, *ibid.*
75 Paul R. Miller, *ibid.*
76 J. S. Gerig, *ibid.*
77 Stanford Mumaw, *ibid.*
78 James A. Steiner, *ibid.*
79 A. J. Steiner, *ibid.*
80 Reuben Hofstetter, *ibid.*
81 J. J. Hostetler, *ibid.*
82 Moses K. Horst, *ibid.*
83 John R. Mumaw, *ibid.*
84 *Ibid.*
85 Roman H. Miller, *ibid.*
86 Gingerich, *Service for Peace*, 280.
87 Ray Horst, paper in files of M.C.C.
88 Ralph Hernley, *ibid.*

Chapter IX

The Church and Her Members Who Accepted Military Service

THE CHURCH IS CONCERNED

As soon as it became evident that a considerable number of men were accepting military service, the leadership of the church manifested genuine concern. In describing the results of the preliminary census of 1942, the Peace Problems Committee, in its report to General Conference in 1943, said: "This is a startling report and challenges our most serious concern." What the causes for the failure were and what ought to be done about it were not altogether clear. The committee raised the question, however, as to whether the church had maintained an adequate discipline on this point: "One of the measures recommended by General Conference and most of our district conferences to aid in holding our position against war service is the exercise of a discipline which treats men who enter the army as transgressors. We understand that in some places this is not being done. Possibly we need improvement on this point."[1]

At the same time the Peace Committee of the Southwestern Pennsylvania Conference said: "The picture with regard to the stand taken by many of our drafted brethren is not a flattering one and should give us as a conference body grave concern." With the receiving of this report, the conference adopted recommendations: making the Peace Committee a standing committee of conference; providing for a systematic visitation of brethren in C.P.S. camps; giving attention to financial assistance to drafted brethren; and looking to a "constant teaching program on non-resistance and peace," with the Peace Committee helping the ministers in outlining such a program. Finally the members of the conference resolved to "continue to stand faithfully on the peace principles of the New Testament as enunciated by General Conference and our own resolutions from time to time."[2]

In May, 1944, the Ohio and Eastern A.M. Conference passed the following resolution:

WHEREAS, The expression of our nonresistant doctrine has been clouded with a failure on the part of some of our young men to be true, and

WHEREAS, Numbers of our people continue to be employed in defense and other questionable industries and to purchase war bonds in lieu of civilian bonds, and

WHEREAS, Our young men of high-school age are facing severe tests, be it

Resolved, That we definitely teach and preach the Scriptural truths on this doctrine and that the ministry of each local congregation or community provide for counsel and fellowship meetings with those who face these problems and those who have become engulfed in these harmful activities, with a view to helping them to become spiritually established and to recover those who have erred, to their former fellowship.[3]

Early in 1944 the editor of the *Gospel Herald* called attention to the failure of one third of the young men to remain faithful to the teachings of the church, and gave some counsel as to what the attitude of the church should be toward them. Recognizing that the membership of these men was "at least in question," he stressed the obligation of the church to

consider them our sons, to remember them with all the kindness of friendship, to pray for God's continual blessing upon them, and to labor for and expect their return to the fold of the church . . . which has given a consistent testimony against the great evil that they have seen . . . . Let us pray and labor that these many sons of ours may not be lost to Christ and to a full-Gospel church.[4]

A month later a second editorial reported a wide reader response to the first, indicating that "this question is one of the most important before us just now." Some of the respondents felt that the first editorial, in saying that the membership of the men who accepted military service was "at least in question," seemed to imply that one could be both a soldier and a member of the Mennonite Church. To this point the editor replied as follows:

. . . engaging in war is contrary to the teaching of the Scriptures and not only a violation of a rule of the church. An acceptance of the full-Gospel teaching will not allow the position that one may be an obedient Christian either in or out of the army. It is not ours to say that no one has ever gone to heaven from the battlefield. We only know it is the plain teaching of our Lord and of the apostles that we should resist not evil, that we should love and not hate, that we should forgive and not take vengeance . . . . We fully agree that the plain teachings of the Scriptures and the stated position of the church make it impossible to retain in church fellowship and good standing one who becomes a part of the military machine. We were simply trying to describe the attitude and practice of the church as a whole. Some deal with the question by an immediate expulsion. Others leave the question open until the return of the boys. Whichever method is used, it should be a decided matter in the minds of all that a full standing in the church must depend upon a repudiation of all militaristic sentiment and participation.

Some of the respondents also raised questions concerning the nature of the prayers to be offered for church members who were in military service. On this question the editor said:

"To pray for God's continual blessing upon them" is not to pray for God's blessing upon their war effort. It should be clear that no Christian can consistently ask God to bless that which He has condemned. It is not even to pray merely that they may be spared and returned to us unharmed. If we pray for this, we should also, as one brother did, pray that no German or Japanese mother may be bereaved through the participation of our boys in the war. But the chief subject of our prayer for these young men should be that God will, as one brother says, "show them the error of their way and lead them to true repentance." The greatest blessing which God could give them would be a renewed conscience against the awful sin of war. And surely we may pray that in whatsoever situation they may come, they may with saving faith lay hold upon Christ as their Saviour.

But these clarifications, which we gladly make, are in no sense a denial of the main point of the earlier editorial, which is that we want to win these boys back to salvation, to fellowship in the church, and to a positive conviction against militarism. The danger is that their having accepted service will create between them and us a sort of strained feeling which will make us cool, in our friendship toward them, and which will make them sense that they are un-wanted and unwelcome in our churches and in our communities. Let us pray mightily that God will give us a breadth of love which can extend open arms of welcome to the prodigals in uniform, as well as to those who have sinned in other ways.[5]

EFFORTS AT RESTORATION

The minutes show that from time to time the Peace Problems Committee considered this matter, and gave counsel to the church by means of recommendations sent to the district conferences through their secretaries. Essential points in these recommendations were that persons who had accepted service in the armed forces be considered as transgressors and out of fellowship with the church; that efforts be made to restore the men to fellowship through repentance and confession; that where these efforts fail, the men be excluded from church membership; and that these efforts be accompanied by instruction and admonition of the congregations as to the nonresistant faith of the church and its Scriptural basis. The Peace Problems Committee also recommended that restored members be required to relinquish all connection with military and veterans' organizations; that such brethren who may be eligible to receive benefits for physical disability while in service take up the case with their local ministers and conference committees; and that members of the church should hold themselves aloof "from all types of government benefits which jeopardize our position as nonresistant Christians."[6]

In August, 1944, the Peace Committee of the Southwestern Pennsylvania Conference recommended: "That when our boys who took up army service return to our homes and communities, we deal with them sympathetically and Scripturally and try to lead them to see their Scriptural error and to draw them back into true fellowship with the church."[7] This recommendation was adopted by the conference. In May, 1945, the Virginia Conference spent considerable time on this question and adopted resolutions:

1. That all such [who had entered the armed forces] shall be considered as by their own choice to have forfeited their fellowship in the church.

2. That we continue to intercede for them at the throne of grace that the Holy Spirit bring strong conviction upon them both of the truth of God's Word and of their personal responsibility for obedience to it.

3. That the brotherhood, and especially the ministry, should seek to maintain friendly personal contacts with all such past members, showing a sympathetic and courteous attitude, and endeavoring to win them back into the fellowship of the church.

4. That the pastors and bishops arrange for an early interview with men returning from military service . . . and with others who have given sympathetic and moral support to the war effort. They shall seek to ascertain their convictions and endeavor to lead them (through repentance and confession) into full accord with our faith and practice.[8]

In August, 1945, the Illinois Conference recognized the situation in its own district, and placed the blame largely on the ministry itself in the following resolution:

Since present conditions reveal to us as a ministry, a laxity of teaching and example on the principles of nonresistance and nonconformity to our own constituency, we as a ministry bow our faces in shame and repentance and humbly beg forgiveness for our neglect and failure to teach and make these principles known and effective. Because of this some have erred and grown indifferent. Therefore be it

Resolved, That we will with the help of God and the aid of the Holy Spirit, pledge ourselves to more faithfully preach and teach these principles to our constituency. Be it further

Resolved, That in dealing with those who have erred on these principles we endeavor by love to effect a restoration to fellowship and to the joy of Christian service.[9]

The Indiana-Michigan Conference a year earlier had expressed itself in a similar way, stressing the need of a revival within the brotherhood for the deepening of the spiritual life, as a basis for a more consistent nonresistant testimony:

WHEREAS, There is evident a manifest lack of conviction on the part of some young people as well as some parents, and

WHEREAS, The doctrine of nonresistance can be effectively adhered to and exemplified only by regenerated and spiritual believers, therefore be it

Resolved, That we as a ministerial body pledge ourselves afresh to preach a full Gospel, emphasizing repentance and obedience, and that we further appeal to all our congregations to cry mightily to God for a deep revival in all of us. May we all raise our voices against sin by unitedly illustrating the life of Christ in all of our manner of life, convincing the world of the power of God with men in this dark sin-stained world.[10]

The Missouri-Kansas (South Central) Conference in 1943 reported a special meeting for consideration of the question: "What discipline should this conference recommend for those who take up military service?"

It was the unanimous feeling that we need to exercise patience and love toward those who have fallen, yet be firm and Scriptural in consideration of each one. We believe we must abide by our previous Scriptural interpretation, as expressed by General Conference in the leaflet, *Peace, War, and Military Service* and by our Missouri-Kansas Conference Discipline. We furthermore wish to do all possible fully to restore our fallen brethren as opportunity comes.[11]

The situation in the Canadian churches, even though under a different government and conscription system, was virtually the same as in the United States. In the Ontario congregations about the same percentage of men had accepted military service as in the United States, although in Alberta-Saskatchewan less than 10 per cent of the men did so. The official attitude of the church was also similar. In 1945 the Alberta-Saskatchewan Conference passed a resolution on receiving fallen members back into church fellowship, and then said:

> *Resolved*, That in applying this resolution to those who have forfeited their membership through the acceptance of military service, or those whose membership has been affected because of participation in related war activities, we adopt the general policy recommended by the Peace Problems Committee of General Conference.[12]

From these conference actions it is clear that throughout the church, persons accepting military service were assumed, by virtue of that fact, to be under church censure. The Alberta-Saskatchewan Conference used the expression, "forfeited their membership through the acceptance of military service." The Ohio Conference spoke of recovering "those who have erred to their former fellowship." The Southwestern Pennsylvania Conference proposed efforts "to draw them back into true fellowship with the church." The Virginia Conference would do this "through repentance and confession." As early as May 1, 1941, the official conference statement of the Franconia Conference said: "Those not willing to file the conscientious objectors' papers or refuse to accept alternate Civilian Service forfeit their membership."[13] The Lancaster Conference, and perhaps others, made similar announcements at the beginning of conscription.

While it was generally assumed that a man accepting military service was not in fellowship with the church, there was actually much variation from conference to conference and from congregation to congregation as to the manner in which the discipline of the church was carried out. In some cases, soon after a man was inducted into the army, it was announced to the congregation that this person, having renounced the principles of the church, was no longer considered a member. This was the regular practice in certain conferences, particularly in the East. In other cases, bishops in charge of congregations followed the policy of waiting until after the man's return from service. An effort was then made to obtain a satisfactory statement of confession. If this effort was successful, the man was restored to full fellowship. In many cases, statements made by men restored to fellowship were genuine confessions of sin and repentance therefrom. In some cases, however, they were little more than statements of general assent to the teachings of Christ and the church, without pointing up very sharply the real issue at stake. In few if any congregations, however, were persons who had engaged in military service considered as continuing in full fellowship without some gesture at reconciliation.

MANY NOT RESTORED TO FELLOWSHIP

Early in 1949 the Peace Problems Committee made an effort to learn the status at that time of the Mennonite young men who had accepted military service. This was done by means of a questionnaire census similar to that used in making the original draft census. Complete returns on the questionnaire were not received, and some of those received were defective. This was evidently due to inadequate records, and in some cases to careless reporting. From the returns it seemed clear, however, that in about one fourth of the cases, when a man accepted military service it was announced that his church membership had been forfeited. In about three fourths of the cases he was officially considered not in good standing, with further action deferred. In a very few cases were there reports of no action, with the individual considered in good standing.

The most important item in the study was that concerning the present status of the men. The returns showed that 3½ years after the close of the war, approximately 32 per cent of the men who had served in the armed forces were members of the church. Approximately 68 per cent had not been restored to fellowship. Of the latter, about one third were reported as having united with another church. Two thirds were either members of no church, or their church relationship was unknown. Chapter IV shows that the number of men who joined the armed forces was approximately 1,300. This means that through her war experience the Mennonite Church lost approximately 900 young men.[14] It should be remembered that these figures, as well as this entire chapter, deal only with the (Old) Mennonite Church. No comparable statistics are available for other Mennonite groups, since in their case no similar study has been made.

NOTES AND CITATIONS

[1] *Report of Twenty-third Mennonite General Conference* (1943), 38.
[2] *Southwestern Pennsylvania Mennonite Church Conference Report* (1943), 13, 14.
[3] *Minutes of the Ohio Mennonite and Eastern A.M. Joint Conferences* (1944), 11.
[4] *Gospel Herald* (Jan. 20, 1944), 36:897.
[5] *Ibid.* (Feb. 24, 1944), 36:1009.
[6] Minutes of the Peace Problems Committee.
[7] *Southwestern Pennsylvania Mennonite Conference Report* (1944), 14.
[8] *Minutes of the Thirty-fifth Annual Mennonite Church Conference of the Virginia District*, 10, 11.
[9] *Report of the Illinois Mennonite Church Conference* (1945), 21.
[10] *Report of the Indiana-Michigan Church Conference* (1944), 4.
[11] *Report of the Missouri-Kansas Church Conference* (1943), 10.
[12] *Report of the Alberta-Saskatchewan Conference* (1945), 6.
[13] Jacob M. Moyer, Abstract of Minutes of Franconia Peace Problems Committee, and accompanying letter, in files of Mennonite Research Foundation.
[14] See returns of questionnaire in files of Peace Problems Committee.

9

Chapter X

The Entire Brotherhood Is Tested

During the war it was not only the nonresistance of young men of draft age that was under test. It was rather that of the entire brotherhood. It was the entire brotherhood that financed the C.P.S. program, and it was the entire brotherhood that had to face such issues as contributions to the Red Cross in wartime, civilian defense programs, work in war industries, the purchase of war bonds, and related questions.

THE RED CROSS WAR FUND

As early as March 19, 1942, the chairman of the Peace Problems Committee had an article in the *Gospel Herald* dealing with "The Red Cross War Fund." This article quoted an itemized statement of the manner in which the Red Cross planned to spend its current annual budget of $65,000,000. The statement showed that 68 per cent of the fund would be used for the support of the war and defense activities, and only 20 per cent for disaster and civilian emergency relief. The article closed with the suggestion that "those who desire to give conscientiously" might use this analysis "as accurate and reliable information as to what the Red Cross will use its money for in wartime."[1]

In the meantime representatives of the Peace Problems Committee and of the Peace Committee of the Lancaster Conference met with local and national representatives of the American Red Cross to discuss possible ways of co-operating with its work without violating the principle of nonresistance. Following these conversations the Peace Problems Committee on May 29, 1942, adopted the following statement:

STATEMENT TO THE AMERICAN RED CROSS BY THE MENNONITE CHURCH AND AFFILIATED BODIES CONCERNING READINESS TO CO-OPERATE IN WARTIME COMMUNITY SERVICE[2]

The Mennonite Church appreciates the valuable emergency service which the American Red Cross is in a position to render in the local community in wartime as well as peacetime, and encourages its local congregations to co-operate with Red Cross chapters to the full extent of their ability subject only to the provision that such co-operation shall not involve participation in the national war effort and thus conflict with the church's historic conscientious conviction against participation in war in any form.

Specifically we encourage our people to offer the following service to local Red Cross chapters in time of emergency:

1. The care of evacuated children in homes.
2. Housing and feeding of refugees in homes and churches.
3. Service as nurses' aids.
4. Service in disaster relief.
5. Other similar emergency service.

We advise that this service be offered under church administration subject to supervision by the Red Cross or any agency designated by the Red Cross, and that the local congregations or conference make plans in advance to administer the service offered. Lists of qualified registered workers, and of facilities, such as homes, including reception capacity, should be prepared so that Red Cross officials may be informed of the resources to be placed at their disposal.

We encourage our people to contribute to the financial support of this emergency service, as well as in all cases of disaster relief, through church channels which will in turn forward such funds to the Red Cross treasury.

Obviously this statement, which was signed by all members of the American section of the Peace Problems Committee, recognized the possibility of wartime air raids within the United States, and anticipated forms of action which in that event might be taken by local Mennonite congregations. Actually, however, this particular type of emergency never developed; hence there was no opportunity for carrying out the proposed program. The final reference to Red Cross contributions, on the other hand, was a practical suggestion which was taken advantage of officially by the Lancaster Conference. Members of this conference were encouraged to contribute to the Red Cross, stipulating their contributions to be allocated to the disaster relief fund. It is also known that many Mennonites outside the Lancaster Conference followed the same plan, although it is impossible to say how many did so.

Another phase of the Red Cross problem was the Red Cross blood bank. In March, 1944, a questioner in the *Gospel Herald* asked whether a sincere Christian could contribute to this cause. The reply to the question was given as follows:

The use of blood plasma is one of the great advances in medical science. Both civilian and military hospitals use and need it in large quantities, although during wartime military needs probably exceed civilian. We understand that it is the plan that every county in the United States is to have a blood bank with reserve deposits of blood plasma for civilian use. Certainly it is not only right, but a privilege to contribute to such a civilian blood bank. Contributions of blood for military use is another question. Those who cannot participate in war in any form will probably feel that they ought not contribute in this form.[3]

CIVILIAN DEFENSE ACTIVITIES

The problem referred to above was closely related to the larger problem of civilian defense activities. Early in the war every community in the nation was organized under the Office of Civilian Defense, for participation in these activities. Civilian defense activities were designed in part as a means of protection in case of invasion or attack. Emphasis was placed on aid to victims of bombing, on fire fighting, on first aid, and on refugee evacuation. In most communities, however, the danger of invasion or attack during the second World War was slight.[4] In actual practice, therefore, the chief function of civilian defense activities was the building of war morale and the maintenance of the war spirit at a high level. In the beginning considerable pressure was exerted to bring about general participation in this program by all citizens. Consequently nonresistant Christians frequently found it necessary to make difficult decisions. They did not wish to appear unwilling to participate in emergency relief measures for the welfare and safety of their own communities. On the other hand, their conscience would not permit them to become involved in an organization for war promotion, disguised as a community welfare program. The Peace Problems Committee received frequent requests for help in the solution of this question, and in general recommended that "our people should be willing to assist in emergencies which might arise, but refrain from entanglements with war agencies . . . ."[5] Specific help was offered in cases of special difficulty.

The Mennonite congregations affected most seriously by the question of civilian defense were those located near the eastern seaboard, where the danger of bombing was greatest. This was especially true of congregations in Virginia, located in the region of the Newport News shipyards, and in close proximity to other potential bombing objectives. It was this situation which led the Virginia Peace and Industrial Relations Committee to appeal to the Peace Problems Committee for help in the autumn of 1942. This appeal led to a special meeting of the committee on November 6, 1942, at which time representatives of the Virginia, Franconia, and Lancaster conferences were present, as well as John L. Horst, the chairman of the Mennonite Relief Committee. The meeting agreed upon the following nine test questions which might be used as a means of deciding the nonresistant Christian's attitude toward participation in any given activity:

1. Does it partake of the nature of a tax?
2. Does it have the force of law?
3. Does it require the exercise of law enforcement?
4. Does it hinder or help the war effort?
5. Does it contribute to human welfare without compromise to our position otherwise?
6. Is it part of, or under the direction of, military authority?
7. Will it lead to relationships detrimental to our faith?
8. Does it offer an opportunity to give a testimony for Christ?
9. Is it in accord with the Gospel of Christ?[6]

At this meeting it also was tentatively agreed that the time had arrived when the church should consider the promotion and organization of service units, trained and prepared to render efficient and constructive Christian social service in needy areas, in times of war or peace, whether

in the home community, in other communities in the homeland, or in
foreign countries. While the service rendered by such units in wartime
might be thought of as an alternative to the militaristic features of the
O.C.D., the committee had in mind a more comprehensive program of
service which would be continuous, whether in wartime or in peacetime.[7]
In order that the problem of civilian defense as well as the idea of Mennonite service units might be given more careful consideration, a special
study committee was appointed. After considerable study, this committee, consisting of John R. Mumaw, John L. Horst, and C. L. Graber, submitted a report which was accepted by the Peace Problems Committee
on February 11, 1943. The report is in two parts, one dealing with civilian defense activities, and the other with the proposed Mennonite service
units. The latter part of the report is referred to at length in Chapter XVI.
The major portion of the section on civilian defense is quoted as follows:

REGARDING CIVILIAN DEFENSE ACTIVITIES

The Office of Civilian Defense was set up originally to organize the civilian population to meet possible air raid emergencies. Its present function has
come to include many other wartime activities. We have learned that the
civilian defense activities are all geared to the total war program. The organization of local civilian defense councils is intended to integrate and promote within the local community such programs as the Federal Government has called
essential to the winning of the war.

These defense councils have two main functioning branches—civilian protection and civilian war service. Under the protection branch the council functions in the mobilization, organization, and training of personnel capable of
rendering efficient service to the community in emergencies resulting from the
effects of enemy action, especially air raids. It includes the work of air raid
wardens, fire watchers, emergency food and housing provisions, auxiliary police
service, auxiliary firemen, rescue squads, emergency medical service, demolition
and clearance, decontamination, and road repairs. The civilian war service
branch is an effort to organize the civilian activities which contribute to the
prosecution of the war. It includes salvage, transportation, war savings, services to service men, recreation, consumer interests, nutrition, health and medical
care, welfare and child care, housing, education, agriculture, labor supply and
training, and plant utilization. These services are all on a volunteer basis.

Many of these activities represent a type of social service which Christians
need not hesitate to promote. We must recognize, however, that this total
program is motivated by the spirit of militarism. It is sponsored with the view
of making definite contributions to the prosecution of the war. For that reason
we believe that active participation in the civilian defense program is a strain
on the Mennonite conscience.

From the Mennonite viewpoint, it appears that our best expression in the
community relationships is the spirit of co-operation. In our use of transportation facilities we can accept inconvenience without complaint. We can comply
cheerfully with the regulations governing rationed commodities. In some lo-
calities circumstances may justify organizing separate units under church
sponsorship. Certain types of service which contribute directly to human welfare are legitimate expressions of our good will to men. Rescue work, evacuation and feeding of refugees, and other deeds of mercy appeal to us. But unless we can find some official sanction to set up our own service units to co-

operate with the O.C.D., we can hardly consider that type of work. Types of service which have to do with the preservation of property appeal to our people. Fire fighting, bomb squads, fire watchers, and the like could become a legitimate service if it could be organized and sponsored by our own group.

The outline of O.C.D. activities includes the promotion of legitimate industries, the efficient co-ordination of which is necessary to win the war. This involves a large number of enterprising Mennonites. The continuation of such employment is justified on the basis of our service and employment before the war and of its present contribution to civilian life. We are motivated by principles of stewardship and are not engaged in our present vocation in order to make a contribution to the war effort.

From these studies of civilian defense activities we have concluded that during the time of war Mennonites will find it increasingly difficult to engage in activities related to emergencies arising from war. The O.C.D. covers so many areas of community life that we can not compete with their local councils. To participate in their organizations will jeopardize our position because their activities are inspired by war purposes. To avoid complications and a compromise of our nonresistant position and to insure our being able to render a social service that is done in the name of Jesus we must set up our own organization to carry on any work of this kind.

It is evident that Mennonite people should render what service we can to the community in the name of Jesus without waiting for a disaster emergency. We believe, too, it would be well that our people should not wait until a time when O.C.D. officials bring moral pressure to bear upon our people to do something. This should be a voluntary and aggressive step arising from within the congregation. In every community there are additional burdens to be carried because of wartime conditions. We should always be ready to lift that burden for purposes that are not for the prosecution of war. There are legitimate community services which cannot function adequately in the community, such as in the case of general hospital duty where there is scarcity of help. It should be our aim to make such significant contributions before local community pressure is brought to bear upon our Mennonite group.

In the light of these observations we recommend listing the following items as alternate service which we can promote and render as Mennonite service units or individuals: cleaning hospitals, donations to blood banks for civilians or the registering of blood types, sewing service, nurses volunteer service (with local chapter), nutrition training classes, first-aid units, firemen reserves, disaster relief units, and such like.

The study committee's complete report ended with a summary of nine conclusions, of which the first two were as follows: "(1) We see no satisfactory way of participating officially with O.C.D. organizations. (2) We believe that any service of that type in the local community should be alternative service under church direction." The remaining conclusions had to do with the proposed Mennonite service units, as discussed in Chapter XVI. It is important to observe that while the permanent peacetime service unit idea took immediate root, and experienced a continuous growth from that point on, public pressure for participation in civilian defense activities had reached its peak by the time the study committee made its report, and declined in importance from that point on. When the Peace Problems Committee gave its biennial report to General Conference in August, 1943, it was able to say: ". . . the course

of the war with the decreasing likelihood of invasion, has reduced somewhat the pressure on our people for participation in defense activities.
The Peace Problems Committee has never felt that the organization of
alternative service activities on a church-wide scale was necessary or
practical under the circumstances, and accordingly has refrained from
recommending such action."[8]

While the Peace Problems Committee was giving serious attention
to the question of civilian defense, district conferences were doing likewise. Earlier reference was made to the Peace and Industrial Relations
Committee of the Virginia Conference. In 1942 this committee reported
to its conference that, "On the matter of selling junk and paper for defense or in special drives it was decided that we should try to avoid participation in special drives for that purpose, but that it is not wrong to
dispose of these things in normal ways and through normal channels."
The committee also reported having considered the question of permitting one's property to be used for defense purposes. On this matter the
committee said: "It was the sense of the committee that we cannot consent to the use of our property for defense or army use, but that we cannot resist the demands made by the government. In any case we should
always show an attitude of courtesy and humbly in the fear of God
explain our position." In 1943 the committee reported to conference
that, with several local brethren, it had been "agreed to raise no objection
to participation in making a survey of evacuee house facilities in the
Harrisonburg community as sponsored by the Office of Civilian Defense.
At the same time we registered our conviction for the need of being
cautious in any relationships we sustain to local defense chapters of the
O.C.D."[9]

In the Lancaster Conference the brotherhood was requested to
co-operate in a program of caring for refugees and evacuee children.
The Red Cross had approached or written many of the churches of the
county, inquiring as to the availability of church buildings for the care
and feeding of refugees who might be forced out of their homes in case
cities were bombed. The report of the Lancaster Peace Problems Committee says: "The plan seemed to be that the churches be made available
and members of the various churches be responsible to operate the kitch-
ens and serve the refugees, the Red Cross to furnish food and supervise
the program. After some discussion of the matter we all felt this . . . to
be in harmony with our position and should be taken up by the various
congregations and as much as possible be supervised by our own groups,
providing the food, serving it, and providing blankets to sleep on." In
the matter of evacuees, the Lancaster Community Service Association,
at the request of the Red Cross, projected a plan for the removal of children from bombed areas. The plan was to bring the children to receiving
centers for identification and physical examination, after which they
would be assigned to homes made available for their care. On this matter

the report of the Lancaster committee says: "After some discussion of
the problem and various implications it was felt that this is in accordance
with the teachings of the Scriptures, and an opportunity to give a testimony which is in line with our position on war."

In line with these sentiments the Lancaster committee on April 20,
1942, adopted the following resolution:

1. *Resolved,* We favor the care of evacuated children in our homes and
are willing to co-operate with the responsible local agency in working out details. We believe that act of mercy to be in harmony with the teachings of
Christ and the Scriptures. Matthew 25:35.

2. Care of refugees. Since the question has come to our various churches
of arranging and providing for any refugees who might pass through this area,
our committee recommends according to Hebrews 13:2 that our churches be
made available for such emergency and suggests that the local congregations
arrange to provide the necessary food and care wherever possible.

Following this action the committee wrote the Lancaster Community
Service Association, sending a copy of the above resolution, stating the
willingness of the Mennonites to co-operate in the care of such children
in case the need arose, and estimating that the various plain church
groups in Lancaster County could care for 2,000 children. On May 11,
1942, the conference itself took official action regarding the use of church
buildings for the care of refugees. This action said: "We favor the use
of our churches for any emergency in care of refugees; providing that
our local congregations be privileged to administer the care needed,
under the supervision of a Red Cross appointee."[10] In addition to the
eastern conferences, other district conferences also adopted occasional
resolutions dealing with the matter of civilian defense in one form or
another. These resolutions, for the most part, were of a general nature,
advising against any action which would violate the principle of nonresistance or the spirit of the official statement on *Peace, War, and Military Service,* as adopted by the Mennonite General Conference in 1937.
Apparently it did not seem necessary in most of the conferences to deal
with the question in a more specific manner.

WAR INDUSTRIES

A closely related problem, and one which resulted in more violations of the principle of nonresistance within the brotherhood than did
civilian defense activities, was the problem of work in war industries.
On this subject the statement on *Peace, War, and Military Service* says:
"We cannot knowingly participate in the manufacture of munitions and
weapons of war, either in peacetime or in wartime." Soon after the beginning of conscription, and more than a year before the United States
entered the war, the Peace Problems Committee urged men registering
for the draft to be very cautious in claiming deferred classification on the

ground of being employed in an essential industry. It warned that even though the factory might not be making war materials at the time, later developments could make it embarrassing for the C.O. who had claimed deferment on the grounds of working in the plant.[11]

In another letter, apparently in reply to an inquiry by a machinist concerning his own particular problem, the chairman of the committee said: "It seems to us that if you do not take part in the manufacture of direct munitions of war, it would be possible to continue your job as a machinist. Many of the ordinary things of life will be used as equipment for soldiers, and it would be difficult to draw the line. I presume that if your job does not involve the manufacture of military airplanes, tanks, and other direct munitions of war, you should continue. You may find, however, that it may come to the place where your conscience will not permit you to continue in the job which you have because of its connections with war, and you will therefore want to seek other employment."[12]

In its report which was adopted by General Conference in 1941, the Peace Problems Committee again emphasized that, "we can have no part in any activities related to the military or contributing to military objectives. This applies to war service, war finance, manufacture of materials of war, and support of military defense activities."[13] The following summer the *Gospel Herald* published an article by the Peace Problems Committee, entitled: "Can Conscientious Objectors Work in War Industry?"[14] In this article the committee said:

> The conscientious objector is not expected by his fellow citizens and the officials of government to take part in war industry. It is clear to most persons who think, that it would be inconsistent for men who cannot use weapons of war themselves to earn their living out of making weapons of war to place in the hands of others. Local boards, when classifying men for military service, frequently point out the inconsistency in applying for IV-E classification while working in a defense plant. One local board chairman in a community where there is a large nonresistant population has several times vigorously expressed his criticism of men who manifest this inconsistency. He is unwilling to grant conscientious objector classification to those who deliberately and knowingly serve in war industry. We can have no quarrel with his position.

While the article was clear in its statement of principle, it recognized that the application of principles to concrete situations is not always easy. For example, a conscientious objector might find himself in a plant, part of which is engaged in war production, and part in civilian production. In such a case should he resign his job? The committee thought it permissible for the man to remain as long as his own section of the plant continued in civilian production. Again, if a C.O. who has worked in a given factory for years, producing civilian goods, now finds this factory gradually changing over to the making of submarine and bomber parts, what should he do? The committee believed that as soon as it became clear that the major production of the plant was for war purposes, the

C.O. should discontinue his employment in that place. "Again, if a man is working in a factory producing civilian materials which are also used by the armed forces, such as clothes, furniture, food, etc., must he break his connection with such a factory?" The committee thought "not, unless the factory was specifically set up for production for military purposes or its output is contracted for war use for the duration of the war. Temporary or partial commitments to army use would not constitute a clear violation of principle."

While recognizing that the making of decisions was not always easy, the committee nevertheless believed that the sincere conscientious objector, who earnestly sought the correct solution in any given situation, would be able to find it.

When principles are clear, and conscience is clean, and obedience to the truth and the right is well heeded, a sincere believer will find his way through to a right solution of all problems along this line, provided he is willing to follow the guidance of the Spirit of God. It is impossible to set up in advance a set of rules which will help him to decide every case automatically. What is essential is that a clear witness is maintained against war and that the labor of a man's hands goes primarily into peaceful civilian needs.

The article reminded the church, however, that as the war continued, the number of factories in which one could find employment not involving war production would steadily decrease. For this reason many who had gone to the city for work would find it advisable to return to the farm where labor was scarce. Others might find it necessary to give up a job at a high wage for one that paid less well. Some might even be compelled to learn new skills. Attention was also called to the possibility of congressional legislation freezing labor in war industries, or drafting labor for such purposes. For this additional reason it was urged that all persons then engaged in questionable employment should make whatever change was necessary in order to make clear their position as conscientious objectors.

There can be no doubt that these diligent efforts on the part of the Peace Problems Committee had a wholesome effect. On the other hand, the fact that such urgent warnings were necessary is evidence that the nonresistant testimony of many brethren and sisters was weak on this point, as much so as in the matter of service in the armed forces. In its report to General Conference in 1943 the Peace Problems Committee said:

For the first time in our history as a nonresistant people we are faced with the problem of pressure to enter war industry. Our committee has endeavored to aid the church to meet this test by counsel and clarification of issues. While in most places the record is good, there are still those who are willing to sacrifice conscience for the sake of lucrative income, and others whose conscience still needs enlightenment. Some local draft boards see this point more clearly than some of our people and refuse to consider men who work in war industry as eligible for IV-E classification as sincere conscientious objectors.[15]

In addition to the efforts of the Peace Problems Committee for the maintenance of a clear testimony in the matter of wartime employment, district conferences and many local congregations also worked diligently on the problem. In 1943 the Peace and Industrial Relations Committee of the Virginia Conference reported that it had helped in determining whether or not the Wayne Manufacturing Company of Waynesboro, Viriginia, was engaged in making parts for aircraft carriers. "This was done in the interests of IV-E classification of certain Mennonite employees. We had a satisfactory interview with the superintendent of the factory and assisted two brethren of the southern district in their claims as conscientious objectors by furnishing notarized statements of our findings. This was written for their use in submitting evidence of conscientious objection to military service to hearing officer."[16] In 1942 the Southwestern Pennsylvania Conference said: "We are concerned that our brethren and sisters refrain from doing work that is recognized as contributing directly to the military effort."[17]

In 1942 the Ohio and Eastern A.M. Conference said:

It does not appear consistent for our members who are conscientious objectors, to knowingly fail to register as such, to voluntarily continue to work in generally recognized direct war defense shops, or to voluntarily purchase war defense bonds, stamps, and such like. We advise that members who work in factories or departments which manufacture munitions and implements of warfare such as tanks, guns, army planes, battleships, etc., be recognized as having the same standing as those who take up noncombatant service.[18]

In 1943 the same conference reported that from its congregations 255 men were in C.P.S., and 104 in military service, while 66 members were working in regular defense shops. This was followed with the statement: "Draft boards are rigid on defense shops, but rather lenient on farm deferments."[19] In 1942 the South Central (Missouri-Kansas) and the Franconia conferences adopted almost identical resolutions concerning "violations among us in some phases of our Scriptural position on peace, war, and military service," and counseled "those who are violators to prayerfully consider our Scriptural position and to order their lives and activities in accordance with the same in the fear of God and with faith in Him."[20] Employment in defense industries, no doubt, was included among the violations here referred to.

While there was a general uniformity in the official position of district conferences on employment in war industries, there was considerable variation as to the discipline actually exercised on the congregational level. An editorial in the January 13, 1944, issue of the *Gospel Herald* refers to an inquiry from a mother who had sons both in C.P.S. and in the army. The inquirer asked why a brother who joins the army is set back from communion, while another who has received a draft deferment because he is engaged in the manufacture of guns, ammunition, and airplanes, has nothing said to him about his inconsistency. The editor's comment was, "The mother may well be puzzled." Sometime earlier an article by a concerned layman had appeared in the same periodical warning the brotherhood against "a looseness in the discipline of members who are violating the Word of God and ignoring the position of the Mennonite Church in such things as taking part in defense work, buying war bonds, and working in factories where war work is the chief aim . . . . We believe that God is displeased with halfhearted attitudes toward these sacred doctrines."[21]

AGRICULTURE IN WARTIME

Before leaving the question of employment in wartime, a word should also be said about agriculture in wartime. During the second year of the war, for example, someone sent the following inquiry to the *Gospel Herald:* "Is it wrong for our Mennonite young men to work for farmers who raise soybeans for market since soybeans are used in manufacturing war materials?"[22] This refers to a particular agricultural product which in some cases was actually used in the production of war materials; and there were good reasons for raising this question. In addition to this, however, the question was sometimes raised whether the ordinary production of food in wartime is not a contribution to the war effort. Is not food essential for the winning of a war?

In order to assist in clearing away some of the confusion on this question, the chairman of the Peace Problems Committee, in January, 1943, had an article in the *Gospel Herald,*[23] entitled "Farming and Fighting." The article reasoned that since the farmer produces no destructive materials, he is not in the same class as the manufacturer of war materials; that since the farmer is a civilian, taking no orders from the military, he is not in the same class as the soldier or the worker in a war industry under military protection; that since farming is a universal peacetime industry, essential to peacetime civilian life and welfare, it is not a war industry, nor in the same class as industry created for war purposes; that since soldiers who use food produced on farms in wartime also used food from the same farms, either as soldiers or civilians, in peacetime, and since even in wartime not more than 10 per cent of the total farm production is used by the armed forces, farming cannot be considered a war industry or as participation in war; that since in wartime the army is fed and clothed first, and civilians are allotted what remains after the army has its share, the farmer who ceases production in wartime is not taking food from the army, but rather from the civilian population.

The article said that propaganda arguments used against nonresistant farmers usually come either from militarists who want to break down the Christian conscience in order to get more war participation, or from weak Christians, often those engaged in war industry or military service, who desire an alibi for their own lack of conscientiousness. "The argument that the government counts farming as war industry and essential to war, strong though it may seem at first glance, proves nothing except the well-known fact that a war cannot be carried on without healthy soldiers and workers. Food never killed anyone or won any war, though the lack of it has killed many and may have lost wars. Wartime slogans are morale builders and not necessarily truthful. Be wise and not misled by them." The article ended by saying that farming in wartime, for the production of food in the same manner that it was carried on in peacetime, is a consistent thing for nonresistant Christians to do. "For nonresistant farmers to change the pattern of farming," however, "to introduce crops specifically for the purpose of furnishing raw materials for the manufacture of war munitions or implements or for army goods, used for no other purpose, would be wrong, and would be an indirect participation in war."

THE MEDICAL PROFESSION

Perhaps no occupational or professional group experienced greater pressure to enlist its services in the war effort than did the members of the medical profession. Younger physicians whose training had been completed, and who were engaged in private practice, were offered commissions in the army or navy with attractive financial considerations attached. The Procurement and Assignment Service set up by the American Medical Association, and recognized as an official consultation agency for Selective Service, served as an agency to recruit medical personnel for the armed forces, as well as to insure an equitable distribution of physicians on the home front. The Procurement and Assignment committees of the various county medical societies surveyed the available personnel of their respective areas and made recommendations for the assignment of eligible physicians to the army and navy, or for private practice in some local community which had no medical service. Physicians who failed to respond to the recommendations of the Procurement and Assignment committees were frequently subjected to considerable social pressure, and if this did not produce the desired results a I-A classification by the local draft board usually did so. Premedical college students were usually given a deferred classification. Then upon admission to medical school, or some time afterwards, they were inducted into the armed forces, although not called up for active service until after their training had been completed. By the close of the war most medical students in the country were in uniform.

Obviously this situation provided some genuine testing for members of the medical profession who had conscientious objections to military service. The total number of physicians and medical students who were members of the Mennonite Church was not large, but it seems clear that the nonresistant record of this small group was as good as the average of members of the church who were called by the draft, if not better. As nearly as the author has been able to determine,[24] the church had fourteen practicing physicians and dentists of draft age, two of whom accepted military service. Of the remaining twelve, two were women. Three were ordained ministers serving as missionaries in India and Africa. One was a former missionary, now engaged in private practice at home. For a time he had a IV-D classification, because of his ministerial status. Evidently because he had no pastoral charge he was reclassified IV-E, but never called up for service. At one time he was approached by the Procurement and Assignment Committee about offering his services to the army, but after explaining his position as a conscientious objector the matter was not pursued further. One of the twelve was deferred on the ground that his services were necessary in the hospital to which he was attached, although Procurement and Assignment placed great pressure upon him to take up military service. One was deferred because of physical disability. Another, a bit older than the average of the group, was evidently considered essential in his home practice. One was classified IV-E and inducted into C.P.S., where he served for a time, later transferring to the United States Public Health Service. Another physician was classified IV-E, but his call was withheld after he accepted an appointment with the Mennonite Central Committee for relief work in Puerto Rico. The remaining member of this group was in the Public Health Service.

In addition to this group of practicing physicians there were about thirty-one men and two women in medical school. One of the women accepted military service. All of the men were given deferred classifications, while pursuing their medical or premedical training, or both. Of this group, at least five accepted military service. Two were inducted into C.P.S. upon the completion of their medical training. Two were assigned to practice in communities which had no medical service. Thirteen entered foreign missionary or relief service, under a Mennonite mission board or the M.C.C., upon the completion of their training. Two accepted assignments with the Public Health Service. Most of the remainder evidently assumed private practice after the completion of their training. It seems clear that of the forms of service accepted as alternatives to military service, the least satisfactory was the United States Public Health Service. This service was too closely allied to the military; it required the wearing of the uniform while on duty, although not while off duty; and toward the end of the war it came to be officially regarded as a part of the armed service and subject to military orders. For this reason two of the physicians who had accepted Public Health commissions during the period of their training, had their commissions terminated at the end of their training, and accepted assignments from Procurement and Assignment in communities which lacked medical service. It would seem that for the future, the Public Health Service would need to be considered as unacceptable for Mennonite conscientious objectors, unless that service comes to be more clearly divorced from the military than was the case in the second World War.

During the time when medical students were generally expected to accept induction into the armed forces, some of the Mennonite medical students experienced genuine difficulty with their draft boards, or even with the administrations of the medical schools where they were enrolled. The two men mentioned above, as placed by Procurement and Assignment to service in needy communities, were so placed only after their cases had been appealed to the Director of Selective Service. Several men were denied admission to certain schools because of refusal to file the application for army induction which accompanied the application for admission to medical school. It was usually possible, however, for the qualified student to obtain admission to some school. Perhaps the medical school with the most sympathetic attitude toward students with conscientious objections to military service was Hahnemann Medical College of Philadelphia, where throughout the war about 20 per cent of the student body retained their civilian status. At least eight or ten Mennonites studied in this medical school at some time during the war period.

While registered nurses were not drafted during the war, pressure was brought to bear upon some members of the profession to join the armed forces. Adequate statistics concerning Mennonite nurses are not available, although the Mennonite Nurses Association reports that during the war years at least 175 members of the Mennonite Church were registered nurses, and at least 100 were student nurses. "The actual figures would probably be somewhat higher if we had a complete record."[24a] From this group the author has learned of only one who joined the armed forces, although there were several cases of former members who accepted service after leaving the Mennonite Church. The Mennonite Hospital of La Junta, Colorado, reports a letter from the state office of the Nurses Association urging nurses who cannot conscientiously enter military service to offer their services to small rural hospitals who were short of help. A number of La Junta graduates responded to this request, with the result that certain hospitals in Colorado and Kansas received needed help in a time of critical shortage of nurses. In at least one case the La Junta graduates received public recognition through the state Hospital Association for the service thus rendered.[24b] The Mennonite Nurses Association also reports 19 nurses as having served in C.P.S. camps, and 38 in foreign relief work, during the war and up to September, 1950. During this time at least seven nurses were engaged in foreign mission work.[24c]

TEACHERS AND PUPILS IN PUBLIC SCHOOLS

Not the least of the testings which came to members of Mennonite congregations and communities were those experienced by the pupils and teachers of the public schools. In some schools, of course, little or no difficulty was experienced. In others, however, pupils and teachers were subjected to war propaganda, and in some cases even to real persecution. In many cases listening to war speeches and the singing of war songs was bound to have an unwholesome influence, as well as unhappy results. In many schools teachers were expected to direct the sale of war savings stamps, and pupils were expected to buy them. At least one Mennonite schoolteacher, in another branch of the church, resigned her position rather than participate in such activity. It is certain, however, that under the pressure of the time too many Mennonites in the public schools, reluctantly no doubt, but nonetheless really, participated in the sale and purchase of war stamps, in drives for the collection of scrap iron, and in similar questionable activities, in violation of their nonresistant principles.

One Mennonite superintendent of a public school described to the author his own experience during the war years. At the beginning of the war the school board informed this superintendent that, while his personal convictions as a conscientious objector would be respected, he would not be permitted to propagandize his pupils in any way, or to speak openly among them of his nonresistant principles. He agreed to this, only to be dismayed by his own helplessness in the situation as he found one or more of his teachers using their classroom situations as a means of aggressively propagandizing their pupils in support of war. There was little he could do in the situation. Had he attempted to stop this propagandizing activity the board would have considered it a violation of his pledge of silence. Thus a Mennonite teacher found it necessary to remain silent about his nonresistant convictions while his teachers were openly working against the principle of nonresistance, and that in a school where perhaps the majority of the pupils came from Mennonite homes. It is not surprising, therefore, that the nonresistance of a considerable number of young men from the Mennonite congregations of this community, particularly those of high-school age, failed to meet the test when they were called by the draft. An understanding of this situation will go far to explain why, throughout the church, a larger percentage of the younger age group accepted military service than was true of the older group. An understanding of this situation also goes far to explain the establishment of numerous new Mennonite elementary and high schools during the war period, as explained in Chapter XIV.

A matter which for a time threatened to become a serious problem was the projected High School Victory Corps program. This was a plan for enrolling high-school boys and girls in units for the promotion of activities such as physical education, food preparation, and agricultural and industrial work in support of war. Its purpose was to orient the high-school youth psychologically for war service, and to give him a start in a type of work which he might continue after leaving school. The government had developed elaborate plans for this so-called "voluntary" program which, if carried through, would have brought tremendous pressure upon thousands of Mennonite young people to compromise their nonresistant principles. The Peace Problems Committee, as well as the Peace Section of the M.C.C., gave serious attention to this problem. Plans for alternative activities for Mennonite youth, to take the place of the Victory Corps, were discussed by these committees, and in a few local communities were rather far developed. Happily, however, the government dropped its plans, and the High School Victory Corps program failed to develop.

RATIONING AND PRICE CONTROL

Another area in which the faith and the sincerity of nonresistant people were tested during the war was in matters of rationing and price control. Both of these procedures as used in the second World War were new experiences for America and for the American Mennonites. The need for rationing arose out of wartime shortages of food, tires, gasoline, building materials, and other common consumption goods. Its purpose was to guarantee a fair and equitable distribution of the goods which were available after the army had taken what it wanted. The American people do not like to be regimented, and indeed there is little that can be said in favor of regimentation as a principle. On the other hand, when only a limited supply of necessary consumption goods exists, ordinary common sense would suggest that some system is necessary to guarantee to each person a fair share of that which does exist.

This was the purpose of rationing, and those citizens who deliberately violated rationing rules were simply using illegal means to secure more than their share of goods. Thus they were violating the law and also insisting on having that which belonged to someone else, and if a Mennonite fell into this error, he was violating his professed principle of nonresistance on both counts. The writer believes that the majority of Mennonites took the right attitude toward rationing and made a sincere effort to comply with the letter and the spirit of the law. It is certain, on the other hand, however, that there were Mennonite violations of rationing rules. Was the extra gasoline secured upon application always used for the purpose indicated in the application? Did "tractor gasoline," purchased for use in Mennonite farming operations, ever find its way into the tanks of passenger automobiles for consumption on the highways? How many other illustrations of violation would it be justifiable to suggest?

Closely related to the rationing program was the fixing of ceiling prices on goods entering the market. The purpose of ceiling prices was to keep the national economy under control, and to prevent runaway inflationary prices during the period of wartime shortages and abnormal demand for goods. Violations of ceiling price and rationing regulations were known as black-market practices. In many cases where transactions were of a nature easily observed by the public, articles were sold at the legal ceiling price, but could be easily obtained only by purchasers who on the side quietly slipped a generous tip into the seller's pocket. In other cases where the transaction was of a more private nature, the exchange was frankly on a level above the ceiling price, payment often being made in currency rather than by check, in order to avoid danger of detection. How many Mennonites were guilty of this illegal practice, whether as buyers or sellers?

In order to stir up the consciences of the Mennonite people, especially on the matter of rationing, the chairman of the Peace Problems Committee published an article in the *Gospel Herald*, first explaining the purpose, need, method, and benefits of rationing, and then closing with these words:

What shall be our attitude toward rationing? First of all, cheerful acceptance. Grumbling, complaining, criticism are unworthy, unnecessary, and useless. They have no place in the Christian's attitude on such matters. For the nonresistant, they are completely out of place. In the second place, loyal compliance. Prompt, accurate, complete, and willing obedience to all regulations, in letter and in spirit is the Christian's response. In the third place, no evasion or hoarding. In the fourth place, loyal support of the government in the purposes behind rationing, and intelligent and wholehearted encouragement of all citizens to support the rationing program.

What then shall we do? We shall reduce consumption wherever possible. We shall restrict the use of tires, gasoline, transportation, etc., to the minimum, and eliminate pleasure travel. We shall wipe out of our midst the careless as well as the intentional "griping" and complaining that is all too much indulged in and we shall patiently, cheerfully, and loyally do our part to bear the common burdens that fall upon all in time of war. Where possible, we shall increase production so that available supplies may increase, and that the time may soon return when free enterprise and free consumption may again be possible.[25]

In a few instances, although not generally, district conferences felt moved to adopt resolutions referring to the above questions. In 1943, for example, the North Central (Dakota-Montana) Conference discussed the question of attitude toward rationing and other wartime measures, and "*Resolved*, That as a church we manifest a conscientious and cheerful regard for all government regulations and restrictions that are not a part of the war machine."[26] Two years later the Conservative A.M. Conference "expressed its conviction that we need to conform with O.P.A. [Office of Price Administration] regulations and abstain from black-market activities in order to hold a Scriptural relationship toward our government."[27]

UNUSUAL EXPERIENCES

Except for the drafting of young men, and the various wartime demands, restrictions, and regulations referred to above, life in the average Mennonite community continued in wartime much as in peacetime. In a few cases, however, there were unusual experiences, the most striking, perhaps, being that of Strasburg, a small congregation of sixty-nine members located near Chambersburg, Pennsylvania. In January, 1942, the government took over 21,000 acres of land in Franklin County for the construction of a huge ammunition depot. All farms, schools, and churches in the area were taken, including the site of the Strasburg Church and cemetery, and the homes of most of the members of the congregation. A correspondent from the congregation in the following June wrote: "We held our communion the last time we had services there. We felt sad to leave our place of worship, but were strengthened when we thought of how our forefathers met their problems. The Lord made a place for us. There was a vacant church belonging to the Church of the Brethren standing out of the area that was taken. They built a church in Chambersburg and worship there, and through their kindness gave us that church . . . . Our congregation was somewhat scattered by getting other homes, but most of them can come."[28] It is possible that this experience had an effect on the size of the congregation. At any rate, the *Mennonite Yearbook* for 1943 reports fifty-one members for the Strasburg congregation, which is eighteen less than the previous year. The *Yearbook* for 1948 lists fifty-five members.

Besides the Strasburg congregation, there were other Mennonite congregations whose church property and homes were threatened with confiscation, for use as government projects, at one time or another during the war, although this is apparently the only case in which the threat actually materialized. Among the congregations so threatened were: Morrison's Cove, near Martinsburg, Pennsylvania; Mount Joy, in Lancaster County; East Bend, near Fisher, Illinois; Salem, near Tofield, Alberta; and the Wood River congregation, near Wood River, Nebraska. Other congregations were located near army camps whose activities were bound to have some influence on the life of the church community. As an illustration, a correspondent for the congregation at Manitou Springs, Colorado, writes:

At present an army camp is being built six miles south of Colorado Springs to house from thirty-five to forty thousand soldiers. This will increase the population to that extent. Already there are fourteen thousand camp workers at work building this addition to our district living quarters. . . . Six miles northeast of Colorado Springs is our C.P.S. camp in which over 140 C.O. boys are at home. Six miles east of Colorado Springs an air training field is to be built in which from three to four thousand American men will be trained for air service in the national army. All these activities added to our neighborhood add to our opportunities and to our responsibilities toward the men, women, and children involved.[29]

PUBLIC OPINION

Another test which nonresistant people are usually expected to meet in wartime is the test of public opinion. When war feeling is running high, conscientious objectors are likely to be looked upon by the public as evading their patriotic duties. Frequently the result is criticism, sometimes bitter hostility, and even severe persecution. During the first World

War, Mennonites suffered a considerable amount of ill treatment, and as a result of that experience it was expected that in case of a future war the opposition would be even more severe. In actual practice, however, the opposite proved to be the case. This may have been due in part to the fact that during the first World War the American people experienced an overdose of hysteria, which caused them to be more cautious the next time. In the second place, the conscientious objector was better known in 1941 than he had been in 1917, and the public had come to understand him.

In the third place, the C.P.S. program was evidence that the objector to war, even though excused from military duty, was nevertheless ready to perform work of national importance, even without pay. In the fourth place, in most Mennonite communities the C.P.S. program, the civilian bond program, the relief program, and related projects were so well and so favorably known that even though there was criticism on the part of some non-Mennonite neighbors, the general attitude was one of respect, if not of agreement. In Kitchener, Ontario, for example, the House of Friendship was maintained largely by the Mennonites. This mission and relief enterprise was established in 1938 to give spiritual and material assistance to unfortunate persons in difficult circumstances. During the war the House of Friendship became an officially recognized agency for the care of transient and homeless persons. The service which the Mennonites thus rendered received public approval as a worthy community service in lieu of defense activities.

Children in the public schools sometimes experienced ridicule, being referred to as C.O.'s and slackers. A few persons lost their jobs because they declined to purchase war bonds, or because their employers did not want to have C.O.'s around. There were very few cases of violence, however. The Oak Grove Church near Smithville, Ohio, the Wellman Church at Wellman, Iowa, and the East Union Church near Kalona, Iowa, were treated with yellow paint by irresponsible persons. In the latter community it was apparently these same irresponsible persons who surrounded the home of Bishop D. J. Fisher one night and dropped a nuisance bomb on the front porch. The bomb exploded, but without serious effect. The acts of hostility in this community were accompanied by a variety of charges to the effect that Fisher was responsible for keeping members of his congregation from joining the army, from purchasing war bonds, and in general from doing their supposed patriotic duty. The offenders in the Iowa community were promptly arrested, however, and in due course of time the feeling of hostility subsided. The responsible non-Mennonite citizens of the community, although not sharing the nonresistant views of the Mennonites, disapproved the rowdyism which occurred. Many of them personally assured D. J. Fisher of their friendship, and *The Des Moines Register*, the state's leading newspaper, published an editorial explaining the views of the Mennonites, and declaring them to be "certainly not a matter for rowdy neighbors with yellow paint and nuisance bombs."[30]

Similar occurrences could be cited in local communities of other Mennonite groups. On one occasion Newton, Kansas, and even the campus of Bethel College at North Newton, were scenes of minor vandalism. While these incidents seemed serious enough at the time, they were, after all, relatively minor incidents. During the second World War, Mennonite congregations and communities in the United States suffered very little persecution.

NOTES AND CITATIONS

[1] Harold S. Bender, "The Red Cross War Fund," *Gospel Herald* (March 19, 1942), 34:1091.

[2] Minutes of Peace Problems Committee, May 29, 1942.

[3] *Gospel Herald* (March 9, 1944), 36:1063.

[4] This is not saying that the danger did not seem real for a time; nor is it saying that in case of a future war it will not be very great. Indeed, in case of a future war it seems unlikely that United States territory will escape bombing.

[5] "Report of the Peace Problems Committee," *Twenty-third Mennonite General Conference* (1943), 36, 37.

[6] The test questions and the idea of service units were first suggested to the Peace Problems Committee by the Peace and Industrial Relations Committee of the Virginia Conference. These ideas were then developed further at the meeting of Nov. 6, 1942, and formulated in the manner given here. See memorandum of the Virginia committee to the P.P.C. Also Minutes of Peace Problems Committee, Nov. 6, 1942.

[7] *Gospel Herald* (March 25, 1943), 35:1106.

[8] *Twenty-third Mennonite General Conference* (1943), 36, 37.

[9] Report of Peace and Industrial Relations Committee of the Virginia Conference (1942), in files of Peace Problems Committee.

[10] Reports of the Lancaster committee in the files of Peace Problems Committee.

[11] Harold S. Bender to H. R. Schertz, Nov. 2, 1940, in Peace Problems Committee correspondence.

[12] Harold S. Bender to Lewis Kauffman, Nov. 5, 1940, *ibid.*

[13] *Twenty-second Mennonite General Conference* (1941), 21, 22.

[14] *Gospel Herald* (June 25, 1942), 35:282.

[15] *Twenty-third Mennonite General Conference* (1943), 38.

[16] Report of Peace and Industrial Relations Committee of the Virginia Conference (1943) in files of Peace Problems Committee.

[17] *Report of the Southwestern Pennsylvania District Mennonite Church Conference* (1942), 14.

[18] *Report of the Ohio Mennonite and Eastern A.M. Joint Conference* (1942), 15.

[19] *Ibid.* (1943), 37.

[20] *Report of the Missouri-Kansas Conference* (1942), 6; Resolutions Passed at the Franconia Conference (Oct. 1, 1942), in files of Peace Problems Committee.

[21] William O. Hobbs, "Maintaining Scriptural Discipline and Nonresistant Faith," *Gospel Herald* (March 18, 1943), 35:1092.

[22] *Gospel Herald* (Aug. 5, 1943), 36:379.

[23] *Ibid.* (Jan. 28, 1943), 35:938.

[24] The author is indebted to H. Clair Amstutz, M.D., secretary of the Mennonite Medical Association, for help in gathering the statistics here given.

[24a] Letter, Dora Taylor to Guy F. Hershberger, Nov. 1, 1950.

[24b] Letter, Maude Swartzendruber, Oct. 9, 1950.

[24c] Letter, Verna Zimmerman, Sept. 28, 1950.

[25] *Gospel Herald* (March 11, 1943), 35:1074-5.

[26] *Ibid.* (July 15, 1943), 36:340.

[27] *Report of the Conservative Amish Mennonite Conference* (1945), 11.

[28] See *Gospel Herald* (Jan. 22, 1942), 34:909; (July 2, 1942), 35:300.

[29] L. C. Miller, in *ibid.* (May 28, 1942), 35:185.

[30] *The Des Moines Register* (June 17, 1942), 10.

Chapter XI

Civilian Bonds

Wars cost tremendous sums of money which are generally obtained through increased taxation and the sale of special government war bonds. In time of war, therefore, nonresistant people find it necessary to decide what their attitude must be toward war taxes and war loans. As to taxes, Mennonites have generally taken the attitude that these should always be paid to the government under which they live. Romans 13 and I Peter 2 teach that government serves a useful purpose for the restraint of evil and the protection of the good. For this reason Christians are to pay taxes, "tribute to whom tribute is due, custom to whom custom."

If anyone objects to the payment of taxes because a portion is used for the financing of war, in which conscientious objectors cannot participate, Mennonites would reply that they cannot participate in any of the coercive functions of government. From the viewpoint of nonresistance, the police function as well as the military is forbidden to the Christian. The coercive functions of the state have been ordained of God, however, for the maintenance of order in a sub-Christian society. Since Christians live in the midst of this society they are commanded to be obedient to its government and to pay taxes for the performance of its necessary functions. Furthermore, the payment of taxes is not a voluntary act; it is compulsory. If the individual refuses to pay his taxes the government will take them by force; and to this act of distraint the nonresistant Christian can not resist. The use which the government then makes of the proceeds is the responsibility of the government, not that of the nonresistant taxpayer.

The lending of money to the government, however, is a voluntary act; it is not a tax. The individual is free to lend or not to lend as his conscience directs. Therefore, if the nonresistant Christian is invited voluntarily to lend of his means for the waging of war, it is only consistent that he should decline to accept the invitation. For this reason the Mennonite statement on *Peace, War, and Military Service* says: "We can have no part in the financing of war operations through the purchase of war bonds in any form or through voluntary contributions . . . , unless such contributions are used for civilian relief or similar purposes." Even though the purchase of war bonds is a voluntary act, as stated above, the experience of the Mennonites during the first World War showed that the pressure of public opinion, and of government war agencies, can become very strong in their insistence that citizens make such purchases. So great was the pressure at that time that many Mennonites succumbed and purchased war bonds, while some of those who refused suffered considerable persecution. This was not a very satisfactory experience. Therefore, as the second World War approached, it was felt that a better solution should be found for this problem. The C.P.S. program was an improvement over the military camp experience of conscientious objectors during the first war. Why should there not also be an improvement over the war bond experience of twenty-five years earlier?

THE CANADIAN CIVILIAN BOND PLAN

Since Canada had entered the war in 1939, the nonresistant people of that country were confronted with this problem in advance of those in the United States. Early in the war the Canadian peace churches appealed to the Dominion Government at Ottawa for an opportunity to make wartime contributions to a cause in harmony with their nonresistant convictions. This appeal was honored on December 11, 1940, when the government announced a loan of $1,000,000 to be recognized by registered non-interest-bearing certificates, the proceeds of which would be used for the alleviation of distress or human suffering due to the war. Here was a bond issue for relief purposes, and not for war, which nonresistant people could purchase with a clear conscience; and the government announced that the purchase of these bonds by members of the peace churches would satisfy as a suitable substitute for the purchase of war bonds. Later it was provided that conscientious objectors who desired to receive interest on their loans might purchase the regular war bond, with a special sticker attached, indicating that the loan would be used for relief purposes, the same as the non-interest-bearing certificates.

The Canadian churches responded generously to this opportunity. During the time of the second Victory Loan in 1942, for example, the Military Problems Committee, representing the Ontario peace churches, sent letters to all Mennonite families asking their co-operation in the purchase of the special types of certificates and bonds. In June, 1945, the Military Problems Committee reported to the Ontario Conference that the total amount of non-interest-bearing certificates purchased to date by all branches of Mennonites in all of Canada was $822,660.16, and the total of interest-bearing bonds with stickers attached was $3,849,750.00.[1] There is no way of knowing what share of this amount was purchased by members of the Mennonite Church.

EFFORTS FOR A SIMILAR PLAN IN THE UNITED STATES

In the United States it did not prove possible to make an arrangement with the Treasury Department as satisfactory as that in Canada. As early as October 24, 1941, however, the executive secretary of the

Mennonite Central Committee reported to the Chicago meeting of church leaders[2] that the M.C.C. was arranging to issue certificates of receipt for contributions made to War Sufferers' Relief and Civilian Public Service. It was the thought that such certificates could be used as substitutes for giving to defense and war drives, such as those of the U.S.O. (United Service Organizations). The secretary also reported the possibility that the Treasury Department would issue a special agricultural bond which could be purchased by nonresistant people as a substitute for defense or war bonds. He said the National Service Board for Religious Objectors was working on this problem.

Following the declaration of war on December 8, 1941, war bond drives were promptly gotten under way, but the problem of a substitute bond had not been solved. Church leaders were doing all they could, however, as can be seen from the following letter of December 16, 1941, sent by the Peace Problems Committee to all bishops of the Mennonite Church:

An urgent issue which faces many of our brethren at the present time, particularly those working in factories, is that of defense bonds. Drives are already being put on in factories, to purchase bonds and stamps, and in other ways pressure is being brought upon our people to participate in bond campaigns. We wish to inform you that we are working diligently on the question of a substitute government bond to be bought by nonresistant people as an alternative to war and defense bonds. We believe that by next week we will be able to report to the church success in arranging for such a bond. Meanwhile, we would like to urge our people to patiently and faithfully maintain their position of nonparticipation in the financing of the war in any respect, in accord with our historic position and the resolution of the 1937 Turner, Oregon, General Conference.

In advising our members along this line, we are not suggesting that they in any way obstruct the sale of war bonds nor that they refuse to support their government in its nonmilitary activities and financing. We need to be very careful in this respect. We should, however, remind our people that there is no compulsion in the purchase of war or defense bonds and that liberty of conscience on this matter is still recognized. Our people should, therefore, be careful not to be stampeded or overwhelmed by any local pressure. If our bishops will inform their ministers and people in general of the prospect of getting a substitute for war bonds, we believe this will help many to hold steady.

Meanwhile, the donation certificates which were promised at the Chicago meeting on October 24, are now ready. They can be secured by writing to E. C. Bender, Treasurer, Mennonite Board of Missions and Charities. You will understand that these certificates are to be used for donations to relief and Civilian Public Service and will not substitute for bonds. Their chief value will be, however, to serve as an alternative to contributions to Red Cross and U.S.O. drives in local communities. They can also be used, of course, as an alternative to war bonds if the donations are sufficiently large to count in this way. In addition to certificates for $10.00 or more, we are also furnishing stamps in denominations of 10¢.[3]

The belief that a civilian bond issue could be announced in the near future was based on the fact that Orie O. Miller and John E. Lapp had an appointment with Treasury Department officials for the following week. It was hoped that this conference would bring current efforts to fruition. The conference was held on December 23, according to schedule, but no conclusion was reached. Then on December 26, 1941, the Peace Problems Committee decided: (1) To "continue every possible contact until a satisfactory solution is found to the problem of defense bonds and defense stamps for our people. (2) That until then a statement be prepared and our membership throughout informed of how their own willingness to subscribe money for government support can be consistently shown."[4]

The Peace Problems Committee looked to the Mennonite Central Committee for help in preparing this statement. This help was received when the latter met in its annual meeting on January 3, 1942. At this time the M.C.C. officially expressed its gratitude for the manner in which the government had recognized the conscience of those who cannot bear arms, and asserted its belief that a similar freedom would be granted "in lesser demands" as well. A ten-point "appeal to our people" was then adopted, of which number six urged "that we do not purchase war and defense bonds and savings stamps, but rather purchase civilian government bonds and savings stamps as they are available." It was then suggested: (1) That M.C.C. certificates and stamps, representing contributions for relief and C.P.S., continue to serve as alternatives to defense bonds and savings stamp purchases, particularly for persons with limited means and for children. (2) That persons "able to purchase bonds of substantial size make use of a statement of readiness to purchase civilian bonds when they become available." The following statement was then approved by the M.C.C., and also by the Peace Problems Committee.[5]

STATEMENT OF READINESS TO PURCHASE CIVILIAN GOVERNMENT BONDS

In consistency with my religious belief and conscientious convictions I cannot aid or abet war or give voluntary support to the national war effort, and for these reasons cannot purchase government obligations, the proceeds of which are used for war purposes. However, I do wish to support my country with such means as are at my disposal, for constructive ends and particularly in works of relief of human need and suffering, and am accordingly prepared and ready to purchase $_____ par value of government obligations that may become available for such purposes, when and as they are approved by the Mennonite Central Committee to this end. I will subsequently make additional purchases as my circumstances and the general situation may warrant.

Date _____ Signed _____

This statement was printed and distributed throughout the brotherhood for use wherever needed.

In March, 1942, the M.C.C. reported that the Treasury Department had not yet issued the hoped-for bonds, earmarked for civilian services, but added that "there is reason to believe that such will eventually be available." The M.C.C. urged that in the meantime the "Statement of Readiness to Purchase Civilian Government Bonds" continue to be used. "These have provided temporary relief of pressure in most cases where wisely applied."[6] Two months later, when the war bond campaign was being actively promoted in the middle western states, the Peace Problems Committee received numerous requests for information and help. In response to these inquiries the committee addressed a letter to all bishops of the conferences in this area, saying that, "There seems to be a general intent to maintain our position on this question. . . . However, a few of our people, possibly because of delay in providing civilian bonds, have been tempted to yield to local pressure and buy war bonds." The letter then emphasized the following points:

1. We are informed by officials in Washington that there is no compulsion to buy war bonds. Whoever buys, does so because he wants to.

2. In places where the "Statement of Readiness to Buy Civilian Bonds" has been presented, bond campaign chairmen have approved it, and our position is recognized.

3. Civilian bonds have not yet been provided, but a meeting held yesterday in Philadelphia reports progress made. The committee will work at this until it is successfully arranged.

4. We would urge that our conferences through their executive committees give advice and counsel to our people, urging them to hold the position we have taken.

5. In some places the M.C.C. certificate of donation to C.P.S. and War Relief is acceptable as a substitute.

Whatever the pressure, there is no need or reason for us to yield on the point of war bonds any more than we expect our boys to yield and accept military service. May it not be said this time as in the last war, that our home people were not as loyal and staunch to our nonresistant faith as our boys who went to camp. Even government officials agree that we cannot consistently purchase war bonds if we ask for exemption from the army.

We do not want to be negative and evade duty. Hence our people should be encouraged to purchase civilian bonds in line with their ability. We are not escaping sacrifice, but rather sacrificing in line with a Christian conscience on war.[7]

THE UNITED STATES PLAN NOT ENTIRELY SATISFACTORY

In June, 1942, the prolonged effort to obtain an issue of civilian bonds at length bore some fruit. The outcome was less satisfactory, however, than the arrangement provided by the Canadian government. Paul Comly French, representing the peace churches through the National Service Board for Religious Objectors, had presented the Canadian plan to officials of the United States Treasury Department on numerous occasions. The Treasury Department finally replied, however, that it had investigated the Canadian plan and considered it too expensive to administer. On May 18, 1942, Orie O. Miller prepared a letter at the direction of the M.C.C., once more setting forth the Mennonite concern, and referring to the Canadian plan as a satisfactory way of meeting the need. This letter, with letters from the other peace groups, was presented to the Under Secretary of the Treasury by Paul Comly French in person. This presentation and conversation resulted in a letter from French to the Secretary of the Treasury asking whether it would be "possible for us to purchase regular issues of Treasury bonds and notes and then redistribute them to our people in smaller denominations through a nonprofit corporation we are organizing." The Secretary of the Treasury replied that this plan would be acceptable. The proposal was that from time to time, as Treasury bonds and certificates of indebtedness would be offered to the public "and which are not designated by their terms as 'war issues,'" the proposed corporation would be notified of the fact. The latter would then have the privilege of buying such amounts of these securities as it could use and distribute them in various denominations to individual subscribers who could not conscientiously buy war bonds.

After receiving this proposal, the interested groups agreed that instead of organizing a new corporation to act as an intermediary for the distribution of the loans, an existing financial organization should be used for this purpose. The organization agreed upon was the Provident Trust Company of Philadelphia. Officials of this banking institution, among whom were a number of sympathetic Quakers, agreed to the plan, and by June 22, 1942, the details had been worked out to such an extent that the program was considered ready for presentation to the interested groups. Accordingly, on June 25, 1942, a meeting called by the M.C.C., and attended by representatives of the various Mennonite and affiliated groups, was held in Chicago. Following an explanation of the civilian bond plan the meeting approved it, and charged the M.C.C. with "the responsibility of representing the co-operating Mennonite and Associated groups in the administration and promotion of the plan."

Orie O. Miller was appointed M.C.C. representative on the Civilian Bond Committee, which represented the N.S.B.R.O. and the constituent groups in negotiating with the Provident Trust Company and the Treasury Department. It was also announced that the Brethren Service Committee had already approved the plan, and that the American Friends Service Committee had it under advisement.

The plan provided that persons wishing to purchase civilian bonds could do so in denominations of $50.00, $100.00, $500.00, or $1,000.00. These amounts, plus a service charge of $1.50 for each bond purchased, were to be forwarded to the Provident Trust Company. The latter would then complete the purchase, and after receiving the registered bond from the Treasury office would forward it to the subscriber. The announcement of the plan in the church papers stated that individuals desiring to make a contribution to a church institution or a charitable institution could do so by registering a civilian bond in the name of this institution. The bond itself, or a receipt from the institution receiving the bond, would then serve as evidence of having discharged a government obligation; and the purchaser would receive credit in the county quota. A receipt for bonds registered in the name of a church or charitable institution would also serve as evidence for income tax deductions.

During the war many industrial organizations followed the plan of deducting a percentage from the employees' wages for the purchase of bonds. Announcements of the civilian bond plan stated that employees could instruct their employers to deduct a similar percentage from their pay, and reserve the deductions until a sufficient amount had been accumulated for the purchase of a fifty-dollar civilian bond, or more. The employer would then forward the amount to the Provident Trust Company for processing. The announcement also said that if purchasers of civilian bonds could subscribe through their local defense bond solicitor, this might be a helpful way of offsetting the pressure by local groups for war bond purchases. Subscribers were warned, however, to take proper precautions that the funds be invested through the proper channels, that is, through the Provident Trust Company. An unsatisfactory feature of the plan was the fact that no bonds were available in denominations smaller than fifty dollars. To remedy this defect the M.C.C. suggested that local congregations set up a plan whereby smaller subscribers would contribute to a fund which would be used to purchase a bond for a group. Individual subscribers would then receive receipts for the amount subscribed individually.[8]

Later, however, the Provident Trust Company arranged to purchase regular Treasury Bonds, costing $18.50 each, and maturing in twelve years at $25.00. Also, to satisfy the increasing number of requests for savings stamps of a civilian character, the Mennonite Central Committee made available a series of M.C.C. Savings Stamps for Civilian Bond Investment. These were provided in denominations of 10¢, 25¢, 50¢, and $1.00. Congregations desiring to make use of such stamps were encouraged to appoint someone as treasurer to be responsible for their distribution. Funds received from the sale of stamps would be held by the treasurer until a given purchaser had accumulated sufficient funds for the purchase of a civilian bond. For the purchase of the smallest bond, the subscriber must submit in stamps, or in stamps and cash, a total of $19.50. This included $18.50 for the bond, plus a service charge of $1.00 as required by the Provident Trust Company.[9] After the bond plan got under way it also developed that the Treasury Department actually did not issue the civilian bonds in denominations of less than $100.00. As a result the Provident Trust Company accumulated a large number of subscriptions for $50.00 bonds which it was unable to complete. Attempts were then made to solve this problem by having the subscribers send in an additional $50.00 and receive a $100.00 bond, or send in an additional $5.50 and receive three treasury savings bonds at $18.50 each.[10]

When the civilian bond plan was announced it seems to have met with general approval. The Southwestern Pennsylvania Conference in August, 1942, adopted a resolution saying: "We strongly urge our ministry to encourage the purchase of such bonds by our people, and that they make arrangements to bring this matter before individual members in some systematic way. It is very evident that it is both inconsistent and unnecessary for our people to purchase war and defense bonds."[11] Later in the year the chairman of the Peace Problems Committee, in a printed letter to ministers in charge of Mennonite congregations, said: "We appreciate the way our people are responding to the Civilian Government Bonds. Thus far 90 per cent of all subscriptions have come from Mennonites and Amish of various branches, and our branch is supplying a large part of this. We consider it our duty to purchase these civilian bonds in line with our ability and what the government expects of those who buy war bonds. We trust each congregation has appointed a representative to handle subscriptions and forward them to the Provident Trust Company in Philadelphia according to instructions sent out."[12]

In 1943 the secretary of the Ohio Conference reported: "Our people are doing quite well in purchasing Civilian Government Bonds."[13] In its report to General Conference in 1943, the Peace Problems Committee said that as of August 1, 1943, about 10,000 Mennonite subscribers had purchased civilian bonds totaling $1,500,000.00. This figure included all Mennonite groups; no information was available as to the share of the Mennonite General Conference constituency, although it was known to be substantial. The Peace Problems Committee was aware, however, that not all of the constituency was supporting the civilian bond plan. On this matter the committee said: "We have no dependable information on this point, but have been informed that in some of our communities there is considerable weakness and that war bonds are being bought by some of our members."[14] Whatever the amount was, it would seem that many of the actual war bond purchases were made by persons who had no great conscience against doing so. While there is no way of knowing what percentage of the brotherhood lacked this conscience, it would not seem unreasonable to assume that the church's weakness on this point was about as great as the weakness reflected in the number of men who accepted military service.

On the other hand, it is also likely that some war bonds were purchased by persons who did have a conscience against supporting the war effort, but who were confused by the unfortunate manner in which the civilian bond plan operated. At first, as said above, $50.00 bonds were declared available, and smaller denominations not. Then, after many people had paid their subscriptions, the smaller bonds were actually issued and the $50.00 denomination declared unavailable. At first it was provided that civilian bonds should be purchased through the Provident Trust Company. Later, however, these same bonds were also made available to the public generally, through local banks. Even though they were not labeled war bonds, they were nevertheless counted as such by local bond drive organizers. In this situation it is not surprising that some conscientious persons were confused; that they honestly questioned the difference between the two kinds of bonds; and that less conscientious persons used this situation as a justification for purchasing war or defense bonds, labeled as such. The Peace Problems Committee recognized this unsatisfactory situation. Its report to the 1943 General Conference refers to "long and wearisome negotiations with the Treasury Department," in an effort to obtain the civilian bond plan in the first place. The committee frankly said that "the civilian bond plan as arranged is not what we wanted, and not altogether satisfactory"; and added that "recently the further handicap has developed that these bonds are now available to the public generally through local banks."[15]

THE PLAN NEVERTHELESS A TESTIMONY AGAINST WAR

It was the committee's opinion, however, that even this unsatisfactory plan was a genuine testimony against war; and that if bonds were purchased at all they should be purchased through the Provident Trust Company. This would constitute a clear refusal, both to purchase bonds designated as war bonds, and to participate in war bond campaigns. To purchase bonds at the local bank during the war bond campaign, even though the bonds were not specifically labeled as war bonds, would nevertheless put the nonresistant Christian in too close alliance with the war effort. In September, 1943, the chairman and secretary of the M.C.C. Peace Section set forth the advantages of the civilian bond plan as follows:

By subscribing through the program provided, we leave a united witness of conscience against war. The plan is not altogether what was desired at the beginning, but is the best that could be gotten. Your committee has consistently recognized this, but we have also consistently pointed out that it is a step far in advance of anything achieved heretofore. By our response and adherence to it we hope eventually to gain greater recognition and respect on this issue.[16]

The Peace Section believed, and rightly so, that, "There is no other way to witness for our position, and still purchase government bonds, than the M.C.C. civilian bond plan." The only alternative would have been a refusal to purchase any bonds whatsoever.

In this connection it may be noted that some brethren felt themselves conscientiously unable to purchase any kind of government bond. In the September 23, 1943, issue of the *Gospel Herald*,[17] John M. Snyder had an article setting forth the view that refusal to purchase any kind of government bond is the only consistent position for the nonresistant Christian to take. Snyder recognized that the civilian bonds did help in registering a protest against war bonds. He felt, however, that they actually served the same purpose as war bonds, especially since the Treasury Department did not clearly commit itself to use the proceeds strictly for civilian purposes. Snyder's objections went further than this, however, since he believed that the nonresistant Christian should not invest his money in government bonds, even in peacetime, for purposes definitely known to be civilian in character. The owner of any kind of government bond, he said, holds title to a portion of the government's capital investment. This makes him party to the operation of the state, which a nonresistant Christian cannot consistently do. Taxes are in a different category, since in this case the government assumes title to the money, and the entire responsibility for its use. In the case of bonds, however, the individual holds the title, making him responsible for its use.

It is not known how many Mennonites refused, for conscience' sake, to purchase any kind of government bond during the second World War; nor how many agreed with the position described above. Very likely, however, the majority of Mennonites would agree that the civilian bond plan as it operated during the war was not satisfactory. The M.C.C. and the Peace Problems Committee would agree fully with this position. It is clear, however, that the M.C.C. did everything it could to obtain a better plan, and failed in this attempt. The civilian bond plan was only a partial success. In the first World War, however, no concessions were granted by the Treasury Department at all; and often the pressure of local communities was such that the individual either had to purchase war bonds or suffer for not doing so, which many did. It would seem therefore that the brotherhood owes a debt of gratitude to the Peace Problems Committee, and to the M.C.C., for the partial success which they did achieve in the second World War.

Furthermore, the fact that the Canadian government did issue a genuine civilian bond, to be used specifically for war sufferers' relief, is evidence that efforts of nonresistant people in this direction can result in success. It is to be hoped, therefore, that in case of a future war the nonresistant people will again ask for such consideration, and that the effort will be more successful than it was in the United States in the second World War. For such success, if it is realized, many people will be highly grateful. The figures show that even under the unsatisfactory plan of the second World War, nonresistant people purchased 33,006 subscriptions, for a total value of $6,740,161.14 in civilian bonds, most of them through the Provident Trust Company. Of this amount, $4,911,277.00 was subscribed by Mennonites of the various groups.[18] The amount purchased by the members of the (Old) Mennonite Church is not known; it was, however, a substantial share of the above amount.

NOTES AND CITATIONS

[1] *Calendar of Appointments of the Mennonite Church of Ontario* (1945), 23.

[2] This was the meeting called by Peace Problems Committee to review the status of C.P.S., described on page 66 ff.

[3] Copy in files of the Peace Problems Committee.

[4] Peace Problems Committee Minutes.

[5] *Ibid.*, Jan. 3, 1942.

[6] *Gospel Herald* (March 19, 1942), 34:1093.

[7] Copy in Peace Problems Committee files, May 13, 1942.

[8] An analysis of the plan, with historical background, is given in "The Civilian Bond Purchase Plan," *Gospel Herald* (July 16, 1942), 35:346-7.

[9] M.C.C. Peace Section: Memorandum covering suggested procedure in use of savings stamps for civilian bond investments purpose. In Peace Problems Committee files.

[10] Provident Trust Company to Mennonite Relief Committee, May 31, 1945. See Peace Problems Committee files.

[11] *Report of the Southwestern Pennsylvania District Mennonite Church Conference* (1942), 13, 14.

[12] Peace Problems Committee letter to ministers in charge of Mennonite congregations, Oct. 30, 1942. Copy in files of Peace Problems Committee.

[13] *Reports of the Ohio Mennonite and Eastern A.M. Joint Conference* (1943), 27.

[14] *Twenty-third Mennonite General Conference* (1943), 38.

[15] *Ibid.*, 37.

[16] "The War Bond Campaign," *Gospel Herald* (Sept. 23, 1943), 36:538.

[17] "On the Civilian Bond Question," *ibid.* (Sept. 23, 1943), 36:538-41.

[18] *The Reporter*, Feb. 15, 1946.

Chapter XII

The War and the Work of the Church

A war of four years' duration was bound to affect the work of the church in numerous ways. The second World War did not only take thousands of Mennonite young men from the life and work of their home congregations, for induction into C.P.S. It also diverted the energies of numerous other men from necessary normal phases of church work, into the new emergency program. The work of the general and district conferences was affected by the war. So was the mission program of the church. The Mennonite Publishing House was confronted with new problems. The schools and colleges of the church found themselves in new situations with respect to enrollment, faculty, administrative staffs, programs of instruction, and in other respects. The relief program of the church came to be greatly enlarged as a result of the war; and the war saw the emergence of a new type of church program in the form of Mennonite service units.

MENNONITE GENERAL CONFERENCE

In 1943 the biennial meeting of the Mennonite General Conference was restricted to delegate sessions. Instead of a mass meeting with thousands of people gathered in a large tent, as had been the practice for many years, the 1943 Conference consisted chiefly of several hundred ministers gathered in the assembly hall of Goshen College. Happily, however, this curtailment of activity was due merely to wartime travel restrictions, and not to any effort on the part of government to thwart the work of the church. The Peace Problems Committee was able to report to this session of General Conference that it had been assured by government officials that "There would be no governmental restrictions on a normal indoctrination of our people according to the historic faith of our church, and that our church publications could continue to publish our peace testimony as before."[1] This statement is amply verified by the continued production of peace literature throughout the entire period of the war, as described in Chapter XVII. As mentioned elsewhere, this session of General Conference increased the size of the Peace Problems Committee so that it now consisted of sixteen members, twelve from the United States and four from Canada. Following 1943 no regular session of General Conference was held until 1947, when the older type of mass meeting was resumed. A special session for delegates was held at Goshen College in

1944, however; and a special session for delegates, with attendants from local congregations, at Souderton, Pennsylvania, in 1946.

Following the termination of C.P.S. and the Selective Service System, on March 31, 1947, the Peace Problems Committee authorized its chairman and secretary to "write an appropriate letter of appreciation to President Truman, General Hershey, and Colonel Kosch for their attitude and consideration through C.P.S. and World War II."[2] Certain district conferences at one time or another sent similar letters to appropriate officials. The Mennonite General Conference at its regular session in 1947 authorized letters to President Truman, Prime Minister W. L. Mackenzie King, and General Hershey. These letters, as signed by the moderator and secretary, together with the replies thereto, are given below:[3]

The Honorable Harry S. Truman   August 28, 1947
The President of the United States
The White House
Washington 3, D.C.
Sir:
The Mennonite General Conference, assembled in biennial session at Wooster, Ohio, August 28, 1947, and representing over 50,000 Mennonites in the United States and Canada, by unanimous action of the delegates present, expresses herewith its grateful appreciation for the provisions of the National Selective Service and Training Act of 1940, in effect from latter 1940 to March 31, 1947, and the executive orders of the President of the United States implementing this act, by which full recognition was given to those whose Christian conscience forbade all participation in war or preparation for it. In accord with the best historic, democratic traditions of our land, sincere conscientious objectors were granted (1) complete exemption from military service and (2) opportunity for service to the nation in work of national importance under civilian direction; also the churches from which these conscientious objectors come were authorized to administer work camps and minister to their members in this service. For these privileges we are grateful to God and extend our hearty thanks to the Congress, the President, and to the Director of Selective Service and all those associated with him in this enterprise.
We pray that our country may never again become involved in war, but if it does, or if any form of military training be established, we petition the Congress and the President to re-establish in principle provisions of the past law for conscientious objectors with a still more complete elimination of military connections from the entire system of registration, induction, and supervision of conscientious objectors while in service and such liberalizing of provisions for the conditions and terms of service as will achieve the best use of the contribution of the conscientious objectors and their churches to the nation, and best comport with the high traditions of democracy, liberty of conscience, and religious faith, which have enriched our American national life and which we cherish as a Christian brotherhood.
Signed in behalf of the Mennonite General Conference,
                                                    Allen H. Erb, Moderator
                                                    Amos O. Hostetler, Secretary

The President's Amnesty Board
Department of Justice Building
Washington, D.C.

Dear Mr. Hostetler: September 10, 1947

There has been referred to this office for acknowledgment your letter of August 28, 1947, addressed to the President of the United States, setting forth the stand of the Mennonite General Conference on the subject of registration, induction, and supervision of conscientious objectors during war.

These statements have been noted and will be given due consideration.

Sincerely yours,
William W. Naramore,
Secretary, President's Amnesty Board

The Right Honorable W. L. Mackenzie King   August 28, 1947
Prime Minister of Canada
Ottawa, Canada

Right Honorable Sir:

The Mennonite General Conference, assembled in biennial session at Wooster, Ohio, August 28, 1947, and representing over 50,000 Mennonites in Canada and the United States, by unanimous action of the delegates present, expresses herewith its grateful appreciation for the provisions made by the Department of National War Services which permitted conscientious objectors to war to serve in Alternative Service Camps or under the Alternative Service Work Administration. In accordance with the democratic tradition of the British Commonwealth of Nations, sincere religious objectors were granted complete exemption from military service and opportunity for service to the nation in work of nonmilitary character. For these privileges we are grateful to God and extend our hearty thanks to the Parliament, the Prime Minister, and the Department of National War Services.

We pray that our nations may never again become involved in war, but in case they do we pray that their respective governments continue to uphold the principle of religious freedom, giving consideration to those who cannot conscientiously participate in warfare, by making provisions for serving their country in a program with a complete separation from all military connections and a liberal administration and conditions of service as will achieve the best use of the contribution of conscientious objectors and their churches to the nation, and best comport with the high traditions of democracy, liberty of conscience, and religious faith, which have enriched our Canadian and American national life, and which we cherish as a Christian brotherhood.

Signed on behalf of Mennonite General Conference,

Allen H. Erb, Moderator
Amos O. Hostetler, Secretary

Amos O. Hostetler, Esq.,   Ottawa, September 2, 1947
Secretary,
Mennonite General Conference,
Topeka, Indiana, R. 1,
U.S.A.

Dear Sir:

The Prime Minister has asked me to acknowledge your letter of August 28th, expressing the appreciation of the Mennonite General Conference for the provisions made by the Government of Canada in the last war in so far as conscientious objectors were concerned.

Yours sincerely.
G. J. Matte,
Private Secretary.

August 28, 1947

Major General Lewis B. Hershey
Sometime Director of Selective Service
Washington, D.C.
Sir:
On behalf of the Mennonite Church we express to you our sincere and grateful appreciation for your administration during your term of service as Director of Selective Service of that portion of Selective Service dealing with conscientious objectors and Civilian Public Service. Without your sympathetic understanding of our position as a church and your consideration of the convictions of our young men who were drafted into the civilian public service of the country and of those who were appointed to represent us in the administration of Civilian Public Service, the solution of the many problems related to the national service of conscientious objectors would have been much more difficult. Together with you we sought, and in a large measure found, a successful way through the problems arising in the course of the great national co-operative experiment of Civilian Public Service. We cannot say we were happy with every detail of the program, but we are satisfied with the general result. In case of need for renewal of Civilian Public Service or some comparable plan, we hope to propose some improvements as a result of our experience.
Please convey our sincere appreciation also to your associates, in particular to Colonel Kosch.
We pray that the blessing of God may rest upon you for your contribution to the cause of religious freedom.
Signed on behalf of Mennonite General Conference,

Allen H. Erb, Moderator
Amos O. Hostetler, Secretary

September 3, 1947

Mr. Amos O. Hostetler
Secretary of the Mennonite General Conference
Topeka, Indiana
Dear Mr. Hostetler:
I want to express to you my deepest appreciation for the kindness of Mennonite General Conference in writing me the letter of August 28, 1947. The association with this group under all the circumstances which must inevitably attend such an association has been satisfactory and heartening to me.
I wish that you would express to your conference the appreciation and the thankfulness which I have always felt toward them for their continual co-operation in the execution of the laws of this nation under circumstances many times most difficult.
I shall send a copy of your letter to Colonel Kosch in California where he has gone since his retirement from active service.

Sincerely yours,
Lewis B. Hershey,
DIRECTOR

DISTRICT CONFERENCES

The district conferences of the Mennonite Church were also affected by the war in various ways. As early as November 9, 1939, the Virginia Conference held a special session "for a discussion of our nonresistant position in the light of international affairs." The European war had been in progress only a little more than two months, and the Selective

Training and Service Act was not to be enacted for another ten months. The Virginia Conference felt, however, that preparation for this eventuality should not be delayed, and passed a resolution urging "the ministerial councils of this conference to arrange for programs on nonresistance so that our members in the various districts become more thoroughly indoctrinated. We also recommend that approved literature on nonresistance be distributed into our Mennonite homes."[4] Throughout the war almost every annual session of every district conference dealt with the question of nonresistance in one form or another, or referred to the influence of the war upon its work. In 1942 the secretary of the Ohio Sunday School Conference reported that the work of its Executive Committee had been curtailed and the secretary's visits to Sunday schools had been reduced in number because of wartime travel restrictions. A similar report was made in 1943.[5]

In 1942 the South Central Conference had apparently written the governor of the state concerning his attitude toward the meeting of the conference in regular session that year. At any rate the conference adopted a resolution of appreciation "for your letter of approval of our church gathering. In response to your recognition of the great need for spiritual development, particularly in this emergency, we wish to assure you that we desire, in the fear of God, to work for the highest welfare of our fellow men."[6] In 1942 the Pacific Coast Conference, on the other hand, was canceled "because of regulations concerning special public gatherings in what are designated as combat zones." In its place, however, a two-day ministerial meeting was held to take care of necessary conference business.[7] In 1944 and in 1945 the Iowa-Nebraska Conference was limited to a ministers' meeting, due to travel restrictions.[8] The Alberta-Saskatchewan Conference was unable to have its annual meeting with the Creston, Montana, congregation which belongs to that conference, because of difficulties in crossing the international border in wartime.[9]

LOCAL CONGREGATIONS

The program and work of local congregations in most cases was not greatly affected by the war. In 1942, however, at least one congregation in Oregon held its regular Sunday evening meetings during the afternoon, because of blackout requirements at night. After making arrangements whereby the meetinghouse could be blacked out if necessary, evening meetings were resumed.[10] In 1942 the rationing of gasoline prevented the congregations at Kouts and Rensselaer, Indiana, from joining the Howard-Miami congregation near Kokomo in their annual union Thanksgiving service.[11] Gasoline rationing also prevented the Indian Cove congregation near Hammett, Idaho, from using a school bus to bring children from the town of Hammett to the meetinghouse for Sunday morning services and special meetings. A correspondent says that because of this situation "many of them are being deprived of Gospel messages and teaching at this time."[12] In order to conserve fuel oil the Morton, Illinois, congregation held its midweek meetings and sewing circle meetings in the homes of members instead of in the church.[13] Because of gasoline and tire rationing, the women of the congregation at Bally, Pennsylvania, organized their own sewing circle instead of meeting with the sewing circle of the Pottstown congregation as they had formerly done.[14] The Metamora, Illinois, sewing circle met bimonthly instead of monthly. During the intervening months garments were taken home by circle members and sewed there, an arrangement which seemed to be satisfactory.[15]

In some congregations the summer Bible school program was handicapped by gasoline and tire rationing. In a stimulating article in the *Gospel Herald* C. F. Yake presented the challenge of overcoming this handicap. Instead of having a large school at one place, involving much transportation, why not have a number of small schools involving less transportation? "There are really a dozen and one different ways in which we can get around the tire shortage and the gasoline rationing . . . . Even if teachers may have to come from a distance, why not use a bicycle? Perhaps some might come on horseback. And what about the horse and buggy?"[16] Congregations found a variety of ways to meet this challenge. The congregation at Carstairs, Alberta, held its summer Bible school one hour each evening for ten days in conjunction with revival meetings.[17] The Yoder, Kansas, congregation had one week of summer Bible school instead of two, but held sessions both in the forenoon and afternoon, instead of forenoon only. In this way the two-week course was covered, while gasoline and tires were used during one week only.[18] During the summer of 1943 the congregation at Nappanee, Indiana, studied the summer Bible school lessons on Sunday evenings in the basement of the church, while the regular evening meeting was in session in the main part of the building.[19]

In some cases travel restrictions may have proved beneficial rather than detrimental. At any rate, the secretary of the Ontario Sunday School Conference reported an upsurge in average Sunday-school attendance during 1942-43, and suggested that this may have been due to restrictions of travel.[20] In certain cities and defense areas the shifting character of the wartime population created abnormal situations, in some cases hindering the work of congregations and mission stations, and in other cases giving them new opportunities for service. In 1943 the Woodland congregation, a mission station at Wichita, Kansas, reported that many of its Sunday-school children had moved away. Also the working hours of the people were so irregular that all revival meetings were postponed for the time being.[21] The Mennonite Gospel Mission at Pinckney, Michigan, on the other hand, found opportunities for summer Bible school and Sunday-school work in the vicinity of government housing projects and trailer camps near Ypsilanti.[22]

PUBLICATION WORK

The publication work of the church was also affected by the war. In his report for the fiscal year 1941-42, the General Manager of the Mennonite Publishing House stated that manufacturing costs had risen "between twenty and thirty per cent during the past few years." While so far it had been possible to obtain the necessary materials, the quality of available paper had already been reduced. It did not seem likely that there would be a serious paper shortage, but as a measure of precaution the House had increased its stock more than 50 per cent during the past year.[23] Early in 1943 the General Manager reported in the *Gospel Herald* that the costs of printers' supplies were still rising; that in some instances they had risen 50 per cent; and that there was a general lowering in the quality of the materials. The War Production Board had also limited the use of paper for 1943 to 90 per cent of the amount used the previous year.

Since the circulation of most of the periodicals published by the House was constantly increasing, however, the curtailment of paper usage was more serious than the 10 per cent would seem to indicate. It meant that a given copy of any of the House publications might at any time need to have its paper content reduced by one fourth or one third. Other limitations were affecting the work of the binding department of the House. It was too early to know how far the working staff eventually would be affected by the war.[24] In April, 1943, the House reported that the paper shortage made it impossible to supply the demand for a third printing of work sheets for the *Primary Sunday School Quarterly*.[25] In midsummer, 1943, the *Gospel Herald* announced that the various Sunday-school quarterlies would be reduced in size by eight to twelve pages each, and occasional issues of the *Herald* would be reduced from sixteen to eight pages in size.[26] The report of the Publication Committee to General Conference in 1943 also announced the discontinuance of the *German Sunday School Quarterly*.[27]

It should be remembered, on the other hand, however, that the exigencies of the war also demonstrated the need of an increasing amount of peace literature which the Mennonite Publishing House did not fail to produce. The record of this achievement is related in Chapter XVII.

NOTES AND CITATIONS

1 *Twenty-third Mennonite General Conference* (1943), 35.

2 Peace Problems Committee Minutes, April 17, 1947.

3 *Twenty-sixth Mennonite General Conference* (1947), 17-20.

4 *Gospel Herald* (Nov. 23, 1939), 32:734.

5 *Report of the Ohio Mennonite Sunday School Conference* (1942), 18; (1943), 5.

6 *Report of the Missouri-Kansas Church Conference* (1942), 7.

7 *Gospel Herald* (June 11, 1942), 35:233.

8 *Report of the Iowa-Nebraska Conference* (1944), 2; (1945), 3.

9 *Report of the Alberta-Saskatchewan Conference* (1941 and 1943).

10 *Gospel Herald* (March 12, 1942), 34:1073.

11 *Ibid.* (Dec. 10, 1942), 35:800.

12 *Ibid.* (Dec. 10, 1942), 35:793, 796.

13 *Ibid.* (March 11, 1943), 35:1073.

14 *Ibid.* (May 13, 1943), 36:145.

15 *Ibid.* (June 3, 1943), 36:193.

16 *Ibid.* (May 28, 1942), 35:181.

17 *Ibid.* (Nov. 19, 1942), 35:729.

18 *Ibid.* (May 20, 1943), 36; 164.

19 *Ibid.* (September 23, 1943), 36:537.

20 *Calendar of Appointments of the Mennonite Church of Ontario* (1943-44), 20.

21 *Report of the Missouri-Kansas Church Conference* (1943), 15.

22 *Gospel Herald* (Sept. 2, 1943), 36:473.

23 *Ibid.* (May 28, 1942), 35:188.

24 *Ibid.* (Jan. 25, 1943), 35:1036.

25 *Ibid.* (April 22, 1943), 36:88.

26 *Ibid.* (July 1, 1943), 36:289.

27 *Twenty-third Mennonite General Conference* (1943), 33.

Chapter XIII

The War and the Mission Program of the Church

A SHORTAGE OF FOREIGN MISSIONARIES

Few phases of the church's work were more seriously affected by the second World War than was its foreign missions program. With the outbreak of the war in 1939, the sailing of missionaries appointed at the last annual meeting of the Mennonite Board of Missions and Charities was delayed for a time, although eventually all of them reached their destinations.[1] In 1940, however, George and Kathryn Troyer were denied permission to return to the India field, evidently because there were children in the family. Being unwilling to permit children to sail to the Far East under wartime conditions, the Department of State refused them passports; later the British government also refused the Troyers permission to enter India.[2] Thus during the year, May, 1940, to April, 1941, only two missionaries went to India, whereas four returned. From now on the war situation made civilian travel to India almost impossible. During the three-year period, 1941-44, only one person sailed for that country under the auspices of the Mission Board. Because of this situation, the India Mission itself had planned to prevent the depletion of its staff as much as possible, by postponing furloughs of missionaries on the field until such time as arrivals from America could again take their place. In the spring of 1942, however, the Japanese army invaded Burma, and an invasion of India itself seemed imminent. Thereupon the American consul urgently advised all Americans in that country not essential to the war effort to leave at once.

Reluctantly the mission made a partial compliance with this request, and decided that those missionaries whose furloughs were due at that time should return to America. As a result, ten workers returned home during 1941-44. The normal number of workers in the India Mission was thirty or more. By 1944 the personnel had been reduced to seventeen. The war was nearing its close, however, and during the next year it was possible to send missionaries again. During the two-year period, 1944-46, the Mission Board sent thirteen workers to India. With others returning on furlough, however, the 1945 report showed only eighteen missionaries actually on the field at that time, and the 1946 report said: "If furloughs are granted normally and those on furlough return normally to the field, there should be twenty-one missionaries at work in our India Mission by January, 1947. This number needs to be built up to thirty again as rapidly as possible if we think merely in terms of attaining our prewar strength."[3] Happily this hope was more than realized within a short time. In 1946, 1947, and 1948, more new workers were appointed, so that the 1949 annual report of the Mission Board was able to show thirty-five missionaries actually on the field, with an additional one teaching in the Woodstock School at Landour. Four India missionaries were reported on furlough in 1949.[4]

Being farther removed from the war theater, the personnel of the Argentine and the Africa Mennonite missions was not depleted to the extent that that of the India Mission was. Nevertheless, the war had its effect. From 1940 to 1946 only three new missionaries appeared on the Argentine field. Four new workers, scheduled to leave in 1945-46, were delayed a year because of difficulty in securing entry permits. After being permitted to sail early in 1947, the church was made sorrowful through the death of Clifford Snyder, one of the four, while en route to the field. In 1946-47 two additional new workers, Lester and Alta Hershey, were scheduled to go to Argentina. Being unable to obtain entry permits, however, they were later transferred to the La Plata Mission in Puerto Rico. During the war the furloughs of the older missionaries in Argentina were postponed as in the case of India. By 1945, as numerous overdue furloughs were granted, the staff of the Argentine Mission was sharply reduced. In 1944 there were twenty-six missionaries on this field, with two on furlough. In 1946 only seventeen were on the field, with eleven on furlough. Even the report of 1949 showed only eighteen on the field, with seven on furlough and two in language school.[5]

In the Africa Mennonite Mission operated by the Eastern Mennonite Board of Missions and Charities, four missionaries arrived in 1940, but none in 1941 and 1942. In 1943, however, Elma Hershberger and George and Dorothy Smoker arrived on the field. Because of hazardous travel conditions in the Atlantic, they sailed down the west coast of South America, then by land from Chile to Buenos Aires, and from there by boat to Africa. Their baggage was shipped directly, however, only to have it sunk somewhere in mid-Atlantic.[6] There were no arrivals on the Africa field in 1944. In 1945, however, the year the war came to an end, there were seven arrivals. During the war years furloughs were also reduced to a low figure. After 1945, however, furloughs as well as sailings to the field began to resume a state of normalcy.

THE WORK OF THE FOREIGN MISSIONS

In addition to a shortage of workers, the war brought other problems to the mission field. For a brief period early in the war, a threatened reduction in subsidies from the Mission to Lepers, an organization in London which subsidizes numerous stations in India, caused a curtailment in the work of the Shantipur Leper Home.[7] The war emergency affected transportation facilities in India, as well as in Europe and America, so that missionary travel within the country was handicapped.[8] In 1942 the war in Burma, with its threatened invasion of India, brought much anxiety to the Mennonite mission in the Central Provinces. A note from George J. Lapp written in late February, but not received until three months later, said:

With the war in Burma so dangerously near Rangoon we are doing some hard thinking these days . . . . Our Indian leaders are thinking hard also and laying plans for possible eventualities . . . . We are hoping for the better and sincerely hope that all plans for India's moving forward unitedly as a nation can become a reality and that the country can remain at peace within its own borders. We are hoping and praying that our missionary forces may not have to be curtailed because of any adverse developments that might take place. Sister Lapp and I long to remain in India even at risk to ourselves if by so doing we can do our part in helping to establish and extend the cause of Christ and the church in this country. We are living a day at a time, these days, and trusting God for protection and guidance. The country is quiet and our work is going on unhindered. Many hundreds of people are reached through the evangelistic touring and village preaching that is done.[9]

Other reports in 1942 told of a shortage in the rice crop. This, combined with war conditions, increased the cost of living so that there was considerable suffering among the poor people of India. Evidently as a relief measure, the government opened a camp for breaking stones for road building in the vicinity of the Mennonite mission. Early in 1942 over seven hundred people were on government work at this place. Some of the Mennonite congregations in India were giving help to their needy members, although the mission as such had not opened any relief work of its own.[10] In 1943, however, the mission reported receipt of funds through the Mennonite Central Committee with which to assist the needy people of its congregations and villages. An All-Mennonite Relief Committee had been organized in which one Brethren in Christ and four Mennonite missions were co-operating. In addition to serving local needs, this relief committee had sent funds, through a Baptist mission and the English Friends, to help relieve the suffering caused by "the disastrous cyclone and tidal wave in Bengal." Some help was also given to war sufferers, and for work in prisoner of war camps.[11]

This unfavorable economic situation tempted some of the Indian church members to violate the principle of nonresistance by joining the army where they received good wages. The report from India to the 1943 meeting of the Mission Board says:

Our church membership has lost more than it gained . . . the past year. The main reason for this is that many of our young men have entered military service. The great cause of this is the economic conditions obtaining at present. There was little work for them here and they could earn more by entering the service. Most of them are in noncombatant service, such as cooks, motor drivers, hospital assistants, laundrymen, and personnel servants, but a few are in active service. This has thrown them all out of church fellowship. Pray that they may realize that they are not in the will of God, and that they may not lose their Christian experience.[12]

The report also says that "the leaders stood firm on the doctrine of non-resistance," which means that the missionaries and the native Indian ministers were united in their testimony for the principle of nonresistance, and in discipline for its violation.

During the war period, when missionaries could not be transported to and fro in a normal manner, various expedients were employed to meet the situation. Provision was made for missionaries whose furloughs were overdue to take briefer six-month furloughs from their regular assignments, while remaining in India. To meet the problem created by the worker shortage, greater responsibility was given to native Christians. This in itself was no doubt a good thing, both for the mission and for the Indian church. After all, the mission was now more than forty years old, and the India Mennonite Conference consisted of eleven congregations with nearly 1,400 members. In these congregations there were seventeen native ministers and deacons. With this growth in numbers and in maturity there was also a growing feeling that a greater measure of control should be transferred from the mission and the missionaries to the Indian church and the native workers. It is possible that the growth of Indian nationalism also had something to do with this new attitude. At any rate, the mission recognized the need for a change.

At the 1945 annual meeting of the Board it was reported that the India Mennonite Conference had completed incorporation proceedings, and was now an "organized body legally empowered to hold property." Accordingly, all church buildings in India formerly held by the Mission Board were now being transferred to the India Mennonite Conference. The name of the mission itself was being changed from "American Mennonite Mission" to "India Mennonite Mission." A new constitution was in process of adoption which provided for the inclusion of a number of Indian brethren in the mission organization, sharing with the missionaries the responsibility of managing the entire mission enterprise.[13] At the 1946 annual meeting the secretary of the Board reported that fourteen Indian nationals had been chosen members of the Mission Council. The secretary then reported that "this new development in co-operation has so far worked out well and much good will and mutual confidence have been expressed. With complete political independence fast becoming a reality for the country of India this new mission government is a natural and inevitable development."[14]

As mentioned above, the annual meetings of 1946, 1947, and 1948 each appointed new workers for India, so that by January 1, 1949, there were thirty-five American missionaries on the field in the India Mennonite Mission. The wartime worker shortage had now been recovered, and conditions were practically normal again. This, with the new constitution and its provision for co-operative administration, indicated that with the second half century of its history the India Mennonite Mission was entering a new era. Problems of Indianization were not easily solved, however. Various experiments were continuing in an attempt to find the best way, or to keep up with the rapidly changing situation. The 1949 meeting of the Mission Board approved the suspension of the experimental constitution,[15] and a combined conference and mission committee in India was now attempting to find new and more fruitful ways of expressing the co-operative spirit. Late in 1949 the Mission Board sent Sanford C. Yoder and Paul Erb to India as fraternal delegates, especially to be present for the fiftieth anniversary observances held during the latter part of the year. These brethren gave valuable counsel on the question of Indianization of the mission program, and in the assuming of ever greater responsibility by the India Mennonite Church.

Since Argentina was not officially in the war, nor threatened by invasion, foreign mission work in that country was not affected in the same way nor to the extent as were missions in India. Nevertheless the war did affect Argentina, and with it the Argentine Mennonite Mission. In 1942 the secretary of the Mission Board reported: "Economic conditions in Argentina are not good. The war has practically destroyed their commerce with European countries, which in normal times purchase large supplies of meat and grain. Prices for produce are very low and many laborers are unemployed. All of this creates a very unfortunate situation in the country."[16] The following year the secretary reported this situation as continuing, with drought and crop failure as added hardships. These conditions affected the work of Mennonite mission stations in outlying districts, because many people whom they had served now moved to the cities in search of employment. As a result "they often lose contact with the life of the believers and not infrequently they give up their connection with the church." On the other hand, it was also reported that from 1940 to 1943 five new stations had been opened, besides new Sunday schools in towns and cities where churches were already in existence.

The secretary reminded the Mission Board, however, that the work in Argentina was not easy. The State Church was growing more unfriendly. The Roman Catholic Church outside Argentina was actively opposing Protestant missions within that country. Furthermore, the international relations of Argentina and the United States were such that no one from the latter country, missionaries included, was very welcome in Argentina.[17] This situation, no doubt, was largely responsible for the delay and even the refusal of permits for missionaries to enter the country, referred to above. The feeling of suspicion toward citizens of the United States is illustrated by the fact that Samuel E. Miller, a Mennonite missionary stationed at Arrecifes, was shadowed by officials for a time, suspected of being a United States government spy attempting to learn whether the Ford and Chevrolet agencies in Argentina were making sales to Nazis.[18] A wartime development of a different character in the Argentine Mennonite Mission was the taking over in 1943 of a mission project among the Indians in the Argentine Chaco, near the Bolivian border, about 1,000 miles north of Buenos Aires. This field of work was obtained from the Emmanuel Mission, when the latter no longer was able to obtain supporting funds from England. Thus wartime conditions led to the opening of a new work which was "enthusiastically entered into by the Argentine Church," and which it was hoped would be "a stimulus to the missionary life and zeal of our brethren in the "Southland." Gasoline rationing, however, prevented the missionaries from moving into the territory by automobile, thus delaying the work for a time.[19]

It had been the policy of the Africa Mennonite Mission to grant furloughs to first-term missionaries after five years of service. During the war, however, this was impossible. One couple who went to the field in 1936 did not return to the United States until 1945. Ray Wenger, who died on the field in 1945, had arrived with his wife in 1938. It is not impossible that his untimely death was brought on in part by his prolonged term of service. The Africa Mission found ample opportunities for work, more than it was able to do. As soon as the war began in 1939, all German citizens in Tanganyika were interned. Among them were about 240 German Protestant missionaries. Thus many missions were left without leadership, presenting a challenge to the Mennonite mission as well as to all others in that territory. The Tanganyika government invited the Africa Mennonite Mission to supply a doctor for the German mission at Bukoba. The Mennonite work itself, however, was only six years old, and the young mission did not feel itself able to accept the invitation.[20]

The native Christians in the Africa Mennonite Mission, like those in the India Mennonite Mission, were confronted with the question of military service. A report from the field in 1942 said that one of the Africa stations "suffered from deserters who have gone to war or after shillings."[21] Another said that "in the medical work it appeared for a time that several of the native workers would be conscripted for military service."[22] A letter from Elam W. Stauffer of the Africa Mission explained that there was "general conscription over the whole district" in which the mission was located. The government required each of the chiefs to produce a specified number of men from his district. The chief then made the selections, and if the selectee had objections he could plead his case when interviewed by the district officer. Stauffer said that no members of the Mennonite mission were compelled to join the armed forces. Some who had religious objections were released by the chief himself after they had stated their cases.

The missionaries had proposed to the provincial commissioner that conscientious objectors be given the privilege of alternative service. The latter took the position, however, that C.O.'s were too few in number to justify such service. Because of this Stauffer believed that the government itself may have influenced the chiefs not to press into the army any persons with religious objections to military service. Despite the lenient policy of the Tanganyika government, there were some nominal members of the Mennonite mission who voluntarily enlisted in the army. Stauffer said, however, that none of these were members in good standing. Either they "were under discipline for some transgression or were so near the border line that we hardly knew what to do with them. We had no members who were otherwise in good standing that enlisted or were drafted . . . . Some of those who enlisted were penitent of their sins by the time they were released and were taken into the church again. These had fallen on other scores too and were reinstated as those who had fallen into sin. We had none to reinstate that served in the forces that had been otherwise in good standing."[23]

NEW FOREIGN MISSIONS OPENED

Anyone seeking evidence of foreign missionary interest in the Mennonite Church should be able to find it in the fact that while the church was administering and financing a heavy C.P.S. program and related projects, and grappling with wartime problems in India, Africa, and South America, it was also taking steps toward the opening of new missions in China and Puerto Rico. In his report to the annual meeting in 1941, the secretary of the Mennonite Board of Missions and Charities said: "For some years there have been those who thought that sometime our church should open work in China. I personally, strongly favor the consideration of such a venture. At present it is impossible, but when peace again returns, this field no doubt will offer unusual opportunities for Christian work."[24] The Mission Supplement of the January 8, 1942, issue of the *Gospel Herald* was devoted largely to information about China as a mission field. This issue of the *Herald*, as well as other publicity which appeared from time to time, was designed to prepare the church for the new undertaking. At the annual meeting of the Mission Board in 1942 the president said that "the Board wishes to be prepared with both personnel and finances to undertake relief and mission work when and if that field opens." The following resolution was then adopted:

Whereas, The country of China constitutes the world's greatest unevangelized population, and

Whereas, The inadequacy of pagan religions and the experiences incident to war have conditioned the Chinese for the reception of the Gospel, and

Whereas, There is exhibited in our constituency a marked growth in prayer concern and giving for that field; therefore be it

Resolved, That we, before God, pledge our readiness and willingness to minister to the tremendous spiritual and material needs of that country, when and as, in the providence of God, He shall open to us the opportunity; and be it further

Resolved, That, pending the opening of doors for our own units to work in China, we suggest that our Board receive contributions for such reliable organizations as are already alleviating suffering and need in that country.[25]

A year later this resolution was followed by definite action. The 1943 meeting of the Board delegated J. D. Graber, who had returned from the India Mission a year before, to go to China to investigate opportunities for relief and mission work.[26] This assignment was carried out and Graber returned from China in time to report to the annual meeting of 1944. While the entrance of workers into the country was still uncertain, the Board nevertheless appointed George Beare, J. Lawrence Burkholder, and Clayton Beyler for relief work in China under the Mennonite Relief Committee. Beare was a missionary on furlough from India. The plan was for him to return to India with his wife where she would resume her work with the American Mennonite Mission, and he would engage in relief work. Burkholder and Beyler were also to go to India, and then as soon as the way opened the three were to proceed to China.[27] There they were to open relief work, which was to be followed by a mission program as soon as possible.

A year later, however, the way had not yet opened for entrance into China, and the prospective China workers were still in India. George Beare had completed his relief assignment and had returned to his mission post. Burkholder and Beyler had been loaned to the M.C.C. for its relief project in Bengal. In the meantime Titus Lehman had arrived in India to join the group, and Verna Zimmerman was appointed to sail in September, 1945.[28]

By 1946 the war was over and it was now possible to proceed with the opening of both relief and mission work in China. The primary concern of the Board, however, was mission work; and it did not seem wise to open two projects in China simultaneously. Therefore it was decided to proceed with the opening of mission work, and to loan the Board's China relief workers to the M.C.C., who had already undertaken work in Honan Province. This was done with the understanding that the workers might be attached to the Board's mission program later on, if it should be considered desirable to carry on relief work as an auxiliary to the mission program. In line with this policy, it was announced at the 1946 meeting of the Mission Board that the relief workers previously appointed for China were now on the field serving the M.C.C. At the same meeting Don and Dorothy McCammon and Christine Weaver were appointed missionaries to China.[29] These appointees spent the following year in further preparation for their work. At the annual Board meeting of 1947 Luella Gingerich and Ruth Bean were also appointed for the China Mission[30] and in September of that year they sailed for the field in company with Christine Weaver and the McCammons. By the close of the year

1947 the five were in West China "engaged in language study preparatory to undertaking the opening of work in the Hochwan area of the Szechwan Province."[31] The group was joined by Eugene Blosser in 1949.

The new work was soon confronted with great difficulties, however, because of the advance of Chinese Communism. The 1950 report of the Mission Board says: "The Communist occupation of the entire country is now complete. . . . Our missionaries are . . . not permitted to leave their city without special permission. . . . The future of Christian work in China is not bright. . . . We continue to be inspired by the spirit of faithfulness of our missionaries to their call as evidenced in their determination to remain at their post of duty as long as possible."[31a] In spite of their devotion, however, the task grew increasingly difficult, so that by the end of 1950 steps were being taken for the missionaries in China to leave the country. Even before this took place, however, the Mission Board had opened another new Oriental mission, in Japan. The M.C.C. relief work in Japan had revealed great possibilities for missionary work in that country. The Board then took action at its annual meeting in 1949, appointing Ralph and Genevieve Buckwalter and Carl and Esther Beck to open the work in Japan. The new appointees arrived on their field of labor in December, 1949.[31b]

In the doctrine and practice of the Mennonite Church there has always been a close relationship between missions and relief work. While preaching the Gospel of salvation, the true missionary is also concerned for the material and social welfare of those whom he seeks to save. Relief and social service, on the other hand, are not a Christian service unless they are permeated with an evangelistic spirit and, wherever possible, integrated with a program of evangelism. The India Mennonite Mission had its beginning in a relief program during the great famine of the eighteen-nineties. During the second World War the M.C.C. and the Mennonite Relief Committee again had a work in India, in close cooperation with the Mennonite missions of that country. While the M.C.C. was carrying on its relief program in China, the Mennonite Board of Missions and Charities was taking steps to establish a new mission in the same country. Hence it was to be expected that, in other places as well, the relief and social service programs of the church would be examined for the possibilities which they might provide for permanent missionary work.

In its report to the annual meeting in 1942 the Missions Committee of the Mennonite Board of Missions and Charities said: "Our present peace testimony in the form of relief work should result in the opening of a great door and effectual in the way of conducting mission work in Europe and Asia."[32] The 1943 report of the same committee expressed a concern for

the possibilities of our C.P.S. boys serving in foreign relief. Inasmuch as we look to relief work as the possible beginning of permanent mission work, it is our concern that utmost care be exercised in the choice of personnel so that the

12

impacts made in the work will be Christian and truly Mennonite and will pave
the way for the opening of permanent missions. It should be expected that
from the relief workers should be chosen some of the permanent mission workers. This conviction was conveyed to our Relief Committee as well as to the
Mennonite Central Committee.[33]

The 1944 report of the Missions Committee expressed a similar conviction. The Mennonite Relief Committee reported to this same meeting
that the M.C.C. had opened a relief unit of six C.P.S. men in Puerto Rico,
two of whom were members of the (Old) Mennonite Church. The
Relief Committee also recommended that Dr. George D. Troyer and a
member of the Executive Committee be sent to Puerto Rico to investigate
the possibility of medical work there, "and that the Relief Committee
stand ready to enter into any relief work which may develop as a result
of this investigation." The secretary's report, in referring to Puerto Rico,
indicated that this was being considered as a future mission field.[34] The
Board acted favorably on this recommendation, and sometime later asked
Dr. Troyer to give a year's service to the M.C.C. unit at La Plata. This
experience, it was believed, would give him a better knowledge of the
people, and enable him to evaluate the evangelistic possibilities of the
island.

Accordingly, Dr. Troyer with his family joined the M.C.C. unit in
December, 1944, where he assisted Dr. H. C. Amstutz in the La Plata
hospital. In May, 1945, S. C. Yoder, secretary of the Mission Board, came
to the island where he and Troyer, with the help of Amstutz and others,
investigated the need and opportunity for permanent mission and medical work. Following the investigation Yoder returned to the states in
time for the annual Board meeting and recommended to the Board that
a mission work be started, including medical and educational services.
The Board acted favorably on this report and adopted a resolution:
"That we take steps to open mission work in Puerto Rico, and authorize
the Executive Committee to proceed with plans for getting workers on
the field."[35]

No appointments of workers were made at the annual meeting in
June, 1945. Shortly afterwards, however, Paul and Lois Lauver were
appointed and sent to Puerto Rico where, in co-operation with George D.
and Kathryn Troyer, they opened a mission station near Aibonito in the
Pulguillas Valley, about twelve miles from the M.C.C. unit in the La
Plata Valley. It was reported to the 1946 annual meeting of the Board
that the new work had been "well begun." Construction of permanent
buildings for the mission was begun in January, 1946. In addition to the
four original appointees, Elmer and Clara Springer had recently arrived
on a short-term basis, while Annabelle Troyer, a trained nurse appointed
by the Board, was with the M.C.C. hospital at La Plata.[36]

The Puerto Rico Mennonite Mission made rapid progress. It was
reported to the 1947 annual Board meeting:

This continues to be a promising field. A church has been organized, members have been received by baptism, and the sacrament of communion has been observed. The latest report (mid-May) indicates that a class of forty is under instruction looking forward to being baptized into church membership. Cottages for missionary residences are being erected, a simple church building was put up, and plans are being studied for the erection of a suitable hospital building. All this is in the Pulguillas Valley.

In La Plata the Mennonite Central Committee requested us to supply for the unit a pastor who is fluent in Spanish and who can gather in the harvest of souls prepared by the service activities of the C.P.S. unit. Early this year Lester Hershey and family accepted appointment to this field and actually took up their tasks there a few weeks ago.[37]

The 1948 *Mennonite Yearbook* listed ten Mission Board workers as stationed at Aibonito, and two with the M.C.C. unit at La Plata. The same source also reported that during 1947 arrangements were made for the Mission Board to purchase the Puerto Rico Reconstruction Administration property occupied by the M.C.C. unit.[38] This transaction, and the appointment of Lester Hershey as pastor of the La Plata Church, were steps in a long-range program looking forward to the eventual transfer of the entire La Plata project to the Mennonite Board of Missions and Charities. This transfer was completed January 1, 1950. It would therefore be correct to say that in Puerto Rico the Mission Board found the earliest and best realization of its hope that some wartime Mennonite relief projects would result in the establishment of permanent mission work.

Two other relief projects considered as possibilities for the beginning of permanent mission work were Ethiopia and Belgium. The Ethiopian project was begun in 1945 under the administration of the Mennonite Relief Committee. As of January 1, 1949, eleven workers were engaged in this project. Daniel S. Sensenig of New Holland, Pennsylvania, appointed as a missionary by the Eastern Mennonite Board of Missions and Charities, was serving as pastor of the unit while looking for a suitable location for the proposed new mission.[39] The relief program in Belgium was largely a project of the Mennonite Relief Committee. As of January 1, 1949, three workers remained on this project. In 1947 a special Belgium Mission Study Committee reported to the annual meeting of the Mission Board, urging the Board to "prepare itself for this task at the earliest possible time, so that the mission effort in Belgium may capitalize to the full upon the relief work of that country."[40] By 1950 both of these hopes were being realized. The 1950 *Mennonite Yearbook* reports the Ethiopia Mennonite Mission in operation, under the Eastern Mission Board with nine workers on the field, or under appointment: Daniel and Blanche Sensenig, Chester and Sara Jane Wenger, Walter and Mae Schlabach, Mary Byer, and Rohrer and Ellen Eshleman.[41] The 1950 annual meeting of the Mennonite Board of Missions and Charities also took action appointing David and Wilma Shank as permanent workers in the Belgium mission.[42] They sailed in September, 1950. Another proposed field of work, interest in which had its beginning in wartime relief, was London. At the 1949 annual meeting, the Mission Board approved a plan for a Mennonite Gospel Center in London as soon as sufficient suitable personnel could be found.[42a]

The forward-looking program of missions in the Mennonite Church during the war years is symbolized in a splendid way by the appointment in 1944 of a full-time secretary for the Mennonite Board of Missions and Charities. For more than a half century all of the Board's officials, except the treasurer, had served on marginal time; and until 1921 this had been true even of the treasurer. Under this Board two foreign missions in India and Argentina, besides many home missions and charitable institutions, had been established and nurtured. By 1944 it had become clear, however, that the work of the Board required the services of a full-time secretary. At the annual meeting of that year S. C. Yoder, who had served as secretary for twenty-four years, was chosen president; and J. D. Graber, who had given two terms of service to the India Mission, was appointed full-time secretary. In his first annual report the new secretary did not merely recite the multiplied problems of the Board, such as the shortage of workers, and transportation difficulties due to wartime exigencies. He also said:

> I believe we are on the threshold of a new missionary expansion. Everywhere one finds a new concern and a new vision. More people are seriously asking, "Lord, what wilt thou have me to do?" than ever before. Many qualified and consecrated young people are coming forward and offering their lives for Christ and the church. For this we are thankful, but with this increasing number of consecrated youth coming forward our responsibilities likewise grow. We must have vision and faith. We must launch out into the deep. We must enter new fields. We must strengthen and renew the staffs in our various fields. All this will require even greater financial support and increasing sacrifices in terms of consecrated youth. But let us not falter as we face the growing responsibility. In faith and trust let us go forward with Him.[43]

Even a year earlier, in May, 1944, the Mission Board had sponsored a ten-day missionary training conference. Some forty young people were enrolled in this conference which was devoted to a study of the India, South America, and China mission fields. There were courses also in the Biblical basis of missions, in the history of missions, and in the organized work of the Board.[44] In 1945 a second training conference was held. The literature announcing the conference said: "We are on the threshold of a fresh missionary expansion. The call for 'labourers' will grow more insistent as closed countries open and as transportation facilities return to normal in the immediate postwar years. Old fields need to be restaffed and new fields need to be entered." An attractive folder, *The Enlarging Vision,* was prepared by the Board and circulated widely in the schools and colleges of the church. It featured the various fields of missionary service, "stressing the historical development, with an eye always toward future expansion."[45]

During the winter, 1946-47, the new secretary of the Mission Board visited the India mission field and the prospective field in China. In his annual report of 1947, he said it was not the purpose of the Board to bring its program "back to normalcy," but rather "the watchward must always be 'ADVANCE.' " Very fittingly, this was the theme of the Board meeting program: "An Effective Witness"; "What Is Our Witness Today?" "How Shall We Extend the Christian Witness?" At this meeting the Board adopted a five-year plan of work, including a goal of sixty-three missionary recruits for regular full-time service in India, Argentina-Uruguay, Puerto Rico, and China, and twenty short-term workers in India and Puerto Rico.[46] Within a short time this goal was on the way to realization. The 1950 annual report of the Mission Board showed that, as of June 1, 1950, the number of workers actually on the field in the foreign missions under its jurisdiction was as follows: India, 37; South America, 20; China, 6; Puerto Rico, 16. In addition to these a number of others were under appointment, including the four appointees for Japan.

HOME MISSIONS

It was not the foreign mission program alone that was affected by the war. Home missions were affected also, although on a lesser scale and in a different way. In 1943 the secretary of the Mission Board reported that the work on the Mexican border in Texas was handicapped by the rationing of gasoline and restrictions on travel. Since centers of worship were being maintained over a wide area, wartime conditions made it difficult to serve them adequately. In the same report the secretary said that "city mission work is never easy, but at present it is especially difficult."[47] The mission at Iowa City, Iowa, reported that some families were moving into other locations where defense jobs offered higher wages, while "a few families object to their children attending Sunday school because of the stand our church is taking on the war problem."[48] The Lima, Ohio, Mission reported that war work with its "around the clock seven days a week" program was a great hindrance to evangelistic efforts.[49] The *Missionary Messenger* reported that city missions in the Lancaster Conference were experiencing a decline in attendance, and that some of this was due to the nonresistant position of the church.[50]

The Peoria, Illinois, Mission reported a decline in the attendance of young people. This was due to the draft, to the shifting of population, and to increased difficulty in reaching the people: "It is becoming more and more difficult to lead the people to Christ. Large pay checks, overtime, and the removing of restraint in a war period are contributing greatly to the hardening of the hearts of young and old. This challenges us to a greater loyalty to Christ and His commission."[51] While these difficulties were real, and there must have been many discouragements in the work of city missions, there were also encouragements. In 1943, for example, the city mission at Los Angeles reported the receipt of $130.00 from the men in C.P.S. camps at Luray, Virginia, and Three Rivers, California, for use in the summer camp work of the mission.[52] Thus the very war which apparently retarded city missions stimulated young men to support them at a time when they were least able to do so. All of this augured well for the future.

FINANCIAL SUPPORT OF MISSIONS

A final word should be said about the manner in which the church supported its entire mission program during the war. In 1937 the Mennonite General Conference, in its statement on *Peace, War, and Military Service,* had said: "We ought not to seek to make a profit out of war and wartime inflation, which would mean profiting from the shedding of the blood of our fellow men. If, however, during wartime, excess profits do come into our hands, such profits should be conscientiously devoted to charitable purposes, such as the bringing of relief to the needy or the spreading of the Gospel of peace and love, and should not be applied to our own material benefit." At the 1942 annual meeting, the Mission Board adopted a resolution urging the brotherhood to observe the spirit of this commitment.[53] In the early history of C.P.S. many brethren had feared that the cost of the program would be so great as to jeopardize the mission program of the church. In February, 1943, however, the chairman of the Peace Problems Committee said that if the spirit of the above commitment is observed "the Mennonite Church will have plenty of money to operate Civilian Public Service camps, to conduct a great relief program, and to promote all the educational and charitable enterprises of the church." He cited the current increase in giving in the church as evidence that "a goodly share of excess income now is being devoted to these purposes." It was his hope that this would continue, since the need for large giving would continue for a long time, "both during wartime and after the war when the destructiveness of war dawns on the world in full and stark reality, and when the need of the Christian Gospel will be greater than ever."[54]

There were a number of ways in which the war retarded the mission program of the church, but a decrease in funds was not one of them. In midsummer, 1941, S. M. King, writing from India, said:

As we receive money each month from the home Board for the maintenance of the work here in India it gives us a feeling of gratitude to the supporting church and to God. Since the outbreak of the present European war the transfer of money to India has been difficult and in some cases impossible. Some European missions are not receiving money from home and in some other cases the transfer is greatly delayed. This has not been the case with the

American Mennonite Mission . . . . We are grateful to the Board for her earnest effort and to God for overruling even in such matters as the transfer of money from the homeland. We know that the giving members of the home church are blessed as they dedicate their offerings to God, and we pray with you that the work here may prosper under His guidance.[55]

A year later a news item in the *Gospel Herald* said:

The General Mission Board reports that there are no overchecked funds for the past month. The fiscal year closed with all overchecks wiped out, including the old building debts on the Ohio Old People's Home and the Detroit mission home. We praise the Lord for this evidence of missionary zeal on the part of the church. That the missionary program of the church has not been made to suffer because of heavy expenditures to carry on Civilian Public Service and Sufferers' Relief is especially commendable.[56]

In 1945 the president of the Mennonite Board of Missions and Charities reported to the annual meeting that:

The financial condition of the Board has never been better than it is now. Since modern missions and finances are necessarily closely tied together, this is a cause of much gratitude to God and to the brotherhood. The increasing contributions in spite of other demands upon the finances of our people no doubt reflect a larger interest in missions and are a challenge to the Board to expand the work in the fields that are now occupied as well as to enter new fields as soon as the political situation makes such ventures possible.[57]

These favorable and optimistic reports were justified by the financial reports of the treasurer of the Mennonite Board of Missions and Charities. The reports showed that from 1935 to 1946 the cash contributions received by this treasurer increased each successive year, except two, from $96,129.53 in 1935, to $183,705.40 in 1941, to $539,184.13 in 1943, to $934,305.31 in 1946. In 1947 the figure declined to $828,357.00. These figures, taken as they stand, are impressive. An analysis of the reports of treasurers of other church boards and institutions would undoubtedly show similar increases for this period.

These figures merely prove, however, that the giving of the members of the Mennonite Church, measured in dollars and cents, had increased remarkably since 1935. They would be more significant if they told us whether or not the increase in giving was in proportion to the increase in the income of the contributors. To obtain this information it would be necessary to know the annual income of the church during the same period, and this information is not available. In 1948, however, the Mennonite Research Foundation did make a study of the income of members of the Mennonite Church for the year 1947. From this study the Foundation estimated that the income for that year was $60,000,000.00, or an average of a little more than $3,000.00 for each member of the church who received an income above $500.00. The Foundation also estimated that the total contributions of the members of the church to all causes, missions, relief, church colleges, and other causes, were approximately $3,000,000.00.[58]

If these estimates were correct, they mean that members of the Mennonite Church, on the average were contributing 5 per cent of their income. While this percentage was higher than that of the average American church member, it was far below the one tenth commonly cited as the goal for which the church should strive. If 10 per cent is the correct goal, it means that the program of advance outlined by the Mission Board for the years ahead was not an unreasonable one. The Mennonite Church was alive at the middle of the twentieth century, and her vision for missions and world service had been greatly enlarged. Of this one could be sure. On the other hand, it was equally certain that the church had by no means achieved what she ought to achieve. It was clear that her program must continue to be one of advance, for she was still far short of her goal. In commenting on the report of the Foundation the editor of the *Gospel Herald* said that now it was certain that the church was giving one twentieth, and not one tenth, of its income: "It is obvious that the increased incomes of these years are going into real estate and automobiles and furniture and the payment of debts and travel and education and luxuries in such proportion as to cut the Lord short of His share. There can be no question that the conscience of the church needs to be sharpened so that we will give more nearly as the Lord has prospered us. Each one of us knows, at least approximately, what proportion of his income he is giving, for we report this figure on our income tax returns. Can we in all good conscience say to our Lord, We have done what we could?"[59]

NOTES AND CITATIONS

[1] *Gospel Herald* (Sept. 28, 1939), 32:548.
[2] *Report of the Thirty-fifth Annual Meeting of the M.B.M.C.* (1941), 8; *Gospel Herald* (Aug. 14, 1941), 34:432.
[3] *Report of the Fortieth Annual Meeting of the M.B.M.C.* (1946), 9, 38.
[4] *Ibid.* (1949), 81, 82.
[5] *Ibid.* (1949), 82, 83.
[6] *Gospel Herald* (Jan. 7, 1943), 35:880, 890ff.
[7] *Report of the Thirty-sixth Annual Meeting of the M.B.M.C.* (1942), 81.
[8] G. J. Lapp, "Anxious Days," *Gospel Herald* (May 14, 1942), 35:148.
[9] *Gospel Herald* (June 11, 1942), 35:228.
[10] *Report of the Thirty-sixth Annual Meeting of the M.B.M.C.* (1942), 17.
[11] *Ibid.* (1943), 13.
[12] *Ibid.* (1943), 68.
[13] *Ibid.* (1945), 8.
[14] *Ibid.* (1946), 8, 9.
[15] *Ibid.* (1949), 13, 65.
[16] *Ibid.* (1942), 8.

17 *Ibid.* (1943), 10.

18 *Gospel Herald* (April 22, 1943), 36:84ff.

19 *Ibid.* (June 17, 1943), 36:252ff. *Report of the Thirty-seventh Annual Meeting of the M.B.M.C.* (1943), 10.

20 *Missionary Messenger* (Nov. 26, 1939), 5; (April 13, 1941), 2.

21 *Ibid.* (April 12, 1942), 13.

22 *Ibid.* (Aug. 9, 1942), 10.

23 Letter, Elam W. Stauffer to Guy F. Hershberger, Feb. 23, 1949.

24 *Thirty-fifth Annual Report of the M.B.M.C.* (1941), 11.

25 *Report of the Thirty-sixth Annual Meeting of the M.B.M.C.* (1942), 29.

26 *Ibid.* (1943), 24.

27 *Ibid.* (1944), 7, 9, 25, 26.

28 *Ibid.* (1945), 13.

29 *Ibid.* (1946), 19, 38.

30 *Ibid.* (1947), 47.

31 *Mennonite Yearbook* (1948), 9.

31a *Report of the Forty-fourth Annual Meeting of the M.B.M.C.* (1950), 18.

31b *Ibid.* (1949), 70.

32 *Report of the Thirty-sixth Annual Meeting of the M.B.M.C.* (1942), 12.

33 *Ibid.* (1943), 17.

34 *Ibid.* (1944), 9.

35 *Ibid.* (1945), 26-28.

36 *Ibid.* (1946), 10, 16-18.

37 *Ibid.* (1947), 9.

38 *Mennonite Yearbook* (1948), 14.

39 *Ibid.,* 10.

40 *Report of the Forty-first Annual Meeting of the M.B.M.C.* (1947), 34.

41 *Mennonite Yearbook* (1950), 41.

42 *Report of the Forty-fourth Annual Meeting of the M.B.M.C.* (1950), 87.

42a *Ibid.* (1949), 12, 19, 64.

43 *Ibid.* (1945), 9.

44 *Ibid.* (1944), 22, 23.

45 *Ibid.* (1945), 34.

46 *Ibid.* (1947), 6, 40.

47 *Ibid.* (1943), 11.

48 *Gospel Herald* (March 26, 1943), 34:1100.

49 *Ibid.* (April 8, 1943), 36:37.

50 *Missionary Messenger* (May 9, 1943), 1; (Oct. 10, 1943), 15.

51 *Report of the Illinois Mennonite Church Conference* (1943), 10; (1945), 12, 13.

52 *Gospel Herald* (Nov. 25, 1943), 36:725.

53 *Report of the Thirty-sixth Annual Meeting of the M.B.M.C.* (1942), 29.

54 Harold S. Bender, "Money and War," *Gospel Herald* (Feb. 18, 1943), 35:1002-3.

55 *Gospel Herald* (July 10, 1941), 34:302.

56 *Ibid.* (May 7, 1942), 35:120.

57 *Report of the Thirty-ninth Annual Meeting of the M.B.M.C.* (1945), 6.

58 Melvin Gingerich, "Questions and Answers on the Mennonite Income Study," *Gospel Herald* (Oct. 5, 1948), 41:924-5. In the report the contributions were estimated at $2,500,000.00, but later revised to $3,000,000.00.

59 *Gospel Herald* (Oct. 5, 1948), 41:923.

Chapter XIV

The War and the Educational Program of the Church

The schools and colleges of the Mennonite Church had always shown an active interest in the peace work of the church. For a long time two members of the Goshen faculty had served on the Peace Problems Committee, and several were closely connected with the work of the Mennonite Central Committee. Others had made significant contributions to peace literature and to the peace teaching program of the church. Goshen College had been the scene of important peace conferences in 1935 and 1939. An active campus organization, with a co-operative student-faculty membership, was the Goshen College Peace Society which had been organized in 1936. Hesston and Eastern Mennonite colleges did not have peace organizations as such. Both schools, however, were vitally interested in the doctrine of nonresistance which was actively promoted on their campuses. On March 5, 1940, for example, E. J. Swalm addressed the Eastern Mennonite College group on "Nonresistance Under Test." About two weeks later Amos Swartzentruber spoke to the group about his recent experiences as an M.C.C. relief commissioner in Europe.[1] Similar work was being carried on by the schools and colleges of the other Mennonite groups, as well.

THE WAR AFFECTS THE COLLEGES

The coming of conscription and the war, however, did not only mean an interest in peace and nonresistance on the part of the faculties and students. It also meant that the work of the schools would be affected in a vital way for a period of years. In October, 1940, the *Goshen College Record* reported that forty-eight students and six faculty members had registered for the draft on October 16.[2] This was the first registration under the Selective Training and Service Act of 1940 which eventually registered all men of the ages eighteen to sixty-five inclusive. The meeting of the Goshen College Peace Society on November 4, 1940, was given to "a discussion on the information needed to fill out the questionnaires to be given to conscientious objectors." Prospective service projects for C.O.'s were also discussed and described, in so far as information was available.[3] On December 4, 1940, J. L. Stauffer spoke to the student body of Eastern Mennonite College, bringing the latest information on conscription and Civilian Public Service.[4]

Since the first C.P.S. camps were not opened until May and June, 1941, the draft did not affect the college enrollment for the year 1940-41.

In the fall of 1941, however, some men who had planned to be in college were in C.P.S. instead. Others did not return to school because it was evident that they would soon be called to camp. In October, 1941, the *Goshen College Record* announced that one student had received his summons for C.P.S. induction within less than two weeks after his arrival on the campus. The induction of another student had been deferred sixty days beyond its original date of October 15. Three others had received camp questionnaires, but hoped to be able to complete the first semester of school. Five men who would have been members of the class of 1942 were already in C.P.S., not having entered school at all in the fall of 1941.[5] In December the *Record* announced that four juniors, including the proctor of the men's dormitory, would not return to school after the Christmas holidays. The semester would not end until late in January, but arrangements had been made for these men to finish their semester's work and receive their credits.[6] During the following years the story was much the same. In December, 1942, it was announced that, because of the draft, at least ten freshmen would drop out of school at the end of the first semester. One senior was drafted during the first semester, and three freshmen dropped out because they were granted farm deferments.[7] In October, 1943, a senior, the business manager of the *Goshen College Record*,[8] was called to camp. In January, 1944, two more members of the *Record* staff were called.[9]

Almost as soon as the United States entered the war the universities and colleges of the nation began to fit themselves into the war program. Most of them, especially the larger ones, established military and naval training units on their campuses. Students who enrolled in these units pursued academic subjects considered essential for that branch of the service for which they were training, and received college credit for work successfully completed. These students were inducted into the service, and were in charge of commissioned officers who provided basic military and naval training. After completing their basic academic and military training the members of these units moved on to regular military camps where their final training was completed. Before the war was over, most of the students in medical and dental schools were in uniform, and at the conclusion of their training were promptly placed into active military service. In addition to the type of co-operation described above, universities and colleges were also expected to support the nation's war program by promoting the sale of war bonds, by providing speakers, by releasing members of their faculties for such essential war services as their specialized training fitted them, and by other means. In many schools the wartime student enrollment was much below the normal enrollment. Thus the military and naval units on the campuses were often welcomed as a means of keeping the enrollments from declining even farther.

Obviously, no Mennonite college could think of participating in this kind of program. It was reasonable to believe, however, that Mennonite colleges did have a contribution to make to the need of the time; a contribution which would also be consistent with their nonresistant faith. It was also felt that it would be advantageous for the various Mennonite and affiliated colleges to take a united stand on the question. Accordingly, representatives of Goshen and Hesston colleges met with representatives of Bethel, Bluffton, Freeman, Tabor, and Messiah Bible colleges at Winona Lake, Indiana, on August 7, 1942, and approved a document entitled, *Mennonite Colleges and Wartime Problems: A Statement of Position and Proposals for Action.* This statement was as follows:

Being by reason of our religious belief and our historic Mennonite convictions committed to the way of life taught and exemplified by Jesus as a way of love to all men and ministry to all human needs, and being accordingly conscientiously opposed to participation in war in any form as a violation of that way of life, we desire to set forth our common position on the problems which face our colleges as a result of the war and the needs, both present and prospective, resulting from it.

1. We propose to continue a strong Christian educational program with emphasis on a type of general college education which will strengthen Christian faith and character and equip young people with a basic philosophy of life which will help them to meet successfully the problems that await them as they go out into the present and the postwar world, and prepare them to render an effective ministry to its needs.

2. We shall continue and strengthen our peace testimony within our schools and churches, and elsewhere as opportunity may afford.

3. We desire to promote among our faculty, students, and constituency positive service to our local communities, to the nation as a whole, and to the world in this time of great need. We pledge ourselves, accordingly, to promote the following forms of service;

  a. To recruit and prepare students and faculty for needed services which we can conscientiously perform; and to cultivate the spirit of sacrificial ministry to human needs.

  b. To promote giving to relief and reconstruction needs, particularly through the Mennonite Central Committee and its program.

  c. To encourage support of the Civilian Public Service Program provided by the government and operated by the Mennonite Central Committee.

  d. To support the sale of Civilian Bonds as made available by the government through the Mennonite Central Committee.

4. We find ourselves unable to accept from the government assignments which would commit us to participation in the war effort, since this would require us to violate our consciences and deny the faith and heritage of the churches which sponsor and support our colleges. Specifically this means inability to participate in the following federal programs:

  a. Recruiting and training men for any branch of the armed services as is required in the government's Enlisted Reserve program, under such plans as the Navy V-1, V-7, etc.

  b. Promotion of the sale of war bonds or stamps.

  c. Promotion of support of the war by any form of propaganda, such as posters, chapel announcements, speakers, material in school publications, and the like.

5. At the same time we shall continue to cultivate a warm spirit of loyalty to our country, and a Christian patriotism which leads to devotion to the high-

est welfare of the land, and which we believe will lead to the finest possible contribution of our nation to the welfare of the entire world. We are devoted to the constitution, and the democratic traditions and institutions of our country, and shall continue to cultivate respect for and loyalty to our democratic heritage, and a desire to improve and strengthen it.

6. We propose to set up a training program for prospective workers in relief and reconstruction service, both at home and abroad, which can be offered to conscientious objectors who are willing to volunteer for service, provided arrangements can be made with Selective Service whereby men in such training can be assigned to such service either before or after induction into Civilian Public Service.

7. We appreciate the freedom of conscience vouchsafed us by our government, and we suggest that each college make its position known to its students and constituency, and to the government agencies involved, with a view to better understanding and greater appreciation of our position, in order that good relations with the government and our communities may be maintained, and our peace testimony as well as our general witness may be more effective.

8. We anticipate that the position we are taking may bring heavier burdens upon our colleges than in peacetime, and therefore solicit from our churches increased support in counsel, in finance, and in prayer, that we may continue to serve well our young people and our churches, and may increase rather than reduce our usefulness.

ACTION

It was moved and passed that we authorize the creation of a committee of representatives of all Mennonite colleges desiring to participate in the civilian service training program, whose duty it shall be to formulate more specific plans to present to the colleges; and that we instruct this committee to work with and through the Mennonite Central Committee and the National Service Board for Religious Objectors in arranging for the program. This committee shall be known as *The Committee for Civilian Service Training in Mennonite Colleges.*

Eastern Mennonite College was not represented at this first meeting of the Mennonite schools. It later endorsed the above statement, however, and its representatives were present at some of the subsequent meetings of the intercollege group which eventually came to be known as the Council of Mennonite and Affiliated Colleges. A good illustration of what Mennonite colleges might repeatedly have been asked to do, had they not stated their position clearly, is found in a visit of army engineers to Eastern Mennonite College on February 3, 1943, to survey the school plant as to its possible use by the War Department for military training purposes. Following this visit J. L. Stauffer, President of E.M.C., wrote to Lieutenant Colonel Byron Bird, Chief of the Engineering Division of the War Department, describing the character of the school, stating clearly the nonresistant faith of the church which the school serves, and enclosing a copy of the church's official statement on *Peace, War, and Military Service.* In view of these stated convictions, Stauffer requested the War Department to grant exemption from the proposed use of the college plant.[10] Apparently the matter ended at this point.

ACCELERATED COLLEGE PROGRAMS

Since the war made it difficult for many college students to complete their courses without interruption by the draft, most of the universities and colleges of the country adopted an accelerated program designed to offset this influence as much as possible. Mennonite colleges also followed this pattern. In January, 1942, Goshen College announced its emergency accelerated program, to become effective in the second semester.[11] The final examination period for each semester was shortened to three days, the spring vacation was eliminated, and one week dropped from the second semester. By this process three weeks were saved, and commencement was advanced from June 8 to May 18. A three weeks' intersession was then held from May 19 to June 5. The regular summer session of nine weeks was held from June 8 to August 7. This was followed by a three weeks' post-session, from August 10 to August 28. This program made it possible for a student to complete two full semesters of work between the close of the first semester in January, 1942, and the opening of the first semester of the following school year. The entire school year of 1942-43 was accelerated, the first semester beginning August 31, and ending December 23, 1942. The second semester began January 5, and ended May 3, 1943. This was succeeded in turn by two spring sessions, each three weeks in length, and a summer session of nine weeks, ending August 13, 1943. By this program it was possible for a student to complete three semesters of work from August 31, 1942, to August 13, 1943.

This accelerated program was followed without modification for three full years, to August, 1945. Thus a student entering the freshman class in the fall of 1942, if he pursued the accelerated program without interruption, was able to obtain his bachelor's degree by May 1, 1945. During the academic year, 1945-46, the second semester ended May 20, followed by one three weeks' spring session and the regular summer session of nine weeks. By 1946-47 the emergency was over, and the Goshen College calendar returned to the standard pattern; the first semester began September 5, with commencement coming on June 9, followed by the regular nine weeks' summer session.[12] The programs of Hesston and Eastern Mennonite College were never accelerated, however, except that for a time their academic years were shortened so as to lengthen their summer vacations by one or two weeks. In the case of Hesston, at least, this was accomplished in part by shortening or eliminating the spring vacation.

Although the wartime program at Goshen College made it possible for students to accelerate their individual programs, they were not required to do so. Many students, especially the women, followed a normal program, taking four full years for the completion of the college course. Besides the men who desired to complete as much of their course as possible before being called by the draft, those who took advantage of the accelerated program were chiefly two types of students: (1) Elementary education students planning to enter the teaching profession as early as possible because of the wartime shortage of teachers. (2) Preprofessional students planning to enter medical, dental, or theological schools at the earliest possible date.[18] Under the Selective Service System theological and pretheological students were deferred and classified IV-D. Medical and premedical students were classified II-A. Deferment of medical students was granted to conscientious objectors as well as to those planning to enter military service, although in certain medical schools it was difficult for C.O.'s to gain admission, or to continue their course.

In January, 1943, Goshen College announced that its accelerated program had been stepped up so as to admit students, particularly men, who had not even completed their high-school course. By this plan a student who had finished three and one-half years of high-school work could enter as a freshman and then receive his high-school diploma after completing one semester of college work. Such students entering college in the spring session could complete two semesters of work by the end of December, 1943. Since one year of college work was a prerequisite for professional deferment, this early admission to college was essential for certain students who might otherwise have been drafted before becoming eligible for deferment.[14] In December, 1943, the college announced that it would enroll senior high-school students under this accelerated plan beginning with the second semester of the college year in January, 1944. By this plan eligibility for deferment could be obtained by September, 1944.[15]

TRAINING FOR FOREIGN RELIEF

It was evident to Mennonite colleges and relief agencies that at the conclusion of the war, if not before, there would be "unparalleled opportunity for relief administration and reconstruction work," a task for which Christian conscientious objectors with college training would be especially qualified. The above-mentioned[16] *Statement of Position and Proposals for Action* adopted by representatives of Mennonite colleges in August, 1942, proposed "to set up a training program for prospective workers in relief and reconstruction service, both at home and abroad, which can be offered to conscientious objectors who are willing to volunteer for service, provided arrangements can be made with Selective Service whereby men in such training can be assigned to such service either before or after induction into Civilian Public Service." Even before this proposal was officially adopted many C.P.S. men had volunteered for foreign relief, and it had been the hope of the M.C.C., as well as of the administrative agencies of the other peace churches, that this type of service could be offered to all men in C.P.S. who desired it. The Goshen College *Annual Report* for 1941-42 also said that a group of twenty-six men on that campus had "definitely volunteered to prepare themselves for the task of relief and [that] it is the intention of the college to set up a program making it possible for them to be prepared to do that service well."[17] This plan was carried through, and during the academic year, 1942-43, a number of student volunteers were enrolled in the Goshen College relief training program. Similar programs were carried on by other colleges of the historic peace churches.

In the meantime Mennonite, Brethren, and Quaker colleges had brought the idea of an official C.P.S. relief training program to the attention of Selective Service officials. This idea met with favor, and the Director of Selective Service gave tentative approval for the establishment of a Civilian Public Service College Training Corps. Admission to the corps was to be open to C.P.S. men who were qualified for relief work, and who were willing to pledge a year or more after the war to such service. In the meantime Selective Service stayed the induction of men with IV-E classifications who were certified by the colleges as members of their own training programs. Then on April 21, 1943, the official C.P.S. training program was finally authorized, when the Director of Selective Service signed an order establishing a foreign relief and rehabilitation project as work of national importance, to be known as Civilian Public Service Camp No. 101. The order said that the work undertaken by the men assigned to C.P.S. Camp No. 101 should consist of "pursuing a course of study in preparation for duty on foreign relief and rehabilitation," and the preparation of materials for such study.

Under this program the "main camp" was to be located in Philadelphia. It was to consist of a small group of research men preparing outlines, bibliographies, mimeographed materials, and other helps for the study of relief and reconstruction, using the library facilities of the University of Pennsylvania for its work. The "side camps" were to be located at various Mennonite, Quaker, and Brethren colleges, where larger groups of students would engage in study. This plan of study and training was to be comparable to the training program carried on in other colleges by the army and navy. The difference was, of course, that after the completion of their training the men in the colleges of the peace churches were expected to engage in foreign relief work, this service to continue for at least one year after the close of the war. If a man for some reason could not be assigned to a relief project immediately after the completion of his training, it was understood that he would be assigned to some other C.P.S. project until such time as the foreign relief assignment could be made.

During the summer of 1943 a special nine weeks' training school, under the auspices of C.P.S. Camp No. 101, was conducted at Goshen College, with the various Mennonite groups co-operating. Sixty-six men were enrolled in this summer school, together with sixteen women volunteers. A similar school for men from Brethren C.P.S. camps was held at Manchester College in Indiana. For men from Quaker camps there were schools at Earlham College in Indiana, Guilford College in North Carolina, and Haverford and Swarthmore colleges in Pennsylvania. The Manchester school enrolled seventy C.P.S. men, and the combined enrollment in the Quaker schools was sixty-two. It had been the plan that during the school year, 1943-44, smaller groups of C.P.S. men would study in preparation for relief work at the four Mennonite senior colleges, Goshen, Bethel, Bluffton, and Tabor, with the various junior colleges cooperating. A similar program had been planned for the Quaker and the Brethren colleges. In the beginning of the program it was specified that not more than 4 per cent of C.P.S. men could be assigned to the relief study program. Even this small percentage, however, meant that over a hundred Mennonite men would receive the benefit of the special training program. It was hoped, however, that as time went on the number might be increased.

The men transferring from the college training programs to the official C.P.S. training school in the summer of 1943, many of whose inductions had been stayed, were now officially inducted into C.P.S. and assigned to C.P.S. Camp No. 101. About one third of the men in the summer training school came directly from the college training programs, and about two thirds were volunteers from C.P.S. camps. The women were selected from applications made to the M.C.C. Since all of the men were C.P.S. men, the entire cost of their training program, including board, room, and instruction, was paid by the M.C.C. The women students were responsible for their own expenses. The educational program was planned by a joint committee of the M.C.C. and the Mennonite colleges. It consisted of courses in Relief Administration; Contemporary World Relief Needs in Europe, China, and South America; Mennonite History; the History and Philosophy of Mennonite Relief; Christian Life; Community Hygiene and Nutrition; and Physical Fitness.[18]

Unfortunately, however, the United States Congress enacted legislation late in June, 1943, forbidding the continuation of the C.P.S. relief training program in colleges. This legislation came in the form of a rider to the military appropriations bill for the year 1943-44. It simply said that none of the military appropriations might be used for the training of C.P.S. men in colleges, or for the general administration of such training. Neither could men so trained be assigned to work outside the territorial possessions of the United States. Since the C.P.S. system was under the general administration of Selective Service, which was manned by officials who received their salaries from the federal military budget, the effect of this order was to forbid Selective Service to assign any C.P.S. men to such a relief training program. Since several of the training schools were actually in session, however, when the law was passed, they were permitted to continue until about the middle of August. Even so, in the case of the Goshen school at least, the closing date came a week or more ahead of the original schedule. Thus, all plans to use C.P.S. men for foreign relief work had to be suspended. Even a small group of C.P.S. men who had sailed for China, by authorization of President Roosevelt, was recalled after proceeding as far as South Africa. This was an advance exploratory unit representing the American Friends Service Committee, the Brethren Service Committee, and the M.C.C. The men returned to the United States in December, 1943.

Even though C.P.S. training units on college campuses were brought to an end in the summer of 1943, it was possible to continue a restricted relief training program within certain C.P.S. camps and units, as part of the regular camp educational program. Ernest E. Miller, who as president of Goshen College had taken a leading part in the original training program, served the M.C.C. as director of relief training under the new plan. The first unit was set up on September 6, 1943, in connection with the mental hospital unit at Ypsilanti, Michigan. By the end of 1943 training units had been set up at Mulberry, Florida; Howard, Rhode Island; Duke University; and Alexian Brothers Hospital in Chicago. The Duke University unit was operated by the Methodists, and the Alexian Brothers unit was operated co-operatively by Friends, Brethren, and Mennonites. The remainder were M.C.C. units. The total enrollment in these units was approximately ninety men and six women. During 1944 two more training units were established; an M.C.C. unit at Denison, Iowa, and a co-operative unit at Beltsville, Maryland. The number of trainees served in 1944 was 135 men and 13 women. In 1945, the relief training units at Denison, Iowa, and Howard, Rhode Island, were discontinued and a new M.C.C. unit was opened at Poughkeepsie, New York. The highest number of M.C.C. relief trainees enrolled at any one time in 1945 was 116. At the close of the year the number of men was 99. With the coming of discharges in large numbers in 1946, the C.P.S. relief training program was brought to an end.

It was the original plan of the training program that about one third of the work given should be devoted to language study; one third to Bible study, Mennonite history, and orientation in the special concerns of the M.C.C.; and one third to the study of subjects directly relevant to relief and work projects. This plan was carried out to a large extent, although at times it was necessary to modify the program because of difficulty in securing qualified instructors. A number of qualified instructors were recruited from the ranks of the C.P.S. men themselves. Members of the faculties of Mennonite colleges contributed liberally to the program. Other instructors were obtained from colleges located near the units, such as Ypsilanti State Normal School, De Paul University, Duke University, Vassar and Bard colleges, Brown University, and the University of Maryland. O. E. Baker of the University of Maryland served the unit at Beltsville without charge. An important part of the training program was the research center at the M.C.C. headquarters in Akron, Pennsylvania, which helped in the preparation of materials useful for the program. These included a booklet on the *History and Principles of Mennonite Relief*, by M.C. Lehman, and materials for the study of Paraguay, by John E. Bender. The Akron office also published a monthly *Relief Trainee's News Letter* which was very helpful.[19]

COLLEGE CREDIT FOR C.P.S. AND RELIEF TRAINING COURSES

An important feature of the relief training program was a provision for the granting of high-school or college credit for certain courses, to such trainees as desired it. In order to be eligible for credit it was required that a course be taught by a qualified instructor, approved by a committee representing the Mennonite colleges and the M.C.C. It was also required that teaching materials, bibliographies, readings, the number of class meetings, and examinations be on a level of quality similar to that of courses taught in the high schools and colleges themselves. To facilitate the administration of this aspect of the program, Roy Umble, a C.P.S. man and a graduate of Goshen College with college teaching experience, was appointed educational liaison between the M.C.C. and the Mennonite colleges. It was Umble's task to secure the approval of the above-mentioned committee for courses seeking credit, to receive reports from instructors, to submit reports to the colleges and the M.C.C. concerning the work done, and to certify individual students for receiving credit. At the end of 1945, the director of relief training reported that up to that time the total registration in credit courses was 479; the total hours of credit courses offered was 86; and the total credits earned by men registered in relief training courses was 797 semester hours. This represents the equivalent of a full semester's work for fifty men. Total registration as the term is used here does not mean total enrollment; it includes only those who completed all course requirements, making them eligible for academic credit. Neither do these figures include women's summer service unit trainees.

It should also be noted here that many C.P.S. men received academic credit for courses pursued outside the relief training program, either in camp, or in a college or university located in the vicinity of the camp. Such credit courses were also administered through the office of the educational liaison. At the end of 1945 the total registration in non-relief training credit courses was 192; the total hours of courses was 35; and the total hours of credit earned was 414, or the equivalent of a full semester's work for twenty-seven men.[20] In addition, a number of C.P.S. men fulfilled or completed their college admission requirements, or even received college credit, by passing the General Educational Development tests provided by the American Council on Education. Those receiving college credit on the basis of these tests were chiefly men entering college as freshmen, following C.P.S., especially such as were not in some highly specialized curriculum. Students who had taken a year or two of college before entering camp ordinarily received very little if any G.E.D. credit. Thus the G.E.D. test plan gave recognition to the educational value of C.P.S. experience, and to independent reading and study, on the part of men whose formal education had been interrupted or delayed. At Goshen College the admission of twenty-six men was based in whole or in part on G.E.D. tests; and twenty-seven men received college credits totaling 293 semester hours. Hesston and E.M.C., as well as the colleges of the other Mennonite groups, also made limited use of G.E.D. tests for purposes of admission and credit. At Goshen College, subsequent study of the records of men granted admission through these tests showed that very few of the men experienced difficulty in their college work. In view of these findings, it seemed likely that the use of G.E.D. tests for admission purposes would be continued on a more or less permanent basis, although with the required test score for such admission somewhat higher than was the case immediately after the war.[21]

During 1945 two special M.C.C. relief training schools, for persons other than C.P.S. men, were held at Goshen College. The first continued from June 11 to 29, and the second from September 12 to 29. A total of twenty-two persons attended these schools. These were persons under appointment by the M.C.C. to serve in some foreign field. Instructors in the courses were P. C. Hiebert and J. N. Byler of the M.C.C., and members of the Goshen College faculty. Another feature of the relief training program which must not be overlooked was the women's voluntary summer service units established in mental hospitals, and integrated with the relief training program. As mentioned in Chapter XVI, two women's units with sixty-one women were operated at Ypsilanti, Michigan, and Howard, Rhode Island, in the summer of 1944. In the summer of 1945 two women's units with a total enrollment of forty-four were operated at Ypsilanti, and at Poughkeepsie, New York. The women's voluntary service units at Cleveland, Ohio; Wernersville, Pennsylvania; and Akron, Pennsylvania, were not integrated with the relief training program.[22]

COLLEGE ENROLLMENTS

It was generally expected that the war would bring a serious decline in the enrollment of Mennonite colleges. Much to the surprise of everyone, however, this did not occur. In 1939-40 the full-time enrollment for the regular nine-month academic year at Goshen College was 270. In 1940-41, the first year to be affected by the draft, the regular full-time enrollment was 256. In 1941-42 the enrollment actually increased to 265. The following year it stood at 266. In 1943-44 there was a decline to 238. In 1944-45, however, the figure had returned to 260. During the following year discharges from C.P.S. began in large numbers. From this point onward there was a rapid increase in the Goshen College enrollment.

In 1945-46 the regular full-time enrollment was 321. It was 566 in 1946-47; 598 in 1947-48; and 636 in 1948-49.

Several factors were involved in these enrollment trends. The accelerated program and the deferment of theology and premedical students retarded the decline in the male enrollment. In 1939-40, the last academic year before conscription, the number of regular full-time men students at Goshen College was 128. The lowest figure during the following three years was 116, and in 1942-43 it was actually 124. The next year showed a sharp decline, however, with only 82 men students. In 1944-45 the figure was 85. In 1945-46, the first year to be affected by C.P.S. discharges, the male enrollment was only 99. Few discharged men found their way to college before the second semester, and even then the number was not large. By the fall of 1946, however, a large number of men had been discharged and the drafting of men had practically stopped, so that during the school year, 1946-47, the male enrollment of Goshen College stood at 299, which was more than twice as large as it had been in 1939-40. The following year the figure was 322, and in 1948-49 it reached the all-time high of 368. Thus in 1948-49 the number of men students was 36 per cent higher than the total enrollment had been in 1939-40.

Beginning in 1943, there was also a notable increase in the female portion of the student enrollment at Goshen College. For a long time it had been traditional for women students to outnumber the men by a small margin. In 1939-40, when the number of men was 128, that of women was 142. In 1942-43, when the number of men was 124, that of women was 144. The next year there was an increase in the number of women students, beginning a trend which continued through 1947-48. There were 156 regular full-time women students in 1943-44; 175 in 1944-45; and 222 in 1945-46. Thus during the latter two years the increase in women students more than offset the decline in men students due to the war. The number of women students was 257 in 1946-47; 276 in 1947-48; and 268 in 1948-49. Mennonite college administrators had long been aware that, even though the enrollment in their colleges had increased steadily through the years, the percentage of Mennonite young people enrolled in college was not yet as high as the percentage of American young people as a whole. In view of this fact, they had anticipated a growth in the enrollment of Mennonite colleges for some time to come. Evidently one of the effects of the second World War was to accelerate the approach of the actual enrollment toward the potential. This increase in educational interest affected both men and women; and the increase in the enrollment of women came in time to prevent a serious decline in the wartime total enrollment, such as that experienced by many colleges.

The very large enrollment of men in 1947-48 and 1948-49 was made up of the "normal" enrollment for the new era, plus the discharged C.P.S. men whose education had been delayed. By the end of 1949-50 these discharged men had completed their education, causing the "bulge" to recede, and permitting the Goshen College enrollment to level off at a new normal figure between 500 and 600. It is interesting to observe that throughout the ten-year period, from 1939 to 1949, the percentage of students who were members of the Mennonite Church varied only slightly. The lowest percentage for any one year was 67, and the highest 75, with the average at about 71. In 1947-48 and 1948-49 the percentage stood at exactly the latter figure. Also, of the remaining 29 per cent, a considerable number had always been Mennonites of other groups. In the postwar years, the proportion of Mennonites in this 29 per cent group increased considerably. As a result, the percentage of Mennonites (counting all Mennonite groups) in the Goshen student body was somewhat larger than before the war. In 1949-50, however, the total number of Mennonites of other groups decreased from 73 to 65. An obvious conclusion to be drawn from the above statistics would seem to be that during the decade of the 1940's the number of Mennonite young people enrolled in college had greatly increased, and that this increase was stimulated by the war and C.P.S. experience. No doubt the fact that money had also been plentiful was an important factor as well.[23]

Enrollment statistics of other Mennonites colleges show trends similar to those of Goshen, although Bethel and Bluffton, both colleges of the General Conference Mennonite Church, experienced continuous enrollment declines from 1941 to 1945, which became rather serious in 1943-45. As in the case of Goshen, the enrollments of these colleges increased again, beginning in the fall of 1945. In 1948-49, Bethel and Bluffton had enrollments considerably higher than they had before the war, although in neither case had the increase been as marked as in the case of Goshen. Before the war, Bethel's enrollment had been from 75 to 100 higher than that of Goshen. In 1947-48 it was about 130 lower. At the beginning of the war, Eastern Mennonite College was a junior college, in process of transition to a senior college. Whatever loss of enrollment the war may have caused in this case was more than offset by the increase due to the change to a senior college. Hence each year following 1939 witnessed an increase in the college enrollment at E.M.C. This increase was slight, yet certain, each year until 1945. From this point on the increase was rapid as in the case of the other colleges. In 1939-40 the college enrollment at Eastern Mennonite College was 52. In 1947-48 it was 192. Hesston College, which is also a junior college, experienced a decline in enrollment in 1943-45. Recovery was begun in 1945-46; and in 1948-49 the college enrollment at Hesston had reached 118. In 1939-40 it had been 51.

In both Hesston and Eastern Mennonite College, the academy or high-school enrollments had always been larger than the college enrollments. Since the draft did not reach below the eighteenth year of age, few academy students were affected by it. It is not surprising, therefore, to find that in each of these schools the academy enrollment increased rather consistently from 1939 to 1947. While there were fluctuations, the trend is unmistakable. At Hesston the academy enrollment was 110 in 1939-40, and 208 in 1946-47. The figures for E.M.C. in these two years were 185 and 269 respectively. No explanation of these increases would be absolutely accurate. It seems reasonable to believe, however, that they were influenced by the prosperity of the time, and by the wartime situation which in many public high schools created an atmosphere unfavorable for boys and girls of the nonresistant faith. In 1947-48 both Hesston and Eastern Mennonite College experienced a decline in their academy enrollments. This may have been caused in part by the growth of the newer Mennonite high schools in their territories, Iowa Mennonite School and Western Mennonite School in the case of the former, and Lancaster and Johnstown Mennonite schools in the case of the latter.[24]

NEW ELEMENTARY AND HIGH SCHOOLS

A further word should be said about the newer Mennonite schools. Five Mennonite high schools came into existence during the period of the second World War. Lancaster Mennonite School was founded in 1942, and Johnstown Mennonite School in 1944. In 1945 three new high schools were opened: Rockway Mennonite School of Kitchener, Ontario; Iowa Mennonite School; and Western Mennonite School, in Oregon. The combined high-school enrollment of these five schools, in 1948-49, was 505. About half of this enrollment was in Lancaster Mennonite School alone. Another development in Mennonite education during the war years was the founding of a number of elementary schools. This movement had begun before the war, but was greatly increased during the war and after. The first of these schools were established at Dover and Greenwood, Delaware, in 1925 and 1928, by the Conservative Amish Mennonite group. By the end of 1940 eight elementary schools had been established, and by the end of 1945 there were twenty-five. In 1946 three more were established, and in 1947 seven new ones appeared, making a total of thirty-five elementary schools. Many of these schools were sponsored by Amish and Conservative Amish Mennonite communities. Many, on the other hand, were Mennonite schools. These elementary schools are located chiefly in Pennsylvania, Virginia, Ohio, Delaware, and Maryland. One is located at Arthur, Illinois, and another at Nampa, Idaho.[25]

It was no mere coincidence that so many of the new schools, both elementary and high schools, were established during the war years. It is true that the movement leading to the founding of some of them began as much as fifteen or more years before the war. This is especially true of Lancaster, Rockway, and Western Mennonite schools. On the other hand, there is no question that the wartime environment in many public schools was unfavorable for boys and girls of the nonresistant faith. As the draft census clearly shows, the high-school age group made the poorest showing in the Mennonite response to conscription. No doubt this situation, pointing up the urgent need for a favorable educational environment for the young people of the church, was the major factor in bringing the new movement to its climax.

WARTIME SERVICES OF COLLEGES AND FACULTIES

Not only did the draft and the war affect the enrollment of the Mennonite colleges. It affected the faculties as well, although very few faculty members were actually drafted. Among those who were inducted into C.P.S. were John P. Duerksen of Hesston, and Roman Gingerich of Goshen College. Both Duerksen and Gingerich served as camp directors during part of their C.P.S. career, the latter also spending some time with the Puerto Rico unit where he was in charge of recreation work. Other faculty members were given leaves of absence for special wartime service assignments. In a few cases these assignments became permanent, resulting in a severance of the individual's connection with his college. One illustration is the case of J. N. Byler who was given a leave from Hesston College to accept an assignment under the M.C.C. in 1941. Byler later resigned from the Hesston faculty and became Director of Relief under the M.C.C. At Goshen College John E. Coffman, assistant librarian, was given a relief assignment in England in 1940. He later also severed his college connections and established residence in England where in 1950 he was serving the M.C.C. on a part-time basis.

Certain members of all three faculties, Hesston, Goshen, and Eastern Mennonite College, served on special assignments at one time or another during the war. In 1940-41 Chester K. Lehman of E.M.C. spent part of the year at the M.C.C. headquarters at Akron. Mary Miller of the Hesston faculty spent two years, 1945-47, in relief work in Europe. From the Goshen faculty, C. L. Graber served with the National Service Board for Religious Objectors as assistant to the executive secretary for nine months, December, 1942, to September, 1943. During the following twelve months Graber was attached to the Akron office of the M.C.C. with responsibility for the general direction of its relief activities. Again in March to June, 1946, he had a three-month leave from Goshen College to serve as special M.C.C. relief commissioner in the Far East. From June, 1942, to January, 1944, Paul Bender served successively as educational director of the C.P.S. camp at Medaryville, Indiana, and director of the camps at Denison, Iowa, and Grottoes, Virginia. Willard H. Smith had a two-year leave from Goshen to serve as M.C.C. relief commissioner in Paraguay during 1944 and 1945. Glen R. Miller was commissioner, with general supervision of the relief program in England, during the year 1944. Lois Gunden was engaged in relief work in Europe from October, 1941, to March, 1944. H. Clair Amstutz was absent from the college for three academic years, 1944-47, for medical service in Puerto Rico. Guy F. Hershberger served as educational director on a part-time basis at the Bluffton-Medaryville C.P.S. camp in Indiana during the academic year, 1941-42.

In addition to these assignments, ranging from one to three years in length, numerous members of all of the college faculties contributed to the C.P.S. educational and relief training programs, in a variety of ways, as administrators and instructors. Ernest E. Miller was general director of the relief training school. During 1943-44 Carl Kreider gave part-time service to Goshen College, and part time to the relief training program. In 1945 Guy F. Hershberger taught courses regularly for two semesters at the Farm and Community School in connection with the C.P.S. camp at Malcolm, Nebraska. For two summers Lois Gunden served as director of the women's voluntary service unit at Ypsilanti, Michigan. Harold S. Bender gave much of his time during the entire period of the war in service for the Peace Problems Committee, the M.C.C., and the educational work of the camps. Members of the Bethel, Bluffton, Tabor, and other Mennonite college faculties gave service similar to that of the Goshen, Hesston, and E.M.C. faculties. In addition to the above more lengthy assignments, faculty members of all the colleges of the various Mennonite groups had frequent single and week-end appointments in C.P.S. camps and units in all sections of the country, serving the spiritual and educational needs and interests of the men.

In addition to the services and activities of the colleges and their faculties and students, as mentioned above, there were numerous other special wartime activities of greater or lesser importance. In the second semester of 1941-42 Goshen College began a regular Red Cross first-aid course, without academic credit, with sixty students enrolled.[26] This course was offered regularly for several semesters. In the second semester, 1941-42, a course in fire fighting was offered, with twenty-seven men registered for the first meeting. A member of the Goshen Fire Department was in charge of the course.[27] On at least one occasion, if not oftener, Eastern Mennonite College conducted an air raid drill.[28] Activities such as these were in line with the supposed need of the time for protecting life and property in case of emergency. In February, 1943, an Emergency Service Committee was organized on the campus of Goshen College. This committee rendered such service as keeping in touch with C.P.S. men; sending them occasional gifts, especially at Christmas time; and arranging for the care of needy children in the local community, who, because of wartime conditions, were not receiving the care they otherwise would have received.

In October, 1945, the Emergency Service Committee sponsored a relief drive in which students contributed money earned by working on or off the campus at a time designated for this purpose.[29] Similar drives were conducted on numerous other occasions. After several years, the Emergency Service Committee came under the sponsorship of the college Y.P.C.A. as a regular Y.P.C.A. committee. In the autumn of 1946, as a result of needs presented by C. L. Graber who had recently returned from his trip as relief commissioner to the Far East, Goshen College students gathered a shipment of books to be sent to a bombed-out college in the Philippines.[30] Similar activities were carried on in all Mennonite colleges. The annual mission drives of the college Y.P.C.A.'s usually included a substantial sum for relief. In cases where colleges were located within driving distance of a C.P.S. camp or unit, visits between the college and the unit were exchanged frequently. In November, 1943, a group of Goshen College alumni who were in C.P.S. gave a program at the annual Goshen College Home-coming.[31] Such exchanges between the colleges and the C.P.S. units included participation in religious meetings, informational discussions, and social and recreational activities.

The activities of student organizations on Mennonite college campuses reveal a real interest in the wartime work of the church and its agencies. Literary societies held meetings and programs devoted to peace and relief themes. At Goshen College the Peace Society was especially active in this respect. The colleges themselves in an official way sponsored numerous lectures and meetings which contributed to the wartime work of the schools in a helpful way. Persons able to give firsthand information, such as officials of the M.C.C., relief commissioners, and relief workers recently returned from their field of work, were especially welcome. During the time when the relief training school was in session at Goshen in the summer of 1943, Paul Comly French, the executive secretary of the N.S.B.R.O., spoke to college and relief training students, giving an inside view of the Board and its work. Among the many other speakers of this type were O. R. Yoder, the superintendent of the Ypsilanti State Hospital, where one of the C.P.S. units, as well as a relief training unit, was stationed. Two outstanding addresses at Goshen College following the close of the war were those by Peter Dyck and C. A. De Fehr, representatives of the M.C.C. who had played a prominent part in the moving of the Russian Mennonite refugees to Paraguay. The other Mennonite colleges, of course, sponsored similar meetings.

Student periodicals on college campuses did a fine piece of work in keeping students informed on the wartime work of the church and the colleges. There were letters from former students, now in C.P.S., describing life in C.P.S. camps. Faculty members now serving in South America or Europe furnished articles or letters which appeared in print in the college papers. College campuses were also frequently meeting places for important committees and groups engaged in the wartime work of the church. On one occasion Goshen College was the scene of a regional C.P.S. directors' meeting; on another occasion of a meeting of hospital unit leaders. The Peace Problems Committee, of course, often met on the same campus. Thus in numerous ways the Mennonite colleges played a most significant role in the wartime work of the church.

C.P.S. MEN RETURN TO COLLEGE

In the second semester of the academic year, 1945-46, discharged C.P.S. men began to appear on the college campuses. Just as student periodicals a few years before announced their disappearance from time to time, now they announced their reappearance. In May, 1947, the *Goshen College Record* announced the appointment of two ex-C.P.S. men as editor and business manager of the college annual, the *Maple Leaf*. Five years earlier the resignation of such appointees to take up C.P.S. service was the common occurrence.

If ex-C.P.S. men were to continue their college education, it was necessary that the cost of their education be met in some way. Since these men had given their time with little or no pay while in C.P.S., it was considered proper that the colleges and the church constituency do something to assist them in meeting this cost. The college authorities, the M.C.C., and official committees of the constituent groups began working on this problem early. As explained more fully in Chapter VII, the Council of Mennonite and Affiliated Colleges and the Mennonite Aid Section of the M.C.C. agreed on a plan of educational rehabilitation whereby the colleges were able to provide grants-in-aid, generally equivalent to free tuition, for as many school months as the student had spent months in C.P.S., with twenty-seven months as a maximum. In the case of Goshen, Hesston, and Eastern Mennonite College, the necessary funds for carrying out this program were provided largely through the Mennonite Relief Committee. From these three colleges, as stated above, about 240 men received C.P.S. grants-in-aid to the total amount of nearly $80,000.00.

FOREIGN STUDENTS IN MENNONITE COLLEGES

A significant postwar development in Mennonite higher education was the bringing of foreign students to the American colleges. In the summer of 1946, Ernest E. Miller, president of Goshen College, and Ed. G. Kaufman, president of Bethel College, went to Europe to investigate the possibilities for such a program. While this has been a postwar development, it was nevertheless, at least in part, an outgrowth of the war-time experience. As early as 1944-45, for example, students of Goshen College, through their Y.P.C.A., had raised nearly $450.00 to assist in bringing foreign students to the campus. In 1945-46 part of this sum was used to assist one student from Puerto Rico who came to Goshen. In the latter year a still larger amount was raised for the same purpose. As a result of the visit to Europe of the college presidents in the summer of 1946, a sizeable group of European students studied in American Mennonite colleges the following year. In addition, there were students from Puerto Rico and Lebanon. Each year since then there has been a good representation of foreign students on Mennonite campuses in America, representing not only Europe, Puerto Rico, and Lebanon, but also Paraguay, Mexico, Ethiopia, India, China, Korea, and perhaps other countries. By the end of the school year 1949-50 this foreign student program had brought to the Mennonite colleges of the United States approximately 140 students, about 40 per cent of whom had studied at either Goshen, Hesston, or Eastern Mennonite College.

To make this program possible, the colleges generally granted the foreign student free tuition. If he could provide the remaining costs himself, he did so. Where this was not possible, funds were obtained from other sources. Each year some funds were contributed by American students. The colleges frequently obtained gifts for the aid of foreign students from interested persons or congregations. The Mennonite Relief Committee had also given much help in the case of students attending Goshen, Hesston, and Eastern Mennonite College. Closely related to the foreign student program was the program of American student tours to Europe which began in the summer of 1947. In a sense this might be thought of as a student exchange program. The American students who were in Europe in the summer of 1947 actually did spend a brief period in study at one of the European universities. In 1948 and 1949, however, the Voluntary Service work project took the place of this study experience.

POSTWAR PROBLEMS AND OPPORTUNITIES

The large postwar enrollment of the Mennonite colleges brought with it a rather serious housing problem. At Goshen College the former men's dormitory was converted into a women's dormitory, and emergency housing in the form of temporary barracks was provided for the men. Available classroom space came to be very inadequate, and auditorium space even more so. Similar conditions existed on all of the campuses, with the result that new building programs were launched at all three schools of the Mennonite Church. Hesston constructed an emergency men's dormitory in 1946, and completed Hess Memorial Hall, a large auditorium-gymnasium, in 1947. In 1948-49 definite plans were laid for a new science building, construction of which was well under way by midsummer, 1950. At Goshen construction of a new auditorium-gymnasium, with space for music classrooms and studios, a bookstore, and student center, was begun in the summer of 1948. This building was completed in 1950 at which time construction of a new women's dormitory was also begun. In addition, plans were being projected for a new chapel and seminary building. At E.M.C. a large chapel was completed in 1943, and the construction of a new women's dormitory was begun in 1949.

All in all, wartime and postwar developments had brought to the Mennonite colleges manifold enlarged opportunities and responsibilities. Student enrollments had grown. Building and financial operations were maintained on an increasingly larger scale. Opportunities for the colleges to serve their constituencies had increased. The wartime experience of the church had demonstrated as never before the need for a trained ministry in the Mennonite Church. The colleges responded to this challenge by establishing the Biblical Seminary, with an enlarged faculty, as a separate school of Goshen College, and by expanding the Bible departments of both Hesston and Eastern Mennonite College. Goshen College was looking forward to the founding of a collegiate school of nursing. All of the colleges were growing more sensitive to the demands of the constituency for instruction in agriculture. In numerous ways the educational institutions were making a greater impact on the life of the church, and were doing more to prepare the youth of the church for a life of service, than ever before in their history.

NOTES AND CITATIONS

[1] *Gospel Herald* (June 13, 1940), 33:221.

[2] *Goshen College Record* (Oct. 25, 1940), 1.

[3] *Ibid.* (Nov. 8, 1940), 3.

[4] *Gospel Herald* (Jan. 30, 1941), 33:941.

[5] *Goshen College Record* (Oct. 11, 1941), 1.

[6] *Ibid.* (Dec. 19, 1941), 1.

[7] *Gospel Herald* (Dec. 31, 1942), 35:860.

[8] *Goshen College Record* (Oct. 12, 1943), 1.

[9] *Ibid.* (Jan. 18, 1944), 3.

[10] Letter of J. L. Stauffer to Lt. Col. Byron Bird, in files of Peace Problems Committee.

[11] *Goshen College Record* (Jan. 16, 1942), 1.

[12] See the annual issues of the *Goshen College Catalog.*

[13] *Goshen College Bulletin*: The Annual Report (1942-43).

[14] *Goshen College Record* (Jan. 19, 1943), 1.

[15] *Gospel Herald* (Dec. 30, 1943), 36:848.

[16] Page 176.

[17] *Goshen College Bulletin*: The Annual Report (1941-42).

[18] *Ibid.* (1942-43).

[19] Mennonite Central Committee Annual Reports (1944-46).

[20] *Ibid.*

[21] Statement from the Dean's office.

[22] M.C.C. Annual Reports.

[23] Statistics are taken from various issues of the *Goshen College Bulletin* from 1939 to 1949.

[24] Statistics are taken from Silas Hertzler's analyses in his articles on attendance in Mennonite schools and colleges in the *Mennonite Quarterly Review* for the period.

[25] See statistics in *Mennonite Yearbook* (1949).

[26] *Goshen College Record* (Jan. 30, 1942), 1.

[27] *Ibid.* (Feb. 27, 1942), 1.

[28] *Gospel Herald* (Nov. 5, 1942), 35:684.

[29] *Goshen College Record* (Oct. 16, 1945), 1.

[30] *Ibid.* (Aug. 6 and Sept. 24, 1946).

[31] *Ibid.* (Dec. 7, 1943), 1.

Chapter XV

Ministry to War Sufferers

The well-known petition of the Mennonites and Dunkers to the Pennsylvania Assembly in 1775 said that they were ready at all times to help those in need or distress, "it being our principle to feed the hungry and to give the thirsty drink; we have dedicated ourselves to serve all men in everything that can be helpful to the preservation of men's lives, but we find no freedom in giving, or doing, or assisting in anything by which men's lives are destroyed or hurt."[1] The 1937 Mennonite statement on *Peace, War, and Military Service* says, "we are willing at all times to aid in the relief of those who are in need, distress, or suffering, regardless of the danger in which we may be placed in bringing such relief, or of the cost which may be involved in the same. We are ready to render such service in time of war as well as in time of peace." These two statements are expressions of a principle taught by the sixteenth-century Anabaptists; a principle which has been practiced more or less consistently throughout Mennonite history. Ministering to the needs of suffering humanity is a manifestation of Christian love, and is properly associated with the principle of nonresistance, both in theory and in practice. It was to be expected, therefore, that in the suffering which accompanied the second World War, the Mennonite Church would find both an opportunity and a responsibility.

SPANISH RELIEF, 1937-40

The Spanish Civil War, which began in July, 1936, may be considered a kind of rehearsal for the second World War. It was proper, therefore, that the Mennonite relief program should begin there also; for the war did bring considerable suffering, particularly on the loyalist side. This Mennonite relief project was undertaken entirely by the Relief Committee of the Mennonite Board of Missions and Charities, hereafter referred to as the Mennonite Relief Committee. The program was officially authorized at the annual meeting of the Board in June, 1937, in a resolution which said, ". . . we look with favor on the idea of opening relief work in Spain whenever in the judgment of our Relief and Executive committees said relief can be given effectively and there are funds available for this purpose." Historic Mennonitism has always held that a Christian ministry to the physical needs of men is an expression of Christian love, and an integral part of the Gospel message. For this reason the church regards its peace testimony and its relief program, not as mere humanitarian efforts, but as phases of its evangelistic program, and therefore properly a work of the Mission Board. This point of view is reflected in the above-mentioned resolution which "assumed that the message of the Gospel will accompany the work of relief for the body . . . . Whatever final commitments are made in the matter of opening work in Spain, the sending of workers, or the determination of policies regarding the work shall be approved by the joint Executive and Missions committees before they become effective."[2]

On September 21, 1937, the Executive, Missions, and Relief committees in joint session approved the gathering of funds and clothing for Spanish refugees. Levi C. Hartzler and D. Parke Lantz, missionary on furlough from Argentina, were approved as workers to be sent to Spain as soon as arrangements could be completed. Reasons for this action as given by the Relief Committee were: (1) The physical need in Spain. (2) The special place for neutral, nonresistant people in the Spanish situation. (3) The opportunity for giving a peace testimony. (4) The spiritual need of the Spanish people. The committee then appealed to the church through its periodicals, and by other means, for the support of the program. Funds were to be sent to the treasurer of the Board at Elkhart, Indiana. Clothing was to be shipped by sewing circles to Elkhart, Indiana, and to Scottdale and Lancaster, Pennsylvania.[3]

Lantz and Hartzler sailed on November 3, 1937, arriving in London on November 8, in Barcelona on November 17, and at Murcia in southeastern Spain on November 23, 1937, where they immediately began their work. Lantz returned in April, 1938, but Hartzler continued on the field until May, 1939. Others who gave a term of service in the Spanish work were Clarence Fretz, October, 1938, to May, 1939; Lester T. Hershey, October, 1938, to the spring of 1940; Wilbert Nafziger, February to December, 1939; and Ernest Bennett, February, 1939, to the spring of 1940. In 1938 the Mission Board reported cash contributions for Spanish relief, for the fiscal year ending March 31, 1938, as $18,151.46. In addition, there were gifts-in-kind, chiefly clothing, valued at $13,115.11. The following year the value of clothing shipments amounted to $12,411.55. When the program closed in the spring of 1940, cash contributions totaling $31,-474.11 for Spanish relief had been received from the churches.[4] Including the gifts-in-kind, the total amount contributed by the Mennonite Church for the Spanish program was about $57,000.00.

Only a portion of the supplies distributed by the Mennonite relief workers, however, was contributed by the Mennonite Church. Following October 1, 1938, much of the workers' time was devoted to the distribution of food contributed through the International Commission for the Assistance of Child Refugees to Spain. When the chairman of the Mennonite Relief Committee returned from Europe in May, 1939, following a review of the Spanish situation, he reported that at the close of the war in the spring of 1939 the Commission had seven ships with relief food and supplies en route to Spanish ports, and that since then further large shipments were being made from the United States and other countries.[5] Following the close of the war, however, the work of the Mennonite relief unit underwent considerable change. It received supplies from the Commission and turned them over to the Auxilio Social, the national relief organization. A report from the workers in August, 1939, said: "We co-operate with them in many ways, as seeing that the food reaches the place where most needed, etc., while endeavoring to carry a message of good will and friendship to the Spanish people from the twenty nations represented by the Commission."[6] This work continued through the following winter, and was finally closed in the spring of 1940.

While it did not establish a permanent Spanish mission, the Mennonite Relief Committee nevertheless considered its Spanish work as a definite witness to the Christian Gospel. In his report of 1939, the chairman of the committee said: "The deep spiritual darkness throughout the land, and the hunger existing here and there for the light is also testified to by all those whom we met . . . . More than ten of Spain's provinces had not a single evangelical witness point." The chairman also reported that the Dutch Mennonite Peace Group was keenly interested in the Spanish relief program and had contributed about $1,500.00 to the work.[7] A report of the Mennonite Relief Committee in the spring of 1940 said that Lester Hershey and Amos Swartzentruber, who had recently arrived in Europe, were returning from France to Spain "to review and close up the work there, and especially to contact again the needy Christian groups with whom our workers have become acquainted and have been helping both temporally and spiritually. . . . Let us pray that the work in Spain may yet lead to some definite Christian activity in that land by our people. Indeed, there are some indications that the clouds under which the evangelical Christians have been laboring may be lifted to some extent." The committee's report to the Mission Board in May, 1940, said that the Spanish work "in its final phases was devoted largely to rendering assistance to Spanish evangelical Christians."[8]

EUROPE, 1939-1945

Before the Spanish relief program was closed, the German armies had invaded Poland and the second World War was begun. Less than three months after the war began, the Mennonite Central Committee sent M. C. Lehman to Europe to investigate opportunities for the relief of war sufferers in countries dominated by Germany. Amos Swartzentruber was commissioned to make similar investigations in England and France, and in countries dominated by them. Lehman sailed on November 19, 1939, arrived at Genoa on December 1, and then proceeded to Germany. With the aid of Benjamin Unruh, a German Mennonite leader, he made necessary negotiations in Berlin for entering Poland, where there was much suffering from the effects of the German invasion. Lehman was permitted to open work on a small scale, which continued until December, 1941, when the United States entered the war against Germany. The Polish work was very much restricted, however. Lehman was not permitted to maintain his residence in Poland, and no relief was to be given to Germans. Periodic visits to Poland were permitted, however, in the company of a German government official, to distribute previously sent relief consignments. The German government permitted relief to allied prisoners of war in Germany, and requested the M.C.C. to extend help to German prisoners of war in Canada. The M.C.C. furnished Lehman a monthly minimum of $1,000.00 beginning March 15, 1940.

The major part of the Polish relief effort was carried on in Warsaw where a quarter of a million people had to depend upon the help of others for their daily bread. Some aid was also given to the Mennonites in Poland, particularly in the form of a grant of $1,000.00 to the congregation at Kazun about ten or fifteen miles north of Warsaw. This congregation of 400 members was completely plundered by Polish soldiers. Some houses and barns were destroyed and the remainder robbed of their furniture, implements, livestock, and food. The pastor of the congregation was shot as a spy. Altogether, seventeen members of the congregation were killed. The pastor's wife, son and daughter, and a hired man died when their home was struck by a bomb dropped from a plane.[9] When the United States entered the war against Germany in December, 1941, M.C.C. relief work in Poland came to an end. M. C. Lehman was interned with the American embassy in Germany and arrived in New York with the embassy officials on June 1, 1942.[10] Later he visited certain German war prisoners in Canada as agreed upon with the German government prior to leaving that country.[11]

On December 30, 1939, Amos Swartzentruber, then on furlough from the mission field in Argentina, was officially commissioned by the M.C.C. to investigate relief needs and opportunities in England and France. He sailed from New York on January 19, 1940, arriving at Liverpool on January 28. He reported the presence in England of many refugees from Austria, Poland, and Turkey. He immediately arranged for the distribution of clothing and bedding and $500.00 sent by the Ontario Nonresistant Relief Organization, and for the further use of $400.00 monthly.[12] Then he went to Paris where he met Lester Hershey and Ernest Bennett who came from Madrid to meet him. They investigated the needs of Spanish refugees in France, of whom there were thousands, and arranged to establish a home for children. Following this Swartzentruber and Hershey returned to America, arriving in New York, April 1, 1940.[13]

In a short time Ernest Bennett opened a home for French and Spanish refugee children at La Rouviere near Marseilles. He was joined immediately by Edna Ramseyer of Smithville, Ohio, who had been serving with the American Friends Service Committee, and who now took charge

14

of the new home. Some of the children in the home were full orphans and others half orphans, with their mothers probably in refugee camps, or employed by the government with no opportunity to care for the children. Next Bennett began the operation of a child-feeding canteen at Cerbere, near the Spanish border, where at the beginning about sixty persons who otherwise might have starved were receiving two meals daily. Other homes for refugees were opened at Perpignan and Banyuls. For a time Bennett assisted the American Friends Service Committee in the operation of the transport department of its work at Toulouse. Early in August, 1940, Harold S. Bender arrived in France and spent a month with Bennett reviewing the work and making plans for the future. Among other things, arrangements were made for the opening of a food and milk distribution program at Lyons.

Henry Wiens of Chicago joined the French work in September, 1940, and Henry Buller in January, 1941. Jesse W. Hoover of the Brethren in Christ Church arrived in France in March, 1941, and remained until November that same year. Henry Wiens returned to America in August, 1941. In October, 1941, three new workers arrived, Joseph N. Byler, Helen Penner, and Lois Gunden. Helen Penner remained until June, 1942. Byler returned in November, 1942, just before all of France was occupied by the German forces. Henry Buller and Lois Gunden were caught by the occupation and interned by the German authorities at Baden-Baden where they remained until they were repatriated in March, 1944. During 1941 and 1942 the French work continued at the various stations opened in 1940. Lyons became the center from which the entire French program was directed. In this city a large food and milk distribution program was carried on. The refugee homes in the South continued to care for many sick and starving children. Many other refugees were assisted by a food distribution program carried on in four small towns near the Spanish border. For many people the aid thus received meant the difference between life and death. In the month of January, 1942, more than 17,000 persons received fifty grams of dried vegetables daily, while another 38,000 received some food during the same month. When J. N. Byler returned in November, 1942, he reported that during his year's stay in France an average of 7,111 people were helped in some manner each month.[14] At the time of the occupation, a large amount of M.C.C. supplies remained on hand. These continued to be distributed to the end of the war under the direction of Augustine Coma, a Spanish refugee in France, who had been working with the M.C.C. personnel.

Following Swartzentruber's report on the situation in England, the work was continued there under the direction of Ted Claasen of Newton, Kansas, a member of the General Conference Mennonite Church, who arrived in London in the late spring of 1940. In the fall of 1940 he was joined by John E. Coffman. Claasen returned to America in 1941, but his place was taken by Peter J. Dyck. In 1942 Elfrieda Klassen and Edna Hunsperger joined Coffman and Dyck. All four of these workers were Canadians, Coffman and Hunsperger from the Ontario Mennonite Conference, Dyck from the General Conference group in Saskatchewan, and Klassen from the Mennonite Brethren in Manitoba. In February, 1944, Glen R. Miller of Goshen College arrived in England as director to have general charge of the relief program there for one year. He was succeeded by Samuel J. Goering of Moundridge, Kansas, in 1945. In 1945 the European war came to a close, making possible the renewal of relief work on the continent. Goering was then appointed director of the entire European area, with his office first in London and later in Basel, Switzerland, which then became the general headquarters of the European relief program. Late in 1945 Howard C. Yoder of Wooster, Ohio, came to England as assistant to Goering, and in 1946 he succeeded Goering as general director of the European area. In addition to the above-mentioned persons, at least fourteen others were engaged in relief work in England under the M.C.C. for shorter or longer periods of time. Among these were the following members of the (Old) Mennonite Church: B. Frank Hartzler, Lucinda Martin, Arlene Sitler, John Thut, and Mabel Cressman.

For some time after the arrival of Ted Claasen in England in 1940, the M.C.C. made contributions to the "Save the Children Fund." Later Claasen assumed responsibility for feeding 100 Polish refugee boys. As the work developed, a clothing depot was opened in London from which clothing was distributed among the needy in many parts of London, as well as other parts of England. In 1941 a large home, Wickhurst Manor, near London, was operated as a refuge for small boys and girls who had been forced out of their homes by bombing or other causes. In Birmingham a home, The Woodlands, was maintained for aged and infirm evacuees from the bombed cities. This project was carried on in co-operation with the Friends Service Committee. There was also work among German war prisoners in England, such as the distribution of prayer books and Bibles. In 1943 Peter Dyck opened a home, Taxal Edge, near Birmingham, for sick and crippled evacuee boys. Mennonite workers gave assistance at South Meadows, an evacuee nursery in North Wales, under the direction of the Liverpool Child Welfare. They also assisted with Spanish refugee children at Plymouth, and with children evacuated from the Channel Islands to North England.

In 1944 the London Center, in addition to being a clothing distribution center, now also became a hostel for homeless children. Clothing was distributed to needy individuals, families, and school children in Coventry, Liverpool, Leeds, and many smaller towns. During the single month of December, 1941, the M.C.C. workers distributed 6,000 German prayer books to as many internees and prisoners of war. During four months, November, 1941, to February, 1942, more than 2,000 people in addition to the German prisoners received some help from Mennonite relief workers.[15] As the war came to a close in 1945, the relief program in England was gradually reduced. By the end of 1945 the projects at Wickhurst Manor and South Meadows, and the children's home at the London Center, had been discontinued. The Woodlands had been taken over by the British Friends as a permanent home for the aged. In 1946 both Taxal Edge and the London Center were closed, bringing the relief program in England to an end except for one worker who remained in the war prisoners' service.[16]

When the war came to a close in 1945, the general headquarters of the European relief area was transferred to the continent. It was temporarily established at Amsterdam and then permanently at Basel, Switzerland. As rapidly as possible new relief projects were opened. At the end of 1945 the M.C.C. reported fourteen workers in France, nine in Holland, three in Belgium, and two at the general headquarters in Basel. The work in France followed the pattern of the earlier work of 1940 to 1942, with children's colonies at Chalon, Lavercantiere, Plottes, Vescours, Weiler, Anetz, and Chevagny. Food and clothing distribution figured largely in the work. The headquarters for the French work was at Chalon-sur-Saone, with Henry Buller in charge; that for the work in Holland at Amsterdam, with Peter Dyck in charge. Here the work was carried on in co-operation with a committee of Dutch Mennonites, and also consisted largely of food and clothing distribution.

Two of the workers in Belgium were M.C.C. appointees engaged in the prisoner-of-war work of the Y.M.C.A., and working under the Brethren Service Committee. A third worker, Cleo Mann, of Elkhart, Indiana, had recently arrived to open a work under the direct auspices of the Mennonite Relief Committee. In addition to the work in Holland, France, and Belgium, there were also five workers stationed in southern Italy. These workers, Delvin Kirchhofer, Arthur Jahnke, Grace Augsburger, Bertha Fast, and Esther Detweiler, were members of the M.C.C. Middle East Unit working under UNRRA. UNRRA transferred them from Egypt to di Leuca and Cesarea in southern Italy, where they were engaged in work among displaced peoples. By the end of 1945 C. F. Klassen of Winnipeg, a member of the Mennonite Brethren Church, had just completed an extended survey of displaced Mennonites, particularly Russian and Polish refugees, in western Europe. It was the hope of the M.C.C. to assist these brethren as rapidly as possible.[17]

EUROPE AFTER 1945

During 1946 the distribution of food and clothing was continued in Holland, with the addition of a reconstruction and transport unit on Walcheren Island. This unit consisted of eleven men engaged in constructing and rebuilding damaged homes. By the end of the year, however, emergency relief needs in Holland had practically ended. In France the M.C.C. program continued as in the previous year, with the addition of a builders' unit of twelve men which began reconstruction of war damaged homes late in 1946. The headquarters of the French builders' unit was at Wissembourg. The work among the refugees in southern Italy continued; beginning with April 1, 1946, Boyd Nelson was the director of this unit. In northern Italy help was also given to the Waldensian people, particularly food and clothing for their hospitals and old people's homes. In Belgium the Mennonite Relief Committee carried on a program of emergency relief, with Cleo Mann as director. Other members of the unit were Paul Peachey, Wilson Hunsberger, and Robert and Rachel Fisher.

No doubt the most significant feature of the Mennonite relief program in 1946 was the entrance of M.C.C. workers into Germany, Denmark, and Austria, with investigations in Poland looking toward the reopening of work there by the Mennonite Relief Committee. On March 28, 1946, Robert Kreider entered Germany as the Mennonite member of a group of eight representing CRALOG (the Council for Relief Agencies Licensed for Operation in Germany). By midsummer shipments of food began to arrive in Germany in large quantities and were distributed through German agencies, notably Evangelisches Hilfswerk, the Protestant relief organization, and Christenpflicht, a German Mennonite relief organization in the American Zone. In October two more M.C.C. workers, Walter Eicher and Cornelius Dyck, entered Germany. In the same month the military authorities in the British Zone approved an M.C.C. child feeding program in which the distribution and supervision of gifts would be in the hands of M.C.C. personnel. In November the French authorities approved a similar program for the French Zone. Late in the year additional M.C.C. workers entered both the British and French zones. In April, 1946, workers entered Denmark to bring assistance to the Mennonite refugees from Prussia located in that country. The workers did clothing distribution and welfare work, with Walter Gering serving as pastor and counselor. At the close of the year there were three M.C.C. workers in the refugee camps in Denmark. In September, 1946, Bertran D. Smucker arrived in Vienna to investigate needs and set up a relief program in Austria. By the close of the year two additional workers had been appointed, and food shipments were coming in. In October Howard C. Yoder and Lewis S. Martin made investigations in Poland. By the end of 1946 negotiations for a plan of agricultural and material aid assistance were under way. Wilson Hunsberger, the first worker, arrived in December, 1946.

By 1947 the relief program in Germany was in full swing. During the year, forty-three M.C.C. workers distributed 4,538 tons of food, clothing, and other supplies. This was more than five times the tonnage distributed in the remaining portions of Europe combined. Shipments continued to be made through CRALOG channels to Evangelisches Hilfs-werk, although by the end of the year this organization was receiving few M.C.C. supplies for actual distribution. Small amounts of food and clothing, however, were still being allocated to it for child feeding, parish distribution, and for use in church institutions and special camps. It was M.C.C. policy, however, to help Mennonite refugees and other needy Mennonites through the European Mennonite organizations, since it be-lieved the work could be most effectively done in this way. Christen-pflicht, the South German Mennonite relief organization, was receiving food for feeding programs in Munich, Ingolstadt, Regensburg, Heilbronn, and Pforzheim. Hilfswerk der Vereinigung Deutscher Mennoniten, the relief organization of the Mennonites in the Palatinate and in the British Zone, distributed M.C.C. food in eight different cities, although this rep-resented only a small portion of the M.C.C. distributions in these areas. M.C.C. workers themselves administered child-feeding programs in nu-merous cities of the British and French zones, including Kiel, Ludwigs-hafen, Luebeck, Krefeld Kaiserslautern, and Gronau. In the month of June alone, M.C.C. workers supplied food to 80,000 people in Germany, including children, old people, convalescents, disabled persons, refugees, and prisoners of war. Basel, Switzerland, continued to be the general headquarters of the European relief program, with Atlee Beechy as direc-tor. Robert Kreider was in charge of German relief operations in the American Zone, Cornelius Dyck in the British Zone, and Walter Eicher in the French Zone.[19]

During the year 1947 the M.C.C. shipped 578 tons of food and cloth-ing to Austria where five workers were in charge of distribution. These included Bertran D. Smucker, the leader, and Johan van den Berg, a Mennonite from the Netherlands. Distribution was made chiefly to con-valescents certified by examining physicians. At times the number of these patients, many of whom were in hospitals, reached 2,000 per week. Besides this program, some help was also given to old and sick displaced persons and to a work camp near Innsbruck. In May, 1947, the M.C.C. opened a relief program in Hungary. By the end of the year, 161 tons of food and clothing had been shipped in for distribution. The work in-cluded a child-feeding program in Jaszarokszallas which reached 459 chil-dren. In other places distribution was made through church conferences, institutions, family units, and in other ways. The center of the work was in Budapest where food and clothing were distributed to an orphanage, a boys' home, a girls' home, and a home for the blind, as well as to an old teachers' home, and to summer camps. Supplementary rations were also provided for university students. The work in Hungary was in charge of Howard Blosser and Delmar Stahly. In Italy forty-three tons of food and clothing were distributed during the year, with attention shifting from refugee camps in southern Italy to assistance to the needy in the

Waldensian valleys of the north. Here attempts were being made to set up a nurses' training program in connection with a Waldensian hospital.[20]

In France the children's colonies continued to be the major project during 1947. The M.C.C. headquarters were moved from Chalon-sur-Saone to Nancy. The new center was a combination of relief offices and a children's home. Beginning in 1947, a new policy of administration of children's homes was inaugurated. Formerly they were administered indirectly through French personnel. From now on they were administered directly by American M.C.C. personnel, although French personnel was employed as before. During the year about twenty-one tons of food and clothing were distributed among the French people. A food-packaging program in St. Die provided two four-pound packages per month for 4,000 old people. While in all of its work it was the policy of the Mennonite Central Committee and of the Mennonite Relief Committee to provide relief to needy people regardless of nationality, creed, or political persuasion, the general trend of the French work in 1947 was to concentrate its effort in an area which would serve the French Mennonites. The work of the Wissembourg builders' unit, for example, included the repair of the Mennonite Church at Geisburg. In Holland there was little emergency relief in 1947. About fifty-four tons of clothing were distributed, but chiefly to orphans and special needy individuals and refugees at Roverestein. A children's home was being maintained at Heerewegen. The Mennonite Center at Amsterdam with Irvin B. Horst in charge included a student hostel, Menno Travel Service, and M.C.C. student exchange. Before the end of the year, the builders' unit at Walcheren had completed its work, and the personnel was transferred. In Denmark the major concern continued to be a ministry to the Prussian Mennonite refugees. The chief responsibility for this work was in the hands of Peter S. Goertz of North Newton, Kansas.[21]

In 1947 the Mennonite Relief Committee continued its work in Belgium, with a building program carried on by a unit of fourteen men at Bullange, and patterned after the programs in Holland and France. Only eight tons of food and clothing were shipped into the country during the year. Perhaps the most important direct relief work was that among the families of men in prison because of collaboration with the Germans during the occupation. During the year Cleo and Nellie Mann were in charge of the Mennonite Center at Brussels, and C. Warren Long of Peoria, Illinois, served as pastor of the builders' unit. The headquarters of the Polish unit was a 420-acre farm with adequate housing facilities made available by the Polish government. From this center a considerable amount of direct relief work was done, with 111 tons of food and clothing shipped in. Some of this work was done among Mennonite refugees. The unique feature of the Polish work was the agricultural program. One phase of this was the operation of the farm. Another was the operation of a tractor unit of twenty-five men. The purpose of this was to increase agricultural production and to instruct native farmers in the use of modern machinery. The tractor unit was directed by the M.C.C.[22]

In 1948, the distribution of food and clothing in Austria and Hungary continued much as in the previous year. In the latter country the program came to an end, however, before the close of the year. Governmental regulations restricted the freedom of private religious agencies to such an extent that the M.C.C. felt it best to direct its energies elsewhere. In Austria the program continued into 1949 without much change. During 1948 food and clothing distribution in Italy centered around Torre Pellice. During the summer months two children's colonies were operated. About 100 children were given three weeks of rest, recreation, and religious instruction, with fifteen Waldensian young people assisting in the teaching. For 1949 the M.C.C. planned to carry on a program in Naples, with welfare, children's projects, and clothing distribution to be carried on in co-operation with the Waldensians.

In 1948 the work in Germany and in northwestern Europe underwent a gradual shift from emergency relief to that of rehabilitation. Feeding projects, however, continued on a large scale. During the four-month period, February to May, M.C.C. feeding centers provided supplementary food three times a week to more than 141,000 persons in the British and French zones of Germany. In addition to this, food was supplied to Christenpflicht in the American Zone, to Mennonite refugee camps, to Mennonite committees in the British and French zones, and to Evangelisches Hilfswerk. Students in five different universities in the British Zone, and two in the French Zone (Mainz and Tuebingen), also received food from the M.C.C. During 1948 children's colonies continued to be operated at Weiler and at Nancy in France, and also at Heerewegen in Holland.

The rehabilitation type of service given by the M.C.C. is best illustrated by the work of the community centers at Heilbronn, Krefeld, Hamburg, Neustadt, and Kaiserslautern. These centers included sewing rooms, shoe-repair shops, reading rooms, recreation facilities, and other projects. At Heilbronn in six months, May to October, 1,341 women used the sewing room to do sewing for themselves and families. In the same period the cobblers repaired 1,051 shoes, and 964 books were circulated from the library and reading rooms. At this center a choir was organized for the late teen-age group, and the girls of the nine-to-twelve age group were organized as a club which did singing and Scripture memorization. The purpose of these centers was to provide the people with opportunities for self-help, and to continue the personal and spiritual witness begun in the distribution of material aid. In the words of the M.C.C. report itself: "Community centers in central Europe have been organized to set the stage for personal spiritual witnessing and interpretation by our workers to the spiritual needs of hungry souls. This we believe is being accomplished."[23]

The builders' units, both in France and Belgium, were discontinued toward the end of 1948. Efforts were made to transfer these units to Germany, but the M.C.C. was unable to obtain permission from the military government to do so. At the close of the year, only three Mennonite Relief Committee workers remained in Belgium. They maintained a headquarters in Brussels, distributed clothing, and carried on a ministry to displaced persons in various camps throughout the country. They co-operated with Pastor Charles Grikman who worked among the Latvians and Russians. The M.R.C. was also supporting two native workers who helped in this ministry. As mentioned in an earlier chapter,[24] it was the hope of the Mennonite Board of Missions and Charities to continue the Brussels Center as a permanent Mennonite Gospel Center. During most of 1948 the work in Poland was centered in the Danzig area, where both food and clothing were distributed. In the city of Tczew, weekly and biweekly distribution of food was given to about 1,000 people, especially mothers, small children, and tuberculosis patients. After the first of October, the center of the work was shifted to Nasielsk, about thirty-five miles north of Warsaw. During the year the agricultural program also continued, with tractors tilling the soil on the Rolin Farm, besides assisting some sixty farmers in the community in plowing and threshing. It was the plan of the Mennonite Relief Committee to discontinue its direct relief work in Poland in the spring of 1949. The M.C.C. had planned, however, to continue some phases of work, especially that with the Mennonites in Poland,[25] although this later proved to be impossible.

THE MIDDLE EAST AND ETHIOPIA

Another region in serious need of help because of war conditions was the Middle East. In the summer of 1943 the M.C.C. sent Delvin Kirchhofer of Dalton, Ohio, and Dr. C. Richard Yoder of West Liberty, Ohio, into this region to study the needs and to report possible opportunities for service. Yoder was a young physician who had served some time in public health work in lieu of military service. The two men left Akron, Pennsylvania, on May 16, 1943, traveling by way of New Orleans and the west coast of South America to Valparaiso, thence to Buenos Aires and South Africa, and then along the East African coast to Palestine. They arrived in Durban, South Africa, in early August, and finally in Jerusalem on October 13, 1943. By mid-January, 1944, they had completed a survey of the relief situation in Palestine and Syria. From here they went to Egypt where they established headquarters in Cairo and worked among the Greek refugees of that area, helping to reassemble families separated during their flight, and making preparations to return them to their homes again. They soon began to ask the M.C.C. for more workers, as well as supplies of clothing. Before the end of the year the M.C.C. had nine workers on this field, with four more en route and three under appointment. Besides Kirchhofer and Yoder, three other workers, Henry Detweiler, Samuel A. Yoder, and Paul Ervin Hooley, were working directly under the M.C.C. Four workers, Marie Fast, Nancy Hernley, Grace Augsburger, and Mary Emma Showalter, were serving on loan to UNRRA. The four en route at the end of 1944 were Bertha Fast, Esther Detweiler, Marie Brunk, and Barbara Zuercher. The three under appointment were Arthur Jahnke, Helen Moser, and Martha Eiman. At least five of the ten women workers in the Middle East were trained nurses.[26]

During 1945 UNRRA succeeded in moving large numbers of refugees to their homes in the Balkans, so that it was possible to close many of the refugee camps. This made it possible to transfer relief workers to other fields. By the end of 1945 Delvin Kirchhofer, Arthur Jahnke, Bertha Fast, Grace Augsburger, and Esther Detweiler had been transferred to the refugee camps in South Italy. Mary Emma Showalter was now in England, and C. Richard Yoder had returned home. On May 1, 1945, Marie Fast of Mountain Lake, Minnesota, lost her life at sea while assisting in the repatriation of a group of Yugoslav refugees. Henry Detweiler, Martha Eiman, Helen Moser, and Marie Brunk were still in Egypt at the end of 1945, but were transferred soon afterward. In September, 1945, Samuel A. Yoder, Paul Ervin Hooley, and Nancy Hernley were transferred at UNRRA expense to Ethiopia, where they opened a relief project under the Mennonite Relief Committee at Nazareth, about sixty miles from Addis Ababa. Yoder and Hooley returned home in 1946, but new recruits were added so that by the end of the year a unit of eleven workers was on the field. G. Irvin Lehman, a minister, was director of the unit. His wife was a registered nurse. The group included an additional nurse, Nancy Hernley Conrad, and a physician, Paul L. Conrad. The other members of the unit were Geneva Alexander, Dorsa Mishler and wife, Ada E. Showalter, Truman Diener, and Jacob R. Clemens and wife.

The Ethiopian work centered around a twenty-five-bed hospital at Nazareth, which was dedicated early in December, 1946. It included both a healing and a teaching program. During 1947 the hospital had an average daily census of thirty patients. The clinic associated with the hospital served approximately ninety-five persons per day. The teaching program included a fully accredited primary dressers' course under the direction of Dorsa Mishler. By the end of 1947 a class of seventeen had completed the course and were certified as hospital workers. At the beginning of 1949 the unit strength of the Ethiopian project remained at eleven, although there had been considerable change in the personnel since 1946. In addition to the medical service the unit provided two teachers for the government schools at Addis Ababa. In 1948 the Emperor Haile Selassie approved a mission project within Ethiopia. The Eastern Mennonite Board of Missions and Charities agreed to administer this project which was to be opened in 1949 at Deder, about 250 miles southeast of Addis Ababa, with Daniel and Blanche Sensenig in charge.[27]

INDIA AND CHINA

During 1942 the need and opportunity for relief work in the Far East began to present itself. Suffering in parts of India, due to famine conditions and threat of war, led the Mennonite and Brethren in Christ missions in that country to organize the Mennonite Relief Committee for India. A modest work, especially among refugees, was carried on in 1942 and 1943, aided by a monthly allotment of funds from the M.C.C. In the latter part of 1943 famine conditions became very serious in the Bengal region, with thousands of people dying in the vicinity of Calcutta, and requiring additional funds and workers of all the relief agencies working in the field. The Mennonite work was under the direction of F. J. Isaac of the General Conference Mennonite Mission at Champa until the return of George Beare. As mentioned in Chapter XIII, Beare and his wife returned to India under the Mennonite Board of Missions and Charities late in 1943, where the latter resumed her work in the American Mennonite Mission. The former then took charge of the relief project, relieving Isaac for his work at Champa.

Early in 1945 J. Harold Sherk of Kitchener, Ontario, a minister of the Mennonite Brethren in Christ Church, arrived in India to assume general direction of the Mennonite relief program. George Beare then returned to his mission post. At the close of the year seven M.C.C. relief workers were on the India field, in addition to the director: J. Lawrence Burkholder, Ralph C. Kauffman, Wilhelmina Kuyf, Titus Lehman, Verna Zimmerman, Vera Yoder, and Clayton Beyler. Most of them had been assigned to China, but were giving their service in India while awaiting permission to enter China. During 1946 the India work continued much as during the previous year. At the close of the year, twelve workers were on the field. In 1947 the partitioning of India created a minority problem with millions of refugees leaving their homes. These found their way to refugee camps which gave relief agencies like the M.C.C. new opportunities for service. The latter increased its staff, so that by the close of 1947 the India M.C.C. unit consisted of sixteen persons. A year later the number was thirteen, with the ministry to refugees continuing as the principal service. During these two years or longer Martin Schrag of Moundridge, Kansas, a member of the General Conference Mennonite Church, was the director of the unit. A number of the India workers were appointed by the Mennonite Relief Committee; for a time some of them assisted in the work of the mission hospital in Dhamtari. Most of their time was given to the M.C.C., however, especially after the development of the refugee problem in 1947.[28]

Another Far Eastern people greatly in need of help were the Chinese, a people whose country had been at war since 1931. In July, 1943, Samuel J. Goering and J. D. Graber were sent to China to investigate opportunities for service there. Goering, a former missionary to China under the foreign Mission Board of the General Conference Mennonite Church, went under the auspices of the M.C.C. Graber, a former missionary to India under the Mennonite Board of Missions and Charities, went under the auspices of that organization and of its Mennonite Relief Committee. It was hoped that these two commissioners would be able to open a relief program in which both the M.C.C. and the M.R.C. could participate, and which would also enable the Mennonite Board of Missions and Charities to open a new mission field. Goering and Graber returned to the United States in May, 1944, and recommended that a unit of workers be sent to the province of Honan.

The M.C.C. then appointed S. F. Pannabecker and P. P. Baltzer, former missionaries to China, to initiate the relief work. J. Lawrence Burkholder, Clayton Beyler, and George Beare were appointed by the Mennonite Relief Committee. Since the war in the Far East made it impossible to enter China in 1944, the M.R.C. appointees went to India to assist in the Bengal famine relief program under the M.C.C., until such time as it would be possible to proceed to China. In addition to Burkholder, Beyler, and Beare, Ralph C. Kauffman of Bethel College had also arrived in India late in 1944 under the auspices of the M.C.C. Pannabecker and Baltzer left the United States in October, 1944, first going to Egypt where they assisted temporarily in the work of the refugee camps in the Middle East. From here they went to India where they assisted in the Bengal relief program, and then proceeded to China, where they arrived at the end of September, 1945. In the beginning they were attached to the American Advisory Committee, doing work temporarily in Hankow, but with an assignment to organize a project in northern Honan as soon as war conditions would permit.

Early in 1946 the M.C.C. was able to open its China program, and by the end of that year it reported thirty-two workers on the field, including the Mennonite Relief Committee appointees who had served for a time in India. The M.R.C. did not attempt to open a relief project of its own in China, the Mennonite Board of Missions and Charities being interested primarily in the opening of a mission project. Several of the M.R.C. appointees were planning to transfer to the mission when it would open, however; and in case it would be found advantageous to conduct relief work in connection with the mission, it was expected that the remainder of the M.R.C. appointees would attach themselves to that project. During 1946 most of the M.C.C. workers in China served for a period of time on detached service with other relief agencies. For the purpose of orientation, most of them were attached to either the Friends Ambulance Unit, the American Advisory Committee, or the Chinese National Relief and Rehabilitation Administration, after which they were assigned to regular M.C.C. projects. At the end of 1946 the M.C.C. unit in China was operating a medical center at Chuhsien-chen, including a medical clinic and a public health program. The M.C.C. unit was also co-operating with the C.N.R.R.A. relief plowing project, an agricultural rehabilitation program.

At the end of 1947 there were forty M.C.C. workers in China. The medical program now included service in seven hospitals and clinics. Four of the men were serving as mechanics and field men for the C.N.R.R.A. tractor program, which included thirty-eight tractors, machinery, tools, and other supplies. Much of the unit's work was with Chinese refugees. During 1947 the M.C.C. supplied 106 tons of food and clothing for distribution in China. Milk amounting to 4,500 servings per month was distributed to the needy at Kaifeng. Two hundred tons of seed wheat were distributed, and 40,000 yards of cotton cloth and 15,000 pounds of woolen yarn were made available through Chinese sources. At the close of 1948, the number of M.C.C. workers in China was twenty-eight. The headquarters had been moved from Kaifeng to Shanghai, because of the advance of the Communist forces. An orphanage at Hengyang was caring for about 250 orphans. The workers at this place included James Liu and wife, native Christians, members of the General Conference Mennonite Mission. At the Chinkiang center, 28,451 persons had been given food in the month of September, and during the six-month period, April to September, 15,099 medical treatments were given. A medical project had also been opened on the island of Formosa, in charge of Robert Hess, M.D., and wife of Mount Joy, Pennsylvania.[29]

OTHER FAR EASTERN AREAS

Other areas in the Far East served by the M.C.C. were the Philippine Islands, Java, Sumatra, and Japan. In 1946 C. L. Graber served as a special M.C.C. commissioner to the Far East at which time he made plans for the opening of the Philippine unit. Dale Nebel arrived on the islands on June 6, 1946, to begin the setting up of a fifty-bed hospital and medical clinic in Vigan. The hospital was opened on October 1, 1946, supplies being purchased from the War Surplus Commodities. By the end of 1946 the unit consisted of ten members, with James Brenneman, M.D., in charge of the hospital, assisted by a native physician. At that date approximately fifty tons of supplies valued at more than $50,000.00 had been sent to this area. In 1947 the hospital was moved to Bangued. At the close of the year, the M.C.C. unit consisted of seventeen members, and a year later the number was thirteen. At this time the work was hampered somewhat because of the lack of a resident physician. An attempt was being made to secure a native Christian physician for the assignment.

In 1947 William H. Yoder arrived in Batavia to await an opportunity for opening relief work in Java. Due to the political situation in the Dutch East Indies the remaining four workers sent for Java were serving in India at the close of the year. By the end of 1948 no work had been opened in Java, but the five workers had found their way into Sumatra where a project of medical services and material aid distribution was under way. The five workers were William H. Yoder, Elaine Snider, Caroline Plank, Bertha Eshleman, and Lowell Steider. In 1947 the M.C.C. also took steps to enter Japan. The organization was granted membership in LARA (Licensed Agencies for Relief in Asia) and one carload of flour was contributed which arrived in Japan on December 16, 1947. By the end of 1948 Robert H. Smith of Grantham, Pennsylvania, had been transferred from the Philippines to the island of Okinawa, where he was serving under the general direction of Church World Service. He was the only American relief worker on the island. The M.C.C. had purchased a prefabricated barrack which was to be shipped to Japan and set up for a community center project. H. G. Thielman and wife of Kitchener, Ontario, had been appointed to take charge of the Japan project.[30]

PUERTO RICO

An important relief project undertaken during the second World War was that in Puerto Rico. The work began with the opening of a C.P.S. unit at La Plata in June, 1943. In the beginning this was a sub-unit of the Martin G. Brumbaugh Reconstruction Unit, a project begun by the Church of the Brethren. At the end of 1943 the M.C.C. unit consisted of eight workers, with Wilbur Nachtigall as director and Delbert V. Preheim, M.D., in charge of medical work. By the end of 1944 the unit had forty members, twenty-four of whom were C.P.S. men. Two years later the unit was exactly the same size, although due to discharges following the end of the war, the number of C.P.S. men had been reduced to eight. A large number of the remaining thirty-two members, however, were ex-C.P.S. men. At the close of 1948 the La Plata unit had twenty-four members. In 1944 the C.P.S. men completed the construction of a twenty-five-bed hospital which immediately met a great need in the country, as well as the approval and support of government officials. By the end of the year two additional physicians, H. Clair Amstutz and George D. Troyer, had joined the unit, as well as Earl Stover, a dentist, and five registered nurses. An educational and recreational program provided training in health, agriculture, and homemaking. At the end of 1945 Harry E. Martens was director of the unit and H. Clair Amstutz, M.D., head of the medical service. At the end of 1948 Justus G. Holsinger was director, with Charles M. Hertzler, M.D., in charge of the medical service.

The importance of the medical service in Puerto Rico is seen from the report of 1945 which says that the hospital and clinics were caring for approximately 900 outpatient clinic calls per month. Patients hospitalized were averaging about 100 per month, and there were approximately 25 major and 60 minor operations per month. The 1946 report says that as many as 1,400 people were being treated monthly in the hospital and clinics. Eighteen young women had been graduated from nurse-aid training courses offered by the hospital. During 1947 arrangements were made for the Mennonite Board of Missions and Charities to purchase the Puerto Rico Reconstruction Administration property occupied by the M.C.C. unit. In the same year the Mission Board also appointed Lester T. Hershey as pastor of the La Plata unit. As said above,[31] these two actions were steps in a long-range program, including the transfer of the La Plata project to the Mission Board. By the end of 1948 the La Plata and Aibonito missions had a combined staff of fourteen workers appointed by the Board, and a baptized membership of sixty-four. The transfer of the property was completed in January, 1950. Of all the Mennonite relief projects begun during the second World War, the Puerto Rico project was the first to develop into a thriving permanent mission program.[32]

RESETTLEMENT OF EUROPEAN REFUGEES

The Mennonite Central Committee was organized in 1920 as an agency of the American Mennonites for bringing aid to their suffering brethren in Russia. In addition to carrying aid to Russia, the M.C.C. during the nineteen twenties and thirties had also assisted 29,000 or more refugees, directly or indirectly, to find their way from Russia to permanent homes in Canada, Brazil, and Paraguay. When the European war came to a close in 1945, the Mennonite population of Paraguay was about 5,400 and that of Brazil about 1,500. From the time the first settlers came to Paraguay in 1930, the M.C.C. followed the policy of keeping in close touch with them, providing the kind of assistance necessary for a people going through the struggles and hardships of pioneer life. Land was purchased for resale to the colonies, and almost yearly one or more M.C.C. representatives from North America visited the Paraguay Mennonites to give aid and counsel in agricultural matters, in road-building construction, in legal, business, and financial matters, in medical service, and in the spiritual life of the colony.

Besides short-term commissioners, workers were sent to Paraguay who remained two years or longer, ministering to the needs both of the Mennonites and of native Paraguayans. During 1944 and 1945 nine such workers were on the field. In 1946 there were twenty-five. At Itacurubi, near the Friesland colony, a child-feeding program was carried on during the summer of 1945 and 1946. In 1946 an M.C.C. unit of three workers was engaged in a hookworm-eradication project in the same area. Several workers were assisting in the schools of the Mennonite colony. No doubt one of the most appreciated services in the Mennonite colony was the medical and dental service of the doctors John R. Schmidt, Herbert R. Schmidt, G. S. Klassen, A. M. Lohrentz, and Alvin W. Gaede who served the colonies at various times from 1941 on. It should also be mentioned that during 1947 and 1948 the M.C.C. had four workers in Brazil engaged in a preaching and teaching ministry among the Mennonites in that country. These workers were R. C. Seibel and wife of Reedley, California, and John E. Kaufman and wife of Inman, Kansas.

The need for this continuing service in Paraguay was greatly augmented following the close of the war, when it was learned that thousands of displaced Mennonites in western Europe were anxiously seeking a new home in the Americas. These were refugees from Russia, Poland, and West Prussia, who came through in advance of the Russian army, and at the close of the war were located in numerous refugee camps in Germany and Denmark. A considerable number had found their way into Mennonite homes in Holland where they were being cared for until they could be moved to permanent homes of their own. After more than a year of strenuous effort on the part of the M.C.C., supported financially by all the Mennonite groups of North America, with the help of American army officials and the Department of State, through the overruling providence of God, the first group of 2,304 Russian Mennonite refugees finally sailed from Bremerhaven, Germany, for Buenos Aires on the Dutch steamer *Volendam* on February 1, 1947.

First 329 refugees, gathered from Dutch homes, boarded the ship at Rotterdam. Then on January 28, the ship sailed to Bremerhaven where another 1,071 were taken on board on the evening of January 29. These had come by train in boxcars from a refugee camp near Munich. More than 900 others in Berlin were anxiously waiting to join the group, but the Russian military officials had consistently refused permission for them to travel through the Russian Zone of occupied Germany. Due to the unlikelihood that permission would be given, the captain of the *Volendam* urged that the ship sail on the thirtieth. C. F. Klassen and Peter Dyck, the M.C.C. representatives in charge of the group, decided, however, to wait another day. Then on the evening of the thirtieth, word was received that the Berlin group had been released. They arrived at Bremerhaven in the early morning of February 1. On the afternoon of the same day the *Volendam* set sail for South America and docked at Buenos Aires on February 22, 1947, with 2,304 Mennonite refugees on board. Peter and Elfrieda Dyck accompanied the group on the journey.[83]

The transfer of these 2,304 refugees to their new home was a satisfying experience; but this was only a beginning, as thousands more were awaiting their turn to migrate. In order to expedite this task, the M.C.C. opened two refugee camps in Germany in 1947, one at Gronau in the British Zone, and the other at Bachnang in the American Zone. These camps served as assembly centers for preliminary interviewing and screening by the International Refugee Organization, at whose expense some of the refugees were moved. The Mennonite refugees, both within and without the M.C.C. camps, were provided regular refugee rations with an M.C.C. supplemental ration. The M.C.C. camps also cared for persons deferred because of poor health, in the hope that proper diet and treatment would enable them to migrate later. The spiritual life of the refugees was a major concern of the M.C.C. Members of the regular staff ministered to their needs as they were able, and their work was supplemented from time to time by special representatives appointed for this purpose. Among such representatives were H. H. Janzen of Winnipeg, John J. Wichert and wife of Vineland, Ontario, Cornelius Wall and wife of Mountain Lake, Minnesota, Peter S. Goertz and wife of North Newton, Kansas, and later H. J. Dyck and wife of Elbing, Kansas.

In addition to the *Volendam* group which went to South America, 452 refugees were able to migrate to Canada in 1947, and 42 to the United States, making a total of 2,798 for the year. In 1948 another 2,445 went to Paraguay, 751 to Uruguay, 3,699 to Canada, and 6 to the United States. In 1949 no migrants were taken to South America, although 1,548 came to Canada and 113 to the United States. The number moved in 1950 was: 85 to Paraguay, 3 to Uruguay, 482 to Canada, and 437 to the United States. Of the above number, 147 cases represent migrations, of either old or new settlers, from Paraguay to North America. After subtracting this number, a computation of the above figures shows that during the four years, 1947 to 1950, the M.C.C. assisted a total of 12,220 European refugees in finding new homes in the western hemisphere. The great majority of these migrants were Russian Mennonites, although at least 380 were non-Mennonites, and a considerable number were Mennonites from Danzig and West Prussia. At the end of 1950, however, about 1,000 Russian Mennonites, and perhaps 6,000 from Danzig and West Prussia, remained in western Germany. While most of the Russians hoped to migrate to the Americas, and it was the plan to move as many of the others as possible, it was obvious that most of the latter would probably remain in Europe permanently. For this reason the M.C.C. was putting forth special efforts to assist these people in the development of land settlement and housing projects within Germany. In October, 1950, C. L. Graber went to Germany for a six-month assignment to assist C. F. Klassen in this task.[34]

Early in 1947 an organization known as Mennonite Resettlement Finance, Inc., was established as a trustee of M.C.C. funds and property, devoted to the migration and resettlement of Mennonite refugees. In 1947 and 1948 the officers of this organization were: E. C. Bender, chairman; J. W. Warkentin, vice-chairman; and William T. Snyder, secretary-treasurer; the remaining members of the board of directors were Elvin R. Souder, C. L. Graber, J. Winfield Fretz, Herman J. Andres, and C. A. De Fehr. At the annual meeting of the M.C.C. in January, 1947, C. A. De Fehr of Winnipeg, a member of the Mennonite Brethren Church, was commissioned to go to South America as M.C.C. and M.R.F. commissioner in charge of receiving and resettling the immigrants arriving on the *Volendam*. When the ship docked at Buenos Aires on February

15

22, 1947, De Fehr was on hand to receive the passengers.[35] It was his task to supervise their movement up the river to Paraguay; to assist in the purchase of land; to help in the settlement of individuals and families on the land and in the villages; and to help the new settlers to acquire tools and livestock with which to begin life once more. De Fehr returned to North America to report on his work to the annual meeting of the M.C.C. early in January, 1948. He soon went to Paraguay again, however, accompanied by John W. Warkentin of Hillsboro, Kansas. These two commissioners were in Paraguay the greater part of 1948, receiving and resettling large numbers of immigrants who arrived that year. Herman J. Andres of Newton, Kansas, was in Uruguay from October 17, 1948, to the end of the year performing a similar task in that country.[36] In 1949 J. W. Vogt and Arthur Jahnke were serving as M.C.C. commissioners in the refugee settlement program in South America. In assisting the immigrants to Canada with their settlement problems the Mennonite Colonization Board, an organization of Canadian Mennonites, performed a task similar to that performed by the Mennonite Resettlement Finance Corporation in South America.

SUPPORTING THE RELIEF PROGRAM

It is obvious that the Mennonite relief program after 1937, which included work in many European countries, in Egypt and Ethiopia, in India, China, Japan, Sumatra, and the Philippines, in Paraguay, Brazil, and Puerto Rico, represented a large outlay of contributions in cash, of gifts-in-kind, and of personal services. It is also obvious that the resettlement of refugees from one hemisphere to another represented an even greater cost. A portion of the latter cost was met by the International Refugee Organization. This organization was not authorized, however, to assist refugees of German origin. Many of the Russian Mennonites were able to qualify for I.R.O. help since their ethnic origin was Dutch. Altogether during 1947 and 1948 the I.R.O. assisted in the moving of Mennonite refugees to the amount of $401,400.00. During the same period, however, the cash contributions to the M.C.C. for this purpose by the various Mennonite groups were $1,040,000.00. In addition to this a total of $220,000.00 was made available in the form of loans. Apart from the resettlement program, the total relief program of the Mennonite Central Committee and the Mennonite Relief Committee during the years 1937 through 1948 represented cash contributions amounting to $3,520,000.00, and gifts-in-kind amounting to $6,100,000.00. The contribution of the (Old) Mennonite Church to the refugee resettlement program (1947-48) was approximately $278,000.00 in gifts and $134,000.00 in loans. Of the general relief program, 1937-48 (not including resettlement), its cash contribution was approximately $1,275,000.00. The value of its gifts-in-kind is unknown. The year 1947 represented the high point in M.C.C. and M.R.C. expenditures for relief and resettlement. In this year cash contributions for both of these purposes were $1,472,000.00, and gifts-in-kind amounted to $2,086,000.00, making a total of $3,558,-000.00. In the same year the total loans for resettlement amounted to $85,000.00.[37]

The bringing of this help *In the Name of Christ* to needy people represented a direct personal ministry of 572 men and women, besides occasional short-term commissioners. The usual term of service of a relief worker was two years, although many served longer than this, and also some for shorter periods. Of the 572 workers who served during this period, 282 came from the Mennonite Church. This represented 49 per cent of the total. Twenty-four per cent of the workers, 137 in number, came from the General Conference Mennonite Church. Forty-six of the workers, or 8 per cent, came from the Mennonite Brethren Church. At the end of 1948 the number of M.C.C. and M.R.C. workers on the field was 217. Of this number, 103 represented the Mennonite Church, 52 the General Conference, and 19 the Mennonite Brethren.

Bringing this large amount of material aid to thousands of people not only required the personal ministry of many persons on the field. It also required the financial assistance of a much larger number of persons at the home base. The average cash contributions for relief, of all Mennonite groups co-operating with the M.C.C. during the period, 1944 to 1949, may be calculated at approximately $4.00 per member per year. The gifts-in-kind, however, represented a large amount of co-operative labor. For gathering and processing clothing in preparation for relief shipments, the M.C.C. maintained five clothing collection centers: at Reedley, California; Newton, Kansas; Ephrata, Pennsylvania; Winnipeg, Manitoba; and Kitchener, Ontario. For food processing there were four centers: Reedley, Newton, Kitchener, and Silver Springs, Pennsylvania. During 1948 five persons were employed either full or part time handling and processing the food in the centers. The collection and packing of clothing, shoes, and soap at the centers required the services of fifteen persons, either full or part time. The work of the clothing centers was co-ordinated through a general supervisor at Akron, Pennsylvania, whose task it was to keep in touch with the centers, providing guidance and encouragement, pointing up needs, and keeping the clothing contributions balanced. To a lesser degree a similar supervision was maintained over the food-processing centers.

In addition to the above-mentioned centers, there were a number of subsidiary centers for collection, but not for processing of food and clothing, as at Kalona, Iowa; Goshen, Indiana; and perhaps at other places. The M.C.C. also maintained cutting rooms at Kalona, Iowa, and Bluffton, Ohio, where new clothing materials in large quantities were cut and distributed to local sewing circles for sewing into garments. The supervisor of clothing centers kept in touch with these centers and with local sewing circles through the *Women's Activities Letter,* which kept all interested persons informed and up to date on the program and its needs. One phase of the work was the "children's projects." Its principal function was the preparation and sending of Christmas bundles by children of the various Mennonite communities. An occasional *Children's News-letter* was circulated for the encouragement of this work. The transportation of food and clothing from the various centers for shipment abroad in itself was no small item. During 1948 four truck drivers were engaged in this task.[38]

Perhaps the one local unit which did more than any other to make possible the relief program of the M.C.C. and of the M.R.C. was the sewing circle of the local Mennonite congregation. In one of these local sewing circles the secretary's record book shows that during the year 1947 the circle had twelve monthly meetings, with an average attendance of 27 women.[39] Each meeting was featured with a period of devotion, usually consisting of singing, Scripture reading, and prayer. At each of the twelve meetings, except one, a quantity of relief clothing was packed and prepared for shipping. The amounts ranged from 75 to 550 pounds, making a total of 1,912 pounds for the year. The one monthly meeting which reported no shipment, however, did report the presence at the meeting of Elma Esau, a relief worker, currently attached to the Akron office of the M.C.C., who gave a firsthand account of relief needs in England, Denmark, and Holland. The last minute in the proceedings for that day reads as follows: "The Executive Committee decided to send $25.00 to M.C.C. for yarn to be sent to the refugee camp in Denmark, which need had been presented by Miss Esau."

The report of one monthly shipment of 140 pounds from the above-mentioned sewing circle gives the detailed contents as follows: "33 dresses, 2 coats, 3 jackets, 2 bathrobes, 11 scarves, 5 hoods, 4 pair gloves, 3 men's suit coats, 3 pr. trousers, 4 vests, 2 shirts, 1 apron, 1 romper, 1 comfort, 9 undergarments, 12 pr. hose, 16 infants wear, 1 baby blanket, 20 sweaters, 15 shirts, 4 blouses, 35 pr. footwear, 1 pkg. knitting needles, 1 baby bottle and nipples." At one meeting the food committee reported that since the last meeting 232 quarts and 1 pint of butter were made for foreign relief. This evidently refers to apple butter. At one meeting it was decided to send clothing and ten dollars each to two couples from Holland then at Cornell University. At the same meeting it was decided to purchase a pressure cooker for a missionary family in India. At one meeting members were urged to bring used fats for soapmaking. At the same meeting twenty hospital gowns were made for the use of the Puerto Rico hospital, and ninety-seven bandages were rolled. At one meeting the women did sewing for a local family which had recently returned from several years of service on the relief field. At another, $25.00 was authorized as a contribution toward the purchase of a refrigerator for a missionary family in India.

As noted above, this sewing circle had a food committee which occasionally did canning for relief. Many, perhaps most of the circles, did food processing in season as well as sewing and processing of clothing. In addition to this, a number of portable canners were in operation in various sections of the church in 1947 and 1948. The method used was for the canner to move into a community and process thousands of pounds of pork, beef, and perhaps other meats which were donated and butchered for this purpose by the members of the congregation. It was this kind of activity in hundreds of Mennonite congregations which made it possible for the M.C.C. in the year 1947, *In the Name of Christ,* to provide needy people in many parts of the world with gifts-in-kind amounting to 11,630,775 pounds, and valued at $2,136,153.59. Mennonite women, even while resting in their winter homes, were doing sewing for relief. A news item in the *Gospel Herald* in 1942 reported that women spending the winter in Sarasota, Florida, representing Mennonite and Amish women from at least eleven states, formed a sewing circle to prepare clothing for relief.[40] This was a commendable way in which to spend one's vacation.

THE WORK GOES ON

As said above, the emergency phase of the European relief program had reached its crest, and a gradual transition to the rehabilitation type of work had begun as early as 1948. Similar changes in the M.C.C. program had taken place in other parts of the world, resulting in a gradual reduction of the number of workers on the field. Even so, the annual meeting in March, 1950, reported a total of 156 M.C.C. and M.R.C. workers still on the field. These were distributed as follows: Latin America (Paraguay, Uruguay, and Brazil), 21; Ethiopia, 15; Palestine, 3; the Far East, 26; and Europe, 91. Of the latter group, 59 workers were in Germany, 8 in France, 4 in Belgium, 4 in Italy, 4 in Austria, 5 in Holland, and 7 in Switzerland. The Swiss group was made up of the personnel in the European M.C.C. headquarters office in Basel. The workers in Holland included the personnel of the Amsterdam headquarters, Menno Travel Service, and the Heerewegen center which served the needs of the Dutch Peace Group, as well as a home for conferences and retreats, both for M.C.C. workers and Dutch Mennonites. The French workers were located in the two children's homes at Weiler and Nancy. The Belgian workers were located in Brussels, the Italian workers in Naples, and those of Austria in Vienna. Ten of the workers in Germany were located in the American Zone which included the neighborhood center in Heilbronn, the I.R.O. work in Stuttgart, and the Frankfurt center which served as headquarters for the Voluntary Service program, as well as a meeting place for student groups and the Frankfurt Mennonites. In the British Zone there were 33 workers engaged chiefly in feeding and clothing distribution work, and in dealing with refugees and displaced persons, at Kiel, Hamburg, Espelkamp, and Gronau. In the French Zone there were 11 workers at the Neustadt community center and transportation service, the children's home at Bad Durkheim, and the community center at Kaiserslautern. The Berlin staff consisted of four workers at the neighborhood center.

During the summer of 1950 plans were being made for a further reduction of the M.C.C. personnel on the foreign field, particularly in Germany. It was generally recognized, however, that the relief program of the M.C.C. would need to continue indefinitely in many areas of the world. As the Korean war developed in the summer of 1950, and then appeared to draw to a close in the early autumn, it seemed likely that this unfortunate war-stricken country would open new avenues of service for those Christians concerned for a ministry to war sufferers.

NOTES AND CITATIONS

[1] *Pa. Archives,* Eight Series, 8:7349. A copy of a contemporary broadside containing the petition is in the Goshen College library.

[2] *Thirty-first Annual Report of the Mennonite Board of Missions and Charities* (1937), 25.

[3] *Gospel Herald* (Sept. 30, 1937), 30:571-2.

[4] *Annual Report of the Mennonite Board of Missions and Charities* (1938, 1939, 1940).

[5] *Gospel Herald* (June 8, 1939), 32:213.

[6] *Ibid.* (Aug. 17, 1939), 32:436.

[7] *Ibid.* (June 8, 1939), 32:220.

[8] *Ibid.* (March 14, 1940), 32:1072; (June 13, 1940), 33:227.

[9] *Ibid.* (Aug. 8, 1940), 33:421; (Jan. 16, 1941), 33:886; (April 3, 1941), 34:21.

[10] *Ibid.* (June 11, 1942), 35:229.

[11] *Ibid.* (Feb. 18, 1943), 35:1005.

[12] "Relief Notes," *Gospel Herald* (March 7, 1940), 32:1036.

[13] *Ibid.* (March 14, 1940), 32:1072.

[14] The sources of information for the relief program in France are the annual reports of the M.C.C., the M.C.C. reports in the *Mennonite Yearbook,* and the periodic relief notes in the *Gospel Herald.*

[15] *Gospel Herald* (April 16, 1942), 35:61.

[16] See annual reports of M.C.C.; the M.C.C. reports in the *Mennonite Yearbook,* and relief notes in the *Gospel Herald.*

[17] Report of M.C.C. Annual Meeting, 1945.

[18] *Mennonite Yearbook* (1947), 7, 11, 12.

[19] Report of M.C.C. Annual Meeting, 1947.

[20] *Ibid.,* 1947.

[21] *Ibid.,* 1947.

[22] *Ibid.,* 1947; *Mennonite Yearbook* (1948), 10; *Report of the Forty-first Annual Meeting of the M.B.M.C.* (1947), 18.

[23] Report of the M.C.C. Annual Meeting, 1948.

[24] Page 167.

[25] *Mennonite Yearbook* (1949), 7, 11. A news item in the *Gospel Herald* (April 19, 1949) reported: "The relief unit in Poland is being liquidated at the request of the Polish government according to most recent information from our workers there."

26 Report of the M.C.C. Annual Meetings, 1944-48; *Mennonite Yearbook,* 1944-49.
27 *Ibid.*
28 *Ibid.*
29 *Ibid.*
30 *Ibid.*
31 See above, page 167.
32 Reports of the M.C.C. Annual Meetings, 1944-48; *Mennonite Yearbook,* 1944-49.
33 *Gospel Herald* (March 11, 1947), 39:1080-81; M.C.C. Annual Reports, 1947-49.
34 Reports of M.C.C. Annual Meetings, 1947 to 1950.
35 *Ibid.,* 1947 and 1948.
36 *Ibid.*
37 Statement of M.C.C. controller's office.
38 Reports of M.C.C. Annual Meetings, 1947 and 1948.
39 The sewing circle of the Goshen College congregation, Goshen, Indiana.
40 "Winter Tourists Do Sewing Circle Work," *Gospel Herald* (Oct. 8, 1942), 35:597.

Chapter XVI

Mennonite Service Units

REPORT OF SPECIAL STUDY COMMITTEE

In Chapter X it was stated that the Virginia Peace and Industrial Relations Committee had presented the idea of Mennonite service units, along with the problem of civilian defense activities, to the Peace Problems Committee in the autumn of 1942.[1] On November 6, 1942, the Peace Problems Committee appointed a special study committee to give consideration to this idea. This committee, consisting of John R. Mumaw, John L. Horst, and C. L. Graber, submitted a report to the Peace Problems Committee on February 11, 1943. That part of this report which deals with Mennonite service units is as follows:

> In addition to the type of service which can be rendered as an alternative to participation in civilian defense activities this committee has thought in terms of creating Mennonite service units for a long-range program of Christian testimony and Mennonite witness. We believe that the make-up of such units will depend largely upon the type of service which they are to render. The type of service will be governed largely by the demands and conditions of the place where the service is to be rendered. It would make some difference whether this service is to be rendered in foreign countries or in some section in America. It would necessarily be governed by different principles if it were intended for disaster and emergency relief or whether it were to serve in a project of more permanent needs. We see the possibility of such service being rendered in times of emergency arising from epidemics, floods, forest fires, and immigration. A service unit of the more permanent type could be set up for relief work in foreign lands such as China, Greece, and other sections of Asia and Europe with a view to establish a definite missionary program along with the relief which we would hope to have continued after the war conditions have been relieved.
>
> A primary concern for Mennonite service units is to maintain a healthy spiritual life within the group. Another vital factor is that these groups must maintain a positive Christian testimony among those with whom they work. There should be one or more spiritual leaders in the group who would be qualified to keep up the spiritual morale and testimony of the unit.
>
> The health of the unit should be given due consideration as well as the service which it might render in health work among the people with whom the unit labors. This calls for a doctor or nurse or worker trained in first aid to be included in the units as the type of service may demand.
>
> Such a unit should have a sufficient number of trained workers in such skills as auto mechanics, carpenter, forester, soil worker, dietitian, cook, etc., to do well the job to which they are assigned. They should include nurses, doctors, businessmen, and those trained for service in teaching and evangelistic efforts.
>
> Each unit should have in it the possibility of one or more Gospel teams in which there are a sufficient number of public speakers and singers to render religious programs. This service unit should consider one of its major duties

the conducting of religious services in the community where they labor and to build up a permanent congregation of Christian people.

These units should be made up of Mennonite people who can by word and by life give a consistent testimony to our Mennonite faith and practices.

These Mennonite service units should in the main be designed to provide an avenue of expression for Christian testimony through our youth. Those who serve should be expected to contribute their time, clothing, and personal equipment, with the cost for unit training or unit equipment, and for maintenance and travel of unit members to be covered by the church through its relief committee treasurer.

We believe any new service of this type or any new field of need which we enter must be related to our whole church program, and particularly to its missionary program. During wartime a Mennonite service unit could be definitely related to our mission program in foreign fields or to established churches in the local community. In times of peace this relation could probably most readily be worked out through our city and rural mission efforts. We believe that any community projects which would be undertaken by Mennonite service units should make some contribution to the life of the community. This, however, should be incidental or secondary to our major purpose of carrying on a missionary witness and Christian testimony within the community.

While the type of service rendered to the community may have its temporal aspects we think this type of social service will render stability to the community in which the group is working. It is the sort of thing which missionaries in the foreign fields have been doing along with their program of evangelism. All that is done in the way of material help and in the meeting of the temporal needs of the community must be done in the name of Jesus. The service unit shall be a Christian witness and testimony from the time of their entering into any relief emergency or long-range program of community interests, continuing all throughout the entire time the project is under way. We have conceived of the possibility of setting up such a service unit in the Terry C.P.S. project in Montana. While the campees are there engaged in a rehabilitation program it would be just as reasonable to expect that out of this shall come a community that has in it a definite Mennonite testimony. We should be able to be the first in that field to set up a Mennonite meeting conducted in true form to our Mennonite practices so that when people begin moving into that section we will then already have had an initial setup to take care of the religious needs in the community.

Inasmuch as we expect these service units to contribute directly to our missionary program we believe there must be an organic relationship between them and the existing organizations which the church has set up for our missionary program. We feel that this type of service must be definitely tied in with the work we are already doing and serve to enlarge our vision of possibilities particularly on the home front. We are inclined to believe that many areas on American soil could be definitely profited by such service, and in order to reach those fields it will be necessary to have someone explore the field as well as to have someone administer the projects which would be undertaken. We have conceived the work of the relief committee as a possible group to which this work could be tied. It may be necessary for the mission board to set up a field supervisor to investigate and promote these projects, but it could be definitely linked up with the work of the relief committee under the mission board.

In any community where a group can be organized, instructions to such groups would come through the relief committee, who would see to it that the Mennonite pattern is followed both in scope of activities undertaken and in the manner in which it is carried on. The relief committee could immediately inspire interest in our schools to set up some activity and training for such Mennonite service units so that during the coming summer we might be able to launch initial activity in this direction. It might be possible for some of the larger congregations to undertake similar projects under the direction of the relief committee. It would not be intended to make this an exclusive school project but that this simply be used as a first step to get the work under way.

We believe the work of establishing Mennonite service units could be best moved forward initially through a close co-operation with our church school organizations. The schools could be made responsible for forming a unit, formulating its policies and selecting from time to time its field of service, scheduling its program, choose its members, provide for the unit training with the understanding that the standards of the church be promulgated.

After this first step, and with some experience in this field we believe the church would be ready to formulate other service units from local Mennonite communities. The organization of such local groups could be adapted to the general pattern that has been derived from a critical review of the first experiences.

SUMMARY OF CONCLUSIONS

In the light of our study and these observations we have come to the following conclusions:

1. We see no satisfactory way of participating officially with the O.C.D. organizations.

2. We believe that any service of that type in the local community should be an alternate service under church direction.

3. We believe that in addition to meeting the present emergency situation we should think in terms of a long-range program of Christian testimony.

4. We believe it would be practical to organize Mennonite service units which shall be distinctly Mennonite in their personnel, work, and practice.

5. We believe this service should be put on a voluntary and nonremunerative basis.

6. We believe the service units should be a particular avenue for youth expression to our Christian faith and Mennonite practice.

7. We believe these service units should be immediately initiated through our church schools and through other church organizations where there is sufficient interest and personnel to undertake it.

8. We believe these service units should include the particular skills existing within our Mennonite constituency as well as the Christian training of those who are preparing for work of teaching and evangelism in the church.

9. We believe these service units should be integrated into our whole church and missionary program.

RECOMMENDATION

We recommend that the Peace Problems Committee consider asking the relief committee under the Mennonite Board of Missions and Charities to be made the administrative agency to carry on this type of service.

We suggest further that the types of alternate service which have been suggested above might well tie in with the interests of the General Sewing Circle organization and with the Nurses' Organization sponsored by this board, and we suggest that the initial work be started through the church schools.

This report was received and approved by the Peace Problems Committee on February 11, 1943. The following day it was submitted to the Executive, Missions, and Relief committees of the Mennonite Board of

Missions and Charities. The report, including the recommendation that
the Mennonite Relief Committee become the administrative agency for
Mennonite service units, was approved unanimously by the three committees and referred to the Mission Board which approved it at its annual
meeting in May, 1943. In reporting the plan to the Mission Board, the
Relief Committee suggested that projects of the proposed service units
might serve as alternatives to civilian defense projects, or to work done
by the High School Victory Corps which at the moment seemed likely
to be generally established. It was also suggested that service units would
provide a suitable form of alternative service for Mennonite nurses, some
of whom felt themselves under pressure to enter military service. The
Relief Committee made it clear, however, that it thought of service units
"not merely as . . . alternative . . . service, nor merely as social service,
but as an avenue of expression of our Christian faith and Mennonite
practice, particularly for our youth, and one which should be integrated
into our whole church and missionary program, without in any way sup-
planting our missionary endeavors. Rather we see it as a providential
opportunity to strengthen our testimony at large and to increase our
ministry in following the Gospel call."[2]

MENNONITE RELIEF COMMITTEE INAUGURATES PROGRAM

Following the Mission Board's approval of the idea, the Mennonite
Relief Committee secured the services of Lester Hershey to study the
organization and administration of service units. His report was presented to the Relief Committee in February, 1944. The following summer
the first Mennonite service unit, consisting of four young people, two
men and two women, was organized in Chicago under the direction of
Lester Hershey. The period of work was eight weeks. The work included
a survey of certain districts on behalf of the Mennonite Mexican Mission,
the Mennonite Home Mission, and the proposed mission for Negroes, as
well as summer Bible school work, home visitation, and the renovating
of the mission buildings.[3] In 1945 Laurence Horst of Peabody, Kansas,
was appointed part-time director of Mennonite service units, and served
until the fall of 1948. In the summer of 1945 three units, with a total of
fifteen workers, were in operation for nine weeks. One of these units
served in connection with the Canton, Ohio, and Detroit, Michigan, missions; the second with the Children's Home at West Liberty, Ohio; and
the third with the Mennonite rural mission at Culp, Arkansas. The work
consisted of summer Bible schools, religious surveys, evangelism and
visitation work, together with manual labor, such as repair and painting
of buildings, construction of equipment, and health and sanitation.[4]

In the summer of 1946 the Mennonite Relief Committee had seven
units, with thirty workers engaged in the service. These were located at
Culp, Arkansas; Highway Village and Pleasant Hill, Illinois; Germfask,

Michigan; and Northern Minnesota. Thus far all of the Mennonite service units had been short-term units and were active in the summer months only. In its report to the Mission Board in June, 1946, however, the Relief Committee expressed the conviction that the church should look forward to "an enlarged all-year short-term voluntary service program in which many of our youth might be used."⁵ In the meantime a subcommittee of the Peace Problems Committee was giving special study to this matter and in a report to General Conference in 1946 recommended not only short-term units, but also long-term service projects and local congregational projects. The report also included a recommendation that a full-time director for Mennonite service units be appointed, that General Conference "encourage our churches to support the program generously," and that it "encourage our young people to enter into service freely."⁶ Although these recommendations were adopted by General Conference, some time was required for them to become fully effective. In 1947 thirteen service units with fifty-six workers were in operation, and in 1948 sixteen units with seventy-seven workers. All of these were short-term summer units under the supervision of the part-time director.

FURTHER DEVELOPMENT

At its annual meeting in 1948, the Mission Board took another step forward in appointing Levi C. Hartzler full-time Secretary for Service and Relief. By this action Hartzler became the executive secretary of the Mennonite Relief Committee, the organization responsible for the administration of Mennonite service units. Hartzler assumed his new duties in January, 1949. In a bulletin issued from his office in the following spring, the new director announced plans for long-term service units and an extended program of short-term units. Special attention was called to the long-term unit in operation at the Kansas City General Hospital since September, 1948. Eleven workers comprised this unit, the men serving as hospital orderlies and the women as nurse aides. They lived in a home owned by the Mission Board and located three blocks from the hospital. The home was in charge of Salina Swartzendruber, who did the cooking and cared for the home in general. The Mission Board's agreement with the hospital provided that service unit members should receive Sunday as their day off. This gave the workers an opportunity to share in the life and activity of the twin city missions. Here they assisted in Sunday school and young people's work, as well as visiting the sick and shut-ins, singing in hospitals and convalescent homes, distribution of tracts, and similar work.⁷

The bulletin issued by the director of Mennonite service units stressed the value of hospital service to young people interested in nursing and medicine. It called attention to

. . . many possible types of institutional units which might be developed and which are to be investigated in the near future. Children's hospitals and children's homes offer opportunities for the care and teaching of children. For example, there is a crippled children's hospital in Ohio where the children are mostly polio victims. This would offer opportunities for service in such areas as occupational therapy. The same opportunities would likely be available in penal institutions such as prisons and reform schools. This latter area is a needy area for a real Christian witness. Certain county homes also offer opportunities for various types of service.

The racial minorities in our country offer a fertile field for real Christian service. Certain colored schools in the South are badly in need of teachers and other personnel. Last summer one unit served at a colored school at Piney Woods, Mississippi, and several teachers taught in the school during the summer. The deplorable condition of our own American Indians suggests another possible service area which is now being investigated. The possibility of service units abroad in connection with our relief and mission efforts is being given further study. The unit in Puerto Rico will be coming under the control of the Mennonite Board of Missions and Charities when the complete transfer of property and service is made from M.C.C. by January 1, 1950.

The short-term program for the summer of 1949 is now in the process of development. Last summer 16 units served in nine states with a total personnel of 77 volunteers. Through the work of these young people 65 decisions for Christ were made, 206 Bibles distributed, 4,900 tracts handed out, 611 homes contacted in visitation, 2,030 homes contacted in community survey, 2,173 pupils enrolled in summer Bible school, 218 children enrolled in youth camps, and four races served . . . .

The above program will be continued and enlarged for 1949 as new areas develop and personnel is secured. Further development of the general hospital program and possible builders' and itinerant evangelism or colporteur units indicate directions into which the short-term service unit program may develop.

The director of Mennonite service units found an expression of the spirit of voluntary service in the words of the Apostle John: "But whoso hath this world's good, and seeth his brother have need, and shutteth up his bowels of compassion from him, how dwelleth the love of God in him? My little children, let us not love in word, neither in tongue; but in deed and in truth."[8] To the question, What is voluntary service?, the director said: "Voluntary service is service rendered in the name of Christ to those in need in our world without regard for remuneration. It is Christian youth's answer today to militarism and conscription, to materialism and selfish competition in business, to the physical and spiritual need of our world." The director then outlined five reasons for maintaining service units: (1) To meet need in our world. (2) To obey the command and example of Christ to help the needy. (3) To enlarge the church's witness in our world. We should follow the example of Christ and the apostles who ministered both to the spiritual and physical needs of men. This broader witness also provides young people whose talents are other than that of preaching and teaching, with an opportunity for service. Because of the great selfishness of our generation, unselfish service rendered in the name of Christ by persons of every talent and skill becomes all the more conspicuous. (4)) To recruit workers for the church's larger program. There is a constant call for workers in all areas of the church's work. Service units give young people an opportunity to do in-service training before making a final decision as to a lifework. At the same time service units give church leaders an opportunity to see young people in action where they can help to direct them into the work of the church for which they are best fitted. (5) To give young men of draft age an opportunity to render significant service while their neighbors are participating in a training period with the armed forces.

M.C.C. VOLUNTARY SERVICE

While the Mennonite Relief Committee was developing a service unit idea which had originally been stimulated by the demand for emergency service in local communities, the Mennonite Central Committee was also developing the idea of voluntary service as stimulated by C.P.S. experience, particularly in mental hospital units. That the men working in these units were doing a worth-while and much-needed service was generally recognized. Practically all of the hospitals were understaffed. Why then, it was asked, should not Mennonite young women form voluntary units, to make a similar contribution in these same hospitals? The idea was acted upon, and the program was begun in 1944 with the organization of two women's summer units in the state hospitals at Ypsilanti, Michigan, and Howard, Rhode Island. These two units were integrated with the M.C.C. relief training program described in Chapter XIV, units of which were in operation both at Ypsilanti and Howard. Sixty-one women were enrolled in the two units, thirty-three of whom were from the Mennonite Church.[9] This experiment was sufficiently successful to have it repeated in the summer of 1945. This time there were five voluntary service units with a total of seventy-eight women enrolled. Four of the units were in state hospitals, Ypsilanti, Michigan; Cleveland, Ohio; Poughkeepsie, New York; and Wernersville, Pennsylvania. The fifth was at the M.C.C. headquarters, Akron, Pennsylvania.[10] Of these units, only the two at Ypsilanti and Poughkeepsie were integrated with the relief training program.

By this time there was a growing conviction within M.C.C. circles that Voluntary Service should find additional avenues of expression. In his report to the 1945 annual meeting of the M.C.C., Albert Gaeddert, then general director of C.P.S., said that public health projects like that of the C.P.S. unit at Gulfport, Mississippi,

could and should be carried over to the post-C.P.S. period. During the C.P.S. period we have worked in an alternative service program in lieu of military service. The voluntary aspect of our service should come when there is no compulsion to do alternative service, and it is our hope that the church will want its young people to be provided with opportunities for this type of service, both within the country and in such areas as Puerto Rico, the Philippine Islands, or abroad. Our thought is not to have this based on a humanitarian basis, but rather that it should be thoroughly Christ-centered and motivated by a deep desire "not to be ministered unto but to minister" in the name of Christ.[11]

This wish of the director found an early realization. Of the four voluntary summer service units in operation in 1946, three were in mental hospitals, but the fourth was at Gulfport, Mississippi. At the close of the year Elmer Ediger, the new general director of C.P.S., reported to the annual meeting of the M.C.C. that the Voluntary Service unit at Gulfport had "overcome initial barriers set up by C.P.S. groups," and that it was "injecting a healthy volunteer spirit and making a significant contribution at the hospital." Some members of the unit were ex-C.P.S. men who continued their services on a voluntary basis from two to twelve months after their discharge. Eleven members of the unit were C.P.S. men, not yet discharged. Most of these men were working on the hookworm control program. Three of the nurses in the unit were giving their service to the local city-county hospital. It was planned to have some members of the unit present the opportunities of the nursing profession to potential trainees in an effort to raise the standards of the hospital. Thought was being given to home relief nursing and to home repair in some of the more needy situations. The hospital had even asked the unit for an instructor in nursing to help reopen the training school. Other workers were concentrating on Sunday school and summer Bible school work, and on recreational and youth activities. In co-operation with members of the Gulfport community, the camp group carried on a large-scale program of collecting old toys through the public schools, and rebuilding them for redistribution.[12]

In 1947 the M.C.C. sponsored six summer service units: two in mental hospitals; one in an institution for epileptics at Skillman, New Jersey; one at Gulfport, Mississippi; one at Cuauhtemoc, Mexico; and the other at the M.C.C. headquarters. A total of ninety-two persons was enrolled in these units. The Gulfport and Cuauhtemoc units were organized on a long-term basis, however, and staffed by one-year volunteers. Brook Lane Farm, the newly established mental rest home at Hagerstown, Maryland, was also organized on a long-term basis; and one-year volunteers were assigned for service there. During the year the M.C.C. accepted twenty-four individuals for one-year voluntary service assignments, as compared with eight for the previous year. In addition, six others were assigned to units for periods of six months or more. Since C.P.S. had ended on March 30, 1947, all of the persons at Gulfport were now on a voluntary basis. The former director of C.P.S., who was now the director of Voluntary Service, said this transition to a completely voluntary basis "was helped greatly by the generous 'volunteer' attitude of the discharged C.P.S. group." Approximately half of the men at Gulfport volunteered for periods of one to nine months beyond their discharge. The transition to a voluntary basis also brought a change from what was primarily a public health program to a more varied program. Besides health activities, workers were also engaged "in religious education in a circuit of thirteen colored schools; in community educational projects such as sewing clubs, boys' shop classes, and visual education; in recreation for the same circuit of colored schools; in family welfare, home nursing, and sanitation work of the surrounding poor white and colored community. It should be pointed out that Mennonite mission activity has been greatly stimulated in the Gulfport community as a direct outgrowth of the camp work."[13]

The Mexican unit began as a summer unit, concerned chiefly with the health improvement needs of the Mexicans and of the Mennonite colonists. The summer's work demonstrated the possibilities of the program, however, so that Melvin Funk, the leader, and two other members continued beyond the summer. By the end of the year, nine workers were serving in the unit on a yearly basis, with three more under appointment. A temporary lying-in hospital was being established to serve until the government hospital could be completed. A vaccination and maternity program was inaugurated, and other forms of health assistance were being given. Two members of the unit were serving as teachers among the Mennonites. The services of the summer unit at Skillman, New Jersey, were greatly appreciated. Moreover, the labor shortage in this institution was so great that it was decided to continue Skillman as the site for year-round short-term units, fall, winter, spring, and summer. This plan had the advantage of providing an opportunity for voluntary service to persons whose labors were required on the home farm during the summer.[14]

By 1948, the Voluntary Service program of the M.C.C. had assumed rather large proportions. Throughout the year, 336 different individuals took part in the program. Of these, 62 were one-year volunteers, 220 were summer workers, and 54 winter volunteers. The new aspects of the program included experimental units in Europe and Canada. To some extent the increase in the number of participants represented a normal growth of interest in the service unit program. Many of the different Mennonite groups were now officially encouraging their young people to share in this work, and some of them were taking steps to organize units under their own auspices. On the other hand, there is no doubt that some of the increased participation was caused by the renewal of conscription, and the rather general feeling that deferred C.O.'s should contribute a year of voluntary service. During the summer a new interest in the longer term voluntary service program became manifest. In October a special printed folder was released, and a few copies with application forms were sent to all of the churches.

From September 1 to December 18, 1948, 52 applications for a year or more of voluntary service were received. The 62 one-year volunteers in actual service during 1948 were assigned to eight different places, as follows: Gulfport, 20; Mexico, 19; Brook Lane, 7; internship for Brook Lane, 6; Florida, 2; M.C.C. headquarters, 2; material aid, 1; Skillman, New Jersey, 5. The summer service assignments in the United States were as follows: Cleveland State Hospital, 15; Skillman, New Jersey, 18; Richmond, Indiana, State Hospital, 16; St. Elizabeth's Hospital, Washington, D.C., 15; Mount Princeton Commonweal, a school for delinquents at Nathrop, Colorado, 6; Brook Lane, 5. A new Voluntary Service venture in 1948 was the three summer units in Canadian mental hospitals. These were located at North Battleford, Saskatchewan; Brandon, Manitoba; and London, Ontario, with a total enrollment of 33 for the three units. The latter two were strictly M.C.C. units, whereas the unit at North Battleford was sponsored by the General Conference Mennonite Church.

Another new venture in 1948 was the two summer service units in Germany. In 1947 a group of students from American Mennonite colleges had traveled in Europe, spending some time studying at a European university. When the second student group took the tour in 1948, the experiment was tried of organizing the group into two service units for a month's term of service each in Germany, one located at Hamburg and the other near Frankfurt. The Hamburg unit had 22 American members, to which were added 19 German, 2 Swiss, 1 English, and 4 Dutch members. The Frankfurt unit had 23 American members, to which were added 20 German and 4 Dutch members. The work projects consisted of the reconstruction and repair of old or war-damaged buildings. In the one case, a hospital for epileptics and mentally deficient patients was being repaired; in the other, an old castle was being rebuilt for use as a Christian youth center. The European Voluntary Service effort was a natural sequence of the M.C.C. relief program. The co-operation of Europeans and Americans in the program provided an opportunity for ministry and understanding, and the rebuilding of faith and hope on the part of the German people.

The summer experiment was so successful that two subsequent projects were undertaken. In October, 1948, a voluntary project with fifteen workers was opened at Sembach in the Palatinate, and continued for three weeks. Its work was the building of a Mennonite youth center for that part of Germany. At Espelkamp near Bielefeld, a project of a continuing nature was opened. Here refugee families were being settled in a wooded area, the site of numerous buildings formerly used for the manufacture of poison gas and munitions. The project of the Voluntary Service unit was to assist the refugees in erecting new homes; to remodel old munitions buildings to be used for a children's, and an old people's home; and to assist in the construction of a Christian workers' school for the Evangelical Church. In this project it was planned that certain of the American personnel should stay for longer periods, while the Germans would be coming and going at regular intervals. It was also

16

planned that some American relief workers who were in Europe on a
two-year basis should be added to this unit. The European Voluntary
Service units were being administered within the framework of the total
European M.C.C. program, with Paul Peachey as director.[16]

There is no doubt that the short- and long-term service units did
much to stimulate interest in the work of the church on the part of many
Mennonite young people, and to deepen the conviction that they should
give a period of service to the church. Following a visit to the various
projects in 1947, a member of the M.C.C. Voluntary Service administrative staff said: "This summer consisted not only of making worth-while
friends, a pleasant social life, and in serving. Unit members also developed an understanding of different branches of the church, caught the
vision of a needy world, gained an understanding of the mentally ill, and
experienced spiritual growth which resulted in a more complete commitment to serve 'In the Name of Christ.'" As evidence in support of the
latter part of this statement, the director of Voluntary Service cited the
fact that of the ninety-two summer unit members of 1947, thirty-nine had
expressed an interest in giving a year or more of service to the church
some time later. Perhaps many were catching something of the vision
expressed by Robert Kreider when he said at the Elspeet conference in
Holland in 1947: "I like to think of the Mennonites as a lay church where
the rank and file pour out their time in the service of the kingdom . . . .
We should be prepared to give several years of our life to the service of
the church. The misery of the hour calls us to be frugal. I wish we could
present a solid front to the world of giving 10 per cent or more of our
income for the work of the church."[16]

In making its plans for 1949, M.C.C. Voluntary Service stressed one-
year service terms, and expressed the hope that by the end of the year
the number so enrolled might reach as high as 200. As a rough estimate
of distribution, the director suggested one third in institutional units,
one third in the Gulfport, Mexico, and Puerto Rico areas, one sixth in
Europe and South America, and one sixth in miscellaneous projects such
as Mount Princeton. European plans included: a between-semester
student project of four weeks at Krefeld, Germany; three or four summer units to provide for about 100 people; continuation of Espelkamp,
with expansion from this base, providing service opportunities for longer
term American workers and short-term Europeans; and other short-
term units of from two to four weeks' duration, as the need would arise.
Tentative plans were also made for about 100 people in summer service
units in the United States and Mexico. Tentative plans for Canada called
for four units with a total of 50 people.[17]

In his report for 1946, the director of M.C.C. Voluntary Service cor-
rectly referred to the spirit of voluntary service among the Mennonite
people which helped to make the organized service units possible. By
way of illustration, he cited what he called "one day volunteer units" on

the home front, consisting of men and women who gather for canning and packing of food for relief, or for similar purposes: "It would be astounding if we had figures . . . on the total number of volunteer days donated on the home front of our relief program this past year. Last year the Smoketown, Pa., cannery alone had approximately fifty volunteers each day for four months, five days a week. This is an illustration of the volunteer principle." A final type of volunteer service which might be mentioned is that in connection with the UNRRA livestock attendant program. This was not an M.C.C.-sponsored program. The M.C.C. co-operated with UNRRA and the Brethren Service Committee, however, in supporting it. Perhaps more than four hundred men were members of Mennonite crews who accompanied the livestock boats. Besides these, there were many others, not a part of Mennonite crews, who also assisted in the program.[18]

M.C.C. AND CONFERENCE PROGRAMS

As mentioned earlier, by 1948 a number of individual Mennonite groups and conferences had taken steps to organize service units of their own, in addition to the Mennonite Relief Committee whose program had been authorized as early as 1943. Even within the Mennonite Church three district conferences had service unit programs of their own in addition to the M.R.C. program. The Ontario Mennonite Conference program was under the direction of A. Leonard Snyder; that of the Illinois Mennonite Conference under Roy D. Roth; and that of the Lancaster Mennonite Conference, through the Eastern Mennonite Board of Missions and Charities, under the direction of H. Raymond Charles. The General Conference Mennonite Church had a voluntary service program under the direction of Erna Friesen; and the Mennonite Brethren Church had also authorized a program. P. C. Hiebert had much to do with the initiation of this movement. Most of the conference service programs were of the short-term type, although the Mennonite Relief Committee and the Mennonite Brethren had authorized both short-term and long-term programs. That of the Mennonite Relief Committee is described earlier in this chapter.

As to the relation of M.C.C. Voluntary Service to the conference programs, the M.C.C. director of Voluntary Service considered it the function of his section "to provide opportunities for those who apply and are qualified, to explore for new projects, to establish experimental units, to assist constituent conference programs as called upon and as possible, and to serve as a clearing and co-ordinating center for individual conference and co-operative programs." He recognized that the programs of the Mennonite Brethren Church and of the Mennonite Relief Committee aimed to provide a type of work more closely related to their respective mission programs than would be possible in the case of the

M.C.C. units. "The extent to which both of these groups utilize M.C.C. services such as application, training, and certain types of project explanation," he said, "is in process of being determined. A meeting with the concerned constituent representatives for clearing and joint planning will be held early in the new year (1949)."[19]

The view of the Mennonite Relief Committee and of its parent body, the Mennonite Board of Missions and Charities, as to the relation of its program to that of the M.C.C., was stated in the following resolution adopted at the annual meeting of the Board in 1946, and endorsed by General Conference in 1947:

We believe that voluntary service work in the United States and Canadian territory should be administered and financed directly and separately by those Mennonite conferences (or their service organizations) which desire to undertake such work. We feel that in addition to the major service programs conducted by the various groups the Mennonite Central Committee may be able to render a service to these groups by way of exploration, information, and co-ordination, and by operating a modest voluntary service program of its own primarily for those groups and individuals who have no program of their own and desire an M.C.C. program. We are willing to have the M.C.C. undertake this service and are ready to support it financially as may be needed, provided a clear statement of policy and program, and annual budget proposals is made available to our committee as a basis for its action.[20]

As said earlier in this chapter, the total number of persons enrolled in short-term Mennonite service units of the M.R.C. in 1948 was 77. With additional workers in the long-term unit at the Kansas City General Hospital, which began in September, 1948, the enrollment in M.R.C. units was somewhat larger than this. According to the report of the director, 89 members of the Mennonite Church were enrolled in the various Voluntary Service units of the M.C.C. in 1948. Thus more than 166 members of the Mennonite Church were engaged in some type of service unit work in that year. The total expenditures of the M.C.C. for its Voluntary Service program during the year 1949 were $40,980.64. Those of the M.R.C. for its Mennonite service units for the fiscal year, 1949-50, were $11,685.82.[21]

NOTES AND CITATIONS

[1] See above, page 120.
[2] Report of Thirty-seventh Annual Meeting of the M.B.M.C. (1943), 24.
[3] Ibid. (1944), 13.
[4] Ibid. 1945), 16.
[5] Ibid. (1946), 22, 23.
[6] Ibid. (1947), 19.
[7] Martha King, "Serving the Master in a Hospital," Gospel Herald (March 22, 1949), 42:279.
[8] I John 3:17, 18.
[9] M.C.C. Annual Report (1944).

[10] *Ibid.* (1945).
[11] *Ibid.* (1945).
[12] *Ibid.* (1946).
[13] *Ibid.* (1947).
[14] *Ibid.* (1947).
[15] *Ibid.* (1948).
[16] *Ibid.* (1947).
[17] *Ibid.* (1948).
[18] *Ibid.* (1946).
[19] *Ibid.* (1948).
[20] *Report of the Fortieth Annual Meeting of the M.B.M.C.* (1946), 24.
[21] Report of the M.C.C. Annual Meeting, March, 1950; *Report of the Forty-fourth Annual Meeting of the M.B.M.C.* (1950), 33.

Chapter XVII

Peace Literature

From 1925 on there was a steady flow of peace literature within the Mennonite Church, due largely to the influence of the Peace Problems Committee. In 1927 the committee published two pamphlets by John Horsch, one a *Symposium on War,* and the other *The Principle of Non-resistance as Held by the Mennonite Church.* Both of these pamphlets, the latter in a revised form, were reprinted in 1939. In 1934 appeared a pamphlet by Wilbur J. Bender on *Nonresistance in Colonial Pennsylvania,* and in 1937 one by Guy F. Hershberger on *Nonresistance and the State.* In 1930 J. S. Hartzler's *Nonresistance in Practice* was published with the encouragement of the Peace Problems Committee, as were Sanford C. Yoder's *For Conscience Sake,* and Guy F. Hershberger's *Can Christians Fight?* both in 1940. The latter had formerly appeared as a series of articles in the *Youth's Christian Companion.*

These were followed by Guy F. Hershberger's *War, Peace, and Non-resistance,* sponsored by the Peace Problems Committee and published by the Herald Press in 1944. J. Irvin Lehman's *God and War* was published in 1942, and John R. Mumaw's *Nonresistance and Pacifism* in 1944. From 1933 to 1941 the *Gospel Herald* published a quarterly peace section written by Edward Yoder and sponsored directly by the Peace Problems Committee. Beginning in 1941 this section appeared bimonthly; and in 1948 it was changed to a monthly section, entitled "Peace and War," and edited by Ford Berg. The *Gospel Herald* also carried several special series of articles, one entitled "Questions for Nonresistant Christians," by Guy F. Hershberger, which appeared during the summer of 1940; and another, "In the Midst of War—Thoughts for Nonresistant Christians," by Harold S. Bender, in the spring of 1943. The *Youth's Christian Companion* published an extended series of articles by Melvin Gingerich on "Christian Youth and the State," beginning late in 1940 and continuing through most of 1944. These articles were revised and published in book form by the Mennonite Publishing House in 1949, under the title, *Youth and Christian Citizenship.*

In addition to the titles mentioned above, a number of peace tracts were published. Among these were: *The Present World Situation and Our Peace Witness,* by Orie O. Miller, published in 1930; *The Sixth Commandment,* by S. F. Coffman, later revised and published in 1937 as *Mennonites on Military Service; War and the Christian Conscience,* by John Horsch, published in 1939; and *What About War?* by Edward Yoder, published in 1940, giving ten Biblical reasons why conscientious objectors cannot take part in war. Some of these books and pamphlets received a rather wide distribution. In 1939 the Peace Problems Committee reported that 6,000 copies of the revised edition of Horsch's *The Principle of Nonresistance as Held by the Mennonite Church* had been distributed. Other tracts and pamphlets had an equally wide distribution, and by 1948 several of the titles mentioned above had been reprinted.

In addition to these publications of the Peace Problems Committee, valuable literature was being produced by other Mennonite and affiliated groups. From 1938 to 1940 the Peace Committee of the General Conference Mennonite Church published a series of pamphlets under the general title, *Christian Peace*, as follows: *New Testament Peace Teachings Outside the Gospels*, by Ernest J. Bohn; *Four Hundred Years of Mennonite Peace Principles and Practice*, by C. Henry Smith; and *Propaganda: How to Analyze and Counteract It*, by E. L. Harshbarger. In 1947 the Peace Committee published an excellent book, *The Power of Love*, a study manual adapted for Sunday-school use and for group discussion. It is a helpful and well-planned textbook. Other publications by members of the General Conference Mennonite Church are: H. P. Krehbiel's *War, Peace, Amity*, 1937; E. H. Epp's *Should God's People Partake in War?* which appeared about the same time; and P. H. Richert's *A Brief Catechism on Difficult Scripture Passages and Involved Questions on the Use of the Sword*. Under Brethren in Christ authorship, appeared E. J. Swalm's booklet, *Nonresistance Under Test*, published in 1938, and O. B. Ulery's *Can a Christian Fight?* in 1942. The former relates the experiences of a Canadian conscientious objector in the first World War; a revised and enlarged edition appeared in 1949.

The peace committees of the various Mennonite groups also worked closely with the M.C.C. and its Peace Section in the field of literature. When the C.P.S. program was inaugurated, it became obvious that the M.C.C. had certain obligations in this area. It early planned the series of six studies, *Mennonites and Their Heritage*, designed for use in the formal education program of the C.P.S. camps. The titles of these booklets, the first of which appeared in 1942, are as follows: *Mennonite Origins in Europe*, by Harold S. Bender; *Mennonites in America*, by C. Henry Smith; *Our Mennonite Heritage*, by Edward Yoder; *Our Mission as a Church of Christ*, by Ed. G. Kaufman; *Christian Relationships to State and Community*, by Guy F. Hershberger; and *Life and Service in the Kingdom of God*, by P. C. Hiebert. In 1943 the M.C.C. published a booklet of sixty-eight pages, *Must Christians Fight: A Scriptural Inquiry*, by Edward Yoder. This booklet, catechetical in character, is a series of fifty-six questions dealing with the Christian attitude toward war, and designed especially to counteract the influence of anti-nonresistant literature by "Fundamentalist" authors and publishers. In 1950 a new edition appeared, revised by John A. Hostetler, with the title, *If War Comes*.

In 1944 the M.C.C. published another pamphlet by Edward Yoder, *Compromise with War*, a reply to the position taken by Charles Clayton Morrison and the *Christian Century* that, since all men contribute to the cause of war, none ought to escape it by taking the position of a conscientious objector. This pamphlet was distributed free to all C.P.S. men. In 1945 the M.C.C. published *The Christian and Conscription*, by Edward Yoder and Don E. Smucker, a booklet designed to help in clarifying the various issues involved in military and alternative service. *Think on These Things* was the title of a tract first issued by the Young People's Christian Association of Goshen College, then published by the M.C.C. in 1945. In 1948 appeared *Before You Decide*, by Howard Charles, an M.C.C. booklet designed especially as a help to youth confronting the issues of a militaristic age. Within a year this booklet had gone through several printings. It had also appeared serially in the *Youth's Christian Companion*. In 1949 the M.C.C. published *Service for Peace*, a comprehensive and authoritative history of C.P.S., of more than 500 pages, by Melvin Gingerich. A pamphlet, *What of Noncombatant Service*, by the same author, was also published by the M.C.C. in 1949. A history of the M.C.C. itself had also been authorized, to be written by John D. Unruh.

In 1951 the Mennonite Publishing House published *Wings of Decision*, by Eunice Shellenberger. This is a novel portraying the wartime experience of a young man who made his decision for conscientious objectors in preference to service in the air corps. Another type of literature coming out of the war experiences was the numerous C.P.S. camp papers and books published by C.P.S. men themselves. In addition, David Wagler and Roman Raber published *The Story of the Amish in Civilian Public Service, with Directory*, in 1945; while Peter Lester Rohrer and Mary E. Rohrer published *The Story of the Lancaster County Conference Mennonites in Civilian Public Service, with Directory*, in 1946. In 1951 the Franconia Mennonite Historical Society published *The Franconia Mennonites and War*, by Willard Hunsberger.

In 1936 the secretary of the Peace Problems Committee expressed the committee's concern for more peace literature in the following words:

> For effective work within our own constituency the committee early noted the lack of Scripturally sound peace literature. Where for example the Friends have dozens of well-written books covering both the historical record of their experience as nonresistants in peace or war, and books giving the apologetic of their position to the outside world, the Mennonite Church had hardly any. The committee feels that the teaching from pulpit, through the Sunday school, and other existing agencies can be most effectively supplemented through the production of such literature and endeavors to encourage such effort in every possible manner.[1]

Even as these words were spoken, the committee's hopes were beginning to be realized in a small way. Fifteen years later, however, a substantial body of solid literature had been produced; and there was evidence that production would continue. In addition to writings mentioned above as planned for early publication, the committee in the spring of 1948 had announced plans for the following: a book on Heroes of Nonresistance, to be written by Elizabeth Bauman and designed for the teen-age level; a textbook of nonresistance for the teen-age group arranged in twelve lessons of one chapter each, to be written by Millard Lind; and a history of the Mennonite Church in the second World War, which is now realized in the present volume.

The Mennonite Central Committee through its Peace Section was not only planning new literature. It was also beginning to extend its services by preparing translations to make Mennonite peace literature available in other languages. In 1949 a German edition of Edward Yoder's *Must Christians Fight?* appeared under the title, *Sollen Christen Sich an Der Kriegsfuehrung Beteiligen?* This edition has been widely distributed in Europe, as well as among the German-speaking Mennonites in North and South America. In 1948 the Doopsgezinde Vredesgroep, the Dutch Mennonite Peace Group, published a Dutch edition of Harold S. Bender's *Anabaptist Vision*, with the title, *De Doperse Visie*. This pamphlet had first appeared in English in 1945, as a reprint of an article in the *Mennonite Quarterly Review*. By the end of 1949 the *Anabaptist Vision* and *Mennonite Origins in Europe*, the first volume of the *Mennonites and Their Heritage* series, had been translated into German; and by the end of 1950 the *Anabaptist Vision* had been translated into French and Italian. The M.C.C. was planning to publish these translations as soon as possible.

Many of the titles of books and pamphlets mentioned in this chapter suggest a close relationship between Mennonite peace literature and Mennonite history and theology. There can be no sound peace program except as it is based on the Bible and Christian theology. Therefore the peace teaching of the Mennonites has always been an integral part of their entire Gospel message. When there has been a vital interest in Bible study, and in the theology and history of the church, there has also been a vital interest in peace and nonresistance. When these have been lacking the interest in nonresistance has also lagged. It is not surprising, therefore, that the increasing interest in nonresistance and the production of peace literature since 1925 went hand in hand with a revival of interest in Mennonite history and Biblical study within the Mennonite Church. For a generation prior to 1925, in fact, Mennonite historians and theologians had begun to prepare the way for a new understanding of Mennonitism, with its theology of regeneration, of discipleship, of brotherhood, and of love and nonresistance. By 1925 this development had reached its productive stage, and the new interest in peace literature and peace teaching can be thought of as one of its fruits.

NOTES AND CITATIONS

1 In an address to the Goshen College Peace Society, March 20, 1936.

Chapter XVIII

Peace Teaching

While a substantial body of useful literature is essential for an effective teaching program, this in itself is not enough. Before it can produce results the message contained in the literature must find its way into the thinking of many people. The tenor and contents of the regular and special features on nonresistance in the *Gospel Herald* before and during the war years indicate that the church was making a genuine effort to accomplish this end. During 1938 and 1939, for example, John Horsch had a number of pointed articles, one dealing with "The Position of the Early Mennonites as Regards the Principle of Nonresistance," and another on "The So-called Noncombatant Military Service."[1] In August, 1942, the Peace Section of the *Gospel Herald* carried a practical article on "The Christian's Duty to Government." This was an extended commentary on Romans 13 and its application to the present situation. The October, 1943, issue carried a helpful article on "John Wesley on War," with extracts from his writings collected by a C.P.S. man. The series of articles by Harold S. Bender, "In the Midst of War—Thoughts for Nonresistants," treated such necessary and practical subjects as the threat of the High School Victory Corps, war profits, rationing, and the implications of the civilian defense program. One article was a frank discussion of the weakness of the church as reflected by the large number of men in the army. Another even treated the practical question of marriage in wartime. The entire series challenged the brotherhood to rid itself of all complacency and indifference, and to hold forth the nonresistant witness of the Gospel.

The large number of individual peace articles in the *Herald*, as well as in the *Christian Monitor* and the *Youth's Christian Companion*, are further evidence that the church as a whole was grappling with the problem. There were informational articles explaining what the church was doing; there were articles from C.P.S. men setting forth their experience; there were questions and answers on practical points of Christian conduct in time of war. An article by John H. Mosemann in 1942 asked the question, "Must Christians Fight?" It set forth the New Testament teaching on nonresistance, analyzing the errors both of utopian pacifism and of Fundamentalist militarism. An article by the chairman of the Peace Problems Committee in February, 1945, reported the possible draft of nurses, and discussed the course which nonresistant nurses should take in such an event. Every week during the war the *Gospel Herald* carried Relief and C.P.S. Notes; and an article or editorial on

238

nonresistance appeared, on an average, not less than one every other week. During 1939 and 1940 these general articles and editorials on nonresistance appeared more frequently than this; in 1940 almost weekly.

The peace study conferences held at Goshen College in 1935 and 1939, as mentioned in Chapter I, served to stimulate the thinking of church leaders. The addresses of the first conference were made available in mimeographed form, and two of them were published in the *Mennonite Quarterly Review*. All of the papers of the second conference were published in the *Review*, and then reprinted as a booklet with the title, *Applied Nonresistance*. These published addresses served as source material which was widely used by speakers and leaders. In 1940 the theme for the annual Christian Life Conference at Eastern Mennonite School was "Nonresistance in Principle and Practice." These addresses were also made available through publication. Through the war years, as well as before and since, many local and regional peace conferences and meetings were held, bringing the nonresistant testimony directly to the brotherhood in all sections of the church. Regular sessions of district conferences discussed the nonresistant and relief theme. Quarterly Sunday-school meetings and harvest meetings did likewise. Mission Board and sewing circle meetings dealt especially with the relief phase of the nonresistant testimony. Meetings of city mission workers dealt with the problem of employment in defense plants. Members of the Peace Problems Committee had frequent calls to set forth the nonresistant teaching of the Gospel to local congregations.

In the spring of 1937 the Peace Problems Committee, in co-operation with the Goshen College Peace Society and official committees of the Illinois Conference, sponsored several peace conferences in that state. That same year the Ohio Mennonite Sunday School Conference devoted one session to nonresistance, including testimonies and experiences of brethren who were conscientious objectors during the first World War. As part of this meeting a special prayer service was held for the young people who were now of military age. One entire session of the 1939 Mennonite General Conference was devoted to the theme of nonresistance. Coming as it did, late in August, just before the beginning of the second World War, it made its impression not only upon the Mennonites themselves, but upon non-Mennonite observers as well. An editorial in a Chambersburg, Pennsylvania, newspaper commented on the timeliness of the nonresistant theme at this conference. This theme, the editorial said, is not new for the Mennonites,

. . . but that thousands should be gathered in a peaceful Pennsylvania valley reaffirming the faith of the fathers in nonresistance at a time when a large part of the civilized world is on the brink of resorting to force, the antithesis of nonresistance, is strikingly coincidental. While millions of men in a tense Europe were answering the call to arms . . . the picture of the somberly clad Mennonite churchmen gravely reiterating their will to peace in all human relations was one of sanity and hope.[2]

While the *Gospel Herald* reported a number of peace meetings and conferences in 1937 and 1938, the number was greatly increased in the years which followed. In 1938 and 1939 the district conferences took action endorsing the General Conference statement on *Peace, War, and Military Service,* and usually there was considerable discussion in connection with this action. On November 9, 1939, the Virginia Mennonite Conference held a special session to consider the nonresistant position of the church "in the light of international affairs." The ministerial councils of the conference were urged "to arrange for programs on nonresistance so that our members in the various districts become more thoroughly indoctrinated." It also recommended the distribution of approved literature on nonresistance into the homes of the conference district, and appointed a special committee "to serve in study and consultation on matters pertaining to problems associated with our Biblical position on nonresistance." In 1940 the Virginia Peace and Industrial Relations Committee reported a series of meetings in the various congregations of the conference for the study of nonresistance. These studies were devoted to Biblical teaching on nonresistance, the Christian and the state, nonresistance in industry, in the home and community, and similar topics. In 1941 the committee reported a nonresistance conference held in each bishop district of the conference. In 1944 it reported consideration of plans for a meeting in each district "of men who are sixteen years old and over to explain again our position on nonresistance. We also encouraged the distribution of copies of *Must Christians Fight.*"

AFTER CONSCRIPTION

In the autumn of 1940, following the enactment of the conscription law, the *Gospel Herald* reported a number of meetings called by church leaders to discuss the new issue with their people, especially the young people most directly affected. During the war there were many peace meetings, specifically so called. At this time, however, every special Mennonite meeting was likely to include a discussion of nonresistance. The *Gospel Herald* reported one meeting in which the official statement of the church, *Peace, War, and Military Service,* was discussed point by point. One congregation reported a Sunday evening meeting for a discussion of military influence, especially the threat of the Victory Corps, in the high school. Another congregation reported a midweek study group of young people which used Edward Yoder's *Must Christians Fight* as a text. As the end of the war approached, thought was being given to the rehabilitation of C.P.S. men, and meetings were reported for the discussion of this theme.

The official publicity of the church's wartime program was good. Relief and C.P.S. information released by the M.C.C. office appeared weekly, with few exceptions, in the columns of the *Gospel Herald.* These notes gave information on every aspect of the subject, such as "C.P.S. Candidates for Service in China"; "The Puerto Rico Unit"; "Statistics on M.C.C. Administered Units"; "Food for the Camps"; "How to Obtain Sugar for Camp Canning"; "Camp Briefs"; and "For Spiritual Service to C.P.S. Men." Special articles explaining various aspects of the C.P.S. program appeared from writers in the Akron office as occasion required. Before the first M.C.C. camp opened at Grottoes, Virginia, in May, 1941, the director had an article in the *Gospel Herald* describing the physical preparations for the opening of the camp, the technical work project which would be carried on by the Soil Conservation Service, and the anticipated social and religious life of the camp. The director evaluated the prospects of the camp as follows: "The operation of the camp, we feel, is not merely a social experiment nor yet simply a governmental experiment, but, from our point of view, an outstanding spiritual opportunity. With the help and support of our constituencies we believe the camp program can be made a vital asset to the spiritual tone and life of our churches."[3] In addition to such articles of an official or semiofficial nature, there were many others of an unofficial character which did much to support and promote the C.P.S. program. The following are a few illustrations: "The Spiritual Significance of C.P.S."; "The Educational Program of C.P.S."; "A Visit to C.P.S."

Occasionally there were articles by non-Mennonite authors expressing appreciation for the C.P.S. program. The August 26, 1943, issue of the *Gospel Herald* reprinted a letter from the *Missoulian Daily* (Missoula, Montana) in which the writer pleaded for tolerance toward the conscientious objectors in the near-by C.P.S. camp, the Smoke Jumpers unit: "I can't understand how we can but help respect these young men for their courage. Imagine, they are helping to protect us and our forests for future use for their country's sake, which all proves that these men are far removed from 'slackers.' . . . So when we speak of them, let us in kindness to them forget the words, 'conscientious objector,' and refer to them as the men who are guarding our forests."[4] A few months later a similar letter was reprinted from a Howard, Rhode Island, newspaper expressing appreciation for the C.P.S. unit at the mental hospital in that city: "These young men, along with some 7,500 others in our nation, have landed feet first in the middle of the Sermon on the Mount. They are serving their nation in the only constructive way they feel is consistent with their Christian understanding . . . . With the Apostle Paul of old, they 'must serve God rather than man,' but who can say in this case that by serving God they are not also serving man?"[5] Some weeks later an article by the superintendent of the state hospital, at Ypsilanti, Michigan, reported that following the coming of the C.P.S. unit to that institution, "there was a marked demand for Bibles throughout the hospital." The superintendent declared the effort put forth by the C.P.S. men to have been well spent: "By their lives and in their work they are living the principles of the

Mennonite Church. They are missionaries at home. They are witnesses for Christ in a State Hospital . . . . They have served their country and their church well. They will find their reward in their own hearts, for they followed in the footsteps of Him 'who went about doing good.' "[8]

It was the Peace Problems Committee's task to help the church at all crucial points, and to make such official announcements as were necessary for this purpose. In January, 1942, for example, soon after the United States entered the war, the chairman of the committee had a pointed article in the *Gospel Herald*, entitled "A Message to Nonresistant Christians." This was a concise statement of the nonresistant position of the church, and of its meaning for the current situation. It encouraged the brotherhood to be generous in its support of relief work and C.P.S.; to remain aloof from war and defense activities of all kinds, and from employment in war and defense industries; and to refrain from purchasing war and defense bonds, but rather to purchase civilian government bonds and stamps. The article urged that profits resulting from war situations be used for relief and charitable work rather than for personal benefit; that "we pray for our rulers and those in authority, and for the speedy restoration of a righteous and just peace in the world"; and that in general the church maintain a faithful and consistent witness.

PEACE TEACHING INADEQUATE

It would seem that the peace teaching program of the church during the second World War was adequate, as far as official advices and announcements were concerned. Necessary information and counsel from the M.C.C. and the Peace Problems Committee were always forthcoming, through the columns of the church papers or by other means. More than official information and counsel are necessary, however, if the brotherhood is to remain true to its faith. The message of peace must find its way into the hearts and lives of the rank and file of the people. It is at this point where a great weakness was manifest in the Mennonite Church during the second World War.

In too many congregations the wartime teaching was of an emergency character, not backed up by a consistent program over a period of years before the emergency arose. Several cases come to mind where congregations had no special meetings for the presentation of the nonresistant testimony until a year or more after the war began, and after some of the young men of the congregation had entered the army. One minister in such a congregation stated publicly to his congregation: "We have made some mistakes here; I trust we will do better from now on." In another case members of the congregation were heard to say: "If we had had such meetings a year ago, some things that have happened here might have been avoided." Reports from various congregations indicated that on the congregational level there was little or no specific teaching on the subject prior to the war. In other cases it was frequently heard that parents of young men of draft age were relatively indifferent as to the course their sons should take.

It must be admitted that most local congregations did not have an adequate long-range program of peace teaching. The same must be said of the church as a whole. It is true that an enumeration of titles of peace books, pamphlets, and articles, as given in this and the preceding chapter, makes an impressive list. Before a book or a pamphlet can do its work, however, it must find its way into a home, and it must be read. How many Mennonite young people during the ten-year period, 1931 to 1940, did not read as much as one peace pamphlet? Books and pamphlets like the peace literature described above are usually printed in editions of 2,000, more or less. The Mennonite Publishing House estimates that during 1931 to 1940 perhaps 4,000 pieces of peace literature, distributed by the House, actually found their way into the homes of the Mennonite Church. This means an average of only one piece for every three or four homes. It is estimated that during 1941 to 1950 perhaps 23,000 pieces, distributed by the House, found their way into these homes, or an average of two pieces per home. This estimate does not include literature distributed directly by the Peace Problems Committee and the M.C.C. Even after making allowance for this, however, there must have been hundreds of Mennonite youths who, in the decade before the war, did no reading on the subject at all. During the following decade, to be sure, the number was much greater. In a sense this was an improvement. On the other hand, however, it points up the emergency character of much of the peace teaching of the church. If the task had really been well done, the figures for each decade would have been much higher than they actually were.

Taken alone, a list of peace articles, or a list of announcements of special peace meetings appearing in the church papers, also seems impressive. This is especially true of the periodicals of the war years. An analysis of the contents of the church papers over a period of years, however, presents a different picture. A recent analytical study[7] of Volumes I to XLI of the *Gospel Herald*, covering the years 1908 to 1948, shows that during this period only 9 per cent of the total contents, calculated in inches of space, was devoted to "Anabaptist" emphases, and that actually only 3.4 per cent of the contents was devoted to nonresistance. When it is remembered that this 3.4 per cent includes all relief notes and other M.C.C. and C.P.S. announcements, it must be concluded that from 1908 to 1948 the *Gospel Herald* did not place enough emphasis on peace teaching.

THE NEED FOR THE FUTURE

All of this suggests that if the task of peace teaching in the Mennonite Church is to be well done, much greater effort must be put forth in the future than has been done in the past. Church periodicals must deal with the subject in a more systematic way. More and better literature must be produced. Ministers and parents must have strong convictions on the question of nonresistance. They must make good use of the information and literature which are available; and they must teach their people continuously, from childhood through the period of youth and on into middle age. The Bible says: "Train up a *child* in the way he should go: and when he is old, he will not depart from it." The task of training up a child cannot be accomplished by waiting until an emergency arises, after he has reached the age of eighteen, and then hastily calling a special meeting and placing before him some literature of which he has never heard before. Training up a child is a continuous task from infancy on.

These are facts of which the responsible church leadership following the close of the second World War was fully aware. Much of the new literature then in preparation was designed for use in a more aggressive type of teaching program. This was especially true of the study booklet, and of the book on nonresistant heroes, projected plans of which are described in the previous chapter. Other studies in progress, especially the historical studies, were designed to provide a more solid foundation of factual material for the educational task which needed to be done in the years ahead. As mentioned in Chapter I, the personnel of the Peace Problems Committee itself was enlarged at the 1949 session of General Conference with the addition of three younger men, all of whom had served in C.P.S. These men, John A. Hostetler, Ernest W. Lehman, and Paul T. Guengerich, represented the age group which would gradually need to take over the leadership in the teaching program of the church in the years ahead. Since the war, a number of the younger men had had valuable experience as members of peace teams traveling through the church under the sponsorship of the Peace Problems Committee, spending several days or a week with a congregation, giving addresses, conducting discussion groups, distributing literature, and having personal conferences in the interest of peace.

Not only had the Peace Problems Committee sponsored peace teams. The peace committees of other Mennonite groups, and the Peace Section of the M.C.C., had done likewise. In the summer of 1948 a total of three such teams gave their full time to this work for a period of two months. During the summer of 1949 five teams were in the field, two under M.C.C. sponsorship, two under the Peace Problems Committee, and one under the peace committee of the General Conference Mennonite Church.

Beginning with the year 1947-48, the Goshen College Peace Society sponsored peace teams which gave numerous Sunday evening and weekend programs in churches within easy reach of the college. Teams from other Mennonite colleges have given a similar service. During the summer of 1949 the Peace Section of the M.C.C. also sponsored a peace team of older men, Harold S. Bender, C. J. Rempel, and Erland Waltner, who were engaged in a similar mission among the Mennonite churches of Europe. Earlier than this, Harold S. Bender had given an entire year, 1947-48, to the service of the Peace Section in Europe. During the year 1949-50 Guy F. Hershberger did likewise. Thus the peace teaching mission of the American Mennonites, as they themselves conceived it, reached far beyond the confines of their own local congregations. This was as it should have been. The doctrine of nonresistance is an integral part of the Gospel of Christ. The great task of the Christian Church is to proclaim that Gospel to all men.

As said in the previous chapter, aggressive peace teaching in the Mennonite Church must be thought of as the fruit of a vital interest in the study of the Bible, and of Mennonite history and theology. It is very significant that several important peace pamphlets of the 1920's were produced by John Horsch, who for a generation had devoted his life to the cause of Mennonite history and theology. It is equally significant that the chairman of the Peace Problems Committee after 1936 should have been Harold S. Bender, the leader in the development of study in Mennonite history and theology in the Mennonite Church since 1925, and the dean of the Goshen College Biblical Seminary since 1944. Others who have had an active part in the peace teaching program of the church have been closely associated with this aggressive interest in Mennonite history and theology, or have been vitally influenced by it. The same can be said of the other Mennonite groups. Where interest in the Bible and in Mennonite history and theology have been strong, there has been a strong peace program. Where these have been weak the peace program has been weak.

NOTES AND CITATIONS

[1] *Gospel Herald* (Nov. 3, 1938, and June 8, 1939), 31:666 and 32:210.

[2] Editorial in the Chambersburg, Pa., *Public Opinion* (Aug. 26, 1939), reprinted in the *Gospel Herald* (Sept. 7, 1939), 32:483.

[3] John H. Mosemann, "Our Camp at Grottoes," *Gospel Herald* (May 22, 1941), 34:162.

[4] *Gospel Herald* (Aug. 26, 1943), 36:451.

[5] *Ibid.* (Dec. 9, 1943), 36:762.

[6] O. R. Yoder, "The Mennonite Witness in a State Hospital," *ibid.* (Jan. 27, 1944), 36:914.

[7] Carl Beck and John D. Zehr, "A Study of the amount and character of Anabaptist emphasis in the *Gospel Herald*, 1908-1948." (MSS. in Mennonite Historical Library, Goshen College.)

17

Chapter XIX

Inter-Group Relations

CHRISTIAN INTER-GROUP RELATIONS

The Christian's task in this world is not an easy one. According to the Scriptures he must keep himself "unspotted from the world." At the same time, however, he is the "salt of the earth"; and it is obvious that salt cánnot perform its curative work without making actual contact with that which is to be cured. Even as Christ ate with publicans and sinners that He might win them to Himself, so must the follower of Christ be in continuous touch with those who are not Christians, or with those whose way of life is perhaps partially Christian, in order that he may win them to a full acceptance of Christ and His way of life. And as Christ mingled with men of His day without compromising His principles, so must the Christian today continually match his principles with and against unchristian and partially Christian principles, without sacrificing his own. The Christian must also remember that he is a follower of Christ, and not Christ Himself. His own way of life is Christian only to the extent that he follows Christ perfectly; and the same is true of other professing Christians.

Some denominational differences, and even some differences between various branches of Mennonites, may be due to an unwillingness on the part of some to follow Christ fully. Other differences, however, may be due to honest differences of opinion as to what Christ and the Scriptures actually teach on this question or that. Furthermore, when such differences exist it must not be supposed that all of the truth lies on the side of any one denomination or group. It is usually true that every group has found light in some area, which others would do well to follow; and that every group has weak spots which might be remedied by learning from others. Every Christian ought, therefore, to affiliate himself with that denomination or group which he believes to be most nearly true to Christ in faith and practice, or in which he believes he can serve Christ most perfectly. Then having made his choice, he ought to be loyal to that group, supporting its principles, and seeking ways and means for practicing these principles more perfectly. In doing so he and his group will frequently find it necessary or desirable to co-operate with other groups in the promotion of a cause in which there is a common interest. If such co-operation is to serve its purpose, the groups must respect each other's views and be ready to learn from each other. On the other hand, an uncritical acceptance of the ways of other groups can be of little value, and may result in the sacrifice of important principles. In other words, profitable co-operation among Christian groups requires Christian courtesy and consideration on the one hand, and critical evaluation on the other.

INTER-GROUP RELATIONS OF PEACE PROBLEMS COMMITTEE

Chapters I and II tell the story of co-operative efforts among the Mennonite conference groups, and of the co-operation of these groups with the Quakers and Brethren and other peace groups, in an effort to meet their common problems arising from war and conscription. The M.C.C. was the central agency through which the Mennonite groups co-operated for the carrying on of their common C.P.S. and relief program, and the giving of a united witness to Christian peace and non-resistance. Examples of Mennonite co-operation with other peace groups are found in the occasional meetings of the Conference of Pacifist Churches from 1922 to 1931, and of the meetings of the Historic Peace Churches from 1935 to the time of the organization of the National Service Board for Religious Objectors in 1940. The N.S.B.R.O. was a co-operative enterprise designed to provide a united approach to the Selective Service System for the operation of Civilian Public Service. From the beginning of these efforts the leadership of the Mennonite Church was conscious of the need for Christian courtesy and consideration, as well as for a critical evaluation of the faith, practice, and programs of the groups with whom it was co-operating.

In 1927, as mentioned in Chapter I, the reorganized Peace Problems Committee outlined its threefold task as follows: (1) A teaching program within the church for the strengthening of its own nonresistant faith. (2) Keeping in touch with government officials and with current legislation affecting the nonresistant faith. (3) Interpreting the nonresistant faith to other Christians. All three of these tasks required continuous contact with the leadership and work of other peace groups. An effective teaching program requires the use of literature; it was therefore necessary to evaluate, for possible use, a large amount of non-Mennonite peace literature. Keeping in touch with government officials and with current legislation affecting the nonresistant faith also meant continuous contact with other peace groups engaged in similar activity. Interpreting the nonresistant faith to other Christians obviously required a frequent interchange of views with other Christians. It meant not only that others were learning from Mennonites; but also that Mennonites were learning from others. Natural and necessary as this procedure was, it did involve certain dangers, and this was disturbing to some members of the brotherhood. Obviously, if the members of the Peace Problems Committee had not been well established in the faith, they might have been tempted to compromise the nonresistant teachings as set forth in the Scriptures. There are many types of pacifism which are not genuine Christian nonresistance;[1] and it would not be impossible for a Mennonite Peace Problems Committee to wander from the path of Biblical nonresistance, or to be led astray by some unchristian or semi-Christian form of pacifism. In the 1920's there were a few church leaders who feared that the new Peace Problems Committee, several of whose members were at that time relatively young, was doing this very thing.

RELATIONS WITH GOVERNMENT OFFICIALS

One reason for this fear was the belief that the committee was going too far in its testimony to government officials. Early in 1927, for example, the chairman and secretary published an article on the "Work of our Peace Committee."[2] This article contained a copy of a letter which the committee had sent to government officials, giving the Mennonite position on war, and encouraging government officials to pursue a policy of friendship and good will in international relations. Good will is the Christian way, the letter said, and, "To the extent that a nation's ideals are Christian to that extent can permanent peace come between it and other nations." The letter commended the government for current efforts at the reduction of armaments and the outlawry of war. It also expressed concern because of certain other trends, such as an increase in military training in colleges and universities, unsatisfactory relations between the United States and Nicaragua, and the sending of troops to China.

How much energy the church should devote to this type of activity is, of course, a question. The preaching of the Gospel is the church's primary task. For it to become or to maintain a lobbyist organization, for the shaping of the nation's foreign policy, would be a perversion of its own purpose and function. Moreover, since there can be no true peace without acceptance of Christ the Prince of Peace, the preaching of the Gospel of Christ will do more for the furtherance of peace than anything else which the individual Christian can do. This does not mean, however, that letters or visits to government officials are not in order. The Gospel must be proclaimed to government officials as well as to all other men; and in doing so it is certainly in order to point out the implications of this Gospel as applied to militarism and to relations between nations. This was the view of the Peace Problems Committee, and the letter sent to government officials in the spring of 1927 was sent with this purpose in mind.

One brother who felt that the committee had gone too far believed, however, that to urge governments to pursue the way of peace was unscriptural. Since they are part of the evil world system, according to Romans 13 the making of war is their duty. Efforts at international peace are a delusion. "Shall the church follow this 'Modernistic Delusion' and run the church into the political arena, seeking to win the nation and the world to the principles of the Prince of Peace, when as yet He Himself is rejected by the nation and the world as a whole? . . . May the Lord save us from leaving our heaven-ordained mission to preach the Gospel, and be turned aside to endeavor to make the world peaceful apart from accepting the Lord Jesus Christ, the Prince of Peace!" The Peace Problems Committee agreed that Christ's program for this age was that of the Great Commission, which commands Christians to preach the Gospel of Christ and to teach men to observe all things which Christ taught. It agreed that as long as the world lies in wickedness, war and force will be used, and that the world can be made better only by bringing Christ to it. The committee also believed, however, that Christians should not withhold the challenge of the way of love from men who have not yet accepted Him. The way of peace is part of the Gospel message itself. Therefore Christ and His way of peace should be proclaimed together. Furthermore, if mankind outside of Christ could in some measure see the futility of war, and perhaps a few wars be averted, would not this be worth while?[8]

Actually, there seems to have been no fundamental difference between the policy of the Peace Problems Committee and the views of its critics. Neither was interested in promoting a program of peace apart from the Gospel of salvation through the saving work of Christ. Nor was either group interested in any peace emphasis other than the Scriptural teaching which had always been held by the Mennonite Church. Perhaps the critics had carried the principle of separation of church and state, and of the Christian from the world, so far as to place the Christian in a position where it is difficult for him to testify to the state and to the world as effectively as he ought. It is also important to remember that democratic America is at least partially Christian, and that many officials desire to operate its government on the basis of Christian principles, as they understand them. Many certainly wish to respect the Christian conscience, and desire to know the wishes and opinions of citizens on all important questions. Members of the Mennonite Church, therefore, and certainly an official body like the Peace Problems Committee, would seem to be under obligation to give testimony to government officials, both concerning the conscience of the nonresistant Christian, and the implications of the Gospel of peace, as applied to militarism and the foreign affairs of the state. Perhaps some brethren had not given sufficient consideration to this point.

RELATIONS WITH PEACE ORGANIZATIONS

Another reason for the fears of certain brethren was the feeling that the Peace Problems Committee had gone too far in its contacts with other peace organizations. Members of the committee had attended occasional meetings of organizations such as the World Alliance for International Friendship through the Churches. The committee had also co-operated with the Conference of Pacifist Churches which met occasionally in the

1920's, the secretary serving as a member of a Continuation Committee for the sponsoring of the meetings. It is true, of course, that the views of some of the persons with whom the committee was working were those of liberal pacifism, rather than those of Biblical nonresistance. The committee itself was fully aware of the difference between Biblical nonresistance and liberal Protestant pacifism. It believed, however, that these various contacts provided an opportunity, first to learn some things of value to the committee, and second to give a testimony for Christian nonresistance. If the Mennonite Church does have the message of Christian peace, ought she not use this opportunity to bring it to others? The committee felt that its position and that of the church was not being compromised, but rather the opposite, because the Mennonite position was being heard by other groups. The criticism was so strong, however, that in December, 1926, the secretary of the Peace Problems Committee resigned as a member of the Continuation Committee of the Conference of Pacifist Churches.

During those years John Horsch, many of whose writings on peace were prepared under the auspices of the Peace Problems Committee, while less critical than others, also expressed a concern because of these co-operative efforts. Horsch himself, however, attended at least one meeting of the World Alliance for International Friendship through the Churches. In a letter reporting on this experience he described it as "eminently worth while for the information afforded." Horsch attended the meeting at the suggestion of the Peace Problems Committee, and apparently had no objection to members of the committee keeping in touch with organizations like the World Alliance, in order to learn whatever of value they had to offer. He continually reminded the committee, however, of the liberal religious views of certain leaders of the pacifist movement, and was greatly concerned that the committee keep itself clear from dangerous connections with them. Apparently he had no serious objection to the writing of letters to government officials, although he seems to have questioned their value. Perhaps the connection of the Peace Problems Committee with the Conference of Pacifist Churches caused Horsch more concern than did its attendance at meetings of organizations like the World Alliance. In the former relationship there was actual co-operation, and therefore more danger of becoming involved in a program not in line with Mennonite doctrine and practice; for he was convinced, and rightly so, that some of the leaders in this movement were liberal in their religious views. Although Horsch never opposed this co-operation to the extent that some did, he no doubt felt relieved when the Conference of Pacifist Churches discontinued its activities.[4]

RELATIONS WITH HISTORIC PEACE CHURCHES

The last meeting of the Conference of Pacifist Churches was held in 1931, and for four years there was no organized co-operative work among the Mennonites, Friends, and Brethren. In 1935, however, co-operative activities were renewed, beginning with the Newton Conference of Historic Peace Churches. As said in Chapter I, the movement for this conference was initiated by H. P. Krehbiel of Newton, Kansas, a minister of the General Conference Mennonite Church. Krehbiel had a concern that the Mennonite churches give proper emphasis to Biblical nonresistance, as distinguished from popular pacifism. He shared the feeling of John Horsch that Mennonites must be cautious in their relationship with pacifist organizations. Since the seriousness of the international situation seemed to demand it, however, he took the lead in renewing co-operative efforts on a new basis. The emphasis of the Newton meeting, as well as later meetings of the Conference of Historic Peace Churches, was one on which the participating Mennonite groups could find more general agreement than was true in the case of the earlier Conference of Pacifist Churches. The efforts which began at the Newton meeting in 1935 eventually led to the organization of the National Service Board for Religious Objectors in 1940, when conscription became a reality.

OPPOSITION TO RELATIONS WITH PEACE ORGANIZATIONS, M.C.C., AND N.S.B.R.O.

While these efforts were generally considered necessary because of the exigencies of the time, a number of brethren nevertheless continued to sense danger in such close co-operation with other peace groups. In 1938, for example, the Virginia Conference adopted a resolution endorsing the 1937 General Conference statement on *Peace, War, and Military Service*, with the following provisions:

1. We express our conviction of belief that it is inconsistent with our nonresistant position to affiliate with religious and political pacifist movements and since some of them are seeking to overthrow our government we urge that a statement of abnegation be included in further publications of any pamphlets for general distribution.

2. We express loyalty and support to our government in so far as it does not require us to violate our religious convictions based upon the Word of God.

3. We favor making appeals to the government in regard to our constitutional privileges for religious liberty and freedom of conscience and commend making contacts with government officials to explain to them our position on nonresistance but we do not favor giving advice to the government in any way.[5]

It seems clear that the framers of this statement did not approve of everything which the Peace Problems Committee had done in the past. The third point suggests that in their mind some of the committee's testimony to government officials had gone too far. The first implies that the committee had gone too far in its relations with non-Mennonite peace organizations. It probably does not mean to say that the committee had affiliated with political pacifist movements which seek to overthrow the government. Nevertheless since such organizations did exist, it seemed necessary to warn against them. Some time later the Peace Problems Committee received a communication with a similar emphasis from the General Problems Committee of the Mennonite General Conference. This communication asked the committee if there were any reasons "why there should not be an immediate withdrawal from active co-operation and participation with pacifist churches whose standards are not in harmony with our own."[6] It is doubtful whether this communication represents a studied conclusion on the part of the entire General Problems Committee. More than likely it was a response to pressure from overly concerned brethren. At any rate, so far as the writer knows, nothing came of this communication.

The most severe criticism directed at the Peace Problems Committee came in the summer of 1941, after the first C.P.S. camp had been opened. This criticism came in the form of an Open Letter to the ministers of the Virginia Conference "Regarding the Unequal Yoke with Popular Pacifism."[7] Based on questionable sources of information, the Open Letter gave a misleading picture of pacifist organizations. There is no question, of course, that the views of many leaders within the pacifist movement are at variance with the teachings of Biblical nonresistance. On the other hand, it is also true that some leaders in the Fellowship of Reconciliation, for example, do have a Christian and a Biblical approach to the question. The Fellowship of Reconciliation is certainly not a communistic organization, as the Open Letter said; and the secretary of the Peace Problems Committee was not serving the interests of a subversive organization as the letter also said. Later investigation also showed that certain Mennonites referred to as members of the F.O.R. were not such at all. The Open Letter said that a Mennonite leader had "dragged the name of the Mennonite Church into printed fellowship with . . . Christ-dishonoring groups," through participation in a discussion group sponsored by the Federal Council of Churches. Whether this participation was desirable or undesirable, of course, depends on what the participant did. If he had joined a Federal Council group in the promotion of a pacifist program, out of line with New Testament nonresistance, there would have been good reason to challenge his action. However, if he testified to a group of pacifists concerning New Testament nonresistance, it was quite another thing. Since the person referred to was apparently the chairman of the Peace Problems Committee, it seems obvious that his participation was of the latter type, rather than of the former.

What the Open Letter objected to most seriously was Mennonite representation on the National Service Board for Religious Objectors. It was granted that government officials could not have been expected to deal separately "with 30 or 40 different pacifist groups." The author was confident, however, that Selective Service would be willing to deal with two groups under this plan. The pacifists would constitute one group, with the Mennonites, and perhaps certain closely related groups, constituting the other. It was therefore urged that the church correct the mistakes of the Peace Problems Committee and of the M.C.C.; and that it withdraw from the N.S.B.R.O., and deal with Selective Service independently.

While the Virginia Conference did not accept the conclusions of the Open Letter without qualification, it did ask General Conference to investigate the organizational setup of C.P.S. as related to the welfare of the church. At its 1941 session, General Conference responded to this request by appointing a C.P.S. Investigating Committee of five men. The personnel of the committee was D. A. Yoder, E. B. Frey, A. J. Metzler, Henry Lutz, and John L. Horst. One of the members represented the Executive Committee of General Conference, one the Interboard Committee, two the General Problems Committee, and one was a member at large chosen by the first four. Due to its increased responsibilities, General Conference also enlarged the personnel of the Peace Problems Committee, so that it now had ten members, six from the United States and four from Canada. The United States members were Harold S. Bender, chairman; Orie O. Miller, secretary; C. L. Graber, treasurer; and three new members, Harry A. Diener, Amos S. Horst, and John E. Lapp. The Canadian members of the committee were S. F. Coffman, Jesse B. Martin, A. L. Fretz, and Milo D. Stutzman.[8]

Even though the C.P.S. Investigating Committee began its work soon after appointment, it was obvious that its report would not be forthcoming until the next session of General Conference in 1943. For this reason, no doubt, individuals and groups who were dissatisfied with the operation of C.P.S. continued to express their views through correspondence with the Peace Problems Committee, and in other ways. The criticisms centered largely around three points: (1) Undesirable relationships with the N.S.B.R.O. (2) Pacifist influence in M.C.C.-C.P.S. camps, due to the presence of certain non-Mennonite campers, and the occasional appearance of pacifist speakers, as for example, representatives of the F.O.R. (3) The inter-Mennonite character of C.P.S., which brought members of the various Mennonite groups together in the same camp. It was believed by the critics that the presence of other Mennonites would have an unwholesome influence on the men from the more conservative groups. In 1943 the *Sword and Trumpet* published an article discussing these various points at length.[9]

In the spring of 1942 all of these points were discussed at a meeting called for the purpose by the Executive Committee of the Virginia Conference.[10] The meeting was attended by sixteen members of that conference; by the director of the Grottoes, Virginia, C.P.S. Camp; by Amos S. Horst and Orie O. Miller of the Peace Problems Committee; and by Henry Lutz of the C.P.S. Investigating Committee.

In regard to the first point mentioned above, Amos S. Horst and Orie O. Miller explained that in 1940 they had attempted to state the position of the church to government officials, and had endeavored to obtain recognition for those who had a conscience against the performance of military service. In doing so, they did not feel that they had engaged in any unscriptural effort to influence legislation. As to becoming involved in questionable activity by virtue of affiliation with the N.S.B.R.O., Miller held that the latter was a service board, not an executive or policy board. Its task was to serve the needs of various groups of conscientious objectors confronted with conscription. The board served the Mennonites by representing their wishes to Selective Service; and it served other types of objectors by presenting their wishes to Selective Service. When the N.S.B.R.O. acted in the latter capacity the Mennonites were not concerned. Since the board was merely a service board, and not a policy-making or executive board whose decisions were binding upon the church, Miller did not feel that the church's association with it constituted an unequal yoke.

This conception of a service board rather than a policy board, or executive board, seemed to satisfy some of the Virginia brethren. Others felt, however, that the Mennonite Church would keep its testimony more clear if it were served by the board without being represented on it. They felt it important to emphasize the difference between nonresistance and pacifism; and they were afraid that Mennonite representation on the N.S.B.R.O. would confuse the issue in the eyes of government officials. The executive secretary of the M.C.C. emphasized the fact, however, that there were three administrative agencies for the operation of C.P.S. camps: the M.C.C., the Brethren Service Committee, and the American Friends Service Committee; and that Selective Service was very conscious of the difference between the nonresistance of men in M.C.C. camps and the pacifism of men in other camps. In answer to a criticism that actions sometimes appeared in the minutes of the N.S.B.R.O. before they did in those of the M.C.C., it was explained that these actions were in line with policies already approved. Furthermore, if any particular action did not meet with the approval of the M.C.C., it could say so at any time, and the N.S.B.R.O. would no longer serve the M.C.C. in that capacity.

Considerable time at this meeting was devoted to a discussion of the Fellowship of Reconciliation and other forms of pacifist influence in the camps. The executive secretary of the M.C.C. admitted that undesirable situations did exist in some camps, and manifested a concern for their improvement. It was agreed that the camp advisory committees could be more helpful than they had been in a few cases. Part of the difficulty was due to non-Mennonite men in certain camps. The fact that one of the camps in question was operated jointly by the M.C.C. and the Brethren Service Committee complicated the situation somewhat. The secretary of the M.C.C. also pointed out that in the past there had been more sympathy toward the F.O.R. within certain Mennonite groups than there was in the Mennonite Church, and that this may have been responsible for some of the difficulty. He felt certain, however, that in these groups there was less sympathy for the pacifist type of thought than formerly, and he believed that the C.P.S. experience had made a contribution to that end. He recognized that the subjection of a weak and confused Mennonite Church to pacifist influences could have resulted in the church losing its nonresistant faith. He believed, however, that actually the influence had been in the opposite direction. The church had not only maintained its nonresistant faith; it had also helped other groups to the attainment of a more Scriptural position than that which they had formerly held. He believed that many young men, as a result of their C.P.S. experience, had a new understanding of nonresistance; that the church was more successful than before in leading its youth to see the difference between nonresistance and pacifism; and that today the church had strength of faith and clarity of thinking sufficient to propagate its faith aggressively throughout the world, and to make Christian nonresistance attractive to many people as it never had been able to do before.

REPORT OF C.P.S. INVESTIGATING COMMITTEE

In the meantime the C.P.S. Investigating Committee continued its work. Early in 1943 it made a preliminary report to the Executive Committee of General Conference. It recommended the appointment of an advisory committee to represent the interests of the church in the camp program, and to work with the Peace Problems Committee in an advisory capacity in all matters pertaining to C.P.S. policies and plans. The Executive Committee of General Conference accepted this recommendation on May 15, 1943, and appointed a committee of five men to be known as the Mennonite Civilian Public Service Policy Committee. The personnel of the committee was as follows: Amos S. Horst, O. N. Johns, Simon Gingerich, Truman Brunk, and J. L. Stauffer.[11]

The final report of the C.P.S. Investigating Committee was made to General Conference in August, 1943. The full report, except for the introductory paragraph, follows:

I. FINDINGS: FAVORABLE AND COMMENDABLE

1. In view of the gigantic task involved in this whole program, the rapidity with which it developed, the many uncertain and indefinite factors that had to be reckoned with constantly, the ever-changing scene due to repeated revisions of government regulations, etc., and that it led us over an untrodden path, our investigations reveal a tremendous amount of careful, prayerful, and painstaking work on the part of those responsible for the whole program.

2. The Peace Problems Committee of General Conference is to be commended for its awareness of the situations confronting us as a nonresistant people, and for its intelligent foresight and planning to meet those conditions. The members of the committee and others who assisted them deserve special commendation for the clear and Scriptural statement on "Peace, War, and Military Service," drawn up a number of years before the present war came upon us.

Other literature which the committee prepared and circulated among our constituency has likewise constituted a commendable and helpful service. The various forms and blanks which were sent out to our ministers to aid them in rendering help to our brethren in registration and classification deserve special mention. Their handling of the many problems incident to the drafting of hundreds of our brethren has been most helpful and is much appreciated.

3. The Mennonite Central Committee has performed a gigantic task in planning for and administering the work of the C.P.S. camps. To a large degree this work has been done economically, efficiently, and to the satisfaction of Selective Service and the general public.

4. We feel that the committees named deserve much credit for their promptness in meeting situations demanding immediate action, for their evident desire for divine guidance, and for their efforts to ascertain the mind of the church on the important questions with which they are faced.

5. There is much to be commended in the conditions found in the camps. Among these is the attendance at religious services and the fine spiritual interest and co-operative spirit shown by a large number of the campers. We feel that among the brethren of our own constituency there is an intense interest in the entire program and a desire to have it preserved as an expression of our peace principles throughout the entire emergency or as long as the military training law is in force. We have found that those who are unco-operative and unspiritual are in the minority.

6. We have found all through the period since C.P.S. has been inaugurated a constant effort on the part of the committees involved to correct irregularities and to improve unfavorable conditions. Specially to be commended are the efforts to remove harmful literature, to bar speakers whose viewpoints were not in accord with Biblical nonresistance, and to appoint brethren to minister to the spiritual welfare of the campers.

II. FINDINGS: UNFAVORABLE AND OPEN TO CRITICISM

In giving these criticisms the committee has kept in mind that there are aspects of C.P.S. life that are abnormal and that there are certain conditions obtaining in camp life which are not ideal in their nature. It is not ideal for young men to be segregated in camp away from home and their home church and accompanying environments. It is not ideal for young men to be deprived of the normal social activities of life. It is not normal for men to perform hard labor without pay. Even the worship services in the camps, where men who are constantly together during week days, constitute the group in religious meeting, lack certain features that contribute vitally toward attendance and interest in the church services in home communities. These and certain other abnormal conditions are inherent in a system taking men away from their home communities to live in segregated groups, and are beyond the control of any of the agencies administering C.P.S.

There are, however, a number of things in the organization, personnel, and work of the committees and boards taking care of C.P.S. that do not come in the above category which we have found militating against safeguarding and promoting the standards and doctrines of our church as expressed in the official statements of General Conference.

1. We find that the interlocking membership of the Peace Problems Committee, the Relief Committee, and the Mennonite Central Committee, which is not the fault of any individuals concerned and which may have certain values, has been a disadvantage in getting sufficient representation and counsel of the church in formulating policies and administering the work of C.P.S.

2. We have found that the sincere attempts of the Peace Committee and the M.C.C. in calling meetings of officials of General Conference and representative brethren in order to decide important matters pertaining to C.P.S. policies and plans, because of lack of time to think matters through carefully, have at times been inadequate to give sufficient consideration to all the implications of the issues in question.

3. We find a danger through the present organizational setup of Peace, Relief, C.P.S. and related organizations, of setting a permanent mold for postwar operations which may lead the church away both from her traditional ways of working and from some of her cherished doctrines and practices.

4. The Mennonite Central Committee.

    a. This committee in its make-up represents a wide variety of constituent groups, some of which are not in harmony with us in certain aspects of doctrine and practice, and hence it cannot adequately function to preserve and promote all our distinctive doctrines and practices.

    b. The Mennonite Central Committee in its organizational setup is only remotely controlled by its co-operating bodies; and hence official checks and ratifications of its actions are largely limited to such as it invites from time to time.

5. The National Service Board for Religious Objectors is made up of such a wide variety of groups, ranging from Biblical nonresistants to pacifists who do not base their objections to war on Bible principles, that there is danger, in our co-operating in its work, of compromising our Biblical position and of being mistaken for pacifist objectors, thus obscuring our testimony as peace-loving nonresistant Christians.

6. Civilian Public Service Camps.

    a. Although conscientious attempts have been made and are being made to improve spiritual conditions in the camps, there are conditions existing that show a need of further improvement. Among these are socialistic and pacifistic influences, sometimes fomented by outside speakers, which undermine the foundations of Biblical nonresistance. At the same time we recognize that some conditions in camps reflect more upon the home churches than upon the camp administration.

    b. The spiritual ministry to the campers has not always been maintained to the degree of helpfulness that it should be for the best interests of the campers, although there has been constant attention given to this by the Peace Committee and the M.C.C.

    c. The problem of discipline has been found in some cases to be a serious one which needs constant attention and more adequate provision in order to enhance the best interests of the campers and the cause in general.

    d. The method of financial support of nonpaying or nonsupported draftees has not been satisfactory.

e. The inclusion in our camps of certain religious and political groups who are not in accord with our principles of faith and practice is cause for concern and deserves efforts for a more satisfactory solution.

7. Literature. Some of the literature, both of the National Service Board and some of the camps, as well as literature placed in the camps, has been found to be objectionable. Too often also we find a lack of spiritual emphasis in the camp papers.

In view of these findings we state the following convictions, together with some recommendations.

III. STATEMENTS AND RECOMMENDATIONS

1. In view of the magnitude of the work of C.P.S., touching as it does such a large number of our young men, many of whom will be the leaders of the church of tomorrow; the inclusiveness of the work, affecting all our conferences, congregations, and the majority of our homes; the far-reaching effects on the standards and practices of the church of the present and the future; the enormous sums of money which the church is investing in this whole program; and the fact that many vital decisions must of necessity be made between sessions of General Conference, and further,

Since the Peace Problems Committee has many interests, of which Civilian Public Service is only one, and since its present membership is in part interlocking with the C.P.S. administrative body, thus limiting the range of church representation on these bodies, and since it is difficult and often impracticable to call meetings of representative brethren to help formulate policies and plans for C.P.S., and since such meetings have their limitations in providing time for careful deliberation in order to ascertain the full mind and desires of the church, we feel the need of providing some means of larger constant representation of the church at large in order to help care for our C.P.S. interests.

In order to meet this need we recommend that General Conference elect an advisory C.P.S. committee of five brethren to work with the Peace Problems Committee on all matters pertaining to C.P.S. policies and plans.

Since this committee shall concern itself solely with C.P.S. work it shall be its duty to study this work, and to determine, as much as possible, the wishes of the church as to its policies and administration so that the standards of the Mennonite Church may be upheld and the spiritual interests of her draftees may be safeguarded and promoted.

It shall be the duty of this committee to work co-operatively with the Peace Problems Committee to which it shall submit any findings and recommendations it may have to give concerning the C.P.S. Joint meetings may be held by the two committees whenever they so decide. Their joint working together shall be of a somewhat similar nature to that of the Executive and Mission committees of the Mennonite Board of Missions and Charities. Together these committees shall plan for any changes in the C.P.S. setup that may be needed to safeguard the interests of the Mennonite Church. These committees shall also jointly decide as to how their concerns for the interests of the Mennonite Church shall be brought to the Mennonite Central Committee when such procedures are deemed necessary.

The Advisory Committee shall effect its own organization and shall report regularly to General Conference, and in the interim between conferences may report to the Executive Committee if at any time it has anything to bring to the attention of that body. Nominees for this committee shall be chosen with the view of representing the church as a whole, and none of its members shall be on the Peace Problems Committee, the Mennonite Relief Committee or the Mennonite Central Committee. The committee may be discontinued any time that General Conference decides that its service is not needed.

2. We feel that because of the many types of conscientious objectors connected with C.P.S. there should be some clarifying statement of our peculiar position as nonresistant objectors, as contrasted with pacifistic objectors, to use as a guide in formulating policies and procedures for the present and the future. We recommend that the Peace Problems Committee, in co-operation with the C.P.S. Advisory Committee (if such committee is authorized and elected), prepare such statement in booklet form. In case no Advisory Committee is authorized we recommend that the Peace Problems Committee prepare such a booklet in co-operation with the Publishing Committee of the Publication Board.

3. Since our co-operation with the National Service Board for Religious Objectors has been subject to question because this organization includes and represents all groups of conscientious objectors, some of whom have little or nothing in common with us except their refusal to participate in war, we call attention to the implications, complications, and compromising influences which may result from our active participation in the work of this organization. (1) This association may cause a subtle weakening of some of our Biblical positions on nonresistance. (2) It makes it easy for people not well acquainted with us to get the wrong impression of our doctrine, position, and practice. (3) It also has the appearance of our being unequally yoked together with people who are not in accord with us in faith and practice.

However, we believe as a result of our investigations, that the activities of our brethren in connection with this body are not necessarily a violation of the principle of the unequal yoke, since none of the decisions or actions of this body are binding upon any of those co-operating with it. Furthermore, neither the beginning nor the continuing of our working through the National Service Board for Religious Objectors was or is primarily our choosing but rather due to the willingness on our part to accommodate ourselves to the desire of Selective Service for a central agency through which it could deal with all C.O.'s.

Therefore, since as a Mennonite Church we have never appointed any official representative on it, and are under no obligation to it, we regard the National Service Board for Religious Objectors as a servant we employ in representing our interest in this work to the government. At the same time, however, we believe our Peace Committee may well look forward to caring for our interests in some way that is less objectionable from the standpoints mentioned. We also realize that abrupt changes in procedure may not be advisable at this stage of the emergency.

4. We urge that in camps where young men of our constituency are in the large majority, the camps should be, as much as possible, staffed by brethren of our church, and that other churches in the M.C.C. be granted the same privilege where similar conditions prevail.

5. We urge that great care should be exercised concerning the appearance in our camps of liberal and pacifistic speakers who are not in harmony with our beliefs in Biblical nonresistance; and that there be a strict supervision both of literature received and published by our camps.

6. Because of the far-reaching implications and possible effects upon the welfare and position of the church of postwar work growing out of the C.P.S. program, we urge that all such plans for the future, as they affect the young men of our constituency, be thoroughly reviewed by our Peace Problems Committee together with the Advisory Committee, if such is authorized by this Conference.

7. We urge that continued attempts be made by these committees to solve the problem of financing campers who are not supported and who are not in sympathy with our beliefs and practices.

8. We urge that continued efforts on the part of committees and conferences be made in behalf of the spiritual welfare of our campers through regular preaching services, spiritual life and Bible conferences, and pastoral visitation and supervision.

9. We recommend the continuance of the practice of calling together General Conference officials and representative brethren when there are issues at stake that call for such a procedure in the opinion of the Peace Problems and Advisory committees.

IV. ADDITIONAL INFORMATION

1. The Executive Committee of General Conference has already in response to a preliminary report of this committee to that body, appointed a C.P.S. Advisory Committee to serve until General Conference takes action on our recommendation.

2. A paper on "Nonresistance and Pacifism" has already been prepared under the auspices of this committee. Two chapters of the manuscript of a book prepared under the auspices of the Peace Problems Committee on "War, Peace, and Nonresistance" deal with the subject of "Biblical Nonresistance and Modern Pacifism." These productions should serve as an excellent basis for the booklet suggested in Recommendation 2 of this report.[12]

The fourth recommendation in Part III of the above report proposes that "in camps where young men of our constituency are in the large majority, the camps should be, as much as possible, staffed by brethren of our church, and that other churches in the M.C.C. be granted the same privilege where similar conditions prevail." This proposal reflects a sentiment expressed in many of the criticisms reviewed above: that undesirable conditions in C.P.S. were due to the mixed character of the camp population, including the mixture of different types of Mennonites, as well as of Mennonites and non-Mennonites. It was believed by many that if the camps were exclusively or largely populated and staffed by members of the (Old) Mennonite Church, the undesirable conditions would be greatly reduced. In January, 1943, the Peace Problems Committee received a letter from a minister objecting to the close co-operation of the various Mennonite groups in C.P.S. and relief, and appealing for the creation of a C.P.S. and relief organization for the Mennonite Church alone.[13] Several weeks later the committee received a proposal that the M.C.C. appoint two general directors for its C.P.S. camps. One of these directors would have charge of camps populated and staffed by the Mennonite Church, the Conservative A.M., the Old Order Amish, and the Brethren in Christ. The second general director would have charge of camps populated and staffed by the remaining groups.[14] As noted above, however, the C.P.S. Investigating Committee went no further than to propose staff members selected from the more conservative groups for those camps where "the large majority" of the campers were from these same groups.

REPORT OF C.P.S. POLICY COMMITTEE

The C.P.S. Policy Committee which had been appointed by the Executive Committee also reported to General Conference in August, 1943. Although it had been in existence only three months, and had had only two meetings, apparently none of them in conjunction with the Peace Problems Committee, the C.P.S. Policy Committee brought to General Conference a series of recommendations largely centering around the idea of segregated camps, in line with the proposals mentioned above. The complete recommendations of the Policy Committee were as follows:

1. That we continue to operate our Civilian Public Service camps and detached service units through the Mennonite Central Committee for the present.
2. That we request the M.C.C. to plan for a sufficient number of camps and detached service units to be directed by an official staff selected from congregations in conferences affiliated, or eligible for affiliation, with the Mennonite General Conference to provide for the young men from the said constituent groups.
3. That the general director for the above-mentioned camps and detached service units be a brother selected from our constituent group.
4. That all official appointments of the said camps and units be made only upon the recommendation of the Peace Problems Committee.
5. That only such members shall be used in any official capacity who have a Christian experience, who have proved themselves to be loyal and faithful, and who uphold the standards of the church as set forth by the Mennonite General Conference.
6. That conscientious objectors who are not of our constituent group but are not hostile to our faith and practice may be admitted to our camps provided they are willing to comply with our policies for camp operations.
7. That we take our position as nonresistant Christians and hold ourselves aloof from non-Biblical pacifism, and that a statement clearly defining our position as nonresistant Christians be posted in each camp.
8. That we discontinue giving financial support to non-Biblical pacifists and members of false religious sects such as Jehovah's Witnesses.
9. That the church provide definite spiritual or pastoral oversight for our brethren in camps and detached service units through the Peace Problems Committee.
10. That our camps be placed under regulations which are consistent with the standards of the church, and also the requirements of the government wherein they do not conflict with our conscience.
11. That the Peace Problems Committee together with the Mennonite Civilian Public Service Policy Committee shall determine the course of action to be taken on critical questions related to the Civilian Public Service program as they may arise.
12. That, if these policies shall be adopted by General Conference, a reasonable length of time be allowed for the transition from the present setup to the proposed, or newly adopted, policies; that we make this transition as rapidly as possible; and that we request the Mennonite Central Committee to make some changes in personnel which are urgent in order to maintain the Scriptural standards and give a faithful witness as followers of Christ.
13. Since the present training and service act terminates in September, 1945, and

Since the present trend indicates a possibility of a continued program by our government to promote military strength in this country, We recommend that the Mennonite Civilian Public Service Policy Committee serve as an additional study committee to explore the implications of any new compulsory military training and service act which may be enacted, and together with the Peace Problems Committee be ready to recommend a course of action that will help to preserve our distinctive nonresistance and nonconformity witness.[15]

RESPONSE TO COMMITTEES' PROPOSALS

The reports of the C.P.S. Investigating Committee and of the C.P.S. Policy Committee represent positive proposals for improvement arising from criticisms which, for more than two years, had been directed at C.P.S. It is interesting to note what came of these proposals. General Conference itself approved the recommendations of both reports, except that it did not continue the C.P.S. Policy Committee. Instead, it enlarged the Peace Problems Committee so as to include twelve members from the United States, rather than six. The United States section of the new committee then consisted of Harold S. Bender, Orie O. Miller, C. L. Graber, and nine bishops: Amos S. Horst, Milo Kauffman, John E. Lapp, O. N. Johns, D. A. Yoder, H. A. Diener, J. L. Stauffer, Simon Gingerich, and J. A. Heiser. The committee then organized itself as follows: Executive Committee, H. S. Bender, chairman; Orie O. Miller, secretary; C. L. Graber, treasurer; Amos S. Horst, Milo Kauffman. Subcommittee on C.P.S. Policy Study and Recommendations, Milo Kauffman, chairman; J. L. Stauffer, H. S. Bender, Simon Gingerich, J. A. Heiser.

In its closing statement the Investigating Committee referred to a pamphlet on *Nonresistance and Pacifism* prepared under its own auspices by John R. Mumaw, and to two chapters of Guy F. Hershberger's manuscript on *War, Peace, and Nonresistance*, also dealing with this subject. Both the Investigating and the Policy committees nevertheless asked for the publication of an official further statement clarifying the nonresistant position of the Mennonites in contrast with unscriptural forms of popular pacifism. The M.C.C. responded promptly to this request and published a statement entitled, *Mennonite Civilian Public Service: A Statement of Policy Approved by the Mennonite Central Committee Executive Committee, September 16, 1943.* This printed statement was circulated in the camps and churches, and was placed in the hands of non-Mennonites assigned to M.C.C. camps, in order that there might be a clear understanding between these persons and the camp management. The statement pointed up the difference between New Testament nonresistance and mere humanitarian or political types of pacifism. It set forth the proper relationship of the church agencies to Selective Service in the operation of C.P.S., as understood by the M.C.C. One of the criticisms frequently directed at C.P.S. was that the Mennonite churches were helping to finance non-Mennonites in M.C.C. camps, some of whom were unsympathetic toward the M.C.C. administration and to the nonresistant views of the church. In fact, recommendation No. 8 of the C.P.S. Policy Committee asked that the church "discontinue giving financial support to non-Biblical pacifists and members of false religious sects such as Jehovah's Witnesses." In order to meet this criticism the new statement said that the M.C.C. was inviting to its camps only those men who, in their own consciences, were in accord with M.C.C. policy.

Non-Mennonite men who wish to serve in M.C.C.-administered units and who are ready to co-operate with this administration and accept its policies are heartily welcome to its camps and projects. They will be accepted up to the limits of M.C.C. administrative and financial capacity, with the understanding that they or their constituencies contribute to their support as much as possible.[16]

A reading of the Investigating Committee's recommendation No. 3 shows that while this committee did not share the extreme views of some of the critics concerning the relationship of the church with the N.S.B.R.O., it did believe that "Our Peace Committee may well look forward to caring for our interests in some way that is less objectionable." This referred to a long-range program, however, and was not a request for immediate change. In the matter of segregated camps the Policy Committee went further than the Investigating Committee. Its recommendations No. 2 and No. 3 asked that the M.C.C. be requested "to plan for a sufficient number of camps and detached service units" to provide for C.P.S. men "from congregations in conferences affiliated, or eligible for affiliation, with the Mennonite General Conference," and that the staffs and the general director for these camps likewise be drawn from these congregations and conferences. Other recommendations of the Policy Committee were designed to implement these two basic recommendations.

Neither the M.C.C. nor the Peace Problems Committee found it practicable to carry out these proposals on a large scale. On March 4, 1944, the Peace Problems Committee did adopt a statement of policy looking to the establishment of camps under its own administration. One such unit was established late in 1944. This was unit No. 2 of C.P.S. Camp No. 138, located at Malcolm, Nebraska, near Lincoln.[17] Camp No. 138 consisted of three units, one operating in connection with the Agricultural College of the University of Nebraska. The other two were organized as farm and community schools in connection with soil conservation projects. The college unit and one of the farm units were operated directly by the M.C.C. Unit No. 2, however, was administered by the Peace Problems Committee for the M.C.C. The camp was located on a farm owned by the Mennonite Publication Board, and served approximately thirty-five men. The principal feature of the educational program was a course in "The Mennonite Community," for which a few of the campers received college credit. This course was taught by a member of the Goshen College faculty, and was supplemented by technical courses at the Agricultural College, and by special lectures and conferences on the life and work of the Mennonite Church. This experiment was successful, and the Peace Problems Committee thought of it as a possible pattern for operation in the event of permanent peacetime conscription, which was then considered a probability. The minutes of the committee at the time of the camp's opening say that the "primary purpose of the camp will be to aid the Peace Problems Committee and the branch of the church which it represents in developing a postwar farm and community program for its own young people, and also to contribute to the formulation of its own postwar plans in case of permanent conscription."[18] Before the Malcolm experiment was a year old, however, the war was over, and it was obvious that C.P.S. discharges would result in an early reduction of the number of camps. It did not seem practicable, therefore, for the Peace Problems Committee to open additional camps at this time.

If there had been a continued or a revised C.P.S. program under peacetime conscription in the postwar period, it is not impossible that the Malcolm pattern would have been extended. The report of the Peace Problems Committee to General Conference in 1946 recommended such a program in case of permanent peacetime conscription. As it was, however, the opening of more camps under wartime conscription did not seem practicable.[19] Moreover, an inquiry by questionnaire had convinced the Peace Problems Committee that the C.P.S. men then in camp were not interested in a drastic change in the organization pattern of wartime C.P.S., such as that proposed by the C.P.S. Policy Committee. The men at the Malcolm Camp had transferred there voluntarily, and were happy with the arrangement, both as to its administration and specialized educational program. Had the war continued, and had the Peace Problems Committee opened a few additional units of the same type, they would no doubt have been successful also. It is doubtful, however, whether a general program of segregation, according to conference groups, under the M.C.C. would have been successful. Inquiry showed that the majority of campers of all groups would not have favored the general disruption of the pattern which had been established. This is not to say, however, that in a new situation such as peacetime conscription a different pattern would not have proved successful.

INTER-GROUP RELATIONS IN RELIEF WORK

As mentioned earlier in this chapter, those brethren who objected to the close co-operation of the various Mennonite groups in C.P.S. believed there were equally valid objections to such co-operation in relief work. It was generally accepted, of course, that there was a large and important place for a co-operative Mennonite program under the M.C.C., for the bringing of emergency relief to peoples of war-stricken countries, and for the moving of European refugees to new homes in North and South America. It was also generally recognized throughout the Mennonite Church that there was a real place for the work of the Mennonite Relief Committee under the Mission Board. There is frequent need for relief work in connection with the Board's mission stations. As mentioned in Chapter XV, steps were taken as early as 1942 looking toward the establishment of Mennonite service units by the M.R.C. From 1937 to 1940 the M.R.C. had carried on a foreign relief project in Spain. Prevailing opinion throughout the church recognized the place in Mennonite relief of both the M.C.C. and the M.R.C., and favored the active support of both organizations. A small group believed, however, that the Mennonite Church should withdraw its support from the M.C.C., and that all of its relief work should be done through M.R.C. This view was expressed in correspondence received by the Peace Problems Committee, the Mission Board, and the Relief Committee. The *Sword and Trumpet* also served as a vehicle for the expression of this idea; and at one time or another two district conferences adopted resolutions supporting this point of view. The opening of work in Belgium, Poland, and Ethiopia under the auspices of the M.R.C. was in part a response to these demands.

In 1944 the Virginia Mission Board took action temporarily withholding relief funds contributed within the conference district, and in May, 1944, the Virginia Conference adopted a resolution supporting this action. The reasons given for this action were the curtailment of opportunities for relief work by current war conditions, and "lack of clarity regarding policy in the present administration of relief efforts by the central relief agencies." The resolution stated further that "upon satisfactory clarification of policy as in harmony with the principles of Christian love and stewardship" the funds were to be released. The executive committees of the conference and of its mission board were authorized to "explore the possibilities of relief work in line with the sentiment herein expressed."[20] In line with this action there was some investigation of possibilities for European relief work through an independent Mennonite agency. Two years later the conference expressed its appreciation for the work of this joint committee and further urged it to "do everything in its power to improve the testimony of Christ in the actual administration of relief and to channel all relief goods through the agency or agencies which most faithfully represent the standards and ideals of our Lord."[21]

While realizing that C.P.S. and the relief program as administered by the M.C.C. had its weaknesses, no doubt the majority opinion throughout the church was that the criticisms directed against the M.C.C. had been exaggerated, that they were frequently due to lack of information, and often unfair. On the part of a few, however, the feeling continued that for the future the Mennonite Church should have little to do with the M.C.C. In 1947 the Pacific Coast Conference adopted a resolution saying that: "The late war is now over and we believe that the great reason for our active participation in M.C.C. is now over . . . . We therefore hereby appeal to General Conference that immediate steps be taken that we, the (Old) Mennonite Church, endeavor to promote our activities under our own Mennonite sponsorship."[22]

The response of General Conference to this appeal was an action approving the policy of the Mennonite Board of Missions and Charities regarding relationship with the M.C.C., as adopted by that Board in 1947. The essential points of this policy were as follows:

1. We express our appreciation (a) for the great service rendered in reaching out aggressively into fields of labor practically girdling the globe and giving us opportunities to give much in personnel and money that would otherwise not have been possible; (b) for the difficult and untiring labors in making a way for thousands of European Mennonite refugees to find new homes in the American continents; (c) for the facilities provided to our Mennonite Relief Committee in government contacts, in arranging for transportation and permits, in furnishing material aid, and in helping M.R.C. workers in travel and in finding locations.

2. We stand ready to continue to co-operate with M.C.C. in emergency types of work which can most advantageously be carried on together, such as the movement of refugees and temporary phases of relief.

3. We feel, however, that permanent institutional work, relief work related to mission work, young people's Christian service units, and any work that may involve church membership, administration, and control can be done more advantageously and in better furtherance of the cause of Christ and the church by individual church groups.[23]

EVALUATION OF INTER-GROUP RELATIONS

From the above account it seems clear that the period of the second World War was a time of searching on the part of the church. C.P.S. was a new experience. Foreign relief was developed on a larger scale than ever before in the history of the church. In both of these ventures the church came in contact with the world in numerous ways that were new to her experience. This was true not only of the Peace Problems Committee and its immediate constituency. All of the American Mennonite groups had the same experience; and all of them were searching earnestly and sincerely to find the way that was Christian, and Scriptural, and true to their Mennonite heritage. How far should Mennonites carry their relationships with other peace groups and organizations? To what extent should C.P.S. and relief work have been carried on co-operatively by the various Mennonite groups, and to what extent should each group have worked independently? In looking back over the wartime experience, what can be said as to the effect of these new relationships upon the life of the church, and upon its spiritual welfare? No doubt these questions can be answered more accurately fifty years from now than at present.

It would seem in order, however, to attempt at least a tentative evaluation at this time.

In doing so it would seem a sound premise to assume the following, as three important duties of the church: (1) To remain true to its faith, and continually to strive for a more perfect understanding of the same. Such understanding comes through a study of the Scriptures, through experience in the work of the kingdom, and through learning from other Christians, all of this under the guiding hand of the Holy Spirit. (2) To bring the Gospel of Christ to all men. This includes the message of peace and nonresistance, which must be proclaimed to Christians and non-Christians alike. (3) To educate its own young people so as to give them: a knowledge of the Gospel and the principles of the kingdom; ability to distinguish between truth and error, both through a study of principles and through practical experience in the affairs of men; ability to do the type of creative thinking which makes for progress. While the wartime experience revealed many weak spots in the life of the church, the present writer believes that the history of the church will reveal one of its strongest spots to have been the manner in which the Peace Problems Committee and the M.C.C. led the church through that experience.

First of all, he believes that the peace leadership of the church did have a sound understanding of the Gospel, and of the Christian message of peace. He also believes that this understanding was increased through the war years; and that this development came through study, through prayer, and through a careful evaluation of other peace groups. Leaders in the peace work of the church frequently testified to others concerning the nonresistant faith, both to those who might be thought of as militarists and to those who would be classified as pacifists. Sometimes their relationships with pacifists were felt by some to have been too close. It must be remembered, however, that this is a task which cannot be performed by preaching down at the pacifist as from a pedestal. This task can be performed only by an honest and sincere exchange of thought. Moreover, Mennonites must always remember that they have not found answers to all of the questions which arise out of their doctrine of peace; that there is much which they can learn from other peace groups, even from those which may not have a sound Christian foundation. Did not Jesus say that sometimes the children of darkness are wiser than the children of light? The Christian must not spurn the recognition of wisdom, even when it is found in possession of one who is not a Christian.

As for the relations of the M.C.C. with pacifist organizations, through the N.S.B.R.O., perhaps no one would consider the arrangement to have been ideal. Under the circumstances, however, it is difficult to see how any arrangement much different from this would have been possible. If the different peace groups were to operate C.P.S. camps, some unified approach to the government was essential. Certainly Selective Service would have refused to deal with a number of administrative agencies separately; and it is doubtful whether it would have been willing to deal with as many as two such agencies, as some Mennonites proposed. Furthermore, since the N.S.B.R.O. was a service board rather than a policy-making body, it does not seem necessary to think of this arrangement as an unequal yoke. Would it not be better to think of it as an opportunity for the co-operating groups, not only to perform the particular task which needed to be done, but also to test their own faith and life in the crucible of experience? Certainly that of the Mennonites was so tested, and today no doubt they have a better understanding of that faith and life than they would have had without it. In addition, this experience and relationship also presented a great opportunity for testimony; and as a result, Mennonite faith and life are more widely and favorably known than ever in their history.

As to the presence of non-Mennonites in M.C.C.-C.P.S. camps, several things need to be said. In the beginning all camps were operated by the Friends, the Brethren, and the Mennonites. Even toward the end of C.P.S. the number of camps administered by other agencies was small. Since approximately 40 per cent of all men in C.P.S. were not from the peace churches, it was obvious that they would need to be cared for in Friends, Brethren, and Mennonite camps. Certainly, if the M.C.C. was to operate C.P.S. camps it could not shrink from its share of this obligation. Moreover, if Mennonites have a message of Christian peace to proclaim, what better opportunity could they ask than that afforded by a group of men under their tutelage in a C.P.S. camp? For successful camp administration, of course, there had to be order and harmony. This could exist only where campers were sufficiently in harmony with the principles on which the camp was operated to enable them to co-operate successfully. Experience showed that some men lacked this qualification, that they were unassimilable in Mennonite C.P.S. The M.C.C. then adopted the policy of admitting to its camps only those men who were able to declare themselves in sympathy with the policies of the camp administration. The camps later operated directly by Selective Service itself were organized to meet the needs of those men who did not fit into the life of the camps operated by the churches.

Naturally, the presence of non-Mennonite men in M.C.C. camps was bound to have some influence on the Mennonite campers. Was that influence good or bad? Closely related to this was the appearance in camps, especially in the early period, of speakers representing various pacifist organizations. Was this influence good or bad? A number of brethren felt that it was definitely not good. In most cases, of course, pacifist leaders visiting M.C.C. camps did not do so at the invitation of the camp management. They considered it their business to keep in touch with every aspect of the peace movement, including C.P.S. camps. Since their work involved considerable traveling they naturally planned their itineraries so as to include visits to camps along the way. In most cases, no doubt, when such a visitor came to an M.C.C. camp, the director out of courtesy invited or permitted him to speak. In some cases the visitor may have been a friend or acquaintance of a camper. To forbid the visitor to speak under these circumstances would have been embarrassing, if not discourteous.

In the long run it is doubtful if these visits did much harm. If M.C.C. directors had accepted the views of the typical pacifist leader; if they had invited numerous speakers of this type to the camp; and if they had promoted their philosophy among the campers, a considerable amount of harm could have been done. The alert C.P.S. man, however, was glad for whatever help he might receive in thinking through his own beliefs more carefully; in understanding more fully the various types of pacifism; and in comparing them with Biblical nonresistance. Perhaps there was no better place for this to be done than in an M.C.C.-C.P.S. camp, in charge of an understanding director who was well established in the faith, and an able leader. In such a camp, with a good morale, a certain amount of contact with popular pacifism was probably more helpful than harmful. The writer's own experience in his relation with several camps would tend to support this view.

It is recognized, of course, that such a procedure has its dangers, as does every educational venture. It is also recognized that camp morale was not always what it should have been, and that some directors were not as helpful as they should have been. A few directors may themselves have been confused on the issue of nonresistance and pacifism. In a few camps undesirable situations existed at times, with an influential group of campers, chiefly non-Mennonites, promoting a point of view and program out of line with Mennonite faith and practice. In one or two cases this expressed itself in undesirable association with liberal religious and pacifist groups located in the vicinity of the camp. In some cases, as mentioned earlier, the non-Mennonite pacifist element created problems of administration. As a remedy, the M.C.C. finally adopted the policy of admitting to its camps only such men as were able to declare themselves in sympathy with the M.C.C. program. The issue of nonresistance and pacifism in M.C.C. camps was serious enough, and because of the confusion which it created there were a number of spiritual casualties.

It is the writer's belief, however, that through the C.P.S. experience the men in camp, and the church as a whole, gained rather than lost in their understanding of nonresistance, and in commitment to the same. The need of the time caused the church to do more effective teaching than ever before; and the literature produced during the C.P.S. period, as described in Chapter XVII, was most helpful. One helpful phase of C.P.S. education was the lectures of Don E. Smucker, a minister of the General Conference Mennonite Church. Smucker had earlier been actively associated with the Fellowship of Reconciliation, and had accepted much of the philosophy of liberal Protestant pacifism. His study of the

Scriptures and of Mennonite history, however, brought his return to evangelical Christianity, and led him to renounce liberal pacifism in favor of Biblical nonresistance, as well as to experience a call to the ministry. His testimony in the C.P.S. camps, accompanied by clear analyses of nonresistance and pacifism, helped some of the men to clarify their thinking.

In this connection it is well to remember that pacifist activity in Mennonite C.P.S. camps, and the concern because of it, was most serious during the first year of C.P.S. After all, C.P.S. was a new experiment in which the historic peace churches, as well as other pacifists, were engaged. It was natural that all of them should have been interested in what the others were doing. It is also true that some pacifist leaders seem to have considered themselves called and qualified to provide the intellectual leadership for all peace groups and peace work. A year of experience, however, showed that this proffered leadership was not acceptable among Mennonites. Most Mennonites, following an examination of liberal pacifism, were more appreciative of Biblical nonresistance than before. As the C.P.S. program continued, therefore, the pacifist issue declined in importance.

It is also important to note that the C.P.S. men themselves believed their camp experience to have been helpful spiritually. In 1946 Paul Albrecht, then on the staff of the M.C.C., made a study, using a "C.P.S. Evaluation Questionnaire," which was sent to a scientifically selected group of men, some in camp and others already discharged. This study[24] shows that of the members of the (Old) Mennonite Church who answered the questionnaire, 81 per cent believed the appearance of non-Mennonite ministers in the camps was helpful, while 3 per cent believed it was harmful; 56 per cent said that their own practice of personal devotions had increased through their camp experience, and 7 per cent said it had decreased; 35 per cent said they held to the church's application of the doctrine of nonconformity more strongly than before their C.P.S. experience, while 14 per cent said they held to it less strongly than before, and 44 per cent said they remained unchanged on this point; 36 per cent said they were more loyal to their home church than before C.P.S., while 7 per cent rated themselves less loyal, and 55 per cent said their loyalty remained about as before; 43 per cent said they adhered to the doctrines of the church more strongly, and 7 per cent less strongly than before their C.P.S. experience, while 46 per cent said they remained unchanged in this respect. The C.P.S. experience gave 66 per cent of the men a greater appreciation of the Mennonite heritage, whereas 2 per cent said their appreciation was lessened. Finally, 78 per cent of the men said their understanding of the doctrine of nonresistance was made more clear through their C.P.S. experience, while 3 per cent said they were more confused than before.

An important aspect of the inter-group relations of C.P.S. was the intermingling, especially in the mental hospital and relief units, of young men and women of marriageable age. As one might expect, this frequently led to marriage, in some cases of partners who were not of the same branch of the church. When the latter occurred it meant the transfer of the church or conference membership of some of these people to the group to which their marriage partners belonged. Although this always meant a loss for one group, it meant at the same time a gain for another group. No statistical study of the losses and gains through marriage in C.P.S. and in the M.C.C. relief program has been made. Casual observation, however, would suggest that in the case of the Mennonite Church the gains would easily offset the losses, if not more than do so.

C.P.S. was a great educational venture, and the educational process is always dangerous. Education is getting acquainted with the world, a search for knowledge, in an effort to discover the truth. It is training and experience in distinguishing truth from error. As new knowledge is acquired it must be evaluated, and choices must be made. When evaluations and decisions are rightly made, the result is progress. When they are wrongly made, the result is retrogression. No one wants to make wrong choices and decisions, and no one desires to make a contribution to retrogression. We cannot, however, cease to learn in order to avoid the danger of making wrong decisions. To cease to learn is to become intellectually and spiritually stagnant, than which there is no worse form of retrogression. Progress comes only through the educational process of new knowledge and experience, followed by correct evaluations and right choices, together with earnest labors to make the truth effective in this world. These can come only as the church is blessed with a consecrated and able leadership, and as the entire church gives itself to prayer and an earnest endeavor to know and obey the will of God. May the church never shrink from the task which God has given her. May she ever go forward in the way which leads to knowledge, and truth, and service for Christ and His kingdom. May she ever trust in God to lead her safely through the rocks and shoals of this dangerous path.

NOTES AND CITATIONS

[1] See Guy F. Hershberger, *War, Peace, and Nonresistance* (Scottdale, Pa., 1944), Chs. XI and XII.

[2] *Gospel Herald* (March 17, 1927), 19:1082.

[3] See papers of the Peace Problems Committee deposited in the Mennonite Archives at Goshen College, especially correspondence of the secretary.

[4] Papers of Peace Problems Committee, Mennonite Archives.

[5] Virginia Conference Report, *Gospel Herald* (Sept. 22, 1938), 31:549.

[6] Peace Problems Committee files.

[7] *Ibid.*

[8] *Twenty-second Mennonite General Conference* (1941), 5:78.

[9] Sanford G. Shetler, "The Civilian Public Service Program," *The Sword and Trumpet* (December, 1943), 11:49-65.

[10] A stenographic report of this meeting is in the archives of the M.C.C., at Akron, Pa.

[11] Communication from the secretary of Mennonite General Conference to the chairman of the Peace Problems Committee.

[12] *Twenty-third Mennonite General Conference* (1943), 45-49.

[13] Sanford G. Shetler to Orie O. Miller, Jan. 20, 1943, in Peace Problems Committee files.

[14] John E. Lapp to Peace Problems Committee, Feb. 10, 1943, *ibid.*

[15] *Twenty-third Mennonite General Conference* (1943), 50, 51.

[16] See the complete statement in Hershberger, *War, Peace, and Nonresistance,* 393-8.

[17] See the Annual Report of the M.C.C. (1944), and correspondence in files of Peace Problems Committee. A similar and earlier arrangement had provided for an Old Order Amish farm unit at Boonsboro, Maryland.

[18] Peace Problems Committee minutes, Aug. 1, 1944.

[19] The Malcolm Camp itself closed Dec. 10, 1946. The minutes of the Peace Problems Committee for Jan. 1, 1947, say: "The committee decided to dispose of the camp and its equipment because of the small likelihood of need for the camp in the future."

[20] *Report of the Virginia Mennonite Conference* (1944), 4.

[21] *Ibid.* (1946), 10.

[22] *Report of the Twenty-fifth Annual Mennonite Church Conference of the Pacific Coast District* (1947), 5.

[23] *Twenty-sixth Mennonite General Conference* (1947), 31, 32.

[24] Paul Albrecht, "Civilian Public Service Evaluated by Civilian Public Service Men," *Mennonite Quarterly Review* (January, 1948). 22:5-18; Melvin Gingerich, *Service for Peace,* Appendix 23.

Chapter XX

Conclusion and Evaluation

These lines are being written about five years after the close of the second World War. Five years is too short a time in which to measure the impact of that war upon the Mennonite Church, or to give a final evaluation of the church's wartime experience. It is possible, however, to diagnose in part the health of the church in those years, and to sense the direction in which the stream of life which flowed from the crucible of war was moving.

PEACE TEACHING

By 1940 the Mennonite Church had made a fair beginning in the field of peace literature and peace teaching. It was only a beginning, however, and operated too much merely at the top level. Conference leaders and members of official boards and committees were well informed. Their public statements, both oral and written, with respect to nonresistance and military service, were clear and unmistakable. The Mennonite Publishing House, the church colleges, and the Mission Board labored together faithfully for the promotion of the cause. Even the rank and file of the ministry seems to have been thoroughly committed to the principle of nonresistance. From this point on, however, something was lacking. With 40 per cent of the young men of the church choosing military service it is evident that the church leadership failed to make its information, its faith, and its convictions fully effective within the rank and file of the brotherhood.

The official statements of the church, as expressed in conference actions, were clear enough. The Peace Problems Committee, through its government contacts, and by means of conferences and the production and promotion of literature, was laboring hard to prepare the brotherhood for the test which was to come. For some reason, however, the effects of these labors were not sufficiently felt among individual members of local congregations. The variety and amount of available peace literature was none too great; but that which was available was not read by young men of military age as it should have been. Church leaders at the top level, and students in Mennonite colleges, were frequent participants in peace conferences where they had adequate opportunity to hear and to think about the great question of nonresistance. Perhaps it was too much assumed, because these were being well taught in the subject, that the same was true of the entire brotherhood. The fact is, however, that hundreds of Mennonite youth of military age knew all too little of what was happening at the top level in the church, and were not hearing

273

so much as one sermon on nonresistance per year. One man in reporting his own experience as a C.P.S. camp director describes what he calls "a lack of clear conviction on the part of a sizable group of Mennonite campers as to why they had chosen to serve in C.P.S. . . . Their background had not given them a clear understanding nor an appreciation of Mennonite principles of nonresistance, particularly as these principles are applied to total behavior . . . . It seemed to me that Mennonite churches of nearly all groups have been very weak in teaching this conviction and appreciation, and this failure of the church was responsible for many camp problems."[1]

The teaching task here referred to is one which must be done at the local level. It is the task primarily of the minister, of the lay leader in the local congregation, and of the parents in the home. For a long time it has been the feeling of many brethren that the weakest spot in the work of the Mennonite Church today is in the area of home training, ministerial teaching, and the pastoral care of the congregation. The experience of the church in the second World War would seem to justify that feeling. The Mennonite tradition of a lay ministry is in many ways a good one, and certain aspects of it are highly worth preserving. This must, however, be a ministry which keeps abreast with the needs of its time.

In the past generation the forward-moving world has brought the church face to face with a host of issues which it had never known before. The organized work of the church, on the higher level, and the institutions of the church, such as the colleges, mission boards, and publication interests, have done remarkably well in providing the means whereby these issues may be met. The ministers and lay workers on the congregational level, however, have not done so well in keeping abreast of the times, and they have not learned to use effectively the means which have been provided for them. If the peace teaching task is to be well done in the years ahead it will not only be necessary for the Peace Problems Committee and the organized work which it represents to move forward in new and larger avenues of service. It will also be necessary for ministers and lay leaders in the local congregation to join hands with the Peace Problems Committee; to acquaint themselves with its work; to make use of its literature; and by means of the sermon, the Sunday school, the young people's meeting, the Mennonite Youth Fellowship, through Mennonite service units, by special study classes, and other teaching means, to bring every young Mennonite, both man and woman, face to face with the challenge of the Gospel in order that he may have a true knowledge of its meaning, as well as an appreciation of the Mennonite heritage, and an understanding of the principle of nonresistance, together with a quality of conviction which will enable him to follow unfalteringly in the path of Christian discipleship.

PREPARATION FOR THE WAR EMERGENCY

What was said about the peace teaching work of the church at the top level can also be said of the organized general preparation for the emergency which was to come. The Peace Problems Committee did its task well. It had devoted fifteen years of thought and energy to a search for the course which should be followed in the event of a future war. Of course, it did much more than this. It had prayed that the nation might be spared from the scourge of war, and it had presented the challenge of Christ and the way of peace to government officials. The Peace Problems Committee was also realistic, however, knowing that until the nations accept this challenge the danger of war would be real. For this reason much time and energy was devoted to a possible plan of action in case of war.

Long before the Military Training and Service Act of 1940 became a law, Mennonite leaders had had many conversations with government officials who came to be well acquainted with the Mennonites and their views on war. Long before 1940 government officials knew that Mennonites were conscientious objectors for religious reasons. They knew that they were not social or political radicals who sought to overthrow the government. But they also knew that, in the event of war and conscription, thousands of Mennonite young men would refuse to serve in the armed forces. While government officials could not share the views of the Mennonites, they nevertheless had respect for them, and for the frank and open manner in which they had been presented. Furthermore, the army's experience in the first World War, and the British experience in the early years of the current war, were sufficient to convince most military men that it would be unwise to attempt to force thousands of conscientious objectors to serve in the armed forces.

Thus in 1940 when representatives of the peace churches, together with other interested persons, offered amendments to the Burke-Wadsworth Bill, providing for civilian service as an alternative to military service, members of Congress as well as military officials were ready to accept them. Years of effort on the part of the peace churches had been well repaid. It is a splendid illustration of the fact that important spiritual and social goals can be reached only through long preparation and diligent labor.

THE C.P.S. PROGRAM[2]

Having reached the goal of 1940, however, what shall we say of the result? How shall we evaluate the C.P.S. program itself? Was it the ideal solution for the problem of the conscientious objector in a militaristic world; or do we look for another? There can be no question that the status of the conscientious objector, and the opportunities for consistent

Christian service, were far more satisfactory under C.P.S., than they were under the conditions of the first World War. Although the law did recognize the C.O. in the first World War, he was nevertheless assigned to a military camp where he had to take his stand in a hostile environment, and where in most cases he had to deal with officers who had little understanding of his position, and even less sympathy for it. Much time was spent in the guardhouse and many men received prison sentences. They idled away their time in camp, with nothing to do but to cook their own meals and to care for their quarters. Only a relatively small number were furloughed from the camps for useful farm service, or for relief work abroad.

In 1940, however, the C.O. did not go to a military camp at all. He was immediately assigned to civilian service in a program of work which was planned in advance as making a contribution to the public welfare, and as acceptable to persons whose conscience would not permit them to do military service. This program represented great progress beyond that of 1917-18. Having said this, however, it must also be said that a careful examination of the C.P.S. program reveals some definite weaknesses. During C.P.S. days much was said about the significance, or lack of significance, of the work program. Then there was the disappointment caused by the government's refusal to permit foreign relief service under C.P.S.; and there was the question of work without pay. These and similar questions were minor matters, however, which could be remedied through improved administration. Indeed, many of them had been so improved before the end of C.P.S.

More important than these matters, however, was the basic question of conscription itself, and of the relation of the church and the state in the operation of C.P.S. Did the churches do right in agreeing to administer the camps? In this administrative task did they become party to the administration of conscription, serving as "'straw bosses' for forced labor and as part of the army machine," and were they "as directly involved in running a part of the Selective Service [conscription] System as are draft boards," as argued by the editor of the *Christian Century*[8]

The Mennonite Church has never taken what is known as the absolutist position, refusing registration and all service under conscription. It has always recognized coercion as an essential function of a state which operates in a sub-Christian society, and as long as the type of service required of the Christian has been such as could be performed with a good conscience, the Mennonite attitude has been one of submission. To perform military service, however, or any other service which is contrary to the teachings of the New Testament, whether under conscription or otherwise, has been consistently refused. And, needless to say, the performance of the state's coercive functions has always been considered contrary to the nonresistant teachings of the New Testament. Therefore, if the analysis of the *Christian Century* referred to above is correct, the

M.C.C. departed from good Mennonite practice when it operated the C.P.S. system. What, then, shall we say of this analysis?

When conscription was inaugurated in 1940, Civilian Public Service was accepted by the Mennonites because it exempted them from military service which they could not conscientiously perform, and because it provided an opportunity for useful and humanitarian services which they could perform. When they agreed, and even offered, to operate camps for their own men, it did not occur to them that they were assuming any responsibility for conscription, or that they were entering an unholy alliance between church and state. Conscription was already a fact, and they were not responsible for it at all. They rather thought of themselves as providing camps, with a suitable social and spiritual environment, as a home for men who had submitted to conscription, and who were willing to serve under the requirements of C.P.S. as specified by Selective Service. The government was responsible for conscription and for the work program of the men. The M.C.C. was responsible for the men in their off-work hours.

Stated in this way, there would not seem to have been any undesirable connection between the church and the state. In actual practice, however, the matter was not so simple as that. The M.C.C. was responsible *to the Selective Service System* for the men in their off-work hours. The requirements of C.P.S., which the men had accepted in theory, took the form of numerous rules and regulations laid down by Selective Service governing the life of the men in camp. Furloughs and absences from camp could be had only by special permission. It was the M.C.C. camp director's responsibility to grant these permits and to report them to Selective Service. He even reported on the number of days per month which the man gave to the work project. It was also his duty to report all violations of Selective Service regulations, and to administer whatever penalty was required.

In an ideal M.C.C. camp situation, with Selective Service regulations reasonable, with the camp administration having a large degree of freedom in determining its own program, with all men having reconciled themselves to conscription, and taking an attitude of co-operation in camp, this would have caused little difficulty. It can also be said that, at least until the last year of C.P.S., the Mennonite experience in camp administration was reasonably satisfactory. Quaker and Brethren camps, however, experienced difficulty much earlier than this. This was largely due to the presence in their camps of a considerable number of men of the absolutist type, who objected to conscription as such, and who were often intense individualists. Many of these men were unwilling to submit to a program operating under controls by Selective Service. They demanded a degree of personal freedom which militated against elementary order in the camp, and which Selective Service was unwilling to condone.

19

Furthermore, as time went on Selective Service seems to have become more impersonal in its relations with C.P.S., and its regulations more arbitrary, than was true in the earlier period. By 1945 the executive secretary of the N.S.B.R.O. expressed the feeling that the church agencies were "having a much smaller part in reaching decisions in conjunction with Selective Service than we previously had."[4] Perhaps Selective Service considered this a necessary means for the maintenance of order among the non-co-operators. Perhaps this in turn increased the spirit of non-co-operation within the camp. Be that as it may, as time went on violations of regulations became more frequent, and Selective Service brought increasing pressure upon the camp directors for the enforcement of these regulations upon unwilling men. Out of this situation came walkouts and strikes in some of the Quaker camps, which in turn brought more Selective Service regulations, and the opening of several government-administered camps.

It was this situation which caused the *Christian Century*, Bishop Oxnam, and other religious leaders to cry out against what they called the unholy alliance between church and state. The state should administer its own camps, they said. The churches should not serve as agents for the administration of conscription, and the discipline of recalcitrant campers. In accord with this view, several groups finally withdrew from the N.S.B.R.O.; and the American Friends Service Committee actually withdrew from C.P.S. and closed its camps, or turned them over to Selective Service, a year before the end of conscription. Needless to say, if M.C.C. camp directors had found themselves attempting to enforce Selective Service regulations in a situation like that described above, they would also probably have done well to resign their positions. Happily, however, until at least the last year, the Mennonite experience in camp administration was reasonably satisfactory.

There had always been some problems, of course, as not all of the men were motivated by the second-mile spirit to the extent that they should have been. During the last year of C.P.S., however, these problems in M.C.C. camps increased. The war was over, and many campers were thinking more seriously of their coming discharges than they were of their current C.P.S. obligations. As members of the camp staffs received their own discharges, younger, inexperienced men took their places, the turnover being very rapid at times. All of this contributed to a lowering of morale, so that M.C.C.-C.P.S. in the end period was not what it had formerly been. While there was never any rebellion in any M.C.C. camp, there was considerable dissatisfaction, and this may have been brought on in part by the influence of what was happening in Quaker and Brethren camps. Even without this influence, however, the M.C.C. camp directors would have experienced more difficulty in the later period than they did earlier. As it was, the necessity of enforcing government regulations upon unwilling and un-co-operative campers, while attempting to serve the church as spiritual leaders of the same men, caused some of these directors to conclude that they could not again serve in this dual capacity.

It would seem that this whole question needs to be seriously considered by the church. Was the C.P.S. camp director actually a sort of mayor, exercising delegated powers of coercion in violation of the New Testament principle of nonresistance? If so, was this status inherent in the C.P.S. system as it was organized in 1941-47, or did it appear only at the point where certain campers no longer felt themselves able to accept happily the regulations of Selective Service? In helping to organize C.P.S., did the M.C.C. assist in developing an undesirable system, without seeing its implications, until it was slowly brought to the point where it was difficult for it to reverse itself, and where it could no longer see the picture as clearly as did those who looked on from a greater distance? Or was the problem a relative one, with the camp director becoming an agent of coercion only under certain conditions which could generally have been avoided? Was the director's position perhaps analogous to that of a public school teacher? A Mennonite employed in this or some other civil service, without experiencing difficulties under ordinary circumstances, might well find himself, under other circumstances, in a situation where he could no longer continue in his position without violating his Christian principles. In other words, was the C.P.S. camp director's position a satisfactory one, providing it was properly safeguarded?

A POSSIBLE FUTURE PROGRAM

Certainly Mennonites are universally agreed that C.P.S., as a method of dealing with conscientious objectors, was vastly superior to the method used in the first World War. In answering the C.P.S. evaluation questionnaire, 72 per cent of the Mennonite C.P.S. men themselves said they believed the church had been wise in deciding to operate the camps, and only 7 per cent considered the decision unwise. Furthermore, in spite of all that was said above about dissatisfaction in the camps, 78 per cent of the men who answered the questionnaire said they believed the Selective Service rules on leaves to have been about right, while only 15 per cent believed they restricted the freedom of the men too closely.

In answer to the question as to what should be done in case of an unfair Selective Service policy, which did not force the camper to violate his conscience, 45 per cent of the men thought they should accept the policy and try to live by it; 32 per cent thought an attempt should be made by persuasion to change the policy, but if this failed it should be accepted; and only 5 per cent thought they should refuse to follow the policy in order to make Selective Service change it. These percentages include Mennonites of all groups. The corresponding figures for replies from members of the Mennonite Church are 39, 46, and 3 per cent, re-

spectively. These statistics certainly do not suggest an attitude of opposition to the C.P.S. system on the part of Mennonite C.P.S. men. In this
connection it should also be said that some of the difficulties which
M.C.C. camp directors did experience were due to the presence in camp
of certain unsympathetic groups, like the Jehovah's Witnesses and the
Russian Molokans, who exercised an unwholesome influence on camp life.
If such un-co-operative non-Mennonite groups had been absent, the
disciplinary functions of the director would have been correspondingly
reduced. Having said this, however, it must still be admitted that Mennonite campers provided enough problems for their directors.

It was obvious that the C.P.S. system was not fully satisfactory, and
that in the event of a future service program under conscription certain
changes and improvements would be desirable. The Peace Problems
Committee and the Mennonite Central Committee were fully aware of
this, and in their various appearances before Congressional committees
and other official bodies, from 1945 to 1951, they specified certain essen-
tials for such improvement. Among the essential points specified were
the following:

1. That complete exemption from the draft be provided for all those
whose conscience sincerely forbids them to accept any form of conscription,
and for whom the only alternative is prison. . . .
2. That full provision be made for completely nonmilitary training or
service under civilian direction for those whose conscience forbids them to have
any part in war . . . .
3. That the entire process of selection, induction, and administration of
conscientious objectors in training or service be completely divorced from the
military program . . . that agencies or individuals attached to the armed forces
or involved in the universal military training program in any way should not
participate in the C.O. program in any form.
4. That the federal government should assume basic administrative responsibility [for any such civilian service program, but that] provision be made
for training or service projects wholly as under the administration of church
agencies and for the release of inductees to these projects at their request . . . .
We believe that a wholly government-administered program in which the
church would have only a chaplaincy relationship . . . would be unnecessary
and unsatisfactory, both to the Government and to us . . . .
5. That the wartime policy of no maintenance or wage grants for C.P.S.
men be discontinued . . . .[5]

The draft law of 1948, which became inactive in 1949, but was
extended in July, 1950, for one year, and activated in August, 1950, provided for the deferment of conscientious objectors. In the event of a
large-scale war it did not seem likely that C.O.'s would continue to be
deferred, although it was impossible to say in advance what program
Congress would adopt concerning them. It was believed, however, that
the above recommendations, if adopted, would provide a program as
much in advance of that of 1941-1947 as the latter was in advance of the
program of the first World War. Like the British law, these recommend-

ations, if adopted, would provide for the person whose conscience forbids him to accept any form of conscription.

The recommendation that the selection, induction, and administration of C.O.'s be completely divorced from the military program was a proposal that the individual declare himself a C.O. at the time of his registration. From this point on his relations would be with civilian government officials only, unless and until a civilian tribunal would find him not a sincere C.O., and assign him for military service. Thus the objectionable feature of the C.P.S. system, by which camp regulations were determined by Selective Service, would be eliminated. The proposal that the federal government assume basic administrative responsibility for alternative service, with adequate provision for projects under church agencies, had in mind a diversified alternative program, including some of the best features of the British, Canadian, and American systems of the second World War. Thus, those men with sincere objections to service under conscription could be left free; those willing to serve in a government-operated camp could be so assigned; and those desiring to serve in a church-operated camp or service project, could be so assigned. Such a program could also have included individual assignments to agriculture, after the pattern followed in Canada during the second World War.

The M.C.C. recommendations provided adequate channels of service for those C.O.'s who would find themselves unhappy in an M.C.C. camp, and perhaps a source of trouble if assigned to it. The peacetime Mennonite voluntary service program, on the other hand, provided a variety of service projects already in operation, for which, in the event of conscription, men could be released; or to which they could be assigned by the appropriate civilian government agency. Under such a plan the M.C.C. project director would not be in a position making it necessary to enforce Selective Service regulations on dissatisfied unwilling men, particularly non-Mennonite men, as was sometimes the case in the last year of C.P.S. Whether the government would be willing to accept these M.C.C. recommendations in the event of war and large-scale conscription, remained to be seen. It was certain, however, as the M.C.C. said, that a wholly government-administered program, with the church having a chaplaincy relationship only, would be entirely unacceptable to the Mennonite churches; and no doubt the government would also find it unsatisfactory.

In June, 1951, Congress finally passed a new draft law. In reality this new law was in the form of an amendment to the Selective Service Act of 1948. Instead of deferring the conscientious objector the new law said that the IV-E registrant shall "be ordered by his local board, subject to such regulations as the President may prescribe, to perform for a period equal to the period prescribed . . . [for conscripted men in the armed forces] such civilian work contributing to the maintenance of the national health, safety or interest as the local board may deem appropriate . . . ."

At the time this volume went to press the Presidential regulations for the administration of the 1951 law had not been announced. Hence it was impossible to give a picture of the operation of the new law as it affected the conscientious objector. A number of points, however, seemed clear: (1) The proposal for the complete exemption of the absolutist was not included in the law. In this respect the new law was less liberal than the proposals of the M.C.C. and of the Peace Problems Committee. (2) The new law did not envision a C.P.S. system, either under church or government administration. Instead of this it seemed likely that drafted C.O.'s would be assigned to civilian work under existing government or private agencies. (3) In this program it seemed likely, or at least it was hoped, that existing voluntary service and relief agencies such as those of the Mennonite Central Committee or the Mennonite Relief Committee could qualify for assignment purposes. In such cases, presumably, the church agencies would be free in the administration of their projects so as to eliminate the undesirable administrative features of C.P.S. (4) On the other hand, the law left the administration of the draft machinery itself in the hands of Selective Service and the local boards, and did not provide for a tribunal system such as had been proposed. (5) Thus, in some respects the law seemed to be more liberal than the M.C.C. and the Peace Problems Committee had dared to hope, while some of its provisions were less liberal than those they had proposed. (6) In midsummer, 1951, the Mennonites of America were at the threshold of a new era with respect to conscription. That this would mean the appearance of numerous new and unforeseen problems seemed certain. It was confidently hoped, however, that the new program would be an improvement over all previous programs for the conscription of C.O.'s, with greater opportunities for a consistent witness and service for peace.

PASTORAL OVERSIGHT OF C.P.S.

Man's spiritual needs are so great that, in this summary, the matter of pastoral care for C.P.S. deserves special mention. As said in Chapter VIII, this was entirely inadequate. In the early days of C.P.S. the directors were ordained ministers who were expected to perform the dual function of camp administrator and spiritual adviser. This was too large a task for one man, even if the two functions would lend themselves to easy combination, which they do not. In the later period of C.P.S., when the problems of camp administration were greater than in the beginning, this dual function was vested in an assignee who was not even a minister. Needless to say, under this arrangement the spiritual ministry to C.P.S. men was inadequate.

It is true that many camp directors and educational directors did remarkably well. It is also true that the campers organized themselves through committees and otherwise to carry on a religious program, which was very helpful. Furthermore, the Peace Problems Committee arranged a plan of camp pastoral visitation by ministers of its constituency, and similar action was taken by other groups. While all of this was helpful, it was inadequate. An adequate spiritual ministry required the services of a pastor who was not a camper. Such service was obtained only when the visiting ministers called at the camp. These visits were not frequent enough, and when they did take place, they were of too short duration. In every camp there were many Sundays, and long periods of time, without the presence of any minister. What was needed in each large camp was a resident pastor who could live with the men and counsel them as one who is intimately acquainted with their needs. This essential arrangement was never realized in C.P.S., and the campers themselves agree that it was one of the greatest weaknesses of the program. Any future program should have more adequate provision for spiritual ministration than was realized in C.P.S.

IMPACT OF C.P.S. UPON THE CAMPERS

It is impossible to measure the total impact which the C.P.S. experience made upon the campers. It is obvious, however, that between four and five thousand men could not spend from one to four years each in Civilian Public Service without something happening to them. Certainly C.P.S. was a great opportunity for spiritual and intellectual development, and the majority of the men took advantage of this opportunity, although of course there were those who did not. In answering the C.P.S. evaluation questionnaire, the men themselves said that their spiritual life, measured in terms of personal devotions, loyalty to the church, appreciation of the Mennonite heritage, understanding of nonresistance, and an understanding of the Christian life and its meaning, had been strengthened. Of the members of the (Old) Mennonite Church who answered the questionnaire, 77 per cent said they had gained new understanding of the Christian life; 66 per cent said their appreciation of the Mennonite heritage had been increased; and 78 per cent said their understanding of Biblical nonresistance had been deepened. Most of the remainder said their understanding and appreciation in these areas remained the same as before their C.P.S. experience. Only a very small percentage said that their appreciation or understanding was less than before.[6]

The C.P.S. work record is also impressive, both because of what was accomplished, and of what was learned from it. It is true, of course, that some of the projects were not as significant as they should have been, and that the efficiency of labor in the latter period of C.P.S. was not as high as it should have been. Nevertheless, the total record of work done is an impressive one. Furthermore, many of the men returned from camp, having developed new skills and interests from which they will benefit personally as long as they live. A majority of the men answering the C.P.S. evaluation questionnaire said that their experience would be of value to them in their future vocations. Even more important was the discovery of new opportunities for service through the work which was done. As an illustration, soil conservation practices learned in C.P.S. will have a beneficial effect on many a Mennonite agricultural community for years to come. Service in mental hospitals, likewise, opened new doors of labor and service from which the men themselves, the church which they represented, and the world in which they labor and serve, will receive continuous benefit.

In short, the C.P.S. experience was a broadening and a deepening experience which enlarged the knowledge and understanding of the men, and which opened for them a new world of opportunities for service. Not the least element in this experience was the development of leadership qualities within the men themselves. Many of them were placed in positions of responsibility within the camp, as foremen, as business managers, educational directors, unit leaders, and camp directors. Most of them did their work well, and through it they experienced a personal development which will be of untold value to themselves and to the church. The alert C.P.S. man learned to rethink his religious faith and convictions, and to make value judgments and decisions which made a positive contribution to the development of his leadership abilities. He became acquainted with men from other Mennonite groups, and from other Christian denominations; he learned how to co-operate with them without sacrificing his own convictions and principles; and he learned what it means to assume a place of responsibility in a world of need, and to make a positive contribution to that need. As said in the previous chapter, all of this constituted an educational experience, and the educational experience always has its dangers. Hence there were some casualties; but no doubt the gains of the C.P.S. experience outweigh its losses.

IMPACT OF THE WAR EXPERIENCE UPON THE CHURCH

If the men in C.P.S. learned something of what it means to assume a place of responsibility in a world of need, and to make a positive contribution to that need, the same can be said of the church as a whole. Too often in the past the conscientious objector was looked upon as something of a slacker. Even Mennonites themselves have sometimes had the feeling that their doctrine of nonresistance is a negative sort of thing which keeps them from doing certain kinds of evil; but which, on the other hand, makes little if any positive contribution for good. By the end of the second World War all this had changed. It is said that in the early days of C.P.S. someone sent a check to the N.S.B.R.O. as a contribution to the C.P.S. program. The donor said he was making his contribution, not because he agreed with the principles of the conscientious objectors, but because he believed the C.O.'s were making a contribution to the cause of religious freedom. This story, be it true to fact or not, symbolizes a great truth. Conscientious objectors and the peace churches were making a definite contribution to society. What is equally important, the Mennonite Church, as never before, was conscious of her place in the world, and of the contribution which she was called upon to make.

In the first place, by the end of the war the Mennonite Church was aware of her contribution to theology as she had never been aware before. Most people now realized, if they had not done so earlier, that something was seriously wrong with modern world philosophies. The world was sorely in need of a quality of Christian faith and conviction which neither the conservative nor the liberal variety of traditional Christianity had been able to provide. Even many leaders of the pacifist tradition were increasingly aware that, in spite of its keen sense of social responsibility, liberal Protestant pacifism was suffering from a shallow optimism, and lacking in theological depth. Consequently many serious-minded Christian thinkers were looking for something new in Christian faith and life.

Happily, two generations of Mennonite historians and theologians had prepared the way for a new understanding of Mennonitism, with its theology of regeneration, of discipleship, of brotherhood, and of love and nonresistance. More than forty-six hundred Mennonites in C.P.S., and hundreds in foreign relief and voluntary service work, were a solid testimony to the faith and life which they represented. Men were inquiring as to the nature of this faith, and Mennonites realized that they were making a contribution to the theological thinking of their day, such as they had not made for many generations. Mennonite young men in C.P.S., in their search for a deeper understanding of the Christian doctrine of nonresistance, came to appreciate as never before the significance of their own faith, and the contribution which their own church leaders were making, not only to the study of nonresistance, but also to an understanding of Christian theology as a whole. When the Conference on the Church and War met in Detroit in May, 1950, churchmen from all denominations listened with respect to the Mennonite point of view, and Mennonite peace literature was cited for serious study in preparation for this conference.

Secondly, during the period of the second World War the Mennonite Church received an enlarged vision as to her place on the mission field. As her modern mission work reached its half-century mark, historians were reminding the church that aggressive missionary endeavor was one of the outstanding characteristics of sixteenth-century Anabaptism. Comparing the need and the opportunities of the earlier period with those of her own time, the twentieth-century Mennonite Church became aware that her own missionary endeavors were by no means reaching as far as they should reach. The increased financial contributions of the church, brought on by the current needs of C.P.S. and relief, stimulated the church to make increased contributions to the work of missions. An increasing number of young people were also ready to offer themselves for mission service, so that by 1950 the Mennonite Church had not only brought the staffs of the older foreign missions to their prewar level. She had also established four new foreign missions, in China, Japan, Ethiopia, and Puerto Rico.

Thirdly, the experiences of the second World War helped to develop within the church a new social consciousness, and a new sense of social responsibility. The Gospel of Christ brings salvation to men, not merely to give them an inner experience of peace with God. It goes much farther than this, giving the disciple of Christ an ethic which enables him to demonstrate the way of Christian love and brotherhood in human relations. Refusal to participate in war is one aspect of this ethic and of this way of life. The teachings of the New Testament, however, and the life of the sixteenth-century Anabaptists, go much farther than this. They go to the root cause of war itself, rebuking exploitation, attitudes of superiority, and the seeking of power and prestige; eliminating class distinctions; aiming at a reasonable amount of property for all, rather than much for a few; doing justice to all men; seeking the way of brotherhood. If these goals are to be reached it means that the church must have a vigorous program for the teaching of this Christian ethic, and also for its practical demonstration.

Unfortunately, Protestant Christianity since the last quarter of the nineteenth century had been divided on this question, moving in two diverging directions, neither of which was in line with the true Biblical position. Fundamentalism placed its emphasis almost entirely upon personal salvation, while largely neglecting the social implications of Christianity. Liberal Protestantism, on the other hand, had concerned itself with the Social Gospel and social reconstruction to such an extent that personal salvation was ignored, or even rejected. During the days when the Social Gospel controversy was at its height it was difficult to maintain a balanced view of the question; and because of the extreme Modernism of the Social Gospel school of thought, there was a tendency in the Mennonite Church to be afraid of all social work as a part of the church's program.

Gradually, however, it came to be seen that neither Fundamentalism nor the liberal Social Gospel truly represent the teachings of the New Testament. Slowly the Mennonite Church came to see what the Anabaptist forefathers had seen long before, that personal salvation must express itself in the building of a Christian society. The experience of the second World War helped to crystallize this conviction, with the result that the social consciousness of the Mennonite Church was greatly enlarged. This brought certain new aspects of Christian service into the work of the church, of which the Voluntary Service program is a splendid illustration. The experience of C.P.S. men in mental hospital work created an interest in this type of Christian service, so that by 1950 the M.C.C. was operating a mental rest home in Maryland, had another under construction in California, and was looking for a location for a third home in the middle states. In these projects the Mennonite Church was taking an active part; and in addition the Lancaster Mennonite Conference had under way a project for the opening of a mental rest home under its own auspices in Lancaster County, Pennsylvania.

Another aspect of the new social consciousness within the Mennonite Church was its growing interest and concern for the building of the Christian community. More and more it was realized that the local church is a group of Christians living together as a community, and that this community must in all of its relationships demonstrate the way of love and brotherhood as set forth in the New Testament. Conferences on industrial relations and Mennonite community life, and similar meetings, were welcomed as a help to this end. The publication of *The Mennonite Community* magazine which was begun in 1947, and which in 1949 became a publication of the Mennonite Publishing House, was another illustration of this interest and concern. It is significant that this new venture was brought to fruition largely through the leadership of a group of former C.P.S. men, and others closely associated with C.P.S. work.

The new Mennonite mission in Puerto Rico, which was an outgrowth of a C.P.S. project, also seemed to combine in a fresh way an aggressive program of evangelization with a constructive program of community building and community service. It was the hope of many that the Puerto Rico mission would be able to demonstrate in a real way what is meant by an integration of individual soul winning with Christian social service, leading to the building of the Christian community in the true New Testament sense. It was also encouraging to know that by 1949 or earlier the Mennonite Board of Missions and Charities was actively exploring the possibility of a new type of home mission program, in which a small group of consecrated young families would find a suitable location in which to build homes, and from which they would aim to combine the evangelization of the surrounding territory with a planned program of community building.

In the fourth place, the experiences of the second World War helped the church to see more clearly than ever before the place of youth in the work of the church. C.P.S., and the relief and Voluntary Service program which followed it, were a "youth movement" in which thousands of young men and women discovered themselves, received a new vision of what life is for, and dedicated themselves to a life of service for Christ and the church. The church, on the other hand, discovered the power which lay within her own youth, and began in a variety of ways to enlist this newly discovered energy for the advancement of the kingdom. The organization of Mennonite Youth Fellowship in 1948 is an illustration of this new vision which was leading to a more complete integration of the youth with the life and work of the Mennonite Church. As these steps were being taken the church was holding up the ideal of a year of voluntary service for the church for every young man and woman. While this ideal was still far from being reached, the fact remained that Mennonite youth had found a place in the life and work of the church, such as would hardly have seemed possible thirty years earlier.

THE WAR EXPERIENCE REVEALED WEAKNESSES IN THE CHURCH

Not the least of the revelations which came out of the crucible of the second World War was that of weaknesses in the life of the church. When 40 per cent of the young men of a nonresistant church accept military service, something is wrong. As said elsewhere in this chapter, this situation made it clear that the church, through more effective teaching and by other means, under the leading of the Holy Spirit, must strive to revitalize the brotherhood and to bring a greater conviction to all of its members on the great question of nonresistance, and on other issues. This lack of conviction manifested itself not only in those young men who accepted military service. Too many of the young men in C.P.S. had failed to grasp the true spirit of Christian nonresistance. Some of these, perhaps, were in camp for reasons of tradition, more than because of a conviction which came out of a deep Christian experience. This represented a definite weakness in the life of the church.

Another weakness which manifested itself in the life of the church during the second World War was the apparent lack of conviction on the part of many members who were not subject to the draft. In many cases the failure of a young man to take the C.O. position was due to the influence of his own father and mother, or other members of the family. One case comes to mind of a father who advised his son to accept military service out of fear that the patrons of his retail store might trade elsewhere, if they learned that there was a conscientious objector in the family. While it is admitted that the civilian bond plan as it was developed in the United States was not satisfactory, yet the fact that some brethren purchased regular war bonds, without serious objection, reveals a regrettable lack of conviction. There were also children in public schools who purchased war savings stamps, and participated in drives for the collection of tin and scrap metal for war purposes; and there were Mennonite public school teachers who participated in these activities. As mentioned earlier, too many Mennonites worked in war industries where they took part in the manufacture of war materials and war equipment. Mennonite businessmen of various types were confronted with numerous temptations to violate the principle of nonresistance in the matter of sales, manufactures, and investments; and there were too many who succumbed to these temptations.

The Bible says that the love of money is the root of all kinds of evil; and its influence is so subtle as to make it exceedingly dangerous. To refuse a sale, or to reject a profitable business venture which violates a moral principle, requires Christian character and strength of conviction. Judas sold his Master for thirty pieces of silver; and many well-meaning people since his day have lost their Christian testimony, and ultimately their souls, by placing the value of the dollar more highly than the teachings of the Gospel of Christ. If in some unhappy future day the Mennonite Church should lose its nonresistant testimony, it may well be that the economic interests of its members will be found to have been the most important cause for its fall.

LET US GO ON

A review of the war experience gives occasion, both for rejoicing and for sober reflection: rejoicing because of the manifestations of vitality within the church; and reflection because of the manifestations of decay which were likewise revealed. Certainly there is much in the record to be thankful for; but there is also much progress which remains to be made. The author can think of nothing better at this point than to quote the writer to the Hebrews, who admonished his readers to "go on unto perfection."[7] Or the Apostle Paul who, "forgetting those things which are behind, and reaching forth unto those things which are before," resolved to "press toward the mark for the prize of the high calling of God in Christ Jesus."[8]

May the Mennonite Church leave her mistakes behind her, and press toward the mark of perfection. May the Lord raise up ministers who will preach with fervor the Gospel of faith, repentance and regeneration. May they ever lead the members of the church in the path of discipleship, love, and brotherhood. May they turn the searchlight of truth on every weak and decaying spot in the body of the church, and may the healing rays of the Gospel cleanse every imperfection. May the conferences, boards, and official committees of the church be staffed with Spirit-filled men, wise, courageous, and diligent, who with wisdom and foresight will plan the program and work of the church. May the publishing agencies find able writers of faith and wisdom who through the production of challenging literature will provide the spiritual and intellectual stimulation so necessary for a live and aggressive church. May the schools and colleges provide an intellectual and spiritual leadership which will train the youth of the Mennonite Church to think clearly, and inspire them to labor diligently in the vineyard of the Lord.

May every local congregation be a genuine Christian community, with faithful ministers to lead and inspire the flock; to challenge, to admonish, and to teach. May every family be blessed with godly fathers and mothers who will bring up their children in the nurture and admonition of the Lord. May every congregation be supplied with an abundance of energetic young people, ready to serve in the Sunday school, in missionary projects, in service units, in the work of the local congregation, and of the church at large. May every member of the Mennonite Church be a born-again child of God, walking in newness of life, in the path of discipleship. May he have a clear understanding of his high calling in Christ Jesus, fully challenged by the contribution to the church and to the world which he is called upon to make. May the Mennonite Church truly be a light of the world, a salt of the earth. May her members be "blameless and harmless, the sons of God, without rebuke, in the midst of a crooked and perverse nation, among whom . . . [they] shine as lights in the world."[9]

NOTES AND CITATIONS

[1] From replies of camp directors, in files of M.C.C.

[2] For a lengthy analysis and evaluation of C.P.S. and its administration see Gingerich, *Service for Peace,* Chs. XXII and XXIII.

[3] "The Future of the C.O. Camps," *The Christian Century* (Sept. 22, 1943), 60: 1063-65.

[4] Quoted in Gingerich, *op. cit.,* 364.

[5] "Statement on Conscription for Military Training, and Provision for Conscientious Objectors," submitted to the President's Advisory Commission on Universal Training, April 10, 1947, and to the Senate Armed Services Committee, March 31, 1948. Subsequent statements by M.C.C. or Peace Problems Committee were largely elaborations or modifications of these points.

[6] See the summary of the C.P.S. evaluation questionnaire, in Gingerich, 478-88.

[7] Heb. 6:1.

[8] Phil. 3:13, 14.

[9] Phil. 2:15.

Index

20

Historic Peace Churches, Conference
of, Ontario, Military Problems
Committee of, 102, 139
*History and Principles of Mennonite
Relief*, 183
Hoarding, 134
Hobbs, William O., 137n
Hochwan, China, 165
Hofstetter, Reuben, 111n
Holland, relief work in, 200f, 203,
212, 217
Holsinger, Justus G., 210
Home missions, affected by war, 169ff
Honan Province, China, 164, 208
Hookworm control, 59, 227; in Para-
guay, 211
Hooley, Paul Ervin, 206
Hoover, Jesse W., 198
Hoover, President, 5
Horsch, John, 234f, 238, 245, 250f
Horst, Amos S., 13, 16, 23, 64, 87n,
90, 92f, 97, 101, 103, 109n, 110n,
253ff, 262
Horst, Irvin B., 203
Horst, John L., 66, 120f, 220, 253
Horst, Laurence, 223
Horst, Moses K., 111n
Horst, Ray, 111n
Hospital units, 59, 91f, 224ff
Hostetler, Amos O., 150ff
Hostetler, J. J., 111n
Hostetler, John A., 235, 244
Hostetter, B. Charles, 89, 94
House of Friendship (Kitchener, On-
tario), 136
Housing problem, in colleges, 192
Howard, Rhode Island, 59, 182, 184,
226, 241
Hungary, relief work in, 202, 204
Hunsberger, Willard, 236
Hunsberger, Wilson, 201
Hunsperger, Edna, 199
Hutterian Brethren, and draft census,
39

If War Comes, 235
Illinois Conference, 239; and draft
census, 40; C.P.S. Committee of,
75, 99; draft status and age, 46;
draft status and church standing,
41f; draft status and education, 43;
draft status and occupation, 45; financial support of C.P.S. men, 75;
local congregation ministry to

C.P.S. men, 104f; restoration of
men who took up army service,
115; service unit program, 231;
spiritual ministry to C.P.S. men, 99
Independent churches, and draft census, 40
India, 207, 209, 214, 216; Mennonite
Relief Committee for, 207
India Mennonite Mission, 157ff, 169;
All-Mennonite Relief Committee,
159; civilian travel to, 157; cost of
living, 159; financial support of,
170f; furloughs, 157, 160; government work, 159; personnel reduced,
157, 159; principle of nonresistance
violated, 159f; transportation facilities in India, 159
Indiana-Michigan Conference, and
draft census, 35ff, 40; draft status
and education, 43; draft status and
occupation, 45; financial support
of C.P.S. men, 76f; local congregation ministry to C.P.S. men 105;
revival, need of stressed, 115;
spiritual ministry to C.P.S. men, 99
Induction, 25f; of members of medical profession, 129ff
Industrial Relations, Mennonite Committee on, 3, 83f
Information sent out by Peace Problems Committee, 19ff
Ingolstadt, Germany, 202
Innsbruck, Austria, 202
Interboard Committee, 84
International Commission for the Assistance of Child Refugees, 195f
International Mennonite Peace Com-
mittee, 7f, 11; function of, 8
International Refugee Organization
(I.R.O.), 212, 214, 217
Iowa City, Iowa, local board, 30f;
Mission, 169
Iowa Mennonite School, 187
Iowa-Nebraska Conference, 153; and
draft census, 37ff, 40; draft status
and education, 43; draft status and
occupation, 45; financial support of
C.P.S. men, 76; local congregation
ministry to C.P.S. men, 104; Pas-
toral Committee (camp), 104;
spiritual ministry to C.P.S. men, 99
Isaac, F. J., 207
Itacurubi, Paraguay, 211
Italy, relief work in, 200, 202, 204,
217

Jackson, Robert H., 14
Jahnke, Arthur, 200, 206, 214
Janzen, H. H., 213
Japan, 165, 209f, 214
Jaszarokszallas, Hungary, 202
Java, 209f
Jehovah's Witnesses, 62, 263, 280
Johns, Ira S., 105, 111n
Johns, O. N., 93, 109n, 255, 262
Johnson County, Iowa, 30f
Johnstown Mennonite School, 187

Kaifeng, China, 209
Kaiserslautern, Germany, 202, 204, 218
Kalona, Iowa, community, violence in, 136f
Kansas City General Hospital unit, 224, 232
Kauffman, Lewis, 137n
Kauffman, Milo, 67, 72n, 109n, 262
Kauffman, Ralph C., 207f
Kaufman, Ed. G., 55, 191, 235
Kaufman, John E. and wife, 212
Kazun (Poland) Mennonite congregation, 197
Keim, C. Ray, 9
Kiel, Germany, 202, 218
King, H. J., 104
King, Martha, 232n
King, Prime Minister Mackenzie, 5; letter to, 150f
King, S. M., 170
Kirchhofer, Delvin, 200, 205f
Klassen, C. F., 7, 200, 212f
Klassen, Elfrieda, 199
Klassen, G. S., 211
Klassen, John P., 54
Koch, Roy, 111n
Korea, 218
Kosch, Colonel Lewis F., 50, 152; letter of appreciation to, 150
Kraybill, John R., 110n
Kraybill, M. R., 87n
Krefeld, Germany, 202, 204, 230
Krehbiel, H. P., 9, 235, 251
Kreider, Carl, viii, 189
Kreider, Robert, 56, 201f, 230
Krimmer Mennonite Brethren Church, and draft census, 36, 39
Kulp, E. W., 90
Kurtz, Ira A., 111n
Kuyf, Wilhelmina, 207

La Junta, Colorado, 30; Hospital, 131
Lancaster Community Service Association, 123f
Lancaster Conference, 116; and civilian defense, 123f; and dependency (C.P.S.), 81f; and draft census, 35ff, 40; and Red Cross, 119, 123f; and rehabilitation, 86; Campee Aid Committee, 74; city missions in, 169; Conference Camp Committee, 101; draft status and education, 43f; draft status and occupation, 45; local congregation ministry to C.P.S. men, 106f; mental rest home in, 286; Peace Committee, 188, 123; Released Campers Aid Fund, 74f; service unit program, 231; spiritual ministry to C.P.S. men, 101; token gifts to C.P.S. men, 74
Lancaster Mennonite School, 187
Lantz, D. Parke, 195
Lapine, Oregon, 91
La Plata, Puerto Rico, 60, 158, 166, 210f
Lapp, George J., 159, 172n
Lapp, John E., 36, 48n, 54, 90ff, 95, 100, 108, 109n, 140, 253, 262, 272n
LARA, 210
La Rouviere, France, 197
Latvians, 205
Lauver, Paul and Lois, 166
Lavercantiere, France, 200
Leeds, England, 199
Lehman, Chester K., 188
Lehman, Ernest, 105, 244
Lehman, G. Irvin, 206
Lehman, J. Irvin, 234
Lehman, M. C., 183, 196f
Lehman, Titus, 164, 207
Liberal Protestantism, 286
Life and Service in the Kingdom of God, 55, 235
Lima, Ohio, Mission, 169
Lincoln, Nebraska, 58, 94
Lind, Millard, 237
Lind, N. A., 72n, 96f, 104, 111n
Liu, James and wife, 209
Liverpool, England, 199
Livestock boat attendants, 231
Loans, war, 138
Local draft boards, 16, 19f, 24, 28ff, 36; and C.O.'s, 20f, 28f; attitude

War and the Christian Conscience,
234
War Department, 26, 64, 177
Warkentin, A., 90
Warkentin, J. W., 213f
War, Peace, Amity, 235
War, Peace, and Nonresistance, v,
234, 262
War Production Board, 155
Warsaw, Indiana, 29
Warsaw, Poland, 197
War sufferers, Europe, 1939-45,
196ff; Europe after 1945, 200ff;
India and China, 207ff; Middle
East and Ethiopia, 205f; ministry
to, 194ff; other Far Eastern areas,
209f; Puerto Rico, 210f; Spanish
relief, 1937-40, 194ff
War Sufferers' Relief, 140
Wartime population, shifting char-
acter of, 154
Wartime profits, 170, 242
Wartime slogans, 129
Washington County, Iowa, 31
Washington County, Maryland, and
Franklin County, Pennsylvania,
Conference, and d e p e n d e n c y
(C.P.S.), 81; and draft census,
35ff, 40; draft status and church
standing, 41f; draft status and edu-
cation, 43; local congregation min-
istry to C.P.S. men, 106
Washita County, Oklahoma, 31f
Wayne Manufacturing Company,
Waynesboro, Virginia, 127
Weaver, Aaron H., 87n
Weaver, Christine, 164
Weber, Newton, 89f, 94, 100
Weiler, France, 200, 204, 217
Wellman (Iowa) Church, 136
Welsh Bill, 5
Wenger, Chester and Sara Jane, 167
Wenger, Ray, 162
Wernersville, Pennsylvania, 184, 226
Western Mennonite School, 187
West Liberty, Ohio, Children's Home,
223
West Prussia, 212f
What About War? 234
What of Noncombatant Service, 236
*Who Will Go for Us and Whom
Shall We Send?* 96
Wichert, John J. and wife, 213
Wickhurst Manor, 199f
Wiens, Henry, 198

Wilson, E. Raymond, 16
Wings of Decision, 236
Wissembourg, France, 201, 203
Women's Activities Letter, 216
Women's voluntary summer service
units, 184, 226
Woodlands, The, 199f
Woodring, Secretary of War, 14
Work in war industries, 124ff, 242
"Work of national importance under
civilian direction," 15, 20, 24
World Alliance for International
Friendship through the Churches,
249f
World War, first, C.O.'s in, 276; Men-
nonite relief program, 8; Mennon-
ites in, 135f, 138f; purchase of war
bonds in, 147
World War, second, C.O.'s in, 275f;
how it affected—colleges, 174ff;
district conferences, 152f; foreign
missions program, 157ff; General
Conference, 149f; home missions,
169; local congregations, 153f;
publication work, 155

Yake, C. F., 154
Yellow Creek C.P.S. Letter, 105
Yoder, C. Richard, 205f
Yoder, D. A., 23, 90, 92f, 95, 105,
109n, 253, 262
Yoder, Edward, 55, 234ff, 240
Yoder, Gideon G., 97
Yoder, Howard C., 199, 201
Yoder, O. R., 59, 190, 245n
Yoder, Samuel A., 206
Yoder, S. C., 66, 161, 166, 168, 234
Yoder, Vera, 207
Yoder, William H., 209f
Yost, E. M., 97
Youth and Christian Citizenship, 234
*Youth in Preparation for Service in
Our Church Schools,* 96
Youth, place of in work of church,
287
Youth's Christian Companion, 234,
236, 238
Ypsilanti, Michigan, 59, 155, 182,
184, 226, 241f; State Normal
School, 182

Zehr, John D., 245n
Zehr, M. S., 92, 102
Zimmerman, Verna, 137n, 164, 207
Zuercher, Barbara, 206

www.ingramcontent.com/pod-product-compliance
Lightning Source LLC
Chambersburg PA
CBHW050359110426
42812CB00006BA/1749